George Clinton

Sponsored by

The New York State Commission on the
Bicentennial of the United States Constitution
and
The Center for the Study of the
American Constitution

George Clinton

Yeoman Politician
of the New Republic

JOHN P. KAMINSKI

MADISON HOUSE

Madison 1993

LIBRARY OF CONGRESS CATALOGING-IN-PUBLICATION DATA

Kaminski, John P.
George Clinton : yeoman politician of the new republic / John P.
Kaminski ; sponsored by the New York State Commission on the
Bicentennial of the United States Constitution and the Center for the Study of
the American Constitution
p.   cm.
Includes bibiliographical references (p.   ) and index.
ISBN 0-945612-18-4 (hc)—ISBN 0-945612-17-6 (pbk.)
1. Clinton, George, 1739–1812. 2. Vice-Presidents—United States—
Biography. 3. United States—Politics and government—1775–1865. I. New
York State Commission on the Bicentennial of the United States Constitution.
II. University of Wisconsin–Madison. Center for the Study of the
American Constitution. III. Title.
E302.6.C6K36   1990
974.7'03'092—dc20   90–6482
[B]   CIP

Designed by William Kasdorf
Printed by Edwards Brothers, Inc.

Published by Madison House Publishers, Inc.
P. O. Box 3100, Madison, Wisconsin, 53704

FIRST EDITION

Contents

Acknowledgments

A book is always the product of more than the author. This work is an excellent example. Three previous scholars have made this biography possible—E. Wilder Spaulding whose 1938 biography served the scholarly community for over fifty years; Harold Hastings whose ten-volume edition of George Clinton's papers preserved the texts of hundreds of valuable documents from the catastrophic state library fire of 1911; and Alfred F. Young whose magnificent *The Democratic Republicans of New York* tells the story of New York during the Revolutionary and early national periods.

This biography is the final product of an idea of state assemblyman Maurice D. Hinchey, who refused to let the bicentennial commemorations pass without paying homage to George Clinton during 1989, the 250th anniversary of the governor's birth. Stephen L. Schechter, executive director of the New York State Commission on the Bicentennial of the United States Constitution, was the most instrumental force in bringing the idea of a new Clinton biography to fruition. He encouraged me to assist in planning a conference on Clinton, to present two public papers on the governor, and then to expand those papers into a full-length, scholarly biography. The New York Bicentennial Commission provided financial support for the research, writing, and publication of this volume.

I have also been most fortunate to have three excellent, experienced editors assist me in refining the manuscript. Gregory M. Britton read the first draft and offered his valuable critique. Richard B. Bernstein read the revised manuscript and brought his vast knowledge of the Revolutionary era to my assistance. My colleague and close friend for a quarter century, Richard Leffler did more than offer his editorial assistance by reading and critically assessing the first draft. Many hours over lunch and commuting back and forth to work were spent discussing every aspect of Clinton's career. I deeply appreciate his insights and encouragement.

The staffs at the State Historical Society of Wisconsin and the New York State Library have been gracious in providing their assistance. J. Kevin Graffagnino also generously supplied me with copies of documents from the H. P. McCullough Collection at the University of Vermont Library. Charles D. Hagermann has taken the manuscript from my floppy discs and adapted it for computer typesetting. Finally, I am indebted to my wife Janice and our children Steven and Laura for their understanding and patience.

For my mother and father.

Introduction

George Clinton: The Enigma

George Clinton is an enigma. He and his counterparts from Massachusetts and Virginia—John Hancock and Patrick Henry—were the most popular governors in Revolutionary America; yet, little is known about them because most of their papers have not survived. Without documents—the raw material from which history is written—historians tend to overlook individuals and events or, worse, fill the void by inventing or repeating myths. Such has been the case with George Clinton.

This study examines George Clinton, the public figure. Because most of his personal papers and many of his public papers were destroyed—first, when the British set fire to Kingston in October 1777, and, later and more significantly, in the disastrous 1911 fire at the New York State Library in Albany—much of what we know about Clinton comes from what others said about him and from the events that surrounded him. To understand George Clinton, one must know the history of New York during his time. The man and the state were indissolubly linked for over forty years. In answering the age-old biographer's question "Does the man make the times or do the times make the man?" it is clear that George Clinton—the public man—was predominantly a product of his times. Without the Revolution and its concomitant social upheaval, George Clinton would have remained a lawyer-farmer of the Ulster County middling gentry. The Revolutionary struggle with Great Britain presented opportunities for young George Clinton as it did for many other gentry. Had no conflict occurred with the mother country, Clinton in all probability would have become a political leader within Ulster County. The imperial and intra-colonial conflicts, however, thrust Clinton forward, first on the county, then on the state, and finally on the national level. To a great extent, Clinton typified many others of the gentry, like Washington, Jefferson, and Adams, who filled the political vacuum created by the Revolution.

Elected governor of New York seven times, Clinton was probably the most effective, most well-liked, and (after Patrick Henry) the most charismatic of the wartime governors. Despite his popularity, or perhaps because of it, divisive partisanship lay just below the surface of the political landscape, while the seemingly united faction of New York whigs—aristocrats, moderates, and radicals—fought for their very lives against the British and their loyalist, Hessian, and Indian allies.

Aristocratic whigs were pleased with the state's new constitution, which they themselves had drafted and approved in April 1777. The constitution gave the new state governor a three-year term and more power than the chief executives in the other states. Public opinion throughout the state seemed to earmark the wealthy, Albany manor lord Philip Schuyler as the first governor; consequently, when the moderate George Clinton was elected governor in June 1777, aristocrats were "hoisted with their own petard." Schuyler, John Jay, James Duane, and other aristocrats consoled themselves that the wrong man had been elected by some quirk of fate. The people would correct their error at the next gubernatorial election in 1780. In the meantime, the aristocrats chose to work closely with Clinton in the Revolutionary struggle, acknowledging that Great Britain and its allies were the real enemy. During the war, many aristocrats not only cooperated with Clinton, but they came to admire and respect him. The boisterous radicalism of his early days in the colonial assembly, in the provincial convention, and even in the Second Continental Congress gave way to a more responsible demeanor. George Clinton had become an extremely capable leader who inspired confidence in others. By the election of 1780, the fledgling nation was at the depths of its struggle for independence—surely not a time to change governors reasoned the citizens of New York. Three years later, in 1783, victory was at hand, and the euphoria of independence assured Clinton of still another term. Aristocrats comforted one another: 1786 would be the time when a proper candidate—an aristocrat, such as Philip Schuyler, Chancellor Robert R. Livingston, or John Jay—would be elevated to the head of state.

State and national politics also came into play in the mid-1780s. Throughout the Revolution, Governor Clinton advocated a strengthened Congress that could wage war more effectively. On occasion, the governor was even more nationalistic than his aristocratic challengers. When the war ended, however, Clinton reassessed his state's position within the Confederation and concluded that a dramatic change in policy needed to take place. He no longer favored a stronger Congress; instead he intended to rely on a strong state government, invigorated with an independent source of revenue—the state impost. Crucial issues arose on which Clinton, whose previous pragmatism was difficult to oppose, and the aristocrats seriously disagreed. Policies on paper money, loyalists, the independence of Vermont, and most of all the relationship of New York to its neighbors and to the federal government all found Clinton and the aristocrats in conflict. Because of the conflicts, political parties quickly emerged, led by Governor Clinton and by Philip Schuyler and somewhat later by Schuyler's son-in-law Alexander Hamilton.

At first, between 1784 and 1786, this political conflict was amicable, at least on the surface. But, in July 1787, Hamilton directly attacked the governor—his wartime friend. Personality became a legitimate and a common issue in political campaigns. Instead of focusing on the significant issues, where Clinton often held the upper hand, Hamiltonians mercilessly impugned the governor's motives. It is this George Clinton—the image created by his enemies after 1786—that historians generally have accepted. Those who know more than the mere outline of New York's history during the Revolutionary era understand that there was more to George Clinton than the parochial Antifederalist who steadfastly opposed any increase of federal power that would come at New York's expense.

One of the latest book-length studies of New York during the Confederation—Linda Grant De Pauw's *The Eleventh Pillar: New York State and the Federal Constitution* (1966)—denigrates George Clinton by asserting that he was certainly not the leader of his party. In fact, De Pauw argues that political parties did not exist in New York in the 1780s. If there were parties, though, she proclaims that Clinton was incapable of being a party leader. De Pauw puts forth Abraham Yates, Jr., as a more likely candidate for party chieftain, while she portrays Clinton as an incompetent who somehow repeatedly managed to get reelected governor.

De Pauw's analysis of New York in general and Clinton in particular is simply wrong. George Clinton was, in the words of his nemesis Alexander Hamilton, "truly the leader of his party"—the "Chairman," the "Chief," or the "Pharoah," as he was called by his contemporaries.[1] Chancellor Robert R. Livingston told Lafayette that "the governor headed the opposition [to the Constitution] with all the weight arising from his office."[2] According to "An Independent Elector" in the *Goshen Repository*, March 31, 1789, Clinton was not only "the leader of a powerful party," but that party took its "tone from him." Clinton won reelection because of the success of his policies, because his personality and performance appealed to the multitude of New York's electorate who rejected the prewar politics of deference to aristocrats, and because he was a consummate politician.

To maintain his political position, George Clinton continually struggled against opposing forces. Deep down, the state's aristocrats—especially

Philip Schuyler—strongly resented Clinton occupying the governorship. Clinton had much the same disdain for his aristocratic opponents. He saw in them a constant danger to republican government, and his suspicions of them remained throughout his life. Although enmity existed on both sides, they both coexisted as best as possible. From the beginning of his governorship, aristocrats—particularly Philip Schuyler—schemed to unseat the yeoman chief of state. Clinton was not oblivious to this secret caballing, but he worked with his opponents in governing the state. In January 1787, Clinton gave vent to his feelings for these aristocratic opponents. In a letter to his brother-in-law Christopher Tappen, Clinton described the changed atmosphere in the legislature upon the late arrival of Philip Schuyler—where previously harmony existed, "malevolent Rhapsody" would now reign.

Within his own party, Clinton differed with the more radical elements, especially in fiscal matters. Regularly he opposed their more bizarre schemes, preferring to stear a course that would preserve the unity of all segments of New York's whig community. Abraham Yates, Jr., and Ephraim Paine led the radicals, but in no way could either be described as the leader of the party. Clinton's moderate course occasionally cost him the support of the radicals and the people.

Above all, Clinton was most attentive to the needs of his primary constituency—the yeomanry, those small freehold farmers who populated the rural counties of New York. He formulated his policies with them in mind, and occasionally the programs they favored reshaped Clinton's position, as was the case with the treatment of loyalists and paper money. For example, Clinton's attitude toward the confiscation of loyalist property was certainly affected by the suffering that yeomen endured during the war and the potential high taxes they faced after the war to pay the public debt, to restore the economy, and, if the legislature decided, to provide compensation for confiscated property. Loyalists, in Clinton's judgment, should be forced to relieve the yeoman's financial burden. Yes, the governor had animus for loyalists, but the governor would have supported confiscation even had he been more equanimical toward them. Yeomen had paid dearly in money and blood throughout the war; their burden now should be lightened by confiscations. Other Clinton policies had their primary focus on the betterment of the state's gentry.

Ironically, it was Clinton's success as governor that led to his downfall. While other states suffered from the economic and social problems so commonly associated with the Confederation Period, Clinton's policies rapidly righted the state's economy. New York was prospering when the Constitutional Convention proposed a new federal Constitution in September 1787. Because the new Constitution called for a revolutionary change in the basic structure of the general government as well as a fundamental alteration in the relationship between the state and federal governments, many New Yorkers emphasized the dangers inherent in such a radical reform. The dangers were enhanced because of the implied powers of the Constitution. In other states, the distressed economic conditions and social unrest may have justified abandoning one form of government for another. But in New York, there was little incentive to make the leap of faith necessary to accept the Constitution.

During the 1780s, George Clinton persuaded New Yorkers that he was a moderate and capable leader. To a certain extent this perception developed because Clinton modeled himself on his image of George Washington. The two men first met in the Second Continental Congress in 1775 and their careers—public and private—intersected thereafter for over twenty years until Washington's death in 1799. Even after Washington's death, Clinton's association with Washington was used to the governor's advantage. In the assembly, gubernatorial, and presidential elections, Clinton was referred to as the friend and counsel of the late president.

In *The Democratic Republicans of New York*, Alfred F. Young likened George Clinton to Andrew Jackson. The democratic leanings of the New Yorker as well as his opposition to a large, all-encompassing federal government presaged the seventh president. During his presidency, Jackson was often called "The Second Washington." Surprisingly, despite the Clinton–Jackson and the Jackson–Washington comparisons, no one has compared George Clinton with George Washington. Although such a comparison does not readily leap to mind, there are many similarities between the men—similarities that first made Washington and Clinton admirers of each other and then lifelong friends.[3] The governor demonstrated his respect and admiration for the commander-in-chief, for example, by naming his only son George Washington Clinton and one of his daughters Martha Washington Clinton. Even after the two men took totally different positions on the new Constitution in 1787, Washington and Clinton remained on the best of terms. While the Constitution and later related issues estranged Washington from other long-time friends—first George Mason, then Thomas Jefferson and James Madison—the first president and New York's first governor remained close. Those occasions where these two men's political and private lives intersected form a central theme in this study.

Clinton was a thoughtful man. Although well educated for the time, Clinton had little formal education. He was trained as a surveyor and he studied law with William Smith, one of the great lawyers of the day. Clinton was fond of books. He took half a dozen volumes with him into combat during the French and Indian War, owned his own personal collection and regularly contributed to the New York City lending library. As governor, he consistently advocated public support for education, in particular a state university and, later in his term in office, public education for all children.

Though intelligent and thoughtful, Clinton was neither a scholar nor a philosopher. E. Wilder Spaulding, George Clinton's first biographer, lamented over fifty years ago that Clinton had not been a philosopher—a shortcoming that Spaulding believed cost Clinton the presidency. This assessment, however, is specious. Had Clinton been a philosopher, he would not have been George Clinton—the pragmatic man of action. To wish that Clinton had been more like Jefferson, Madison, or John Adams is pointless.

George Clinton was a man who dealt with and understood solid, practical realities, whether on the farm or the battlefield; whether serving in the courtroom, the legislature, or as chief executive. He was eulogized as "a practical statesman." Despite his pragmatism, or perhaps because of it, Clinton had a strong belief in the morality of politics and in constitutional government. Whatever his personal preferences and whatever was most expedient, Clinton believed that he had a duty to protect the constitution under which he served. Except for a brief flirtation during the direful years of the Revolution with a government of broad general powers, Clinton steadfastly supported government—both at the federal and state levels—that adhered strictly to a written constitution. Government should vigorously enforce all the powers specifically delegated to it and should never seek to expand its authority through a broad interpretation of constitutional powers. Only with this kind of limited government could individual liberty and state sovereignty be preserved. As an executive—both governor and vice president—Clinton abided by his principles. James Duane, a political opponent, admired the governor's "inflexible Regard to Justice, good order and publick Faith."[4]

During the war, George Clinton displayed a special quality, a rare ability to inspire devotion and confidence—to give men the willingness to endure deprivation and the faith to persist in seemingly endless campaigns against enormous odds. Alexander Hamilton believed that Clinton was "an excellent officer, the people have Confidence in him, will once act with zeal and Serve with Spirit and perseverence under him."[5] After the war, he was able to command obedience and devotion. Again, Clinton was a leader—not a philosopher. Before the bitter personal disputes that came between the two friends, Hamilton referred to Clinton as "a man of integrity and passes with his particular friends for a statesman; it is certain that without being destitute of understanding, his passions are much warmer, than his judgment is enlightened."[6]

As an ardent republican, George Clinton despised aristocracy and monarchy. He believed that they threatened the fundamental principles for which he had fought during the war. Governor Clinton and his followers feared, and probably with some justification, that their political opponents were sympathetic to these elitist ideas.

Despite his egalitarian and republican persuasion, George Clinton repeatedly violated one of the cardinal maxims of the Revolution's republican ideology—the concept of rotation in office. Instead of serving briefly and returning to the community as a private citizen, Clinton was elected for six consecutive three-year terms before retiring from office. Clinton retained his governorship for two reasons: first, he and his supporters feared that their aristocratic opponents would succeed him and do damage to the republic that they had been so instrumental in creating; second, Clinton simply enjoyed the challenge of the governorship, he liked the pay (£1,500 annually), and he was successful at it.

Although he was greatly admired by the people, and despite his democratic predilections, Clinton had a strong distaste for demagoguery and mobocracy. On at least two occasions—Shays's Rebellion that spilled over into New York from Massachusetts in early 1787 and the doctors' riots in New York City in April 1788—Clinton called out the militia to suppress violence. The people as well as their leaders, Clinton believed, were obliged to live within the constraints of the constitution and the rule of law. Armed force and intimidation were the last means to be used to redress grievances against government and were to be exercised only after all peaceable means had been exhausted. As a man of the people, Clinton understood New Yorkers and what they wanted from state government. For over twenty years, George Clinton gave the people of New York the kind of government they had fought to establish during the Revolution.

In assessing the significance of historical events, it is often interesting and sometimes illuminating to speculate about what might have happened if circumstances had been different. If Governor Clinton had supported the impost of 1783 in conformity with the wishes of Congress, would the country's economic problems have been solved? With an independent source of revenue, the Confederation Congress might have been able to address the country's serious social, economic, political, and diplomatic problems. Once amended, the Articles of Confederation might have been further amended, eventually evolving into a parliamentary system of government.

Supposing the proposal of the Constitution remained unchanged, what would have happened had Governor Clinton not been so vigorous and steadfast an opponent of the new plan of government? What if Clinton had followed a more pragmatic stance similar to John Hancock's? Would a mild Federalist—a thought that truly boggles the mind—like George Clinton have been acceptable as the country's first vice president? Such a combination as George Washington and George Clinton would have been a powerful team to unite the new nation geographically as well as ideologically, predating the Republican-fashioned Virginia-New York coalition of the 1790s. And, if Clinton had been the first vice president, would he have been elected president after Washington. Would President George Clinton have experienced the same problems—political and diplomatic—faced by John Adams as president? Would Thomas Jefferson have been elected president in 1800 or would he have served as Clinton's vice president—a reversal of their roles from 1805 to 1809?

Obviously these questions are unanswerable. No crystal ball exists that allows us to replay history with changes of significant events here or there. The usefulness of such counterfactual questions, however, is abundantly clear when we see how dramatically altered American and world history might have been if George Clinton's stance on two key issues had been different. Although the times did allow George Clinton to emerge from the obscurity of Ulster County, his decisions did have a significant impact on the course of the new American nation.

To a great degree, Clintonism was the logical response to national forces. Just as in colonial times when the Livingstons, as the out-party, took the revolutionary position and the Delanceys as the in-party became tories, so too did the Clintonians and Anti-Clintonians gravitate to politically polarized positions because of outside circumstances. Both Clinton and his opponents were nationalists during the war. As peace approached, however, Clinton perceived that his state was threatened by the actions of Congress and some of the neighboring states. After the peace, Clinton and his increasingly consolidated statewide party advocated policies that benefited New York over the Confederation. Ironically, it was conservative Alexander Hamilton who gave Clinton the idea to favor New York over the Confederation. In mid-February 1783, Hamilton suggested to Clinton that the army might not disperse peacefully after the war. To prepare for such a dangerous situation, Hamilton suggested that the state legislature set aside a large tract of land and make liberal grants to every officer and soldier who decided to become citizens of the state, thus tying their personal interests with those of New York. Acknowledging his affection for the union, Hamilton saw its weaknesses, as any "prudent man" could. Clinton took his advice and made generous land grants to soldiers who would provide a measure of safety for New York against the aggressive tendencies of its neighbors.[7]

In response to Clinton's introspective state policies, Anti-Clintonians shifted toward a more nationalistic perspective—a position they would have supported even if they had controlled the state government. In their effort to obtain control of the state government, conservatives, such as, Philip Schuyler, John Jay, Alexander Hamilton, sought to strengthen the federal government. With the two parties on a collision course, the personal popularity of the governor and the effectiveness of his policies gave conservatives little hope for immediate success. Eventually, Anti-Clintonians would try to regain control of the state by changing the federal government. In the meantime, the state addressed its immediate postwar problems.

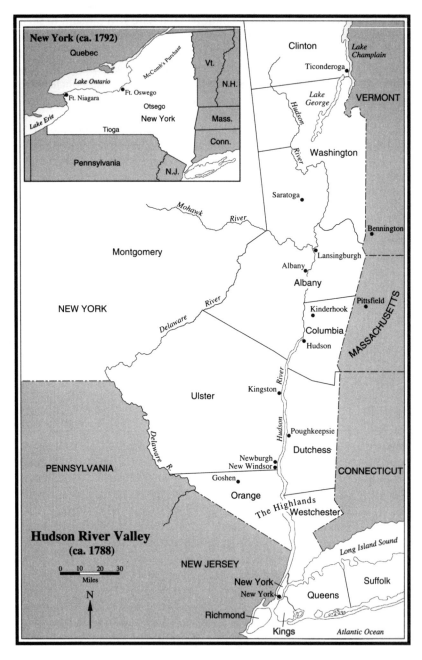

The Hudson River Valley, ca. 1788.
University of Wisconsin Cartographic Laboratory.

I

Preparing for Leadership

1. Laying the Foundation

George Clinton was born on the family farm on the New York frontier in Little Britain, Ulster County, on July 26, 1739. His great grandfather William Clinton seems to have been a royalist who escaped to France when the Cromwellian revolution succeeded in the middle of seventeenth-century England. William left France and moved successively to Spain, Scotland, and Northern Ireland where he established his estate, "Glengary." When William Clinton died, he left his son James Clinton (the grandfather of Governor George Clinton) a two-year-old orphan. Later, in a less violent English revolution, James Clinton supported the winning side as he endorsed William of Orange in the late 1680s. For his services, James was rewarded with an estate in the county of Longford in central Ireland, a county largely populated by English and Scottish Presbyterians under the early Stuarts. James's son Charles, the father of Governor Clinton, was born in Longford in 1690, and there he married a young Irish woman named Elizabeth Denniston.

As Presbyterians, the Clintons faced discrimination from the growing intolerance of the Anglican-dominated government. Consequently, Charles Clinton leased his estate to Lord Granard and along with 400 other dissenters chartered a vessel for Pennsylvania. The Clintons sailed for America on May 20, 1729, aboard the ship *George and Anne*. On the tragic voyage, the Clintons lost two of their three children to a measles epidemic that killed more than ninety passengers. On October 4, after more than five months at sea, the ship landed, not in Pennsylvania, but on Cape Cod. The following year the Clintons moved to Ulster County, New York, where they established a homestead at Little Britain, a few miles west of the Hudson.[1]

Because farming in Ulster County was difficult for the Clintons, Charles supplemented the family income in other ways. Milling, surveying, and speculating in land earned Charles extra money as well as the respect of his neighbors. His surveying talents and knowledge of the land attracted the attention of Cadwallader Colden, the province's surveyor general. As early as 1731 Colden employed Clinton in the onerous chore of surveying the newly-populating New York frontier. After almost twenty years of service, Colden was so pleased with Clinton's abilities and demeanor that in 1748 he recommended him to Governor George Clinton (1686?–1761—a distant relative of our Clintons) as "a person I can safely trust who on all occasion has shown the greatest regard for your Excellency and your family as well as for me."[2] The governor offered Charles Clinton the office of sheriff of the city and county of New York or any other position within his power; but, content with his private life in Ulster, Charles declined the offer. The governor, however, was so taken with his namesake, Charles Clinton's nine-year-old son George, that he named the boy clerk of the court of common pleas of Ulster County. The appointment would take place upon the death of John Crook, the incumbent. Crook died in 1759, whereupon on August 30 George Clinton was appointed clerk by letters patent under the seal of the province. Christopher Tappen was named deputy clerk. On December 12, 1760, Clinton was reappointed during good behavior, and he occupied the post for the remainder of his life—a fifty-three-year sinecure.

Because there were no schools in Ulster County as George Clinton grew up, Charles Clinton employed a private tutor, Daniel Thain, a young Scottish clergyman recently graduated from the University of Aberdeen. Thain's curriculum probably emphasized those practical subjects the young Clinton would need to prepare himself for surveying as well as the upcoming clerkship.

The Clinton family attended the Bethlehem Presbyterian church on the road to New Windsor. In 1773 George was made a trustee of the New Windsor district, but there is no evidence that he regularly attended services. Throughout the revolution, he displayed a strong streak of anti-Anglicanism, probably because Anglicans in New York were usually loyalists. For the most part, however, it seems that George Clinton, like many of his fellow revolutionaries, tended toward deism. The sense of God's general presence and approval of the Revolution permeated Clinton's writings. But he understood that God alone would not bring victory and preserve liberty—that Providence left for men to work out.

George Clinton probably left home in 1757 to enlist on a privateer during the French and Indian War. At eighteen, he signed on as a steward's mate on the *Defiance*, a ship of sixteen guns with a crew of 140. The

Defiance set sail from New York City on a ten-month voyage to the Caribbean, during which it captured three prizes, one or two with the assistance of other privateers. Although Clinton probably received only a small share of the prize money, he learned a great deal about military discipline and the teamwork necessary to survive in warfare.

While George Clinton was off in the Caribbean, his father had been appointed lieutenant colonel in the militia and his brother James received a captain's commission. George arrived too late to join them in the campaign against Fort Frontenac, but he enlisted in the spring of 1760 as a subaltern in his brother's company for the march against Montreal. On August 4, 1760, the twenty-one-year-old soldier wrote what he thought might be his last letter to his "Honoured Father." The 10,000 British troops plus their Indian allies were soon to leave their encampment near Fort Ontario for the assault on Montreal. Because the commanding general gave "Orders that No Officer Shall take his Chest with him," Clinton and his brother "Jamy" wanted their father to know where to claim their possessions if they should be killed. Both brothers stored their silver-hilted swords. George also laid away two silver buckles, one pair of shoes, four fine shirts, nine stalks [i. e., wine glasses], his new beaver hat, one silver clasp, two waistcoats, a small trunk with papers and writing instruments, six books (including a two-volume political and military history of England and a book of poetry), a teapot and three cups, saucers, and plates, three coarse shirts, one pair of trousers, a kilt, and one pair of stockings. Embarrassingly, Clinton told his father that he had "Sow'd" his watch in the "fertile Soil" of the Mohawk River. He hoped, however, to replace it with "a frenchman's."[3] After the capture of Montreal, Clinton, with this limited experience, retired from the military. He, along with most of the other American officers during the Revolution, would learn on the job.

When Clinton returned from Montreal in December 1760, he resumed his court clerkship that he had inherited the previous year. Because he needed legal training to perform his duties properly, Clinton went to New York City to read law with William Smith. One of the noted Whig triumvirate (along with William Livingston and John Morin Scott), Smith was recognized as one of the most prominent attorneys in the province. Others who studied law with him included Robert R. Livingston and Gouverneur Morris. According to an outline in Smith's papers, the subjects necessary for a lawyer were

1. The English, Latin and French Tongues.
2. Writing, Arithmetick, Geometry, Surveying, Merchant's Accounts or Bookkeeping.
3. Geography, Cronology, History.

4. Logick and Rhetorick.
5. Divinity.
6. Law of Nature and Nations.
7. Law of England.

With this broadly based education, the eminent Whig attorney molded his pupil; it was said that Clinton was a "Creature" of William Smith.[4] The combination of studying with Smith and living in radical New York City—infested with the rabble-rousing Sons of Liberty—provided Clinton with a valuable learning opportunity. Clinton himself said that "if I am a rebel Billy Smith made me one. I have been advised by him, have followed his course in whatever I have done and if I am a rebel I am a rebel of his making."[5] The student did become a rebel, but the teacher remained loyal to the king.

On September 12, 1764, Clinton was admitted to the bar. The following year, at the age of twenty-six, he began a year's tenure as Ulster County surrogate. In addition to practicing law, Clinton continued to survey. From March to June 1764, he surveyed the boundary line between New York and New Jersey. Ironically, he also surveyed a 4,000 acre tract for Sir Henry Clinton, the British general who ten years later would be an arch enemy of the surveyor-lawyer turned governor. Clinton continued to practice law and survey, but he also took up farming and milling. He evidently prospered because, by the time of his father's death in 1773, the young Clinton valued his assets in bonds and notes at £1,466, a substantial sum for that time.[6]

2. The Lawyer Becomes a Legislator

For decades colonial New York politics was dominated by a struggle between two aristocratic parties led by the manorial Livingston family of the Hudson River Valley and the mercantile Delancey family primarily of New York City and the southern counties. When the imperial conflict between Parliament and its North American colonies began in 1763, the Livingstons had been in control of the assembly for three years. As the "in party," the Livingstons—usually the anti-Parliament party—either supported Parliament's policies or opposed them as mildly as possible. As the "out party," the Delanceys—usually the court party—took a more strident, popular stance against Parliament. In the spring of 1768, as the conflict between Parliament and the colonies intensified, New York's royal governor Henry Moore dissolved the Livingston-controlled assembly and ordered new elections. Ulster County freeholders, overlooking members of the governor's party such as Cadwallader Colden, Jr., the lieutenant governor's son, chose instead two Whigs, forty-year-old Charles DeWitt of Kingston and the twenty-eight-year-old lawyer George Clinton of New Windsor.

When the new assembly convened in New York City in October 1768, Clinton found himself strangely out of place. As a new member of the Whig-Livingston family, he could expect to play only a minor role in the dramatic events that were anticipated. Although opposed to Parliament's policies embodied in the Quartering Act of 1765 and the Townshend Duties of 1767, Clinton still swore the obligatory oath of allegiance to the Crown and to the royal governor. Assemblyman Clinton was no radical. He hoped to serve his county and assist his party, which still had a small majority in the assembly, in opposing objectional British policy, but he had no thought of independence. More often than not, however, when the inevitable anti-Parliamentary issues came before the assembly, Clinton sided with his Ulster County colleague, and with Philip Schuyler, Abraham Ten Broeck, Philip Livingston, and Pierre Van Cortlandt, who served as the nucleus of the anti-British party.

The assembly's resolutions denouncing Parliament's defense of the Quartering Act again forced a disgruntled Governor Moore to dissolve it in January 1769. In the elections that month, Ulster County reelected its two Whig assemblymen. In much of the colony, new assemblymen replaced incumbents as the Delanceys regained control of the assembly. Despite the loss by the Livingstons, George Clinton returned to New York City in April 1769 a more confident man—a leader of the gentry, standing second only to the aristocratic Philip Schuyler. Clinton had served a short apprenticeship; he was eager to be involved—he was ready to lead. Unfortunately for the young Ulsterite, the Livingstons were so outnumbered (18 to 8) that little could be done to further their revolutionary effort. While other colonies actively opposed Parliament's efforts to tax America, more often than not the conservative Delanceys avoided direct legislative confrontation.

In December 1769 the Delancey-controlled assembly authorized £2,000 for the support of the British troops in New York. Clinton voted against such an appropriation. Alexander McDougall, one of the leaders of the radical Sons of Liberty in New York City, used the assembly's vote as an excuse to attack Parliament, Lieutenant Governor Colden, and the Delanceys in a seething pamphlet. The day after the pamphlet appeared, the assembly denounced it as a "false, seditious, and infamous libel." With the exception of Schuyler, all of the assemblymen—including Clinton—endorsed the denunciation. On February 7, 1770, McDougall was arrested. The Delanceys pressured McDougall to admit his guilt, but Assemblyman

Clinton stood up for the author's rights. McDougall refused to ask for mercy and the assembly committed him to jail. Only five assemblymen— Clinton among them—opposed the sentence. This action helped establish Clinton's reputation among the patriots. In fact, the McDougall affair marked a turning point in the Revolutionary movement in New York.[7] The Delanceys would now forever be the party loyal to the Crown, and the Livingstons would cooperate more closely with the radical Sons of Liberty in New York City. Clinton, it seems, took the same important step toward becoming a radical. When Lieutenant Governor Colden prorogued the assembly on January 27, 1770, Clinton left the charged atmosphere of New York City and returned to the relative tranquility of Ulster County a changed man.

3. An Advantageous Marriage

About a week after returning to Ulster, the young lawyer secretly crossed over into Columbia County and on Wednesday evening, February 7, 1770, married Cornelia Tappen, the twenty-six-year-old daughter of Peter Tappen, "an eminent, substantial, burgher" of Kingston.[8] The marriage had been planned for some time as the marriage certificate was dated October 28, 1769. But, for some reason, the couple wanted to avoid the hoopla of a large wedding. Three weeks after the elopement, Clinton wrote to his friends informing them "that shortly after my return from New York I completed that long talked of business of getting married." He requested "the pleasure of having some of my most intimate friends and acquaintances stop and spend the evening with me on Friday next."[9]

Cornelia Tappen, born on November 19, 1744, possessed "an ingenuous, friendly, placid disposition." She was described by the ardent tory chronicler Thomas Jones, a New York supreme court justice before the Revolution, as "a pretty Dutch girl."[10] Unfortunately, though, Mrs. Clinton's health would plague her throughout her life, perhaps contributing to the reluctance that the Clintons shared about entertaining. This deficiency was more than compensated for by the devotion that both Cornelia and George felt for each other.

The marriage also benefited George's career by linking him with one of the dominant political families in Ulster County. The Tappen connection assured Clinton of a solid base from which to operate. Clinton particularly benefited from the alliance he formed with Cornelia's brother, Christopher, a trustee and clerk of the town, described as "a young fellow of influence, of fortune, and well respected at Kingston."[11] Other prominent connections made by the marriage included Gilbert Livingston of Dutchess

County and Dirck Wynkoop of Ulster. Thomas Jones wrote, "In the Dutch towns in the Province of New York, (Kingston is entirely so) the inhabitants are all related. Cousins in the fifteenth degree are looked upon as nearly related, as cousins-german are in an English town. The Tappen family, in consequence of this kind of consanguinity, was related to almost the whole town. Clinton, in right of his marriage, of course, became also related." Spitefully, Jones recollected that the young "Clinton had art, cunning, and a good share of understanding. . . . He made the most of his connection. He became popular in the Corporation."[12] The Tappens and their relations were strong opponents of Parliament's new colonial policies. With this patriot backing, George Clinton could pursue his radical political course without fear of being turned out of office by his constituents. Ulster County would strongly support its favorite son throughout his career.

After their marriage, George and Cornelia moved to a farm in New Windsor overlooking the Highlands of the Hudson. Here his first two daughters, Catherine (1770) and Cornelia (1774) would be born. Here they would stay until the dangers of war would force them to move.

4. The Call to Congress

Throughout the early 1770s, the Delancey-controlled assembly kept New York out of the Revolutionary struggles as much as possible. During this time, Clinton maintained his leadership role among the minority Livingstons. In January 1775, the Delanceys, by a vote of 11 to 10, defeated a motion made by Clinton to approve the resolutions of the First Continental Congress. Although professing loyalty to his sovereign, Clinton warned the assembly "that the time was nearly come, that the colonies must have recourse to arms, and the sooner the better."[13] Called to order by the chair, the outspoken Whig apologized and the house proceeded with business. When a resolution was considered exempting New York from all internal taxes levied by Parliament, the Ulster firebrand moved on March 8 and again on March 24 that Parliament had no right whatsoever to tax the colonies. This kind of radicalism did not go unnoticed. When a popularly elected provincial congress was called to replace the assembly, Ulster freeholders overwhelmingly elected George Clinton as one of their three delegates. It was this radical legislative body that on April 22, 1775, appointed Clinton to the Second Continental Congress "to meet the Delegates from the other Colonies, and to concert and determine upon such measures as shall be judged most effectual for the preservation and reestablishment of American rights and privileges, and for the restoration of harmony between Great Britain and the Colonies."

George Clinton took his seat in Congress on May 15, 1775. It was at this time that he met George Washington. The young New Yorker was immediately attracted to the Virginian's poise and demeanor, although neither at the time suspected that their future public and private careers would intertwine for the next two decades. Clinton strongly supported Washington's appointment as commander-in-chief of the American army in mid-June 1775. On his journey northward to take command in Massachusetts, Washington addressed the New York provincial convention. When the delegates asked for assurance that he would resign his commission after the conclusion of hostilities, Washington told the New Yorkers that becoming a soldier did not relieve him or his fellow officers of their duty as citizens. He promised the convention that he would relinquish his authority as commander-in-chief as soon as it became expedient. Clinton admired this American Cincinnatus who left his farm to serve his country in time of need. No doubt Clinton, who had left Congress for ten days to attend to "troop business" in New York City, felt honored to host a public dinner for the country's new military leader. The New Yorker would have liked to have accompanied Washington to Boston and there actively support the patriot cause in the army, but Clinton returned to Congress.

Not enamored with legislative service in Philadelphia, Clinton nevertheless dutifully joined the radical forces. In attempting to convince John Jay to attend Congress, South Carolina delegate Edward Rutledge denigrated the New York delegation: except for Clinton, the New Yorkers "never quit their Chairs." According to Rutledge, "Clinton has Abilities but is silent in general, and wants (when he does speak) that Influence to which he is intitled."[14] Loyalist Thomas Jones, however, reported that Clinton "took an active part, was violent and decisive against Great Britain, he ridiculed all terms of accommodation, condemned all thoughts of reconciliation, and even, in an enthusiastic speech, went so far as to wish a poniard [a dagger] in the heart of George the tyrant of Britain, and would gladly contribute towards a handsome reward to any person who would perform so religious, so glorious, and so patriotic an act."[15] This extreme rhetoric continued to gain notoriety for the thirty-six-year-old congressman. Thus, after the Continental Congress requested in November 1775 that New York appoint commanders who would call up the militia to protect the Hudson from possible British attacks, the New York committee of safety, serving during the recess of the provincial congress, appointed Clinton on December 19 brigadier general of the combined brigade of Ulster and Orange County militia. He was happy to leave Congress to take a field command. According to Gouverneur Morris,

Clinton "had an aversion to councils, because (to use his own words) the duty of looking out for danger makes men cowards."[16] Before leaving Congress, Clinton supported the adoption of the Declaration of Independence. He left, however, before the New York provincial congress authorized its delegation to the Continental Congress to sign the Declaration.

5. The Militia General

General Clinton returned home eager to assume his command. He realized that New York was in a life-and-death struggle. Perhaps a majority of New Yorkers could be expected to remain loyal to the king. Those New Yorkers who took up arms against Parliament's policies were taking terrible risks— risks that put their property and their lives in jeopardy. Those unfriendly to the patriot cause must be considered as enemies and be treated accordingly. To this end Clinton actively pursued two goals: one military and the other political. Politically, according to the jaundiced eye of Thomas Jones, Clinton was

> in full power, as absolute and despotic in Ulster, as the French King in France, and as cruel and arbitrary as the Grand Turk. He tried, condemned, imprisoned, and punished the Loyalists most unmercifully. They were by his orders tarred and feathered, carted, whipped, fined, banished, and in short, every kind of cruelty, death not excepted, was practised by this emissary of rebellion in order to compel them (those within his jurisdiction) to obey, conform to, and execute the laws, rules, and recommendations of Congress.[17]

Whether Clinton's anti-loyalist activities were as harsh as portrayed by Jones is impossible to determine. There is little doubt that Clinton believed the patriot cause imperiled by loyalists. With little guidance available to him from a legislature or executive, with no laws yet enacted governing policy toward loyalists, Clinton's only aim was to secure control of the counties within his jurisdiction, thereby protecting those citizens endangered by the British and their allies. He may have felt justified in treating loyalists severely. Later, as governor, however, Clinton would stand against the tide in enforcing state laws that protected the rights of loyalists. But in these early days of the Revolution, General Clinton could not rely on unwritten laws or rights for an enemy capable of destroying him and his cause. The general could rely only on power.

Clinton's military command increased steadily. In August 1776 the provincial convention added Westchester County to his brigade, and the following January Clinton's authority was extended over the Dutchess

County militia. With the command of the militia of four counties, Clinton received orders from the provincial convention to march to and defend the Highlands of the Hudson. For the next two years Clinton's primary military concern was to fortify the Highlands and to block the river from British navigation. "To me," he reported to the New York convention, "it appears a Matter of the utmost Importance that the River should be obstructed which being effectually done will be [of] more real advantage to the United States than 10,000 Men [in] the next Campaign & it is more than likely wou[l]d change the seat of War."[18] To these ends he constructed two forts, guarded the passes through the Highlands, ran a huge iron chain across the river, and stationed two armed vessels in the Hudson immediately above the chain. Repeatedly he responded to the urgent appeals from the state convention and from Commander-in-Chief George Washington by calling out the militia. When the militia hesitated in turning out, Clinton spurred them on: "The season is approaching when in all probability you may be called upon to defend your County ag't the Attacks of a Tyrannical ministry and it will reflect great Dishonour on a County so forward in every other Respect in the Cause of Liberty to be found so extremely negligent in so important a Matter."[19] When this prodding failed, Clinton was quick to recommend to his colonels that company commanders be punished if they failed to furnish their quota of men.[20]

Clinton was an optimistic leader. On those occasions when bad news arrived, he consoled his men by saying that "we must learn to bear the sound of bad as well as good news; indeed, it would be unreasonable to expect the chance of war always in our favour."[21] Clinton, however, was not immune from depression himself. On several occasions in the spring of 1777, Clinton told the New York convention that he wanted to resign his militia command because, he wrote, "I find I am not able to render my Country that Service which they may have Reason to expect of me, considering the Importance of the Command they have honored me with."[22] The general did not wish to retire totally from military service. On the contrary, he told the convention that he would "most chearfully turn into the Ranks & do the Duty of a private & from the Knowledge I have as an Officer of the necessity of Discipline and Subordination I trust at least I shall be an Obedient Soldier."[23] The convention always refused its general's request, telling him that it was impossible to accept his resignation and reaffirming "the high Sense they entertain of your Abilities to serve your Country in this important Hour [and] the Confidence reposed in your Zeal and abilities by the Militia in General."[24]

Clinton often suffered from his own success. He had three primary tasks to achieve: to fortify the Highlands, to raise militia, and to enlist recruits for Washington's army. When he succeeded in obtaining enlistments for the Continental Army, he reduced the number of men available for service in the militia. By working as vigorously as possible on the fortifications, the price of private labor rose significantly above the pay of the militia. Men were unwilling to serve in the militia when they could make double or triple the wages by working on the fortifications.[25]

Raising militia proved to be a never-ending chore for Clinton. Men were naturally reluctant to leave their farms shorthanded or their families unprotected to defend against a threat that often never materialized. Clinton described his problem to Continental Army Major General Israel Putnam: "The Militia which I ordered to this Post & who came in with great Expedition almost to a Man according to Custom begin to be extreamly uneasy. They want to go Home, their Corn is suffering, their Harvest coming on, and they cant see that it is likely there will be any Thing for them to do here suddenly." Clinton asked the old general, "What shall I do with them? If I consent to their going Home they will Return when ordered again with great Chearfulness. If I dont, they will go (many of them at least) without Leave."[26] More often than not, Clinton let his troops go home, hoping they would return. He allowed the same latitude to his colonels, suggesting, however, that militia would be more effective if stationed a good distance from home.

Despite his problems in raising troops, by mid-September 1777 Clinton was pleased to tell the New York convention that the posts in the Highlands "are in so respectable a state of defence, as to promise us security against any attack on that quarter. This, together with the several obstructions in Hudson's River, has probably induced [British] General Howe to alter his original plan and to adopt another."[27] The convention was so pleased with Clinton's performance that in mid-March it recommended to Washington and the Continental Congress that Clinton be appointed commandant of the Highlands posts with the rank of brigadier general in the Continental Army. On March 25, 1777, the New Yorker was elected Continental commander and commissioned brigadier general, a rank he would retain throughout the war.[28] He modestly accepted commission. Thanking Washington for his congratulations, Clinton indicated that his "precarious State of Health & want of Military Knowledge" induced him to prefer "a more retired Life than that of the Army." But "early in the present Contest I laid it down as a Maxim not to refuse my (but tho poor) Services to my Country in any way they should think proper to appoint me. On this Principle I cant refuse the Honor done me by Congress in the present Appointment & shall be happy if in my Best Endeavours to serve my Country in the Military Line shall at my Time prove so successfull as to merit your Excellency's Approbation."[29]

George Clinton, Defender of the Hudson.
Courtesy of the State Historical Society of Wisconsin.

II

The Wartime Governor

6. The General Becomes Governor

By contrast with the temporary peacefulness in the Highlands, the British steadily advanced in the southern parts of the state. The New York convention, dominated by conservative Whigs, regularly moved from town to town, trying to keep one step ahead of the advancing British army. While fleeing, the convention drafted and, on April 20, 1777, adopted the state's first constitution. Most New Yorkers admired their new charter, but John Jay, its principal author, knew that "unless the government be committed to proper hands, it will be weak and unstable at home, and contemptible abroad."[1]

Three candidates for the office of governor surfaced quickly. Conservatives aligned behind Philip Livingston, the former speaker of the colonial assembly and now a delegate to the Continental Congress. Urban radicals supported John Morin Scott, while yeomen held up George Clinton. John Jay also garnered considerable support, but he announced that he would rather serve as chief justice rather than governor. As the election approached, opposition to Livingston's candidacy surfaced. Philip's brother William had been elected governor of New Jersey in 1776, his cousin Robert R. Livingston had been appointed state chancellor, and his nephew by marriage John Jay had just been appointed chief justice. Because such a family monopoly seemed improper, conservatives switched their support to Continental Army Major General Philip Schuyler, the forty-three-year-old manor lord from Albany County.[2] Jay could think of no better person to fill the three-year term of governor.[3] As the gubernatorial election approached, the five-man state committee of safety composed of John Jay, Charles DeWitt, Zephaniah Platt, Mathew Cantine, and Christopher Tappen (Clinton's brother-in-law) recommended to the county committees that Schuyler be chosen governor and George Clinton be elected lieutenant governor. The committee reported that Schuyler would have "many Votes in the Upper counties" and there was "no Doubt of his accepting the Office." The state constitution, the committee reported, was "universally approved. Let us not loose our Credit in committing the Government of it to men inadequate to the Task. These Gentlemen are respectable Abroad, their Attachment to the Cause is confessed & their Abilities unquestionable. Let us endeavour to be as unanimous as possible." Referring to radical Scott, a heavy drinker, the committee of safety acknowledged that "Interest is making for others; But we hope Care will be taken to frustrate the Ambitious Views of those who have neither Stability, uniformity or Sobriety to recommend them."[4]

As the campaign progressed it appeared as if Schuyler would be elected governor, but Clinton's chances dimmed for the lieutenant governorship. Some of Clinton's backers endorsed him for governor; others went along with the committee of safety and supported him for the second position. Jay believed that "by being pushed for both offices [he] may have neither." Furthermore, John Morin Scott had received many votes for the top position—votes that in a direct contest between the aristocratic Schuyler and the yeoman Clinton surely would have gone to the latter. In addition, reports circulated that late groundswells arose in Albany for James Duane and General Abraham Ten Broeck for the second position.[5] Some voters, however, resenting the committee of safety's intrusion, especially its recommendation of Schuyler, cast their ballots against the conservative candidate.[6]

Despite the committee of safety's recommendations, a last-minute, one-sided surge of votes from soldiers propelled Clinton to victory as both governor and lieutenant governor.[7] A tabulation of the election returns indicate that Clinton received 1,828 votes, Schuyler 1,199, Scott 368, Jay 367, Robert R. Livingston 7, and Philip Livingston 5. Clinton's support came from soldiers and yeomen of Ulster, Orange, Dutchess, and the northern part of Westchester not occupied by the British. Schuyler's votes came mainly from the tenants of the three northern counties of Albany, Tryon, and Charlotte. Scott's votes were spread among six counties, while Jay received support from Tryon and his home county of Westchester. The soldiers voted 963 to 187 for Clinton over Schuyler. Even without the overwhelming endorsement of the soldiers, Clinton would have been elected governor. In the lieutenant-governor's race, Clinton received 1,647 to Pierre Van Cortlandt's 1,098 and Abraham Ten Broeck's 748.[8]

One explanation for Clinton's victory can be found in the state constitution's establishment of the secret ballot for gubernatorial elections. Anti-Livingston feeling ran high in Dutchess and Ulster counties. In previous elections, tenants cast their oral vote for the candidate supported by the Livingston lords. The secret ballot changed that deferential pattern. In Dutchess County Clinton received a 206 to 132 edge. William Smith, Clinton's old mentor, reported that "the People of Dutchess and Ulster were perswaded in chusing a Govr. to name no Livingston nor any in Connection with that Family & hence Clinton was preferred to Jay & Schuyler."[9] The secret ballot had skewed gubernatorial elections leftward; the same phenomenon would occur when ballotting replaced voice voting in subsequent legislative elections.

Incredulous at the first reports, Schuyler wrote John Jay that he had heard that Clinton "has a majority of votes for the Chair. If so he has played his Cards better than was expected."[10] Two weeks later, the aristocratic Schuyler again wrote Jay to express his hope that "Gen. Clinton's having the chair of Government will not cause any divisions amongst the friends of America. Altho' his family and connections do not entitle him to so distinguished a predominance; yet he is virtuous and loves his country, has abilities and is brave." Schuyler told Jay that he pledged his loyalty and hoped that Clinton would receive, the "support, countenance and comfort" of "every patriot."[11] Not until August, however, did Schuyler offer Clinton his personal congratulations. In writing for reinforcements, Schuyler assured the new governor that "I shall embrace every oppertunity to make you sit as easy in the Chair of Government as the Times will admit. Your Virtue; the Love of my Country and that Friendship which I have always and with great Truth professed are all so many Inducements to it."[12] Clinton thanked the general for his "kind Congratulations" and assured him "that the Friendship you express for me is reciprocal and that every Thing in my Power shall tend to a Continuation of it."[13] Schuyler gave his support readily because he believed that Clinton would be unable to handle the difficult affairs of state, and that he would be called upon to play a crucial role in the government. In fact, the gubernatorial election of 1777 signaled the dismemberment of the old Livingston party. With the election of Clinton as governor, yeomen had seized control; they would not easily relinquish their power. Aristocrats never felt safe as long as their opponents controlled the state government; they would cooperate with Clinton in fighting the common enemy, but they always looked for the day when the right man would be elected governor. Eventually, failing to unseat Clinton, the aristocrats would work to strengthen and control the general government as a means to restrain the policies of the popular New York governor.

Clinton was notified of his election on July 9, 1777. The day before, Assembly Clerk John McKesson addressed a letter to "His Excellency the Governor" hoping that "no Considerations will induce you to decline the

Office. I pray God, it may be continued to you while you live & that you may execute it with Spirit & Dignity."[14] On June 11, Clinton responded: If left to his own wishes, he told the council of safety, he would accept neither office, but he felt duty-bound to accept "the Free Suffrages of the Public." He told the council that it could expect him to attend and take the oath of office as soon as he could safely leave his military post. Elected governor, Clinton believed that his simultaneous election as lieutenant governor was "a Nullity." To avoid any confusion and possible delay in a new election, however, Clinton formally resigned that office.[15]

News of Clinton's election traveled quickly. Lieutenant-Colonel Alexander Hamilton, Washington's principal aide, wrote to Clinton's immediate military superior, Major General Israel Putnam, "It is regretted that so useful an officer is obliged to leave the posts under his superintendency at a time like this."[16] Before relinquishing his military command, Clinton reported to Washington that "It is with a Degree of Pain that I am under a Necessity of asking Permission at this Time to quit the present Service especially as the Designs of the Enemy are not fully known & sh'd the Business of my new appoitnm't admit of it, I will most chearfully return to the army until the Fate of the present Campaign is determined."[17] Washington wrote the New York council of safety that "The appointment of General Clinton to the Government of your State, is an event, that, in itself, gives me great pleasure, and very much abates the regret I should otherwise feel for the loss of his Services in the Military line. That Gentleman's Character is Such, as will make him peculiarly useful at the head of your State, in a Situation so alarming and interesting, as it at present experiences."[18] Lieutenant-Colonel Pierre Regnier of the Fourth New York Battalion offered his heartiest congratulations to the new governor. "In Congratulating your Excellency," Regnier wrote, "I Congratulate my self, together with the Good People of this State for the Good Choice they have made of one, which Bravery, Courage, Prudence, Perseverance, and Desinterestedness, is the Least of your Qualities, and the only one fitt to be their Ruler in a So difficult and Critical time."[19]

The ministers of the Reformed Dutch Church of Kingston, among other well wishers, congratulated Clinton on his election—"the highest Honor the Subject of a free State can possess." The church was "uniformly attached to the cause of America" and believed that "Religion and morality" justified this "glorious revolution." The ministers admonished Clinton to set the proper precedents "from your vigilance, impartiality and firmness" in preserving inviolate the state constitution and the rights of the people. The governor was counselled that "nothing can more promote the general good than placing confidence in established characters & raising merit to distinguished power."[20]

The governor-elect thanked the Dutch ministers for their support and agreed with them "in thinking that the Constitution gives the fairest Promisses of Happiness." Clinton vowed "to preserve inviolate and thereby secure to the People those Civil and religious Liberties which it [the state constitution] has with the utmost Liberality and Wisdom been attentive to establish and guard."[21] In responding to a committee of Kingston gentlemen, Clinton promised "under the double Tie of Gratitude & Duty . . . faithfully to discharge the important Trust reposed in me by strictly adhering to the Principles of the Constitution so wisely calculated to secure the Rights & promote the Happiness of a free People."[22]

In his first address to the newly elected state legislature assembled at Kingston on September 10, 1777, Governor Clinton praised the late convention for its constitution which marked "the line between the executive, legislative and judicial powers." The governor told the legislators that it was his and their joint responsibility to set precedent for future office-holders. Each branch of government should "remain within the several departments in which the constitution has placed us, and thereby preserve the same inviolate, and repay the trust reposed in us by our constituents when they made us the guardians of their rights." Clinton did not urge this restraint because he feared a domineering legislature. Rather, he used the opportunity to state his own personal philosophy of government: "it shall always be my strenuous endeavor on the one hand to retain and exercise for the advantage of the people the powers with which they have invested me; on the other, carefully to avoid the invasion of those rights which the constitution has placed in other persons."[23]

Three days later the assemblymen responded by congratulating the governor "on his election, and assuring him of the confidence reposed in him by the Assembly and the people." The assemblymen thoroughly approved Clinton's "intention to retain and exercise" all executive powers. They intended to do the same with legislative powers.[24] Alexander Hamilton perhaps summed up the feelings of most New Yorkers: "Governor Clinton will do all in his power to promote objects, in which the state he Commands in is so Immediately Concerned."[25]

7. Outnumbered in the Highlands

Throughout the remainder of the Revolution, upstate New York continued to be one of the primary theaters of battle, while New York City and the six lower counties remained occupied. Repeated threats of a major British invasion or of limited forays up the Hudson from New York City forced the state to maintain its guard. With British General John Burgoyne and

Colonel Barry St. Leger converging on the state's northern frontier, British commander Sir Henry Clinton planned to sail from New York City up the Hudson to rendezvous with them. On September 23, 1777, Burgoyne told Sir Henry that "an attack or even the menace of an attack upon Fort Montgomery must be of great use, as it will draw away great part of their force. . . . Do it, my dear friend, directly."[26] Five days later Burgoyne told Sir Henry that he had abandoned his lines of communication to the lakes because he expected reinforcements at Albany.[27] First, however, Sir Henry attempted to deceive Washington, whose army was stationed outside Philadelphia.

On September 19, General William Howe's army occupied Philadelphia, forcing Congress to abandon the capital. Believing that Sir Henry Clinton, recently reinforced by three to four thousand fresh British and Hessian troops from Europe, planned to send a large force to strengthen Howe for a combined attempt to defeat the main American army under Washington, Congress and the commander-in-chief immediately sent for reinforcements from the New York Highlands. Other militia from the Highlands were sent to strengthen Philip Schuyler's defense against Burgoyne. Only a handful of congressmen worried about weakening the defenses of the Hudson. Washington's army appeared vulnerable as a British flotilla of forty ships sailed out of New York harbor toward Delaware Bay carrying an estimated 3,000 regulars and Hessians and 2,000 loyalists. By the time most of the American troops were on their way to Philadelphia, the British fleet turned and sailed for the Hudson. Alarmed, Washington wrote to his generals ordering them to return to the Highlands and to call out the Connecticut and New York militia. The commander-in-chief also wrote Governor Clinton on August 1 imploring him to resume command of the forts on the Highlands "if you possibly can, consistent with the duties of the Office upon which you newly entered." Washington anxiously awaited word.

The commander-in-chief had good reason to worry. The entire northern frontier was collapsing. In June 1777 General Arthur St. Clair abandoned Fort Ticonderoga without a fight; and, on July 7, General Schuyler, in command of the northern army, reported to Washington that Burgoyne would meet with little opposition as he advanced to the Hudson:

> My prospect of preventing them from penetrating is not much—They have an army flushed with victory, plentifully provided with provisions, Cannon and every Warlike Store—Our army, if it should once more collect, is weak in Numbers, dispirited, naked, in a Manner, destitute of provisions, without Camp Equipage, with little ammunition, and not a single piece of Cannon.[28]

Schuyler asked Washington to send him tents for 4,000 men, 500 camp kettles, a large quantity of muskets, ammunition, cartridge paper, twelve heavy cannon with travelling carriages, sixteen field pieces with ammunition, a competent number of artillerymen and all the equipment necessary for them—horses, harness, and drivers. For the next month, Schuyler continued his despondent barrage, ending on August 13 with a prediction that Burgoyne would soon be in Albany.

Schuyler's dispirited army, most of whom were New Englanders, despised their haughty, arrogant general. Colonel Udney Hay of New York reported to Governor Clinton that "Misfortune and fatigue have broken down the discipline and spirits of the troops and converted them in a great degree into a rabble. They seem to have lost all confidence in themselves and their leaders."[29] Even Alexander Hamilton, Schuyler's future son-in-law, began to doubt the New York general, telling Robert R. Livingston that Schuyler appeared to be "Inadequate to the Important Command with which he has been Intrusted. There seems to be a want of firmness in all his Actions." The "settled durable panic" that had struck the northern army was "a Reflection upon the Leader."[30] On August 4, Congress relieved Schuyler of his command and appointed General Horatio Gates of Virginia as his successor. The prospects in the north appeared grim. If Sir Henry were able to combine with Burgoyne's army, New England would be isolated from the rest of America—the war could be lost. The situation on the northern frontier was so desperate that John Jay called for Governor Clinton to mobilize the entire state militia to oppose Burgoyne. Unfortunately, however, General Israel Putnam, in command of all the forts of the Highlands, had allowed most of the militia in the area to return to their farms because he felt the danger was not imminent. Hamilton had confidence in the governor: "Genl Clinton is an excellent officer, the people have Confidence in him, will at once act with zeal and Serve with Spirit & perseverance under him." Clinton, Hamilton said, could render the greatest service by stopping Burgoyne's behemoth.[31]

Governor Clinton knew exactly what Washington wanted. The governor could easily have declined Washington's request, because of the demands of his civilian office. But Clinton realized the gravity of the situation and he could not refuse Washington. In fact, the governor probably understood that only he had any chance to succeed in this crucial assignment. Sir Henry's forces could not be allowed to link up with Burgoyne.

The governor agreed to take command of the forts. Washington wrote General Putnam that he was "glad to hear that Govr. Clinton has determined to resume the Command at Fort Montgomery, for there cannot be a properer man upon every account."[32] General Gates's arrival in the north also had a miraculous effect on the troops. Governor Clinton reported that "Gates has already reached the army and as I understand . . . things begin to wear a new face. No one talks any longer of retreating and means are already taking for an advance."[33]

Washington held little hope that the Highlands forts could withstand the expected British assault. His aim was to slow Sir Henry's advance sufficiently to give Gates a chance to reorganize. If Governor Clinton could inflict significant casualties on the British attackers from the south, perhaps Sir Henry would retreat back to the security of New York City. Surrender of the forts without a fight—a repeat of Ticonderoga—would be disastrous strategically and a terrible blow to the morale of both the army and the people. Washington reported the bleak prospects to Congress in the most optimistic light. The commander-in-chief felt "great confidence in the activity and bravery of Governor Clinton"—he would be courageous and aggressive, and the British attackers would "meet at least with a Spirited, if not a Successful opposition."[34] Perhaps Sir Henry's attempt to relieve Burgoyne might be totally frustrated.[35]

The British assault on the Highlands commenced during the first week of October 1777. Sir Henry Clinton led a flotilla of forty ships with no fewer than 4,000 soldiers, mostly British regulars and Hessians. The American defenders consisted of about 600 men—mainly militia, half of whom were unarmed. George Clinton assigned his older brother James command of Fort Clinton while across Popolopen Creek the governor himself commanded the weaker and incomplete Fort Montgomery. On October 6, the British attacked the governor's advance picket of thirty men. The guard volleyed and then retreated to Fort Clinton. The British then moved to attack the forts from the rear. Governor Clinton parried by sending 160 men with one artillery piece—all that he could spare—to block a pass through the Highlands. After a courageous fight in which the British suffered heavy casualties, the guard slowly retreated to the fort. Defending themselves in hand-to-hand combat with fixed bayonets, they disputed "the ground inch by inch." Clinton sent another sixty men led by Captain John Lamb with a single cannon from Fort Montgomery to harass the enemy until reinforcements could arrive from General Putnam on the opposite side of the Hudson at Peekskill. Repeatedly the British were driven back by New York grapeshot and "well-directed fire from the muskets, which made great havoc among them."[36]

Defeated in their frontal assault, the British troops dispersed into the woods and encircled the small American force. Understanding the better part of valor, Lamb ordered the cannon spiked and retreated to the fort. Within minutes, at about 2:00 P.M., both forts were surrounded. Three hours later, a British officer—Lieutenant Colonel Mungo Campbell—appeared with a white flag to discuss terms of surrender. Governor Clinton sent Lieutenant Colonel Livingston to "know his business." Campbell demanded that the Americans "surrender in five minutes, and thereby prevent the effusion of blood." The brazen American emissary boldly responded "that he had no authority to treat with him," unless the British "meant to surrender themselves prisoners of war," in which case the Americans assured him they would be "well treated." If the British did not intend to surrender, they could resume their attack on the forts because the New Yorkers were determined to defend them "to the last Extremity." Incensed at this audacity, the British resumed the attack and "a most incessant fire kept up till night." Without reinforcements, Governor Clinton reported that, after eight or ten assaults, his 600 troops were overwhelmed "soon after dusk, when the enemy forced our lines and redoubts at both posts, and the garrisons were obliged to fight their way out, as many as could, as we were determined not to surrender, and many have escaped." The escaping soldiers made their way "under cover of the Night, and by getting in the Mountains, have eluded the vigilance of their pursuers, and are hourly coming in."

Sir Henry lost about three hundred men and fifteen officers in capturing the forts. Many of these fatalities occurred during the last three to four hours of the attack when "the musketry was incessant within forty yards, and less a greater part of the time."[37] Lieutenant Colonel Campbell in command of the attack was killed in the first assault. Angered by their losses at Fort Montgomery, the Hessians gave no quarter as they bayoneted unarmed prisoners until stopped by some British officers. About half of the defenders were either captured or killed, Fort Montgomery suffering the more serious losses. Stephen Lush, the governor's aide was among the captured. In making his retreat from Fort Clinton, General James Clinton was stabbed with a bayonet, but survived when the weapon veered off the garrison's orderly book in his breeches pocket. He was able to make good his escape in the forest west of the fort even though the bayonet had wounded him in the groin. Governor Clinton himself barely avoided capture by descending a steep cliff and crossing the Hudson under cover of darkness. As he reached the shore with British troops searching for survivors, the governor hailed a boat that had just embarked. Recognizing the governor's voice, an officer ordered the boat to return. When Clinton saw that the boat was loaded to the gunwale, he ordered it off, determined to make his escape by swimming across the river. The officer in the boat refused to obey the order and offered his spot to the governor, preferring to chance capture so that the governor could safely escape. Rather than continue the dispute that endangered all, both men got into the boat, and ever so slowly the overloaded vessel made its way safely across the Hudson.[38]

Immediately Clinton started to reorganize his forces. Several captured British spies—couriers from Sir Henry to Burgoyne—all carried the same message that the Hudson was now open and Burgoyne should move his forces for a rendezvous with Sir Henry's army at Albany.[39] Governor Clinton, however, hoped to prevent the British from cutting the chain across the river or from "penetrating by land." He was determined to offer "every kind of opposition in my power, and if I should not be in force, to check their progress effectually, I shall try to throw myself between them, and the most Capital Objects, retireing Northward, 'till I am sufficiently reinforced to make a Stand against them."

The governor reported to the council of safety and to Washington that though the loss of the forts was important, "the manner in which they were defended has given such Gen. Sattisfaction as to elate & not depress" spirits. Clinton realized full well that there would be criticism for having lost the forts that he had only a month earlier told the legislature were secure. He knew that the loss of the forts would be viewed as a serious defeat, and he was willing to take the blame. His officers and men had "behaved with the greatest spirit and bravery."[40] Heartened by their stand, Clinton felt confident that the militia would "turn out pretty generally to oppose the Enemy."

The small band of New York militia and Continental soldiers gained universal praise for their heroism. Connecticut General Samuel Holden Parsons admired "the courage and bravery displayed by the troops (principally militia from New York) who defended the Post . . . No terms would be accepted, but with fortitude seldom found, they undauntedly stood the shock, determined to defend the Fort or sell their lives as dear as possible. The Fort was finally taken, merely for want of men to man the lines, and not for want of spirit in the men." "The garrison was defended with the utmost bravery; no men could do more."[41] From Little Britain, John Palsgrave Wyllys wrote his father about the victories in the north and in the south as well as the loss of the forts of the Highlands. "If ever [a] place was well defended, that was—by a handful of men—& with little Loss—Of near four hundred men, scarce a third is missing—it was carried by storm after repeated attacks; with the loss of numbers & some principal Officers, both British & Hessians."[42]

Attending the legislature in Kingston, Gouverneur Morris placed the blame not on Clinton but on General Gates. Morris charged that Gates "keeps all the strength of the Country idle while the Enemy are making their inroads and sacrificing the bravest of our Inhabitants." According to Morris, King George should "knight" Gates. Morris also censured Israel

Putnam. "Old Putnam," Morris bellowed, "is an old Woman and therefore much cannot be expected from him. Had he reinforced the Governor, Everything would have been not only safe, but glorious."[43] Morris wrote to Chancellor Livingston that the legislature was "hellishly frightened." "The Post was lost for Want of Men to defend it." Despite the loss, Morris was optimistic. "The Governor is safe and writes that the Enemy have indeed got the Fort but he can assure us they have paid for it. . . . We shall get our Spirits again and then perhaps be so full of Valor as to smite the Air for blowing in our Faces. We fought gloriously below. The Militia behaved as well as they could do. We shall beat them. We should soon do so if we have as good Officers as our Governor."[44]

General Parsons, somewhat ashamed that reinforcements had not arrived in time from Connecticut, reported to Governor Trumbull that "my countrymen seem again roused from the stupor which had seized them." The brave defense of the forts had stimulated the people "to more vigorous exertions, and to the exercise of a degree of patience, submission and perseverance necessary to accomplish anything great, or save the country from inevitable ruin." Seen from this perspective, "we may consider the event as fortunate, rather than as an event from which any ill effects will flow."[45]

A New England soldier rendezvousing with the remnants of Clinton's command on the west side of the Hudson, described the governor. "Never had a man a more absolute Ascendancy over people, than he has over the Inhabitants of this part of the Country—They are now gathered round their *Chief*—a stout hardy race—armed with good, long Musquets—in high Spirits—exulting in their behavior at Fort Montgomery & wishing for another opportunity—In short they do not appear like Dutchmen; but have the manners of N. England, from whence I believe they sprang— Their Governor deservedly has their Esteem–few men are his Superiors."[46]

Washington pointed no fingers of accusation; he knew that Clinton's situation was hopeless from the beginning. The commander-in-chief consoled the governor: "It is to be regretted that so brave a resistance did not meet with a suitable reward. You have, however, the satisfaction of knowing that every thing was done that could possibly be by a handful against a far superior force. This I am convinced was the case."[47] Washington believed that "from the bravery of the Garrison of Fort Montgomery," Sir Henry "purchased victory at no inconsiderable expence."[48]

The loss of the Highlands forts bound Washington and Clinton together. Washington knew that he had sent Clinton to certain defeat and perhaps to his capture or death. As distasteful as this was, the general had no alternative. The outcome of the war might depend on keeping Burgoyne's and Sir Henry Clinton's armies apart.

Governor Clinton understood the grave responsibility he accepted by resuming command of the forts. He knew the danger he faced—both to his reputation and to his personal safety. But the governor was loathe to back away from either responsibility or danger. He welcomed the opportunity to serve Washington, and he appreciated his commander's confidence. When Clinton emerged unscathed, Washington was relieved, while the governor knew that he had done everything possible to follow the general's orders.

As the British withdrew in mid-October, they marched into Kingston and avenged their heavy losses by setting the state capital ablaze. Governor Clinton lamented that after a forty-mile forced march in twenty-four hours his regrouped forces were about three miles away when the "lawless & Cowardly banditti" destroyed the town.[49] At the same time, Burgoyne's advance was halted and, without reinforcements from New York City, he surrendered in mid-October.

The loss of the Highlands forts is an event that has slipped into obscurity. Most historians ignore Forts Clinton and Montgomery, and concentrate on the far more important events occurring almost simultaneously around Saratoga—to many, the turning point in the Revolution. Those historians who have commented on the activities in the Highlands, have usually censured Israel Putnam for his inactivity and indecisiveness. Some historians, using Hamilton's 1789 political propaganda as their evidence, blame Governor Clinton for failing to secure the passes that allowed easy access to the forts.[50] A close analysis of the record—both the events themselves and the written record afterwards—suggests a different conclusion. The Highlands forts were simply indefensible in their undermanned condition facing a clearly more powerful attack. Reinforcements from the east side of the river would have helped, but Putnam refused to believe that Sir Henry's main targets were the forts on the west bank. Even when the battle commenced in its full fury, Putnam felt that it was a divergence as he braced for the full force of the British attack—an attack that never materialized.

Far from failing, however, Governor Clinton's mission was a measured success. Washington feared the loss of the Highlands forts not because of their own innate strategic importance. Rather, the forts were constructed to serve as a barrier between British forces in Canada and in New York City. Washington's primary purpose in sending Governor Clinton to the forts was accomplished. Sir Henry Clinton's flotilla was delayed and his army suffered significant casualties. Instead of having free access to the Hudson and quickly racing to Burgoyne's aid, Sir Henry soon realized that his army was in no position to assist the imperiled Burgoyne. Sir Henry returned to New York City leaving Burgoyne to suffer the consequences on the northern frontier. Although there is no way of knowing for certain,

Governor Clinton's valiant defense of Forts Clinton and Montgomery probably had a significant impact on the events unfolding just a few miles to the north. Had Sir Henry Clinton's forces not met with stiff opposition at the Highlands, the southern British army could have linked with Burgoyne's beleaguered troops, forming an unbeatable force in upstate New York. The relatively obscure loss of these two little forts probably had a profound impact on the entire war effort.

Throughout his career, Clinton would be honored for his valiant defense. Only in the "H.G." letters during the 1789 gubernatorial campaign did Alexander Hamilton minimize Clinton's military heroism. Three years later, in the aftermath of the contested gubernatorial election of 1792, "An Ulster County Farmer" remembered the fateful events along the Hudson.

> We have, through a long and perilous war been eyewitness of the conduct of our present governor. . . . Shall we forget his gallant stand at Fort Montgomery, in which, though vanquished, his defeat had all the beneficial effects of victory? Ask the warworn veteran, to whom the British standard bowed on the plains of Saratoga, if the affair at Fort Montgomery did not contribute to the success of our arms in the north, by defeating the intended junction of the British forces, and thereby enabling him to lay the foundation of our treaty with France, and to erect that temple of liberty, at the shrine of which, we at this day bend in silent adoration.[51]

In his funeral oration for Clinton, Gouverneur Morris remembered that Clinton's defense of the forts "was such as to raise the apprehension of having their [i.e., the British] retreat cut off, should they remain in the upper Hudson long enough to make an useful diversion in favor of Burgoyne. That vaunting chief was therefore left to his fate. And thus the obstacles opposed in the Highlands shed a propitious influence on that northern campaign, whose brilliant issue at Saratoga, arrayed in our defence the heads and armies of France and Spain."[52]

Six weeks after the loss of the forts, the Continental Congress directed General Washington to inquire "into the conduct of the principal officers" in command. Washington named a three-man court in February 1778, whose findings Washington reported to Congress in mid-June 1778: "That those Posts were lost, not from any Fault, Misconduct, or Negligence of the Commanding Officers, but solely thro' the Want of an adequate Force under their Command to maintain and defend them." On August 17, 1778, Congress resolved to accept the report, and two weeks later it appeared in the *New York Packet*. Governor Clinton, however, was not satisfied. He had not received a copy of the findings, and he felt that he was not entirely exonerated. He believed that he might later be charged with a foolhardy attempt to save the forts against desperate odds and that through ignorance or negligence he had "made so great a Sacrafice to so vain an Attempt" when he should have preserved the soldiers and stores "by evacuating the Forts." Obviously Clinton knew what Washington wanted him to do; Clinton merely wanted the record to show that no blame was to be placed on him for putting up a fight. Clinton told Congress that "the Respect I owe my own Reputation added to the Desire I have of preserving the Confidence which the Garrison reposed in me, and of which they gave me the highest Proof leads me to think it my Duty to inable myself to evince the Propriety of my Conduct on that Occasion."[53] President of Congress Henry Laurens embarrassedly wrote Clinton to apologize for the neglect. The report of the court of inquiry, Laurens wrote, totally exonerated Clinton of any guilt and "signifies the entire approbation by Congress of your Excellency's conduct as Commander of the Forts."[54] Even General Horatio Gates, who was not one to praise those outside of his immediate circle, declared that "the noble defence of Fort Montgomery, will, to the latest posterity, adorn the name of Clinton."[55]

8. Further Defenses for the Hudson

As Sir Henry Clinton's army returned to New York City, Washington, through his aide Alexander Hamilton, ordered General Putnam to send two Continental brigades and a militia regiment to reinforce the main army located near Philadelphia. Washington feared that the armies of Henry Clinton and General William Howe would combine, and threaten the main American army. An appalled Hamilton arrived at Putnam's headquarters at New Windsor on November 9, 1777, and trembled at what he found. Putnam had done nothing; he had ignored Washington's order in favor of pursuing his favorite "Hobby horse"—a grand assault on New York City. Hamilton then issued a direct order from Washington to forward the reinforcements. But Putnam seemingly had lost control of the situation. The two brigades refused to march because they had not been paid for six to eight months, and in fact soldiers in one of the brigades had mutineed.

At this point George Clinton took charge. He prevailed upon one of the brigades to march partway to Washington's army, "in hopes by getting them once on the go, to get them to continue their march." The governor also borrowed more than $5,000 on his own credit to pay the disgruntled troops. He advised Hamilton to forgo the militia because by the time they reached Philadelphia, their enlistment would expire and they would return to New York. Instead, Clinton suggested that all of the Continental troops under Putnam's command be sent to Washington's aid. Clinton believed that the only immediate danger in the Highlands came from small maurauding bands. The militia could offer sufficient protection from this enemy; Washington, on the other hand, needed all the support he could muster. Hamilton reported to his commander that no reliance could be placed on Putnam, but that "Governor Clinton will do every thing in his power." Hamilton wished that Putnam would be recalled from the command and that "Governor Clinton would accept it. The blunders and caprices of the former are endless."[56]

With the danger in the north diminished and with Sir Henry Clinton moving toward Philadelphia, the governor continued to strengthen the fortifications on the Hudson. Clinton warned the state senate that any delay in this critical matter "may be attended with the most fatal consequences to the public in general, and to this State more particularly."[57] As a further defense for the Hudson, the governor recommended constructing a fort at West Point, placing a chain across the river at that point, and posting some gunboats above the chain.[58]

Clinton's concern for the safety of the Highlands was so strong that in June 1779, he again took command of a militia regiment and marched to the Highlands. Knowing the importance of unified action and not wanting to appear hungry for power, Clinton wrote an extraordinary letter to Continental Army Major General Alexander McDougall of New York. Clinton said that he would assume "the Character of a Brigad'r Genl. in the Continental Army," and as such he would become subordinate to the popular McDougall. If, however, an out-of-state general superior in rank to McDougall should take command, Clinton could not continue in such a subordinate capacity. The militia would not allow their governor to serve under the command of an officer from another state.[59] Ten weeks later, New York's Chief Justice John Jay, then serving in Congress, wrote Clinton, "The Exertions of our State have placed her in a very respectable Point of View, and permit me to tell you, that your march to the Highlands has given occasion to many handsome things being said & written of you here."[60]

9. Slaughter on the Frontier

In spite of the repeated dangers to the Hudson, the most frustrating and disconcerting problem the governor faced was the defense of the frontier. For over three years the entire perimeter of the state—in particular, the Mohawk River Valley—was under the constant threat of attack from enemy bands of 50 to 500 men, consisting of British regulars, loyalists, and the hostile tribes of the Iroquois Nation led by Chief Joseph Brant. No one knew exactly where or when these brutal raids would occur. The uncertainty and vulnerability of settlers created near panic situations. Seemingly coming out of nowhere, the guerilla bands would swoop down on isolated farms and villages, killing, mutilating, and scalping the men who refused to swear allegiance to the king; burning homes and outbuildings; and taking women, children, and the elderly prisoner to Canada. Those who could not maintain the pace of the retreating marauders would be left to perish in the wilderness. A dozen villages were razed completely. The raiders destroyed vast quantities of grain and escaped with large numbers of cattle and horses. This deprived the Continental Army and the state militia of much-needed provisions, and played havoc with the local economy.

Because the frontier settlements could not be protected properly, many farmers left their homes and fields as they brought their families to safety. Continually on alert, the militia became "worn out affording the Inhabitants Protection against" these depradations. Only sporadically would American forces and their Indian allies do battle with a raiding party. Sometimes the outnumbered pursuing militia would become victim themselves to tories and Indians who lay in ambush for them.[61] The inability to provide protection for these frontier settlers weighed heavily on Clinton. Endless petitions were submitted to him for troops to be stationed at various frontier locations to guard against "the Enemy on every Side of us."[62] Clinton wrote to the state's delegates in Congress that many settlers "are desirous of removing unless I can assure them that such Posts will be taken or such offensive Measures pursued as will tend to protect them." The governor anguished over his dilemma: "to defend them by a Militia harrassed as ours are will be impossible—to encourage them to stay will be to make myself in some Measure chargeable with the Evils that may fall upon them in Consequence of such Encouragement—to advise them to break up their Settlements only increases the Evil, for Frontiers and defenceless Frontiers will still remain 'till Hudson's River becomes our Western Boundary." Clinton asked Congress for some indication that posts would be established or that offensive measure would be taken. If there were such prospects, he would "by general Assurances induce the Inhabitants to remain on their Farms. If otherwise common Humanity dictates the Propriety of removing them in Time."[63]

Repeatedly the governor informed the legislature "that notwithstanding the provision made for the defence of our frontiers, a part of them has again been desolated by a merciless enemy." The legislature directed that a force of 700 men be raised for the frontier service; but the governor explained that, "when compared with the extent of country to be guarded, and with what has since appeared the strength of the enemy employed against it, you will discover [that force] to have been insufficient."[64] The governor regularly sought assistance from George Washington, knowing full well that the commander-in-chief did not have the necessary resources and that those resources might be better used elsewhere. Clinton apologized for his numerous pleas for assistance by stressing "the weak and distressed situation of the state."[65] All too often Clinton's expectations were realized when no reinforcements were sent. Washington asked the zealous governor to be patient and understanding; the sacrifice would be worth it; "in the course of events," victory would be theirs.[66] In writing from Congress, John Jay told Clinton that "the Security for the Frontier" lay entirely with Washington, and that the commander-in-chief's "Respect for New York, & the personal Regard he assures me he entertains for the Governor" will draw his attention to our exigencies and afford New York "all the Security in his Power to give."[67]

In a letter to Clinton, the wealthy Albany County manorial lord James Duane expressed the despondency of New Yorkers over the crisis on the frontier: "The Destruction of our western frontier, is the Destruction of our Granary, & will be severely felt; and what is worse the Inhabitants, finding they are not protected, will loose Confidence in the present Government."[68] The only way, in Clinton's judgment, to stop the raids was to go on the offensive. In June 1778, he wrote militia General Abraham Ten Broeck "that no Force that can be collected will be able to afford full Protection to the Inhabitants unless the flying Party by whom they are distressed can be routed at the Places where they usually rendevouz. This I am informed is Unadilla. I woud, therefore, advise an Expedition against that Place."[69] Before the governor could organize such a campaign, warriors of the pro-American tribes of the Iroquois Nation—the Oneida and the Tuscarora—attacked and burned Unadilla and another place called Butter Nuts, taking ten prisoners and releasing one New Yorker held in captivity.[70] In early September 1778, the governor wrote Colonel William Butler stating that he was "more than ever convinced, that offensive Operations ag't the Savages & Tories is absolutely necessary."[71] Later in the month Butler's Continental troops again attacked and destroyed Unadilla and two other settlements, making the frontier somewhat safer until the following spring. As the weather improved in the spring, the guerilla raids resumed with greater frequency and ferocity. Clinton wrote to one of his militia colonels urging him to do "something which may give Confidence to the Inhabitants who are now deserting their Settlements and reanimate the Militia who seem to have lost their fine spirits."[72] Eventually, after stronger pleadings from the governor, Washington authorized generals John Sullivan and James Clinton (the governor's brother) to initiate a pincer movement against the Indian settlements. This successful campaign in August and September 1779 again temporarily quieted the frontier. The governor planned a diversionary expedition under his leadership that also planned to attack "a collection of Tories and Indians who had erected" some fortifications at Shohawkin and Coulatee. General Washington, however, would not allow the governor to lead the mission. The deteriorating situation along the Hudson required the governor to remain available to call up "the Militia to his Aid."[73] When the raiding on the frontier resumed, however, Clinton on two occasions, in May and October 1780, took command of the militia himself and pursued a band of the raiders, but on both occasions the enemy escaped by boat as the militia neared.[74] The legislature on a number of occasions gave the governor "almost unlimitted Powers" to coordinate wartime activities with Congress and foreign allies, and this coupled "with the Attention due to our extensive Frontier (which is seldom a Day without being invaded on one Quarter or another)" presented Clinton with "almost an intollerable Burthen" leaving him "without one Moment's Leisure."[75] This pressure was relieved somewhat when Governor Clinton finally found an effective officer for this frontier fighting when he coaxed Marinus Willett out of an early retirement from Continental service and commissioned him in the militia. Willett, called "The Devil" by the Iroquois because of his relentless pursuit, commanded a regiment of almost 500 men on the northern frontier. Colonel Levi Pawling commanded another 500 soldiers on the southern frontier. Together, these two regiments gave the patriots a presence on the frontier, but Clinton readily admitted that the task of defending the vast frontier was too large for them. "To cover every settlement," the governor lamented, "would so divide [even] a much larger Force than the present is as to prevent their being suddenly able to collect & oppose any large Body of the Enemy."[76] "Despite all of these efforts, General Schuyler described the frontier as "one general Scene of ruin & desolation."[77] "The inhabitants," Schuyler reported, "are all on the wing, ready to fly."[78]

Peace came to the frontier only after the preliminary treaty of peace arrived in 1782. Even then, the situation was dangerous. Governor Clinton reported to Washington, "The frontier Settlements were never in a more defenceless Situation. The Idea of Peace has thrown them off their Guard and I fear will prevent even that Degree of Exertion which may be necessary for their Safety against the smallest Parties. My anxiety for them is therefore proportionably increased."[79] Only when word of the peace treaty eventually reached the British forces in Quebec and at the Northwest posts did hostilities cease.

To compound his military problems, the governor had to provide for the large numbers of refugees made homeless by the enemy attacks on the frontier. In addition, he had to safeguard families and communities from their hostile loyalist neighbors as well as from occasional bands of roving banditti and marauding American soldiers.

10. Stemming the Mutinies

Throughout the war, supplying the army with the basics—food, clothing and pay—remained a critical problem. When the Continental Army and militia were not well provided for, the dangers of mass desertion or mutiny became very real. Despite the military difficulties facing the state, New York was expected to supply the Continental Army, the French navy, and its own militia with food, clothing, arms, ammunition, and pay. Often money was unavailable to purchase supplies. On several occasions, Clinton as both general and governor used his own money or borrowed against his own credit in order to obtain necessary provisions or provide loans to impoverished state officials.[80] During his first winter as governor, Clinton was besieged with pleas from his militia colonels for food and clothing to see the troops through the season. The governor also received similarly urgent messages from Washington and from a committee of Congress in mid-February 1778 appealing for provisions for the Continental Army, then languishing at Valley Forge. Washington reported that the army was in a "dreadful situation." "It is more alarming than you will probably conceive." "For some days past, there has been little less, than a famine in camp."[81] The congressional committee pleaded that something had to be done to provide sustenance for the soldiers. The alternatives were "Mutany, Desertion, a Spirit of Depredation & Plunder ending at last in a total Dissolution perhaps of our whole Army."[82] Judging from Clinton's previous service, the congressional committee hoped that the governor would "amply supply our Deficiency." Washington told Clinton that he expected "every thing within the compass of your power, and that the abilities and resources of the state over which you preside, will admit." In particular, the army needed cattle "to be at camp in the course of a month." Clinton quickly replied that New York was itself in a desperate situation. "Having been long the seat of war, it has been ravaged, plundered & greatly exhausted." American armies in both New England and in the Middle States drew upon New York for provisions, as did the enemy forces in New York City and the southern counties. "Notwithstanding these Difficulties," Clinton ordered that 100 head of cattle and 150 barrels of salt pork be sent to Valley Forge "without a Moment's Delay." The governor assured Congress and Washington that New York was committed to "the Ameri can cause" while the "attachment the People have to the commander-in-chief, will excite them to the most vigorous Exertions for the Relief of his army." Although Clinton could not promise more provisions, he assured Washington "that our most Strenuous Endeavours to procure them shall not be wanting."[83] Within a week, the governor informed Washington that another 1,700 barrels of salt pork were on the way. Washington thanked Clinton: "The readiness with which you comply with all my requests in prosecution of the public service has a claim to my warmest acknowledgments."[84]

Provisioning problems persisted. By mid-1780 Washington's profoundest fears about an army mutiny materialized. The Connecticut enlisted men in Washington's army, now stationed at Morristown, New Jersey, demanded to go home. After some tense moments the mutiny was quelled; but Philip Schuyler, in camp with Washington, realized that "we have too much reason to apprehend that it will shew itself soon and more seriously unless provisions arrive." Officers went on bread-and-water rations so that the soldiers could have the last of the meat.[85] Washington feared that similar uprisings might spread to the Continental units in New York at West Point and Fort Schuyler.

On January 1, 1781, the Pennsylvania Line stationed at Morristown mutinied. Several officers were killed and wounded in a vain attempt to suppress the uprising. The mutineers paraded with arms, seized the division's artillery, and marched toward Philadelphia to present their grievances to Congress. Officers, watching for an opportunity to regain control, accompanied them, hoping to keep them from plundering the countryside.

Washington feared that the entire war effort had reached a devastating crisis. Would all the discontented recruits disobey their officers? Would there be wholesale desertions? On January 4, Washington reported to Clinton that the Continental officers in command of the forts on the Highlands of the Hudson could not guarantee their commands. The commander-in-chief needed the governor's assistance. If the Continental soldiers revolted, only the New York militia could be counted on to protect the forts. If the militia failed to fill the breach, the forts would easily fall because, with the Hudson entirely free of ice, the way was open for a major British assault from their New York City stronghold. If the forts fell, the British would control the Hudson, and divide New England from the rest of the states—their strategy since the beginning of the war.[86] "Under these circumstances," Washington believed "it indispensably necessary" that Governor Clinton stay as near the forts as possible. The governor's "influence with the militia would give a spring to their exertions," and Clinton's advice "would be of infinite service." Washington asked Clinton to forgo the legislative session about to convene in Albany and visit him at headquarters. The next day Clinton responded that he was on his way to attend the commander-in-chief and that during this alarming situation, he would unhesitatingly render Washington "every assistance in my Power."[87]

On January 13, Washington wrote Clinton that the Pennsylvania mutiny had worsened. British emissaries within the soldiers' ranks had been discovered fomenting discontent, but the troops refused to turn over the conspirators to the officers for prosecution. It seemed that unless the soldiers' demands were met, they might go over to the enemy. The situation was desperate as Washington readied a Continental detachment to march from the New York forts to suppress the mutineers. How much support, Washington asked, could he expect from Clinton and the New York militia? The governor responded that 1,000 men could be assembled within three or four days. Some could reach West Point on the day that they were called up to service; most would be there the following day.[88] A grateful Washington responded the next day: "I had the honor last night to receive Your Excellency's Letter . . . and am happy to inform you that there probably will be no occasion to march the Detachment, nor consequently to call the Militia to our aid." A committee of Congress had negotiated a settlement with the rebellious soldiers.[89]

Within days of the settlement of the Pennsylvania Line's mutiny, another rebellion broke out among the New Jersey enlisted men. Washington refused to tolerate any more insubordination. Immediately he ordered a detachment of Continental soldiers from the forts on the Highlands "to compel the mutineers to unconditional submission, to listen to no terms while they were in a state of resistance, and on their reduction to execute instantly a few of the most active, and most incendiary Leaders." Washington hoped that the New Yorkers would "do their duty," but, in any case, he preferred "any extremity to which the Jersey Troops may be driven" rather than to take part in another compromise that would only encourage further mutinies. Civil liberties, Washington wrote Clinton, would be endangered if armed soldiers could dictate "terms to their country."[90]

On January 26, Clinton reported to Washington that he was forced to leave the Highlands because of a threatened insurrection among the troops in Albany. "I think it my Duty, therefore, to be near them & prevent if possible the Spirit of Discontent from spreading." If, during his absence, Washington needed the support of the New York militia, Clinton authorized the commander-in-chief to call upon the brigade's colonels directly. An application to Clinton in Albany "might be attended with too much Delay."[91] By the end of the month, however, the governor reported that "The Spirit of Discontent which had reached the Troops" in Albany "has subsided and I am in Hopes a Repetition is not to be apprehended."[92]

Governor Clinton was such an effective force in New York that on several occasions the British attempted to kidnap him. In mid-August 1781, Washington sent an express rider to warn the governor that six enemy agents were on their way to abduct him. The commander-in-chief, who obviously had a well informed spy network, told Clinton the names of the kidnappers and of the individuals who were expected to harbor them.[93] In responding to a letter from Philip Schuyler in which he told of an unsuccessful attempt to kidnap him, Clinton expressed his credence in Washington's warning because all of the conspirators were "well known to me & from their characters render the Account more than probable." Clinton told Schuyler that this was "the third Party which have been out on this business & of which I have been apprized in the course of the Spring & Summer." Usually the kidnappers were watched closely and often arrested for committing other crimes.[94]

11. A Stronger Congress

A logical answer to New York's and the country's problems was to strengthen Congress under the newly-proposed Articles of Confederation. Many New Yorkers, including Governor Clinton, advocated a more powerful Congress with an independent revenue. Voluntary contributions made by the states simply did not work. On February 13, 1778, Alexander Hamilton wrote his friend Governor Clinton a remarkable letter.[95] Hamilton, serving as aide-de-camp to Washington at Valley Forge, complained bitterly that not only was Congress poorly attended, but it lacked the wisdom and courage it had shown earlier: "Folly, caprice a want of foresight, comprehension and dignity, characterise the general tenor of their actions. . . . Their conduct with respect to the army especially is feeble indecisive and improvident. . . . they have exposed the army frequently to temporary want, and to the danger of a dissolution, from absolute famine. . . . If effectual measures are not speedily adopted, I know not how we shall keep the army together or make another campaign."

Congress suffered "the present falling off" because "the great men who composed our first councils" had taken positions in the army or as civil officers of their states. "The only remedy then," according to Hamilton, "is to take them out of these employments and return them to the place, where their presence is infinitely more important." Hamilton acknowledged the importance of the state governments, but in his judgment, "it is infinitely more important to have a wise general council; otherwise a failure of the measures of the union will overturn all your labours for the advancement of your particular good and ruin the common cause. You should not beggar the councils of the United States to enrich the administration of the several members. . . . How can the common force be exerted, if the power of collecting it be put in weak foolish and unsteady hands?" Only through a strong and effective Congress, suggested Hamilton, could the war be won.

Hamilton felt uneasy about putting these bold thoughts on paper. He would confide only "to those in whom I may place an entire confidence." It was time, he admonished, "that men of weight and understanding should take the alarm, and excite each other to a proper remedy." Hamilton, himself, felt unable to accomplish much; he could only "hint" at the problems. It was up to Clinton to take the lead. New York was generally better represented in Congress than the other states, but the governor should try to get John Jay, Robert R. Livingston, and Philip Schuyler appointed. More importantly, Clinton should use his influence to give "the alarm to the other states, through the medium of your confidential friends." "Indeed," Hamilton pleaded, "it is necessary there should be a change. America will shake to its center, if there is not."[96]

The busy governor responded to Hamilton on March 5, a month after the New York legislature had unanimously adopted the Articles of Confederation. Though Clinton signed the act adopting the Articles on February 16, he believed them to be defective. If Congress were strengthened beyond the provisions of the Articles, "even their Want of Wisdom but too Evident in most of their Measures would in that Case be less Injurious." Could our soldiers "subsist on Resolves," Clinton lamented satirically, "they would never want Food or Cloathing. Resolves are most Powerful Expedients. They are to fill, to Cloath, to Feed, & pay our Armies, at least this is the Language which the late Conduct of our Masters speak."[97] Hamilton was pleased that the governor's "ideas" corresponded so closely with his own.

As spring neared, however, Hamilton felt more "melancholy" than ever. The army, he said, was adequate to assure victory in the next campaign, but the weakness of Congress "will, in all probability, ruin us." Hamilton told the governor that he dwelt "upon the faults of Congress because I think they strike at the vitals of our opposition [to Britain] and of our future prosperity, and with this idea I cannot but wish that every Gentleman of influence in the country should think with me."[98] Clinton was of the same mind.

The commander-in-chief also appreciated Clinton's efforts in strengthening Congress. "In the confidence of friendship," Washington thanked the governor for his support. The weakness of Congress and the lack of support from the states "have uniformly appeared to me to threaten the subversion of our independence. . . . I should acknowledge, to the honor of your State, that the pernicious system I have complained of has not influenced your councils; but that New York is among the few that has felt the necessity of energy, and considering its situation, has done everything that could be expected from it. I doubt not a perseverance in the same plan; and that Your Excellency's influence will be as it has been, successfully employed to promote it."[99]

In early August 1780 delegates from the states of New Hampshire, Massachusetts, and Connecticut met in Boston to discuss efforts to coordinate activities and to strengthen Congress' powers. The delegates called another convention to meet in Hartford in November 1780, and New York was invited to send representatives. In transmitting the invitation to the legislature on September 7, Governor Clinton declared that the powers of Congress must be increased: "When we reflect upon the present situation of our public affairs, it is evident our embarrassments in the prosecution of the war are chiefly to be attributed to a defect in power in those who ought to exercise a supreme direction, for while congress only recommend and the different States deliberate upon the propriety of the recommendation, we cannot expect a union of force or counsel." Clinton believed that Congress ought to be vested "with such authority as that in all matters which relate to the war, the requisitions may be peremptory."[100]

The legislature appointed three delegates to the proposed conference—Philip Schuyler, John Sloss Hobart, and Egbert Benson. Schuyler wrote his son-in-law that "A Spirit favorable to the common cause has pervaded almost both houses, they begin to talk of a dictator and vice dictators, as if it was a thing that was already determined on. I believe I shall be sent with Instructions to propose that a Dictator should be appointed."[101] On October 10, the legislature passed a joint resolution instructing its delegates to Congress to declare in Congress that it was New York's earnest wish that throughout the war or until a confederation government was adopted, Congress should "exercise every Power which they may deem necessary for an effectual prosecution of the war," and that whenever a state failed to provide its quota of men, money, or provisions, "that Congress direct the commander in chief without delay to march the Army or such part of it as may be requisite into such State, and by a military force compel it to furnish its deficiency." Congressman James Duane told the governor that the resolution "does Honour" to the legislature's "Zeal and publick Spirit."[102]

The Hartford Convention met in November 1780 and proposed that George Washington be given dictatorial powers. Congress should also be given the power to levy tariffs to pay the interest on the public debt and should have coercive power to force the states to comply with its dictates. Furthermore, the delegates advocated that Congress be vested with broad implied powers in addition to the limited powers specified in the Articles of

Confederation. By the end of March 1781, the New York legislature endorsed the convention's proposals. Although they went further than the governor expected, he too endorsed the recommendations.

On February 5, 1781, in response to what he and the legislature believed to be an unfair congressional requisition on the state, Governor Clinton wrote an extraordinarily blunt letter to Congress. In fifteen pages, the governor detailed the pain and anguish of New Yorkers in a moving history of the five years of war. Clinton warned Congress that New York could not be expected to withstand the combined attacks of British regulars, Hessians, loyalists, hostile Indians, and rebellious Vermonters if Congress sapped the state's strength to overcome the lack of support from other states. Clinton admitted that "There are great Deficiencies"; but he replied with a rhetorical question: "And whence the Cause?" The governor suggested two possibilities: Congress either did not have the power to enforce its laws and compel each state to do its duty, or Congress neglected to exert the coercive power that it had. New York would not presume to say "whether Congress has *adequate* Powers or not? But we will without hesitation declare that if it has them not it ought to have them, and that we stand ready on our Part to confer them." But the governor argued that Congress had already exercised "extensive Powers." It had waged war, absolved its citizens of allegiance to the Crown of Great Britain, emitted money, entered into treaties, sent and received ambassadors, and given dictatorial powers to the commander-in-chief. "No Objection has, that we know of, been made by any State to any of these Measures. Hence we venture to conclude that other states are in Sentiment with us, that these were Powers that necessarily existed in Congress, and we cannot suppose that they should want the Power of compelling the several States to their Duty and thereby enabling the Confederacy to expel the common Enemy."[103]

Governor Clinton ended his request for lower taxes with a plea for understanding. "We are the Seat of War and immediate Witness of it's Distresses. The Danger to us is imminent and therefore Reflections on the present increasing Calamity of the Country affect and alarm us." New York did not wish to censure any particular state—"Remissness tho' in different Degrees, is chargeable on all." The solution to the crisis was simple. "The Strength and Resources of the Country are sufficient and nothing is wanting but the exercise of a supreme coercive Power properly to draw them forth and combine them."[104] In essence, Clinton called for Congress to assert itself.

A month later, on March 1, 1781, Maryland became the last state to approve the Articles of Confederation. Ten days later Congress notified the states that the first federal constitution had finally been adopted.

Governor Clinton relayed the message to the state legislature on March 19, declaring that "This important event, as it establishes our union, and defeats the first hope of our enemy, cannot but afford the highest satisfaction; and I trust that this state will be as distinguished for its faithful adherence to this great national compact, so essential to the peace and happiness of America, as it has hitherto been for its exertions in the common cause."[105] Despite this optimistic face, the governor knew the future was uncertain and that the situation remained desperate.

The dreadful financial and military situation facing the country encouraged Congress in February to propose a federal tariff of five percent on all foreign imports—the impost of 1781—earmarked to pay the interest and principal on the war debt. New York acted swiftly and ratified the impost on March 19. Eleven other states adopted the impost, but Rhode Island refused. Because the Articles of Confederation required that amendments to the Articles be adopted by all thirteen state legislatures, the impost died.

Although America's military prospects had brightened after Yorktown in October 1781, the country was still in a financial morass. New York's military plight also persisted. Governor Clinton wrote John Hanson, President of Congress, in November 1781 expressing his concern "that there is more than a Hazard that we shall not be able without a Change in our Circumstances, long to maintain our civil Government." Alluding to his letter of February 15th and to various resolutions passed by the legislature at its last session, he assured Hanson that New York was completely federal: "I trust there can be no higher Evidence of a sincere Disposition in the State to promote the common Interest than the alacrity with which they passed the Law for granting to Congress a Duty on Imports and their present proffer to accede to any Propositions which may be made for rendering the Union among the States more intimate and for enabling Congress to draw forth and employ the Resources of the whole Empire with the utmost Vigor." The governor admitted that the state had few resources at present to pay its federal taxes, but, he predicted, when the British evacuated New York City and peace was established, New York would prosper. Clinton assured the president that New York at that time would "chearfully consent to vest" Congress "with every Power requisite to an effectual Defence against foreign Invasion and for the Preservation of internal Peace and Harmony." "As an Individual," Clinton could not "forbear declaring my Sentiments that the Defects in the Powers of Congress are the Chief Source of present Embarrassments and as a Friend to the Independence and True Interests and Happiness of America, I could wish to be indulged in expressing an earnest Desire that Measures might be taken to remedy these Defects."[106]

Concurring with Governor Clinton's opinion, the New York legislature, meeting in special session in July 1782, resolved that Congress ought to be given additional taxing authority and that a general convention be called to revise the Articles of Confederation. These resolutions were forwarded to Congress, but New York Congressman Ezra L'Hommedieu informed Clinton that they would not have the desired consequences because "very few States seem disposed to grant further Powers to Congress."[107] By mid-January 1783, however, Congressman Alexander Hamilton felt more optimistic, as he explained in a letter to Governor Clinton. "Every day proves more & more the insufficiency of the confederation. The proselytes to this opinion are increasing fast, and many of the most sensible men acknowledge the wisdom of the measure recommended by your legislature at their last sitting. Various circumstances conspire at this time to incline to the adoption of it, and I am not without hope it may ere long take place."[108]

Hamilton's optimism was not borne out by later events. The reduced British threat made states less willing to transfer their power to Congress. The New York resolutions were considered by various congressional committees, but in September 1783 a final committee recommended that action be postponed. The following month, Clinton wrote to Washington that he was "fully persuaded unless the Powers of the national Council are enlarged and that Body better supported than it is at present, all their Measures will discover such feebleness and want of Energy as will stain us with Disgrace and expose us to the worst of Evils."[109]

12. A New Danger

As the war wound down and the army suffered through another winter of shortages, the danger of mutiny actually seemed to increase. With a treaty of peace imminent, the soldiers wanted to go home. Less threatened by the British, Congress felt it could renege on promises made to the army. The combination of events was explosive. Major William North, Baron Von Steuben's twenty-eight-year-old aide-de-camp, typified most soldiers when he wrote: "I am heartily sick of the War." Congress should surely do something for the army—but Congress, in North's judgment, had "no honor."[110] Major Nicholas Fish, a twenty-four-year-old veteran with seven years of combat experience, knew not what to expect:

> I think public Justice is at this moment become indispensable, and will prove the only means of keeping the Army together.
>
> Should Congress continue deaf to the voice of Justice, and the real interest of the Country, by withholding pay from the Troops, & persever-

ing in their iniquitous system of parsimony, I am apprehensive we shall be reduced to the sad alternative of dismissing them, or disbanding the Army; should the latter be preferred, I am well assured that no other can ever be raised and then farewell to the Liberties and Independence of this Country.[111]

As the commander-in-chief waited for the definitive peace treaty to arrive, he realized the volitility of the situation at his headquarters in Newburgh, New York. If he disbanded the army, he might jeopardize negotiations or encourage a new British offensive that would prolong the war. Confederation Secretary for Foreign Affairs Robert R. Livingston warned "that the conclusion of the Treaty is still very uncertain. . . . Britain still seeks rather to divide her Enemies, than to be reconciled to them; tho' this suspicion may not perhaps be well founded, yet such conduct is so conformable to the general Tenor of British Councils, to the Character of the King, and his first Minister, that it is at least the part of prudence to be upon our guard against it." Whatever the British intended, Livingston advised that "the peace must still depend upon so many contingencies that no preparation for another Campaign should be omitted on our part."[112]

Unpaid and unfed and with no immediate visable enemy, the soldiers longed to return to their families and farms and were willing to object when Congress demanded they stay. Washington knew that his officers and men were disgruntled; understandably he feared another mutiny. His fears were realized in March 1783 when a number of officers—New Yorkers among them—plotted to blackmail Congress into meeting its commitments for back pay and retirement benefits. The army would not disband if Congress did not fulfill its obligations. Hearing of the plot, Washington summoned the officers together and deftly stifled the Newburgh conspiracy.[113] The commander-in-chief was aware of the close parallels between the American war for independence and the English Civil War. He was not about to become another Cromwell leading a glorious, successful revolution for liberty into the depths of tyranny that would eventually end in monarchy. The governor, close at hand, watched events unfold and realized the dangers republicanism faced; he was grateful that Washington was in command. The governor would soon come to understand that he, like Washington, would be called upon to preserve the republicanism of the revolution against the conspiracies of a dangerous aristocratic junto.

13. Business With the Commander-in-Chief

Three months after the Newburgh conspiracy, the army had become so serene that Washington felt at ease taking time off for private business. For three weeks, from July 18 to August 5, he and Governor Clinton toured upstate New York looking for land investments. They traveled more than 750 miles together throughout the frontier, making a list of potential tracts upon which to bid. The first two bids—at Saratoga Springs and the area on which Fort Schuyler stood—were rejected. Finally Clinton purchased 6,071 acres on the Mohawk River between present-day New Hartford and Clinton, a few miles southwest of Utica. Washington complimented Clinton on the "advantageous terms in the purchase. . . . you certainly have obtained it amazingly cheap."[114]

Although the land was shared equally between the governor and Washington, Clinton paid for it with his own money, charging Washington seven percent annual interest on his debt. In December 1783 Washington arranged for over $2,000 owed to him by the Confederation government to be transferred from the federal treasury to Clinton as the first installment on his debt. A second payment came in April 1785. In November 1786 Washington informed Clinton that he was "endeavouring by the sale of Land, to raise money to pay for my Moiety of the purchase on the Mohawk River," and the following June Washington paid the balance of $840.[115]

From the very beginning of their business venture, Washington displayed his total confidence in the governor, asking that Clinton "take the trouble of doing with my moiety the same as you would do with your own at all times and in all respects."[116] In late 1795, because of the difficulty of getting deeds signed by both Clinton in New York and President Washington either at the capital in Philadelphia or at home at Mount Vernon, Washington gave Clinton the power of attorney "in the management and sale of the Lands in which we are jointly interested."[117] On February 28, 1796, when Washington wrote asking what lots remained unsold in their joint venture, Clinton informed his partner that they still owned seven lots consisting of 1,446 acres valued at over five dollars per acre. Further, Clinton recommended that the land not be sold soon, because "The soil is good and in proportion to the rapid settlement of that Part of the Country the value of those Lands continue to increase."[118] The speculative partnership had been profitable for both men. With almost twenty-five percent of their land still available, the investment had already returned a handsome profit. The two old surveyors had done well as a team.

During this three-week trip in 1783, Clinton and Washington had ample opportunity to get to know each other very well. The two men had plenty of time to reminisce and discuss the future. They each looked forward to the day when they could relinquish their commands and return to the more placid rural life. No longer would they be the commander-in-chief and the governor. They would be two friends tied together by mutual business interests and by a strong patriotic desire to see the fulfillment of the republican experiment they had been so instrumental in bringing about. But all too soon their brief escape ended and they returned to their responsibilities.

14. The Governor's Advice

On March 17, 1783, Congressmen William Floyd and Alexander Hamilton sent Governor Clinton a copy of the provisional peace treaty. Three weeks later, on April 8, Washington notified Governor Clinton that official word had just been received "announcing a Certainty of the glorious Event of a general Peace." The commander-in-chief could now plan his retirement—to think about fulfilling the promise he had made eight years earlier to the New York assembly. When, he asked, should he step down? How should the ceremony take place—in person or by letter? Should he write a farewell address? If so, to whom should it be addressed and who should be asked for advice?

After much consideration, Washington decided to announce his retirement and give his advice to the fledgling nation in a formal letter to the state executives. He would leave the final plans for the ceremonial retirement to Congress. The commander-in-chief now began to prepare his farewell address—perhaps the most important letter of his career—an address he styled as his legacy to the country.

Less than a week after he informed Clinton of the official news of the peace, Washington wrote to the governor seeking advice on the country's peacetime military establishment. Washington wanted the states to maintain a peacetime army, but he knew that, as commander-in-chief, his motives would be suspect. He understood that war-weary Americans—always wary of a peacetime standing army and the dangers it posed to liberty—would balk at a commanding general's recommendations for a perpetual military establishment. Despite these apprehensions, the war demonstrated to Washington that the system of state militias had so many shortcomings that a new system had to be devised. George Clinton was one of the men to whom Washington turned for advice on this sensitive subject.

Three days after Washington wrote his letter requesting advice, Clinton responded.[119] Characteristically, he expressed his inadequacy to address so important a topic. With that necessary qualifier, the governor plunged in. Clinton believed that a regular, ongoing American army was absolutely necessary to garrison the frontier posts and to guard the country's magazines. This garrisoning army would "by no means be sufficient for Defence in case of War." But Clinton knew that Americans would never accept the kind of standing armies then in vogue in Europe. By the same token, the Revolutionary experience had "abundantly evinced that it is hazardous and expensive to the last Degree to leave the Defence of a Country to its Militia." America needed a new kind of military establishment—an army ready at a moment's notice, yet an army under civilian rule that could "be most speedily reduced to Order and Consistency."

To provide for such an army, Clinton proposed that "a sufficient number of Officers . . . be retained in Service" at the end of the war. The officers would be paid only when they were on active duty, but they would "be entitled to certain Encouragements of the negative kind such as exemptions from serving in the Militia or in any of the burthensome Offices of Society, together with some such positive Distinctions (if any should be necessary) as would not tend to give the most distant Cause of Jealousy or Apprehension among the most scrupulous Republicans." These benefits would have to be significant enough to convince the officers to remain in the army "and be at the Call of their Country."

To guarantee a steady supply of qualified new officers, Clinton proposed an education program under which one college in every state would establish a professorship, offer courses, and grant degrees in military science. A distinguished army officer would make annual visits to inspect the course offerings and "report to the proper Office." All vacancies in the army should be filled from graduates with these degrees—no commission should be conferred upon anyone without a sufficient number of the required military courses.

The governor also recommended that all officers should serve on active duty on a rotating basis. Every officer should at one time or another serve at the western posts. In this way they would gain experience without "the Mischiefs which in Time of Peace might arise from too long a continuance in Command at fixed Posts."

It was of special importance, the governor advised Washington, that the union of the states be retained.

> In all our Peace Arrangements we ought, I conceive, to have an Eye to the Support of the foederal Union as the first and principal Object of national Concern. Influenced by this Consideration I would prefer an Establishment (however feeble it might appear) that is calculated to maintain that intimate Connection between the different States which gave us Success in War and upon which I am persuaded our Happiness

and Importance will depend in Peace; and it is this which would induce me to wish to preserve even the name of a *Continental Army* as well as to cherish that Sense of military Honor which is so nearly allied to public-Virtue as not to admit of Distinction; but which from the peculiar Situation of our Country may otherwise be too soon extinguished.

15. The State Reunited

Although the peace treaty had been signed, British forces still occupied New York City and some of the southern counties. Governor Clinton eagerly anticipated the day when American forces would reclaim the city. On April 8, the day that Washington informed him that the peace treaty had been signed, Governor Clinton appointed Egbert Benson as a special emissary to call on Sir Guy Carleton, the commander of the British forces in New York City. Benson was to arrange a convention that would expedite the peaceful departure of British troops.[120]

Benson arrived in New York City on Friday evening, April 11, and met with Carleton the following morning. The British commander "declared his Willingness to adopt any Measures which might tend to preserve Peace and prevent every kind of Misunderstanding or Contention, and that he was much disposed to enter into a Convention for that Purpose." But Carleton would suggest no terms, steadfastly insisting that the initial terms be proposed by the governor. Benson confided to the governor that Carleton acted with "an evidently designed Evasion & a Desire to turn the Conversation to other Subjects." According to Benson, the British commander was "not seriously disposed to enter into a Convention . . . he only intends to save appearances to negotiate and by that means to effect a Delay."[121]

On May 6, Washington, Clinton, and Carleton met at Tappen, New York, to discuss the British evacuation. At this meeting Carleton only agreed to withdraw from Westchester County. For the next six months the governor communicated sporadically with Carleton to plan the exchange of power. Neither the Americans nor the British wanted violence to erupt during that delicate transition when British troops were leaving and the American forces were entering the city; consequently, a slow and orderly evacuation was planned. As the time for British withdrawal neared, Clinton asked Washington if New York Continental troops in Westchester County could move closer to New York City, and, "if there should be no impropriety in it," that these troops "be subject to my Direction while they remain there."[122] Appreciative of all the support he had received from the governor, Washington happily informed his friend that the troops would be moved forward and that it struck him "very forcibly" that Clinton should have command. Washington informed Major General Henry Knox, then commanding the American forces outside the city, that Knox and the governor should coordinate the plan to enter.[123]

On November 25, the long-awaited day arrived. As a last act of defiance, the British cut away the halyards and greased the flagpole in the fort as they left. As soon as the Continental forces secured the city, General Knox raised an American flag on a newly-erected pole, fired a thirteen-gun salute, and notified Washington and Clinton that the formal entry could proceed. The commander-in-chief and the governor, side by side on horseback, escorted by a body of Westchester light cavalry, led the procession. Eight long years of exile had ended. Civil government had been restored. In honor of the glorious event, a song was composed and sung to the tune "He comes! He comes!"[124]

> They come! they come! the Heroes come!
> With sounding fife, with thund'ring drum,
> Their ranks advance in bright array,
> The Heroes of AMERICA.
>
> He comes! 'tis mighty WASHINGTON!
> Words fail to tell all he has done;
> Our Hero, Guardian, Father, Friend!
> His fame can never, never end.
>
> He comes! he comes! 'tis CLINTON comes!
> Justice her ancient seat resumes.
> From shore to shore let shouts resound,
> For Justice comes with Freedom crown'd.
>
> She comes! the white rob'd Virgin, Peace,
> And bids grim War his horror cease;
> Oh! blooming Virgin with us stay,
> And bless, oh! bless AMERICA.
>
> Now Freedom has our wishes crown'd,
> Let flowing goblets pass around,
> We'll drink to Freedom's Fav'rite Son,
> Health, Peace, & Joy to WASHINGTON.

That evening Clinton expressed his gratitude to Washington and his officers at a grand dinner at Fraunces' Tavern. The city council ordered no illumination for Monday evening, December 1, as a splendid fireworks display lit the evening sky.[125] The governor hosted another gala dinner at Cape's Tavern honoring Washington and the French minister, the Chevalier de la Luzerne.

Various groups formally addressed Washington and Clinton thanking them for their years of service. A group of recently returned New York City exiles told the governor that his "vigilant and assiduous services in the civil line" as well as his accomplishments in his military capacity had earned for him "that reputation, which a brave man, exposing himself in defence of his country, will ever deserve. . . . Your example," they said, "taught us to suffer with dignity."[126]

The governor thanked the returned exiles for their confidence in him; and, anticipating their desire for revenge against loyalists, asked the exiles to support the government in the difficult period of readjustment. "A reverence for the laws is peculiarly essential to public safety and prosperity, under our free constitution." He pledged that he would "endeavour steadily to discharge my duty, and I flatter myself that this state will become no less distinguished for justice & public tranquility, in peace, than it has hitherto been marked, in war, for vigour, fortitude, and perseverance. . . . Let us," he said, "shew by our virtues, that we deserve to partake of the freedom, sovereignty and independence, which are so happily established throughout these united states."[127]

16. The Commander-in-Chief and the Governor Part

The time for Washington to leave New York had arrived. Congress, meeting at Annapolis, awaited the formal resignation of their army's commander-in-chief. The governor bade his comrade-in-arms—his friend—goodbye, not knowing if they would ever see each other again. For Washington and his officers it was a time of "undescribable emotions."[128] He would miss them all, particularly the man who had never failed him throughout the war, the man he had learned so much about as they traveled through upstate New York together, the man who had become a dear friend.

Washington resigned his commission to Congress on December 23, 1783, and arrived home at Mount Vernon on Christmas eve. Four days later, after the excitement had died down, the former commander-in-chief wrote a brief letter to the governor.

> I am now a private Citizen on the banks of the Powtowmack, where I should be happy to see you if your public business would ever permit, and where in the meantime I shall fondly cherish the remembrance of all your former friendship.
>
> Altho I scarcely need tell you how much I have been satisfied with every instance of your public conduct, yet I could not suffer Col. Walker . . . to depart for N. York, without giving your Excellency one more testimony of the obligations I consider myself under for the

spirited and able assistance, I have often derived from the State under your Administration. The Scene is at last closed. I feel myself eased of a load of public Care. I hope to spend the remainder of my Days in cultivating the affections of good Men, and in the practice of the domestic Virtues; permit me still to consider you in the Number of my friends, and to wish you every felicity.[129]

Washington and Clinton in Triumph, 1783.
Courtesy of Museum of the City of New York.

III

Shaping the Empire State

17. The State Faces Peace

George Clinton emerged from the Revolution as the most popular man in New York State. Despite the machinations "of some designing men" and his personal protestations that he had "little Reason to wish a continuance in an Office attended with so much Fatigue & Trouble & which has already almost ruined my Private Fortune," Clinton was reelected governor in 1780 with little opposition. The people, Chancellor Livingston wrote to Clinton, were "disposed to do justice to your merits."[1]

Three years later, with peace at hand, opposition to a third term for Clinton arose from both the aristocratic and radical fringes. Five months before the spring election, in responding to a letter of support from Chancellor Livingston, Clinton expressed his thoughts about his political future.

> I cannot say that I experience any anxiety about the Issue of the ensuing Election—If I know myself I shall be able chearfully to submit to the Sense of the People be that what it may—If Ease Pleasure or Profit were to be consulted I should have no Reason to be sollicitous about my Continuance in Office—But these I flatter myself you believe were not the Motives which induced me to accept of it in the first Instance and that no Consideration will now be sufficient to induce me to desert the Service of my Country while the Hour of Danger continues or betray the Wishes of my Friends by yielding to the Intrigues of a Cabal.

Clinton thanked the chancellor for his support and assured him "that this Mark of your Approbation of my Conduct will always be remembered with gratitude."[2]

Clinton's main challenge in 1783 came from Philip Schuyler and the fiery radical Ephraim Paine. Schuyler, Clinton's lifelong nemesis, was described "as confident of his success as ever Sancho was of succeeding to the government of his Island." Two days before the elections, Thomas Tillotson, the chancellor's brother-in-law, felt that Clinton "will procure his election to the Government although he has the distinguished Talents of Schuyler and Paine to parry, which by the bye, is no small matter, when you consider that two to one is odds even at football." A day after the opening of the polls, Margaret Beekman Livingston, the chancellor's mother, reported from Clermont that the "people are much devided." She hoped that Clinton would win but "fear[ed] Pain[e] will git in, altho some say that there is no fear but that the old Govr. will be in again." Despite the "infinite pains" taken by Schuyler's friends, Tillotson reported that Clinton received more than 5,000 votes to Schuyler's 600 and Paine's 500.[3] Philip Van Rensselaer, Mrs. Schuyler's cousin, congratulated the governor for "the Great Election in your favor," hoping that Clinton would "with more satisfaction Enjoy that office than you have done for several years past."[4] The citizens of Albany paid tribute to Clinton who, "both as a citizen and a Soldier," contributed so much to the success of the Revolution. The magistrates of Tryon unanimously supported his reelection as an indication "of our Entire Approbation of your Conduct,"[5] while the freemen of Fredericksburgh Precinct in Dutchess County believed that it would be the height of "ingratitude, cruelty, and baseness" to turn out the man most responsible for holding the state together during the long, arduous war.[6] Congress demonstrated its appreciation by brevetting the governor a major general, and Clinton's fellow Continental officers elected him vice president of the state chapter of the Society of the Cincinnati. For seven years, George Clinton had done a remarkable job as governor, commander-in-chief of the state militia, and Continental Army general. No other man could claim such service; and, throughout that service he remained true to his principles and to his moderate life style. The governor was a powerful political force with which to reckon. In whatever direction he chose to lead, many New Yorkers would follow.

Up to this point, Clinton had been a staunch advocate for giving Congress more power, so that it could accomplish the national tasks charged to it by the Articles of Confederation. But, whether Clinton still was committed at this time to a strengthened Congress is uncertain. Sometime in 1783 or early 1784 Clinton's attitude toward Congress changed. A number of factors contributed to this alteration.

Most New Yorkers believed that their state had shouldered an inordinately large share of the war's burden. The southern counties, including New York City, had been occupied by the British for virtually the entire war. The British occupying army posed a constant threat to the rest of the state; therefore, the New York militia always had to be ready to counter any

British maneuvers. New York also had to contend with Burgoyne's invasion in 1777, with the repeated raids on the frontier, and with about half its
population remaining loyal to the king. At no time during the war was
New York free from conflict or the seemingly endless task of provisioning
the contending armies.

Despite these problems, New York paid a large proportion of its
congressional requisitions. Other states, with fewer wartime burdens, did
far less to meet their financial obligations to Congress. The governor and
the legislature were aware of the failure of other states to pay their fair
share. On February 5, 1781, Governor Clinton wrote Congress to ask that
New York's share of the Continental requisition be reduced. A month
later, the state legislature addressed its constituents. Acknowledging that
taxes had become oppressive, the legislators explained that the money was
needed to defend the state and to meet the demands of Congress. They told
the people that "it becomes us, without deranging the general system,
faithfully to represent our situation [to Congress], while we endeavor to
comply with their requisitions. This we have done, and have reason to
hope for every relief which the present emergencies will permit them to
afford." Whatever Congress decided, the legislature hoped that the people
would "cheerfully submit to every equitable mode which the legislature
may devise to draw forth the resources of this state, and by that means
prevent us from being exposed to the censure of those whom we charge
with neglect." In the meantime, while awaiting Congress' response, the
legislature suspended the latest state tax, and admonished New Yorkers to
persevere in the struggle for freedom; the end was near. "Let us steadily,
unanimously and vigorously prosecute the great business of establishing
our independence. Thus shall we be free ourselves, and leave the blessings
of freedom to millions yet unborn."[7] Despite New York's eloquent plea,
Congress refused to reduce its share of federal expenses. Explaining Congress' apparent insensitivity, the state's congressional delegates told Clinton
that "There can be no doubt but the Requisitions made on our State must
undergo a Revision, Congress See the Necessity of it . . . But finding it
would lay a foundation for much Altercation as other States might Claim
a Reduction of their Quotas, it was thought most advisable to wait for the
Representation of the Legislature as a ground for Reasonable abatements."
In the meantime, nothing was expected from New York "but what the
Legislature shall Judge compatible with their Distresses."[8]

With the return of peace, the governor and the legislature were
unwilling to continue paying an unfair portion of federal taxes. Now, the
people were told that their state government should not commit its tax
dollars to Congress while other states neglected their responsibilities.
Governor Clinton was particularly apprehensive about congressional req-

uisitions because, on March 4, 1783, Congress decided to apportion requisitions among the states for past expenses on the basis of the ability of the states to pay future requisitions. This did not bode well for New York. The richest areas of the state, for example, had been occupied throughout the war, thus depriving New York of the revenue from these lucrative areas. Now Congress was going to levy taxes on New York as if these productive areas had always been paying state taxes.[9] In addition, Congress, in compliance with the Treaty of Peace, advised the state not to seek revenge against or compensation from loyalists who had lived in the occupied area; loyalists in other areas of the state whose property had been confiscated and sold to pay for the war were to be compensated. With this, Governor Clinton had had enough. It was time to reassess New York's position within the confederation.

As Clinton awaited the legislative session in January 1784, he had good reason to be proud of the state's accomplishments. New York had played a critical role in defeating the mightiest nation in the world. Monarchy and aristocracy had been vanquished in, and driven from, America. Liberties threatened in the 1760s and 1770s had been restored. The future seemed bright when viewed against the somber days of 1780. But Clinton saw trouble on the horizon. A quarter-century-old dispute over the ownership of Vermont lay unresolved in Congress. Massachusetts had unexpectedly claimed jurisdiction to almost half of New York's territory. The British still occupied the western posts at Niagara and Oswego, and Congress appeared unwilling to assist New York in dislodging them. The Treaty of Peace provided that loyalist property should be protected and that past confiscations should be compensated. Trade with the British West Indies, so profitable before the war, was now severely limited by a British Order-in-Council threatening the state's economic recovery. Finally, Congress again sought an independent revenue in the form of federal duties on imports, which, in effect, would disallow state duties and require higher taxes on land. All of these issues, Clinton knew, would bring New Yorkers into conflict with their neighbors, with Congress, and among themselves.

On a more personal level, the governor shared his brother's disillusionment with Congress for its refusal to promote James to the rank of major general. For the entire war, James Clinton had quietly and competently served as a brigadier general. On one occasion, Congress bypassed James and promoted a subordinate above him. The governor's brother remained silent. But when Congress repeated the slight, James found it impossible, "Consistent with my Honor or my feelings" to continue in the army. Both George and James Clinton believed that Congress had deliberately snubbed New York in not rightfully approving the merited promotion.[10]

Despite these potential conflicts, the governor remained committed to the union. "Viewing, as I trust you will," he told the legislature in January 1784, that "the blessings we now enjoy as effects flowing from our union, you cannot but be attentive to every measure which has a tendency to cement it, and to give that energy to our national councils which may be necessary to the general welfare." Clinton believed that an anti-American trade policy had been adopted by Great Britain under the "presumption that the confederated power of the United States is not adequate to prevent the innovation. It becomes therefore our interest and our duty, to undeceive them, and if the powers given by the confederation, are not competent for the purpose, to enlarge them; for it is obvious that any partial exertions of the states, individually, to correct this evil, will prove ineffectual."[11]

To meet the state's domestic problems, Clinton developed a coherent plan to defend New York's interests against perceived threats from its neighbors and from Congress, just as he had defended New York from British threats. However, when stronger powers for Congress would benefit New York—powers that would assist Congress in foreign affairs, especially in its efforts to remove British trade restrictions—Clinton would endorse such measures. In purely domestic matters, the governor would put New York concerns above all others. Later, Alexander Hamilton would refer to the governor's policies as "Clintonism." Clintonism was devised by the governor and his advisors as a reaction to the aggressive policies of Congress and New York's neighbors. One of the most dangerous situations, and a crisis that helped to destroy Clinton's wartime nationalism and forge his postwar policy was the independence movement in Vermont.

18. Vermont Secedes

Throughout the war, Vermont was a constant irritant to New York. New York's claim to Vermont—at that time called the New Hampshire Grants or simply the Grants—had long been disputed by New Hampshire and Massachusetts. Settlers from New York and New England received land grants from their colonial governments that sometimes overlapped. Before the Revolution, New York aristocrats received huge grants in the hopes of extending their Hudson Valley manorial system east of Lake Champlain. Later, New Yorkers—such as George Clinton and John Jay—received grants in recognition of their service. Occasionally these conflicting land grants caused disputes that sometimes erupted in violence. In 1764, the king in council ruled in favor of New York's claim, and New Hampshire and most New England settlers in the region acquiesced. But, in 1777, New England settlers in the Grants, led by Ethan Allen and his Green Mountain Boys, declared their own independence from both New York and Great Britain. New Englanders in Vermont would not help other Americans achieve freedom while they remained under the rule of the oppressive Yorkers.[12] Congregationalists in Vermont made the extraordinary argument that they could never feel safe under New York rule because their "*religious* rights and privilidges would be in danger from a Union with a Government" whose constitution tolerated all religions and excluded any from being established.[13]

Throughout his life, Clinton had a blind spot when it came to Vermont. He never saw the parallel between Vermont's struggle for independence and America's. Vermonters, in his judgment, were traitors who had taken "ungenerous Advantage of our Situation" to secede from the state.[14] As governor, Clinton was sworn to protect and defend his state and the rights and property of its citizens. The Vermont insurgents violated these rights and struck at the core of New York's sovereignty. While others might compromise to avoid violence, Clinton was adamant. At the same time, he was realist enough to know the limitations placed on his state, especially during the Revolution; but he would not bend his principles—he would not voluntarily surrender the state's territory or its citizens' property. Clinton wrote to Thomas Chittenden, the new governor of Vermont, expressing his hope that New York and Vermont could keep their dispute "out of Sight" and concentrate on the common enemy. Despite the need for cooperation in fighting the British, Clinton officially informed Chittenden that nothing he or New York did publicly or privately could remotely be construed as recognizing a separate and independent Vermont.[15]

Despite their fury against Vermont separatists, Governor Clinton and the New York legislature were willing to offer a carrot along with the stick. The governor issued a proclamation granting amnesty to all the rebels, while the legislature on February 21, 1778, passed resolutions promising to honor all land claims held by New England settlers under grants or purchases from New Hampshire or Massachusetts. These lenient measures were aimed as much at satisfying New England supporters of Vermont as the Vermonters themselves. Clinton reported to New York's delegates in Congress that, since his proclamation, many of Vermont's New England adherents no longer espoused their cause but admit that the rebels ought to submit to New York's jurisdiction. Although significant numbers of the Vermonters accepted these generous terms, most did not.[16] Like Clinton himself, they would not budge from their demands. That being so, Governor Clinton believed that he had few options: "I fear the Duties of my Office will shortly constrain me" to use force to subdue the "revolted Citizens."

New York believed that the Vermonters got encouragement from the inaction of Congress in the dispute. Governor Clinton asked the president of Congress for "an explicit and unequivocal Declaration of the Sense of Congress" on Vermont. Only such a public statement would "remove an Opinion which these People universally entertain" that Congress really supported Vermont independence but could not openly declare its sentiments because of the adverse effect it would have in New York.[17] Such a stand by Congress would also stifle separatist movements in other states.

The governor regularly urged New York's congressional delegates as well as the president of Congress to raise the Vermont issue. Not until Congress made its determination, he told the delegates, would New York be able to determine its strategy toward Vermont. By mid-July 1778, after "many fruitless applications" to Congress, Clinton felt that he acquitted himself of his duty and that New York would not be liable to censure should civil war break out in Vermont. Congressman Gouverneur Morris reported in June 1779 that all agreed "that lenient measures were most proper to be pursued," rather than "to see Americans embruing their Hands in the Blood of each other."[18] The governor angrily responded expressing his concern for Congress' procrastination. Rumors suggested that the Vermont rebels were aided "by at least individuals in Congress & Servants of the public which I have Reason to fear were but too well founded." Continental Army General John Stark from New Hampshire was reportedly cooperating with the Vermont rebels. Vermont sentenced several loyal Yorkers to banishment, and Stark assisted in carrying out the sentence by imprisoning the exiles in Fort Arnold under military guard. Clinton complained to General Washington, who presented the matter to Congress. Two months later, Clinton wrote New York's delegates to Congress suggesting that Congress' failure to discipline Stark "may be considered as countenancing these unwarrantable Measures" against the liberties of citizens of the state of New York. If these allegations gained credibility, Clinton predicted that New Yorkers would be alienated from Congress, and the war effort would suffer. The longer Congress waited, the stronger the malcontents became. The governor ominously warned that events in Vermont were "fast approaching to a serious and alarming crisis, and unless Measures are speedily adopted to prevent it, we shall very soon be involved in a civil war," as well as a revolution.[19] In October 1778, Clinton informed the legislature that the honor of the state and the safety of the country required action. If Vermont were allowed its independence, other insurgents would follow the example and secede from their states. Such "turbulent and unruly Dispositions" could only serve to "gratify our inveterate Enemies by creating internal Divisions, and render the Confederation a mere dead Letter."[20]

On May 4, 1779, committees of nine towns in Vermont meeting in Brattleborough petitioned Clinton for assistance. The petitioners apologized for "applying for Protection during the Continuance of the War with Great Britain," but their situation had become desperate. Estates and livestock owned by citizens loyal to New York had been taken and special confiscatory taxes had been levied on individuals who refused to serve in the Vermont militia. Since the protection of individuals and their property was esteemed the principal end of government, the petitioners claimed the protection due them in return for their allegiance to New York. If Congress and New York refused to protect them, they would be forced to join the usurpers.[21]

On the Fifth of May, Colonel Eleazer Paterson of Hinsdale asked Clinton for direction. Should he expect New York to support his militia regiment in defending the property and rights of those settlers loyal to New York? Would the governor send the Albany County militia to help defeat the Green Mountain Boys? If New York was unwilling or unable to fulfill its obligation to protect persons and property, Paterson asked that his resignation be accepted.[22]

Ten days later, the governor asked the petitioners and Colonel Paterson for patience. He hoped that violence could be avoided, and he was certain that Congress would act soon to support New York's claims. Well affected citizens should upon all occasions avoid acknowledging the authority of Vermont, except when there was "no alternative left between Submission and inevitable Ruin." This, the governor said regretfully, "appears to me the only proper advice I can give" until Congress' sentiments on the dispute were known. If, however, any violence or bloodshed should occur in those towns loyal to New York, Clinton would offer "all the assistance in my Power, and I trust it will be sufficient for your Safety and Defence." Furthermore, Clinton promised that if any indication arose of the Vermonters planning to "reduce you by force of arms," he would order the militia to their defense instantly. The governor concluded by again asking the loyal settlers for patience in awaiting Congress' decision.[23]

In mid-May 1779, an agitated Clinton wrote to John Jay, now serving as president of Congress. Events in Vermont, he stormed, were "fast approaching to a very serious Crisis which nothing but the immediate Interposition of Congress can possibly prevent." How much longer, Clinton rhetorically asked, could the loyal inhabitants of Vermont be expected to wait for protection from New York and Congress? Clinton expected that he would "be obliged to order out a Force for their Defence." New York did not want to use force, but "Justice, the Faith of Government, and the Peace and Safety of Society, will not permit us to continue longer passive Spectators of the Violences committed upon our Fellow Citizens."[24]

Within the month, Clinton's worst fears came true. Ethan Allen and about 500 militiamen descended on several of the towns loyal to New York and arrested their civil and militia officers, including Eleazer Paterson. Allen berated the townspeople, and in a show of maddening force, struck several individuals with his sword. Defying the state of New York, he declared that the Green Mountain Boys would "Establish their State by the sword, and fight all who shall attempt to oppose them."[25]

Immediately upon receiving the news of Allen's attack, Clinton sent an express rider with letters to President Jay and New York's congressional delegates. "The Vermont Business," Clinton asserted, "is now arrived at a Crisis." He had already alerted the militia to ready themselves. The legislature was scheduled to meet in a few days. In the meantime he would make the necessary arrangements "to repel this Outrage." In addition to the Albany militia, he planned to send another 1,000 soldiers to Vermont—soldiers previously intended for the defense of the frontier and for the completion of the state's Continental quota. Clinton warned Congress to act quickly, as the legislature would not be patient.[26]

Congress received Clinton's urgent letter on June 1, 1779, as it sat as a committee of the whole discussing, coincidentally, the Vermont problem. Allen's violence solidified opinion against the Vermonters, but Congress proceeded cautiously. On June 1, a resolution passed almost unanimously calling for a congressional committee to visit Vermont to ascertain the situation. (Opposition to the resolution came from a handful of delegates who wanted a more vigorous response.) Furthermore, Congress expressed the desire to protect the honor of all the states involved as well as the rights of individuals.

New York's congressional delegates also responded to their governor's letter on June 1, saying that they were pleased to find that New England delegates "came very generally into the measure and appear sincerely disposed to terminate those unhappy Disorders." The delegates felt that violence should be avoided—we should "rather suffer a little than shed blood." The moderate congressional action was more likely "to succeed and if treated with neglect by the People of the Grants, the greater Degree of Indignation will such neglect create through all the States." The opportunity was at hand for an end to the jealousy between New York and New England. Perhaps the crisis created by Allen's raids would benefit New York by leading to a speedy solution.[27]

In a separate confidential letter to the governor, Congressman James Duane, who owned extensive tracts in the Grants, expressed his concern. Duane believed that the congressional committee might well convince a large number of the rebels to return to their duty, but he also feared that the committee might solidify them in their opposition. Duane found this an undesirable "Hazard, altho' it is preferable to the Effusion of American Blood." Much depended on the honesty of the New England delegates—some of whom had instigated the Vermont rebels in the first place. Duane was willing to take a chance, hoping "to bury all animosities in everlasting oblivion."[28]

While he awaited Congress' response, Clinton called out the militia in response to a British foray up the Hudson. Since many members of the legislature were in the militia, this delayed the scheduled legislative session. When the governor received Congress' letter, he was livid. He was astonished that "Congress have passed over in profound Silence the Remonstrance on the Seizure and Imprisonment of the principal Officers of Government" in those towns loyal to New York. How could Congress say that it wished to protect the honor and justice of all states and individuals involved in the dispute when New York civil and militia officers were illegally imprisoned by Ethan Allen, a colonel in the Continental Army? New York's honor and authority had been given "a bold stab." The appointment of a committee, in Clinton's judgment, would only strengthen the rebels who would consider it "as an implied acknowledgment of their authority." It was his opinion that the committee ought not to visit the Grants, at least not until the New York legislature had a chance to consider the congressional proposal.[29] The governor announced that he would leave his field command and call the legislature into session over the Vermont crisis. He told General Washington that New York would soon have to apply "force to force."[30]

Worse news arrived for Clinton from the Grants. Ethan Allen boasted that two-thirds of Congress supported the Vermonters. Allen's agents seized 100 pounds of gunpowder from loyal settlers in Westminster, and talked of imposing confiscatory taxes. It was estimated that Allen had 3,000 militia under arms, 2,000 of whom would willingly fight New York. An additional 1,000 militiamen from Berkshire County, Massachusetts, would join Allen if needed. Allen admitted publicly that he had seized the loyal settlers as a direct challenge to New York. If Congress did nothing to censure Allen, that would be overt proof of either its support of the Vermonters or its impotence. If New York failed to send its militia to rescue the prisoners, a clarion call would be heard by all settlers that New York was incapable of protecting its citizens in the Grants. Clinton knew that if he sent the New York militia, Allen and the Green Mountain Boys awaited them.[31]

Congressman James Duane told Governor Clinton that his censorious letter had "made a serious Impression" on Congress. A special committee considered the letter and on June 16 recommended that all of the prisoners captured by Ethan Allen be freed immediately. Congress, however, still hoped that its investigatory committee would succeed, and declared that the committee was not a diplomatic recognition of Vermont. Furthermore, Duane warned that if New York sent militia to the Grants, "Friends and Relations of the Revolters" in New England would flock to Allen's aid even in defiance of their state governments. Now it was the governor who was asked to have patience.[32]

Clinton candidly wrote President Jay about his fears. He believed that various members of Congress had "countenanced & encouraged the Revolters." The governor questioned "their Integrity." It was clear that by its refusal to take decisive action, Congress had aided the rebels, who gained strength daily while the war effort sapped New York. Clinton foresaw that after the war, supporters would desert New York in its attempt to recover the Grants. In fact, at that time "some of our Neighbors will more readily venture [to] avow their Cause & openly step forth to their assistance." The governor wondered at the coincidence of British attacks on the frontier and up the Hudson along with Allen's raids against New York settlers. Such a coincidence "carries with it something like the appearance of a concerted Plan, and excites suspicions unfavorable" to the rebels. Clinton hoped that such a coordinated strategy had not occurred.[33]

Two members of the congressional committee—John Witherspoon and Samuel J. Atlee—reached the Grants in mid-June 1779 and met with Governor Chittenden. Chittenden promised that loyal New Yorkers would "not be molested till matters are finally settled," if they agreed to serve in the Vermont militia and defend the frontier against the British.[34] The New York settlers objected that this plan called for submission to Vermont as "the Groundwork of the Conciliation." The settlers showed the congressmen Clinton's letter which directed "the Subjects of New York to oppose every Exertion of the Vermont authority whether in raising Men or Taxes." The New York settlers advised Clinton to be assertive.

> New York . . . has it now in its Power to compel Congress to do the State Justice in the Vermont Business. But, if the Legislature suffer the Oppertunity to pass unimproved, Vermont will in all probability succeed & be an eternal & inveterate Foe to the remainder of the State; whereas, Spirit properly exerted at this time, will almost infallibly get a final Decision of Congress in favor of the Rights of New York. A temporary Settlement will establish Vermont.[35]

New York settlers discussed their plight and decided that their situation was indefensible unless New York acted. For several years they had suffered for their allegiance, hoping that Congress would support New York's claims. They eagerly hoped the congressional investigatory committee would see the injustices committed against New York and its loyal citizens. By now it was evident that the committee not only offered no solace, but recommended submission to Vermont authorities and their actions, which both Clinton and the settlers believed treasonable. Unless New York exerted "itself immediately with spirit," Vermont would become independent, and loyal New Yorkers would be forced to "submit to the Powers that are, though with great Reluctance."[36]

Clinton was outraged at the congressional committee's recommendations. He refused to sanction the enlistment of New York citizens in the Vermont militia. After all, these could well be the troops that the New York militia would one day fight. The governor offered to put his objections in writing but the committee declined to accept.[37] At the end of August, Jay asked Clinton to empower Congress to settle the Vermont dispute. Jay believed in the possibility of an amicable solution balancing New York's rights against the "apparent equity" of "hearing the revolters." The important issue, Jay argued, was jurisdiction—who would administer the area—not the actual ownership of the land, since "we have vacant lands enough to do justice to individuals who may suffer by a decision against them."[38] A few days later, Jay told Clinton that he had "intimated" in Congress that New York would not pay its taxes until Congress settled the Vermont issue.[39]

On September 24, 1779, Congress finally made a concrete proposal that would resolve all Vermont disputes. Each of the disputing states was to pass an act authorizing Congress to serve as arbiter, while, in the interim, Vermonters promised not to harm settlers claiming allegiance to another state. In deciding the issue, Congress provided that the three disputing states would be ineligible to "vote on any question" related to Vermont, thus making it extremely difficult to obtain the nine state delegations required to decide boundary matters.[40] Despite the disappointment with what Congress had done up to this point, on October 21, 1779, New York passed such an act. Massachusetts and New Hampshire balked, and Congress reverted to its do-nothing policy.[41]

The controversy escalated when the Vermont General Assembly on October 20, 1779, authorized a delegation to Congress to present its case for independence, and Massachusetts decided to renew its claim of jurisdiction.[42] By April 1780 all hope of compromise seemed lost, and loyal New York settlers again feared for their safety and property. New arrests occurred and the Vermont legislature contemplated wholesale confiscation of Yorkers' land grants. Settlers with New York land titles were dispossessed, and, if they balked, they were banished and warned not to return on pain of death. Those who refused to leave were imprisoned. Settlers with New York grants appealed to the New York legislature. Despite Clinton's promises of aid, the state did not have the resources to help.[43] Just as it appeared that Yorkers in Vermont had no recourse but submission,[44] word arrived that Congress had ruled against independence, and that another committee would be sent to the Grants to determine whether New York or New Hampshire should be granted jurisdiction.

Congress' action buoyed Yorkers but antagonized Vermonters. The Vermont legislature announced that all New York grants not brought in at its next sitting would be voided. The Yorkers faced the dilemma of submitting to the usurpers or being thrust into "an unequal & bloody Conflict, with a ferocious Sett of Men." Again the Yorkers pinned their hopes on Congress, while the Vermonters announced "the Doctrine that Congress have no right to adjudge whether the Grants shall be a State . . . and consequently that the People of Vermont may justly oppose the Decision of Congress should it be against them."[45] Clinton wrote the state's delegates in Congress that he had information that some loyal Yorkers planned to resist the Vermonters with force. The governor urged Congress to take immediate action to prevent violence before a judicial determination could be made. Clinton warned the delegates that "once we are involved in War and Bloodshed, both Parties will disregard Congress either as a Mediator or Judge."[46]

By June 1780, Congress had decided to avoid a final decision in the Vermont controversy until after the war. Maryland Congressman Daniel of St. Thomas Jenifer hoped "that Congress will have more wisdom than to take final Order in this Business, before our independence is established; we have business enough on our hands without carving out more at this time."[47] During the interim, Congress reprobated the actions of Vermont authorities, asserting that they ought to abstain from all further "acts of power as a separate and Independent State." Clinton hoped that Congress' action would "preserve the Peace of the Country until the Dispute can be judicially determined" after the war. The governor called on the Yorkers to raise a company of militia to help patrol the Hudson River Valley.[48]

Congressman John Morin Scott saw things differently. He told the governor that Congress was not an honest broker; the small states were using Vermont as a pawn in a larger game. Maryland and New Jersey, which had no western lands of their own, intimated that they would support New York's position on Vermont if New York ceded some of its western territory to Congress. Scott believed that delay would discourage the Yorkers and strengthen Vermont; "the sooner we press the Matter to its Crisis the better."[49] Scott's cynicism had its effect on Clinton. By October 29, 1780, Clinton was convinced that Congress' delaying tactics would not work to New York's favor, and he urged New York's delegates to push for a final decision. Clinton told Congressman James Duane that he was not surprised at Congress' delaying tactics. For a year, Clinton wrote, it had appeared to him that the Vermont rebels "were encouraged & supported in their Revolt" by Congress, whose "Delay was studied to strengthen their opposition." Clinton believed that many New Yorkers had trusted "that Congress would take up the matter & decide upon it & enforce their Decission." Congress' "Evasion" of the issue and the subsequent "encouragement afforded to the Revolters" caused "universal Disgust to all Ranks of People" in New York. In confidence, Clinton told Duane that "the most sensible among us" felt that Congress had "a premeditated intention to make a sacrifice of this State to answer the political views of others & of interested Individuals." Clinton had become so disillusioned that he alerted Duane that the legislature at its next sitting might withdraw the state's congressional delegation and with it "the Resources of the State which have hitherto so lavishly been afforded to the Continent." New York would then be able to devote all of its resources "for our own Defence."[50] Duane acknowledged that the governor's remarks were "well founded," but counseled patience. "Those who are convinced of the Justice of our Cause wish it to yield to the pressure of our publick Affairs, and that we shoud give no Room for complaint that we embarrass the national Councils with a partial Concern while the Preservation of the common Liberties demands all our Efforts for a vigorous and decisive Campaign."[51]

On October 30, 1780, Governor Clinton received ominous news of an expected British invasion from Canada. Clinton ordered General Abraham Ten Broeck to prepare his Albany militia to offer the Vermonters—both rebels and loyal Yorkers—"every Protection in the Power of the State."[52]

Throughout the contest over the Grants, Vermonters hinted that they would join forces with the British if Congress or New York attempted to restore the latter's rule. In November 1780, Clinton reported to General Washington that evidence had been obtained linking Ethan Allen with the enemy. Regularly thereafter rumors circulated and more evidence surfaced linking Allen with the British. Governor Clinton hoped that only Vermont's leaders were involved in this treason, and that, when the traitors were exposed, the majority of the people would desert them. Realistically, however, Clinton knew that most Vermonters knew exactly what their leaders were doing. The governor believed it was "wisest to suppose the worst and be prepared accordingly."[53]

On November 22, 1780, Governor Chittenden wrote Clinton "to make a positive Demand on the Legislature" to relinquish the state's jurisdiction over the Grants. In exchange, Vermont militia would join New York troops in defending the frontier from the attacks of the British and their Indian allies.[54] Ira Allen delivered the letter which was opened before Clinton arrived in Poughkeepsie for the legislative session. Lobbying efforts convinced frightened frontier legislators that the exchange of jurisdiction for protection was a fair bargain.

Led by Philip Schuyler, New York's senate caved in. On February 22, 1781, it passed resolutions calling for the state to cede its jurisdiction over the Grants. Before the assembly finished its consideration of the resolutions, Governor Clinton arrived and threatened to prorogue the legislature if such a measure appeared imminent. The governor's enemies charged him with "an unwarrantable stretch of power" in interpreting his constitutional authority of prorogation. Clinton's supporters, however, "looked up with admiration at his uncommon fortitude, in . . . preserving inviolate what he and some of them deemed the undoubted rights of the state."[55] To capitulate to the rebels "would not only be ruinous to this state, but also destructive to the general peace and interest of the whole confederacy."[56] To General Alexander McDougall, the governor admitted that pride was also involved. To cede jurisdiction of the territory "woud have reflected lasting Ignominy & Disgrace upon the State & this Consideration alone ought to have forbid it.[57] At this point, a letter arrived from Congressman Duane suggesting that "a speedy & just Decision of the Controversy by Congress" was at hand. The letter "changed the Sentiments of some & for the present stopped the Mouths of all."[58] The assembly did not pass the resolutions.

A few days before New York's senate had passed its cession resolutions, the Vermont legislature, in secret session, passed an act confiscating all of New York's ungranted land in Vermont. Clinton obtained a copy of the act and used it to his advantage. The Vermonters appeared duplicitous—openly extending the hand of friendship and cooperation while secretly stealing New York's possessions.

The constant demands of the war coupled with the dispute with Vermont emotionally drained the governor: "I most devoutly wish this unhappy Controversy was decided. I wish for a just & Honorable Decission; but I am perswaded almost any that Congress can have in Contemplation is better than further Delay." In a way, Clinton hoped that Congress would resolve the conflict by ruling against New York. Congressionally sanctioned statehood for Vermont would eliminate the humiliation that New York and Clinton would face by capitulating to the brazen Vermonters. Clinton could easily rationalize submission to Congress "with a degree of Honor."[59]

But Clinton did not get his *deus ex machina*. Sensing that New York's legislature was willing to relinquish its claims, a congressional committee on August 7, 1781, intimated that Vermont might be granted statehood if it acknowledged proper borders for New York and New Hampshire, and if it respected the property of settlers who claimed allegiance to other states. Although personally supporting "coercive measures," Philip Schuyler reluctantly supported this proposal, but neither the New York nor the Vermont legislatures accepted the proposal.[60]

New York then tried to raise militia among the settlements on the eastern shore of the Hudson. Governor Chittenden warned Colonel Peter Yates "to desist" or "the Consequences will be inconvenient." Colonel Yates stood his ground, telling Chittenden that he would honor his oath as an officer in the New York militia. The confrontation exploded when Colonel Henry Van Rensselaer arrested a private in his New York regiment. The man—"a Certain Fairbanks"—was in reality a colonel in the Vermont militia. Fairbanks escaped from Van Rensselaer, collected his men, and conspired to kidnap New York militia General Leonard Gansevoort. The plot was discovered and a minor skirmish erupted between the two militias. Escalation appeared likely.

Clinton saw the actions of the Vermonters as part of a larger plan coordinated with the British attacks on the frontier. The governor told General Gansevoort that he had avoided direct confrontations with the Vermont rebels for fear of endangering the frontier settlements. New York, however, could not allow flagrant acts of war to go unpunished. Clinton ordered Gansevoort to "maintain your Authority throughout every part of your Brigade" and enforce the laws of the state. More fighting occurred in December 1781 as Vermonters in Schachtekoke and Hoseck refused to join the New York militia and barricaded themselves in blockhouses. General John Stark, the Continental Army commander at Albany, who was notoriously sympathetic to the Vermonters, refused to interfere in the dispute without orders from his superior. As the small contingent of eighty New York militia prepared its assault on the blockhouses, word arrived that 500 Vermont militiamen with a cannon were only a few miles away and were rapidly approaching. When the Vermont militia was within sight, the New York troops hastily retreated. Gansevoort realized that his troops were no match for the Vermonters. He discharged the militia and notified Clinton of the embarrassing turn of events. The rebellious Vermonters had extended their control from the banks of the Connecticut River to the eastern shore of the Hudson. The governor pleaded for congressional assistance against this new attack.[61] Congress, realizing the impossibility of a settlement acceptable to both sides, refused to get involved.

After a year of intermittent tensions, Congress reconsidered the Vermont issue, when, in December 1782, it resolved that the violent measures taken against loyal New York settlers were "highly derogatory to the authority of the United States and dangerous to the confederacy." Congress instructed Vermont to compensate individuals who had been banished or whose property had been conficated. No further discriminations should take place against loyal Yorkers. Congress threatened "to enforce a compliance."[62]

But when Congressmen William Floyd and Alexander Hamilton forwarded the resolutions to Clinton, they told him that Congress' threat was hollow; Congress would never use force against Vermont. The resolutions, however, benefited New York in "that they will give a complexion to the future deliberations on the subject and may induce Congress the more readily to adopt some moderate medium." New York's congressmen recommended that the state take this opportunity "to conciliate the inhabitants of the Grants" and to ameliorate anti-New York feelings in other states. They believed that many Continental soldiers had been given grants in Vermont to tie them to the new state. New York should go out of its way to confirm their titles. Apparently sensing how furious and betrayed Clinton felt, the delegates advised him to pursue a moderate policy overall.[63]

Three weeks later, Clinton responded to the delegates. Although short of a fair policy, Congress' resolutions exceeded the governor's expectations, and he was not without hope for "a just and favorable Issue." He believed that the legislature was "disposed to every liberal Act that may consist with the Honor of the State." He lamented that Congress, not long before, could have "spoken decisively on the Subject," and everyone would have obeyed. Congress still possessed such authority if it acted from strength. Unfortunately a handful of congressmen from a few states "encourage the Revolters in their Opposition."[64] On January 1, 1783, Hamilton candidly advised the governor to seek an amicable compromise with Massachusetts and New Hampshire because Congress would never settle the issue.[65]

In February 1783, a disappointed Clinton reported that Vermont's leaders treated the congressional resolutions with "the utmost Contempt." Several of the banished settlers, who had returned to Vermont expecting compensation, were imprisoned and threatened with execution. Vermont was not yet willing to comply with Congress' wishes if those wishes did not include independence.[66]

In July 1783, President Meschech Weare of New Hampshire sent Clinton resolutions from his legislature "making Overtures for an Amicable settlement of a Boundary Line between the two States." The Grants, the resolutions suggested, should be divided along the summit of the Green Mountains. Clinton refused to consider the proposal. He claimed that there was no support for it in the legislature and he argued that it now appeared as if Congress would soon settle the issue in favor of New York. New Hampshire obviously "would be perfectly satisfied" with getting half a loaf when the expectation appeared that Congress would give it nothing. The governor felt that such a compromise was probably unconstitutional because the legislature did not have the authority to "Dismember" the state. Furthermore, such a settlement would be "improper," because it would alienate those loyal settlers living in the eastern portion of the Grants.[67]

Clinton clearly was not ready to compromise. His obstinacy was at least partly due to his belief that the Continental Army was now prepared to act against Vermont. Clinton claimed to have information that the bulk of the army, even those who had formerly supported Vermont independence, now believed that the rebel leaders were "Traitors to the American Cause that ought to be subdued & punished." Furthermore, even if this animosity did not exist, the army would fulfill its duty by carrying out the decrees of Congress. "The Discipline of our Army," Clinton asserted, "is too perfect to admit a doubt of this." The governor also believed that, despite their ferocious reputation, the Vermonters would easily capitulate when faced with an armed force. Even "a very small Force would be sufficient to induce the bulk of the People to Submission," while the most guilty leaders would take refuge in Canada.[68]

The Vermonters, Clinton suggested, were displeased with the prospects for statehood as outlined in Congress' resolution of August 7, 1781, in which Congress set the western boundary of an independent Vermont at a line twenty miles east of the Hudson. Such a line, the Vermonters realized, would leave Bennington and most of the western towns in the Grants out of the new state. Statehood without these towns would be impracticable. Clinton believed that the circumstances favored New York and a decision should be pushed in Congress before the coming of peace with the British.[69] Two days later, the governor sent New York's congressional delegates several affidavits containing accounts of treasonable activities by the Vermont leaders. In addition, he reported, instead of compensating loyal Yorkers who had been ill treated, Vermont authorities continued their persecution. Clinton believed that "the Public Peace and the Faith and Dignity of Congress" required immediate congressional action.[70] No such action was ever taken.

Peace came to America in 1783, but the Vermont controversy continued. On February 19, 1784, the New York *Independent Gazette* warned its readers that commotions still raged in Vermont and that unless Congress acted "to heal those animosities, which have too long subsisted, . . . the consequences must be destructive and fatal, and probably involve this State in a dreadful warfare." But the Vermont controversy had become larger than an issue of who would control the land between the Connecticut and Hudson rivers. Sectional politics added to the confused set of issues and passions that embroiled Vermont. New Englanders hoped to add Vermont to the Union, thus adding one vote to its congressional voting bloc. (Each state had one vote in the Confederation Congress.) Southerners, however, could also add. Some Southern delegates to Congress openly declared that they opposed settling the Vermont issue because it would "give a ballance to the Eastern *Scale*.[71] Congressman Hugh Williamson of North Carolina wrote his old friend James Duane that "If Vermont must be independent, which I fear cannot be prevented, I wish to see at least two Southern States formed at the same Time." Williamson believed that the Southern and Middle states would always support federal measures; he hated "to see a phalanx of 5 dead Votes [i. e., New England] against us on every interesting Question."[72]

New York's delegation reported to the governor on April 9, 1784, that Congress has determined "not to do any thing about that matter, expecting that in Time we shall be obliged to consent that [Vermont should] . . . become a seperate State."[73] Congressman Ephraim Paine suggested that not one state supported New York's position. If Vermont was to become independent, Paine hoped it would be soon, because, in a few years, the rebels would be able "to dictate their own boundaries." The alternatives seemed simple to Paine: let Vermont become free and join the union or have New York "raise the power of the State and Crush them immediately."[74]

19. The Loyalist Problem

More than any other state, New York had a severe problem with loyalists. Approximately half of the state's population in 1776 remained loyal to King George. A high percentage of residents in New York City, Long Island, and the other southern counties that were occupied by British troops throughout the war opposed the patriot cause. Tenants, in general, looked to the crown for support against their aristocratic manor lords, especially if those manor lords were whigs. Some tenants, even those residing on tory estates, hoped that the crown might reward them after the war with parcels of lands taken from the rebel manor lords. Many frontier New Yorkers pledged their allegiance to the king out of fear from marauding loyalist bands and their Indian allies. In fact, many areas of the state experienced the depravities of civil war.

One of Governor Clinton's most controversial policies during and after the war dealt with the state's treatment of loyalists. In the early days of his militia command, Clinton declared that he would "rather roast in hell to all eternity than be dependent upon Great Britain or show mercy to a damned Tory."[75] He realized that New York patriots were involved in a life-and-death struggle and loyalists were their enemy. "The Conduct of many of these Traitors was so daring and Insolent that a sudden & severe Example [was] absolutely necessary to deter others from the Commission of like Crimes."[76] Tories lurked throughout the countryside, some actively supported the British, and others offered covert assistance to the enemy. No one knew how many more bided their time until the opportune occasion arose to strike out against the patriot cause. Clinton believed it "essential to the Internal Peace & safety in the Country . . . to apprehend or destroy" the "Tory Rascals."[77] To these ends, the governor wholeheartedly agreed that dangerous loyalists should be imprisoned or banished and their property confiscated.

When no legislation existed to guide Clinton, he felt justified in clamping down on loyalists. As the state legislature enacted laws governing loyalists and as Clinton matured in command—both as a general and as governor—he distinguished between vigilante violence and legal means of dealing with tories that were sanctioned by the legislature or its agents, the committees for detecting and defeating conspiracies. Clinton became intolerant of unauthorized attacks on tories, whether by private citizens or by soldiers. Whenever such acts were reported, Clinton demanded investigations and punishment of the guilty parties.[78] On one occasion he personally intervened to save two tories from being tarred and feathered.

Throughout the war, the legislature passed various bills to restrict the movement of loyalists or to confiscate their property. As a member of the council of revision, the governor sometimes opposed these bills. Such was the case with the March 1779 bill to attaint almost 300 people of high treason, which Clinton thought "neither founded on Justice or warranted by sound Policy or the Spirit of the Constitution."[79] Once, however, confiscation bills became law, usually over the veto of the council of revision, the governor saw to it that they were enforced. In addition to his constitutional responsibility to execute the law, fiscal necessities and the refugee problem caused the governor to enforce confiscations.

In March 1777 the legislature created the commissioners of sequestration who seized loyalist estates and rented them at moderate cost to whigs, giving preference to refugees who had fled from British-controlled areas. As the wartime economy and military conditions worsened in late 1779, the legislature enacted a law confiscating loyalist property, but not yet authorizing its sale. The last step was taken in March 1780 when the conservative opposition (always opposed to any measure that threatened the right of private property, for fear that their own property might be endangered) was defeated and the legislature ordered the sale of loyalist property. By the end of 1782, the state realized over $3,600,000 from the sale of confiscated estates.

As a strong advocate of the right of private property, George Clinton opposed the confiscatory legislation in principle. However, the governor supported confiscation partly because of the state's financial need, the danger that loyalists posed to the war effort, the suffering of refugees who had been dispossessed by British and tory actions, and his ideological desire to remake New York into a republican, and more nearly egalitarian, society. In an effort to redistribute land holdings, confiscated estates were to be sold in lots not to exceed 500 acres. The 455 confiscated lots in Dutchess County sold under the act of March 1780 (414 of which had belonged to two manor lords) were sold directly to 401 individuals. Over forty percent of those who purchased the land were tenants who had previously worked the land and paid taxes on it. Now they owned their land. This redistribution of the land occurred repeatedly when confiscated estates consisted of tenant-run farms. Speculators, on the other hand, concentrated their purchases on confiscated town lots and unoccupied frontier lands. But, even in these areas, speculators, eager for a profit, were more likely to sell their holdings than were the aristocratic manor lords who clung to their huge neofeudal estates for social as well as economic ends.[80]

The confiscation program was the most concrete indication of the social aspects of the American Revolution. To be sure, the process of land redistribution had been underway for a long time as hard pressed manor lords occasionally sold portions of their estates to raise cash. But New York's confiscation program wrought immediate change. A freehold was now more attainable for many New Yorkers. George Clinton was pleased with these results. He worried, however, that "some of the states" might try to claim confiscated estates in New York "as a common Interest" for the entire country.[81]

Clinton's aristocratic opponents saw only ill consequences from these seizures. A distressed John Jay wrote to the governor from Spain that "New York is disgraced by injustice too palpable to admit even of palliation. I feel for the honour of my country."[82] Chancellor Livingston lamented over "the violent spirit of persecution which prevails here." He dreaded the ramifications "upon the wealth, commerce & future tranquility of the state." All too often, the chancellor told John Jay, the persecution had ulterior—not patriotic—motives. "In some few it is a blind spirit of revenge & resentment, but in more it is the most sordid interest. One wishes to possess the house of some wretched Tory, another fears him as a rivale in his trade or commerce & a fourth wishes to get rid of his debts by shaking off his creditor or to reduce the price of Living by depopulating the town." The confiscatory program convinced the chancellor "that the more we know of our fellow creatures the less reason we have to esteem them."[83] He worried that the yeomen would not stop with the tories: "The warm & hotheaded whigs who are for the expulsion of all tories from the state & who would wish to render the more moderate whigs suspected in order to preserve in their own hands all the powers of Government."[84] The political struggle over confiscation assured Clinton of the animosity of the aristocratic Schuylerites. The struggle over the treatment of loyalists persisted after the restoration of peace.

Congress posed as great a threat to the state's anti-loyalist program as the conservatives. Article V of the peace treaty of 1783 prohibited loyalist confiscations in the future and called upon the states to compensate those loyalists who had lost property. In March 1783, Congressman William Floyd assured the governor that the treaty's provisions were mere show. Most congressmen, Floyd told Clinton, believed that the article had been inserted into the treaty so that the king and his ministers could say to loyalists that "they had attended to their Interest as far as Lay in their power on the Settlement of a peace." Congress would suggest that the states compensate their loyalists, but the states need not accede to the recommendation.[85]

Governor Clinton thoroughly opposed granting compensation to tories. They had, he maintained, wreaked havoc during the war and had lived in safety and relative luxury behind British lines. Agreeing with the governor, the state legislature on March 31, 1784, resolved that it saw no reason to compensate loyalists whose property had been confiscated, because Great Britain had no plans to compensate Americans who had suffered from the wanton destruction caused by British regulars, tories, and their Indian allies. The "Rules of Justice" did not require, nor would "the Public Tranquility" allow, the restoration of citizenship or property to the enemies of America.[86] The state would keep the confiscated property as partial remuneration for its wartime expenses.

When the British evacuated New York City in late November 1783, the governor worried that the victorious returning exiles would seek vengeance against the remaining loyalists. Repeatedly Clinton called for "a firm attachment to our most excellent constitution, and a steady support of good government, domestic tranquility, and the national justice and honor."[87] He would not tolerate illegal acts of violence, but he was not ready to extend a forgiving hand to his former enemies. The crisis climaxed on May 12, 1784, when the legislature passed an act that disenfranchised all but a few specially-excepted loyalists. Counties and local municipalities followed by passing resolutions that denied loyalists the right to return and claim property."[88] Not until the spring of 1786 did the hostility toward loyalists sufficiently subside that the legislature repealed the disenfranchisement act passed two years earlier.

Clinton was at first ambivalent about the state's postwar anti-loyalist policy. Had it been solely his choice, he probably would have allowed loyalists to resume their normal political activities even though he believed that most tories would become supporters of his political opponents. But Clinton soon realized the strong attitude held by his primary constituents—the yeomen—who were unwilling to welcome back their former enemies. This political combination made Clinton's decision relatively easy. Since his instincts always warned against an abandonment of the yeomen, the governor joined the anti-tory forces. The yeomen appreciated

Clinton's stand, and the state profited tremendously from the confiscations. The anti-loyalist policy, however, cost the governor dearly, as the aristocrats who had grudgingly supported Clinton during the war now abandoned him. From now on, Clinton could expect united political opposition.

20. The Western Lands Endangered

The British occupation of New York City and the lower six counties and the Vermont insurgency were not the only threats to New York's territorial integrity. Beset with military, fiscal, and supply problems, Governor Clinton also found himself fighting off the ravenous territorial appetites of New York's sister states. The small states without western land claims pressured New York to cede its western lands to Congress in exchange for their support on the Vermont dispute; and Massachusetts renewed an old claim to much of western New York.

After John Sullivan and James Clinton conducted their successful campaign against the pro-British Indians in western New York in August and September of 1779, arguments were put forth that the land (only 100 miles west of the Hudson) was conquered territory. Since Continental troops had taken the area from an independent nation, it was suggested, that the land now belonged to Congress. John Jay recommended to Governor Clinton that New York establish posts in the territory and treat it as its own. The state's former chief justice, about to leave on a diplomatic mission to Madrid, told Clinton that New York "had too much Forbearance about these matters." New York should follow Virginia's lead and lay claim to its rightful possessions.[89]

Jay soon refined his views on the state's lands. In his judgment, New York had "unquestionably more Territory than we can govern." He recommended to the governor that Vermont be given its independence and that New York cede its far western territory to Congress. The benefits to be derived from releasing Vermont would be far greater than the problems associated with keeping it. Since the extreme western territory of New York, according to Jay, "lies beyond the convenient Reach of Government, the Retention of it would rather incommode than benefit us." The vast quantities of land "would always be the object of Envy and Jealousy to the other States, and perhaps the Subject of Dispute." New York should cede the western territory to Congress "in a way that would conduce to the Credit and Interest of the State." Jay knew that the governor would be able to develop such a plan, making New York look generous and accommodating.[90]

Chancellor Livingston, serving as a delegate to Congress, echoed Jay's recommendation. In a letter written to the governor on the last day of November 1779, Livingston reported: "I find a violent inclination in most of the States to appropriate all the western Lands to the use of the United States, & in proportion, as they feel the weight of taxes, that inclination will increase, till I fear it will at last overpower us." The chancellor believed that New York should "contrive to make a sacrafice of part to secure the remainder." This tactical cession should be done while New York's title was still treated "with some respect."[91]

Livingston recommended that the legislature establish the state's boundaries along the northern border with Pennsylvania, north to Lake Ontario, along the southern shore of the lake to the St. Lawrence River, north and east to the bounds of Canada, and eastward to New Hampshire. These boundaries would secure Fort Niagara and the navigation of Lake Ontario. Both Congress and the state could use their western lands to raise revenue and help maintain the value of their paper currency, which would be accepted for purchases of land. Virginia had already tried to seize New York's western land. That attempt was warded off when Virginia was unrepresented in Congress. Livingston believed that New York ran a high "risk . . . by being too insatiable in our demands."[92]

The governor responded favorably to Livingston's suggestions. Clinton had long suspected that people in some states intended not only to claim the western lands but the confiscated loyalist estates as well. Experience taught Clinton that public bodies were more influenced in their decisions "by motives of Policy & a Desire of pleasing their immediate Constituents than by a Regard to Equity." With this in mind, the governor agreed with Livingston that it was in New York's interest "to give up a Part of our western Lands, if by this we may be able to enjoy the Remainder free from every Claim." Under this impression, the governor, "for my own Part," supported Livingston's proposed boundaries as "it would leave us Territory nearly as extensive as the Influence of Governmt could reach, and beyond this I do not for many Reasons conceive it to be our Interest to hold Lands."[93]

The following month, the legislature passed an act "to facilitate the completion" of the Articles of Confederation. Desirous of "accelerating the Federal Alliance," and knowing that some states refused to adopt the Articles until the western lands were ceded to the United States, the legislature "authorized and empowered" its delegates in Congress to propose a change in the state's boundaries to reflect a cession of land to Congress.[94] On September 6, 1780, Congress formally asked the other states with western lands to emulate New York's "wisdom, generosity & Candour."[95] Soon Virginia too ceded its entire holdings northwest of the Ohio River, conditional upon Congress explicitly guaranteeing Virginia's jurisdiction over its remaining claims. New York's delegates to Congress used their discretionary authority to set the actual western and northern boundaries of the state. They opted not to emulate Virginia's requirement of a guarantee to all other land because "it might have been liable to a construction that we were seeking a Benefit instead of confering a favour." But the delegates felt that it would be imprudent for them to accept Virginia's cession with its qualifier, "when our own [jurisdiction] was not secured in the same manner." Consequently, they provided that New York's cession was conditional upon a special act of the legislature "unless our State receives the same Guarantee from the Confederated States as any other" state receives for land cessions.[96] Two weeks later, Clinton responded, saying that the legislature was unwilling to pass a law confirming its cession until it knew what guarantees Congress gave to Virginia for its cession.[97]

Despite New York's and Virginia's generosity, the western lands remained a major political issue. On October 9, 1782, Congressman Ezra L'Hommedieu wrote to Governor Clinton that "the Back Lands . . . influences the Politicks of almost all the States." He was uncertain whether Congress would accept New York's cession.[98] Three weeks later, however, Congressman James Duane informed the governor that Congress had accepted New York's cession but had suspended Virginia's conditional cession. Duane believed that New York's cession would honor the state "as well as promote its Interest."[99]

A year later, as peace neared, the Massachusetts delegates to Congress surprised everyone by claiming that all of the territory in western New York rightfully belonged to Massachusetts under its charter of 1629. This assertion, made on the floor of Congress, shocked the New York delegates but evoked no hostile reaction from anyone else. Duane and L'Hommedieu recommended to Clinton that the state immediately fight the claim in a federal court (actually, a specially appointed committee chosen by the disputants and Congress) as provided by Article 9 of the Articles of Confederation. In the meantime, New York should "use the most vigorous Efforts for settling this Country under their Authority, for no Respect ought to be paid to a State Pretention which has laid dormant more than One Hundred & fifty Years."[100] Incongruently, at this same time, the two states amicably appointed commissioners to establish a mutually agreeable boundary between eastern New York and western Massachusetts.

On June 3, 1784, Massachusetts presented a petition to Congress formally claiming western New York and requesting a federal court to decide the case. Congress read the petition and ordered that agents from the two states present their states' cases before Congress on December 6. On August 20, 1784, Governor Clinton called a special session of the legislature. The governor delivered his opening speech on October 18 and told the legislators about Massachusetts' claim. Three days later, the senate tendered its incredulous response. "After all the severe calamities" of the war, New Yorkers had looked forward to a postwar period of peace, recovery, and prosperity. No one anticipated another attack—especially an attack by a brother in arms. Had Massachusetts forgotten the last eight years? "Among the first to make a common cause with our sister State of Massachusetts. Among the first in strenuous and expensive exertions to maintain the war; and distinguished above all others by the weight and duration of our sufferings, we flattered ourselves that we had some claim to her friendship."[101]

On November 12, the legislature appointed five agents to represent the state before Congress. James Duane, John Jay, Robert R. Livingston, Egbert Benson, and Walter Livingston would try to save the state's territory. The New York and Massachusetts agents met in Congress on December 6, 8, and 10, when Congress resolved that they jointly appoint judges "to constitute a court for hearing and determining the matter in question, agreeable to the ninth of the Articles of Confederation." The agents reported on December 24, listing nine judges, five of whom would be considered a quorum. Congress was authorized to fill vacancies and to choose the location where the court would sit.

The federal court was called to meet in Williamsburg, Virginia, on the first Tuesday in June 1785. Delay followed delay, and it soon became obvious that the necessary five judges would not attend. Once it became clear that Congress was unable to resolve the dispute, Clinton authorized the state's newly created land office to sell land in the disputed territory. In 1786 both states passed acts authorizing their agents to meet together and come to some amicable solution outside the cumbersome judicial machinery specified by the Articles of Confederation. Once again, as with Vermont, Congress was unable or unwilling to act, and New York suffered because of it.

The agents met in Hartford, Connecticut, on November 30, 1786, and agreed on a compromise. New York would retain jurisdictional control over the land, but Massachusetts would retain the property rights. The state of New York lost the value of a huge section of its land; Massachusetts had gained a windfall.

As a preface to its printing of the agreement, the February 26, 1787, issue of the New York Gazetteer indicated that this compromise "affords an important lesson to States and Nations in general, when it is considered how much blood and treasure have been expended in territorial disputes much less valuable and extensive." The agreement also served as a important lesson for George Clinton. He had fought the British for eight years and finally was victorious. He had fought his neighbors both in and out of Congress—and he and his state lost. Clinton and many other New Yorkers felt little reason to continue supporting a government that offered them little protection.

21. The Western Posts

By the time of the Revolution, the British had established eight forts or posts around the Great Lakes to assist them in the fur trade. Seven of the eight posts were on land that, by the provisions of the Treaty of Peace, would become American territory, and five of those were in New York— Niagara, Oswego, Oswegatchie, Point au Fer, and Dutchman's Point. Throughout the war, these forts served as staging points for the numerous loyalist and Indian raids on the frontier. As the war wound down, New York was eager to garrison these forts in order to regain control of the lucrative fur trade, assert hegemony over the Native Americans in the area, and assure its claim to its western territory. For these reasons, on March 27, 1783, New York's legislature passed concurrent resolutions calling for the state to occupy these posts when the British evacuated them under the provisions of the Treaty of Peace. If the posts were not occupied immediately upon the British evacuation, New Yorkers feared that Indians would destroy them. But New Yorkers had other reasons for wanting to occupy the forts with their own soldiers. The actions of Congress and the other states on Vermont, and the expressed desire of some states to expropriate western lands for the benefit of the United States, convinced Governor Clinton and the legislature that New York's western lands would be endangered if Continental troops occupied the forts.

Since the Articles of Confederation prohibited states from having peacetime standing armies except for garrisoning forts deemed necessary for the state's defense, New York asked Congress to declare the number of soldiers necessary to properly man the forts. The legislature believed that no more than 500 men would be necessary. These 500 soldiers were to be taken from New York troops already under Continental command, who had enlisted for three years' service beginning in April 1781. Congress was asked to declare that these soldiers henceforth would be "in the immediate Service of this State, and not in the Pay or Service of the United States." Embarrassingly, however, impoverished New York was unable to afford this; and the legislature asked Congress to provide "immediate Subsistence" and munitions for the units and to charge these expenses against the state's account with the Confederation.[102]

On April 1, 1783, Clinton sent the resolutions to Alexander Hamilton and William Floyd, the state's delegates in Congress. The congressmen reported that on April 4 the resolutions were sent to committee, but that they thought "it improbable Congress will accede to the idea."[103] Two months later, Hamilton informed the governor that on May 12 Congress had agreed to a "temporary provision" instructing General Washington to garrison the evacuated forts with three-year Continental soldiers—a plan Hamilton endorsed as "more for the interest of the state than to have them garrisoned at" New York's expense.[104] Congress needed more time to fashion a permanent peace establishment.

Governor Clinton viewed this action by Congress with great suspicion. To make matters worse, Washington wrote to the governor in mid-August, urgently asking New York to supply £500 to "Contract for Boats and to defray the contingent expences of the operation." If New York could not supply the funds, the expedition would have to be delayed until the following spring, by which time Indians might destroy the forts.[105] Despite his objection to Continental units being used to garrison the forts, Clinton told Washington that the necessary funds were available and that he would "convene a Council without Delay & lay before them your Excellency's Requisition."[106] Before the funds were sent, however, Washington informed the governor that the British had no plans to evacuate soon, and that the preparations of the soldiers had been "suspended until further Orders."[107]

On August 23, an angry George Clinton demanded from the state's delegates "a particular detail of the motives which influenced the determination of Congress" to use Continental rather than New York forces for garrisoning duty. Ezra L'Hommedieu responded on September 3, that neither he nor James Duane were at Congress in May when the matter had been determined. Alexander Hamilton and William Floyd were in attendance. It was L'Hommedieu's understanding, however, that Hamilton "had suppressed" the legislature's concurrent resolutions so that they "had been unknown to any Person in Congress," because Hamilton had "determined that it was best for the state that the Posts should be garrisoned with Continental Troops." L'Hommedieu told Clinton that an extract of his letter demanding an explanation of events had been sent to Hamilton, who was now in Albany.[108]

L'Hommedieu explained the situation that had existed in Congress when he arrived in August. He found many state delegations in favor of garrisoning the frontier posts "by the States in whose Territory they were, and not by the Continent." L'Hommedieu had suggested to Duane that they write Clinton to see if the legislature had a preference so that they would know how to vote when the issue arose in the debate over the permanent peace establishment. Duane responded that Hamilton had given him the legislature's instructions when the latter left Congress. L'Hommedieu and Duane agreed that "as soon as an Opportunity presented" they would try "to procure a [congressional] Resolution agreeable to the Instructions as we supposed we had no right to Judge of the Propriety, of a Measure directed by the Legislature." L'Hommedieu, however, told the governor that the posts would not be evacuated before the spring and maybe not within a year. Furthermore L'Hommedieu had been informed confidentially that "Virginia have it in Contemplation whenever an Opportunity presents to take Possession of Niagara, on Pretence that the Posts with Lands to the eastward of it are within the Limits of that State."[109] Clinton's fears were confirmed. He was eager to hear Hamilton's explanation for disregarding the legislature's explicit instructions.

Hamilton responded on October 3. He had immediately turned the concurrent resolutions over to a committee appointed to consider the peace establishment, but that committee's report had been suspended to take up another plan. Opinion in Congress at the time was "unsettled as to the most eligible mode of providing for the security of the frontiers." A large number of delegates, including Hamilton, believed that federal soldiers would more equitably share the defense burden of the exposed states, such as New York and were eager for Congress to assert itself in this and other ways. The Articles of Confederation seemed to prohibit a federal peacetime army; but without such an army, the safety of the country, in fact the very existence of the union, would be endangered. Rather than solving this dilemma, Congress postponed the final peace establishment and, because of the lateness of the season, decided temporarily to send federal units "already on foot" to garrison the posts.

Hamilton explained that he believed that the legislature's only fear was that the forts would be left undefended when the British evacuated. He admitted that he "saw with pleasure rather than regret, the turn which the affair took," but he was sorry if Congress' action "contravened the intentions of the legislature." Hamilton told the governor that New York's geographic position "strongly speaks this language—strengthen the confederation—Give it exclusively the power of the sword."[110] Clinton and Hamilton had come to a parting. For some time, a pattern had been forming—now the two men knew that they were pursuing different ends. Clinton wanted New York strengthened and was profoundly suspicious of Congress' assertions of power; Hamilton's vision of America focused on the national level.

Congress reconsidered the garrisoning problem in the spring of 1784. On April 9, New York's new delegates to Congress, Charles DeWitt and Ephraim Paine, warned Governor Clinton about possible attempts to seize the state's northwestern lands: "Upon the whole Sir it is our opinion that the utmost Vigilence ought to be exercised to prevent any encroachment on our Territory as we are to expect no protection otherwise than from our own arms."[111] Ten days later, the delegates laid New York's concurrent resolutions before Congress, but consideration was postponed in favor of another proposal. Congressman Paine reported on April 29 that Congress would not give New York an estimate of the number of soldiers needed to garrison the forts until it had decided on a final peacetime establishment. Paine told the governor that if the state planned to raise troops to garrison the posts, Paine and his colleague would "protract the Determination of Congress upon the Subject of arangements in order to give an op[p]ortunity to our troops first to get Possession." In Paine's judgment, it was important for New York to garrison Niagara and Oswego because "it appears to be the general Sense of the Delegates that the western Country ought to be Considered as belonging to the united States in Common." The congressman told Clinton "that there is not the least Prospect of any Protection or assistance from Congress and that it is high time for our State to tak[e] the Same measures as though it was Sorounded with open and avowed Enemies."[112]

The governor had reached that judgment a month earlier. On March 19 he commissioned Nicholas Fish as a special secret emissary to Sir Frederick Haldimand, governor general of Canada. Fish was to determine the exact time when British units would evacuate "and make such arrangements with him for the transaction of that business, and our taking possession, as may tend to promote the mutual convenience and interest of both parties." If Haldimand was unprepared for an immediate evacuation, Fish was to make arrangements with him so that he would give New York notice of the withdrawal. Clinton told his agent to report back with "all the dispatch in your power."[113] Haldimand received Fish coldly telling him that the forts would be turned over to Congress, not to a single state. Furthermore, he announced that the forts would not be relinquished until Americans honored the provisions of the peace treaty in their treatment of loyalists and in removing roadblocks to the collection of debts owed British merchants.[114]

As Congress continued to consider the garrisoning problem, it became evident that most congressmen did not want New York to control the forts. Massachusetts appeared to be willing to bribe Congress with promises of a cession of some of the western lands it hoped to obtain from its claim on New York. To ensure its new western holdings, Massachusetts wanted its soldiers to occupy the forts. Congress appeared ready to send Continental forces from West Point—which were predominantly from Massachusetts—to occupy the forts as soon as the British evacuated. Congressman Paine reported that "the Chagrin was very visible when Congress were tould plainly that New York would not Suffer the Massachusetts troops to march into that Country."[115] The opposition of New York coupled with the objections of several states to sending Continental units in general, killed the proposal to send Continental forces to garrison the forts. New York's threat to raise soldiers, "though the assent of Congress was refused" forced Congress to devise a plan that at least gave the appearance of being acceptable to New York and a majority of the states.[116] Congress, therefore, passed resolutions calling for a regiment of 700 men to be raised among the militia from New Jersey (110), Connecticut (165), Pennsylvania (260), and New York (165) to garrison the forts, with Pennsylvania supplying the commanding lieutenant colonel. New York was still dissatisfied. What was Congress trying to do by sending "foreign" soldiers into New York? On June 4, the day after Massachusetts formally filed its claim for New York's western lands, Congressman Charles DeWitt warned Governor Clinton: "I hope the Legislature have taken every precaution respecting the W. Territory. I believe Sir a Plan is formed and perhaps wrought into System to take that Country from us."[117] By this time, Clinton, who had once put his faith in Congress to render justice, needed no convincing that Congress was now New York's enemy rather than its friend.

22. The Impost: A Harbor for Whose Benefit?

Congress emerged from the Revolution in desperate financial condition. Saddled with a huge wartime debt, the Articles of Confederation gave it no authority to levy taxes with which to pay interest or principal. With no coercive power over states or individuals, Congress could only ask the states for requisitions. At the height of its wartime power, Congress never received more than half the revenue it requested. Now, without the menace of the British army as an incentive, states were even less willing to fulfill their financial obligations to Congress. All states had suffered during the war, and they were eager to fund their own recovery programs. Alexander Hamilton sensed the forlorn situation of national affairs: "There are two classes of men . . . one attached to state the other to Continental politics." In his view, "the seeds of disunion [were] much more numerous than those of union."[118]

During the early months of 1783, Congress considered alternative solutions to its financial problems. On April 18, it agreed on a unified economic plan that, among other things, called upon the states to grant Congress the power to lay federal import duties for twenty-five years. Revenue from this impost of 1783 would be earmarked to pay the war debt.

New York's two congressmen—Alexander Hamilton and William

Floyd—split their vote on the proposed economic plan. Ironically, Floyd, the future Antifederalist, supported the proposal, while the nationalist Hamilton opposed it because it was too weak. Despite his opposition, Hamilton urged Governor Clinton to support the impost of 1783.[119] But, without fanfare, the governor had already changed his political orientation, and, with him, a majority of the legislature had also changed. A month before the impost of 1783 was proposed, the legislature repealed its March 1781 approval of the impost of 1781. A new state impost, enacted in November 1784, was to be the cornerstone of Clinton's recovery program. As such, it could not be surrendered to federal use. Annual revenue from the state impost during the Confederation years ranged between $100,000 and $225,000, and represented from one-third to over one-half of the state's annual income. Such a revenue would allow the legislature to levy low real estate taxes or perhaps none at all. The governor saw the benefits to be derived from this horn of plenty; after all the ill-treatment the state had received from its neighbors and from Congress, Clinton was reluctant to surrender New York's most valuable asset—an asset that would greatly benefit the yeomen who formed the great bulk of the governor's supporters.

Some New Yorkers had ideological reasons for opposing a federal impost. In a series of masterful newspaper articles, opponents of the federal tariff, led by Abraham Yates, Jr., argued that an independent revenue for Congress would be dangerous. No one argued against the propriety of Congress having a revenue with which to pay the public debt, but Congress should not have the *power* to raise income independent of the states. The states should retain the power of the purse themselves and grant Congress the funds it needed.

Yates and others feared that Congress would use its taxing power to create a powerful bureaucracy that would soon become oppressive. To collect revenue, Congress would appoint "collectors, deputy collectors, comptrollers, clerks, tide-waiters, and searchers." Troops and ships would be maintained to enforce the tariff. Special courts would be created to try offenders. The old specter of imperial harassment seemed about to reappear. Opponents of the impost argued that when the federal government augmented its power, Congress' voracious appetite for authority would be satiated only when it had "swallowed entirely the *sovereignty of the particular states*."[120] With the consolidation of power in Congress and the loss of state sovereignty, the rights so dear bought during the Revolution would also be lost. The newspaper barrage succeeded as the state senate defeated the impost eleven to seven on April 14, 1785.

On February 15, 1786, Congress asked New York to reconsider its rejection. State Senator Philip Schuyler, in a letter to his political lieutenants in Albany County, held little hope for passage, but he vowed to do his best to adopt the impost, "for the honor, for the interest and *for the security of the peace* of the state." He was not at liberty to tell them what he meant by the "security of the peace of the state." All he could say at that time was "that we have it in our power by *our prudence*, not by our *strength* to avert disagreeable consequences—we may be driven to do by compulsion that which ought to flow spontaneously from our Justice and from neighbourly considerations."[121] A month later, a pessimistic Schuyler elaborated on his fears. If the legislature refused to pass the impost, "the consequences are seriously to be apprehended." Connecticut had already sent emissaries to Vermont and to western Massachusetts to seek their cooperation in compelling New York's compliance. Such a combination, Schuyler asserted, "will be powerful, and if once hostile disturbances arise, heaven only knows where they will end."[122] Schuyler was not alone in predicting violence. President of Congress Nathaniel Gorham of Massachusetts believed that it was only "the restraining hand of Congress, (weak as it is), that prevents N. Jersey and Connecticut from entering the lists very seriously with N. York and bloodshed would very quickly be the consequences."[123]

Animosity toward New York raged throughout New Jersey and Connecticut. Half of all foreign goods imported into these states came through the port of New York. In effect, New Jersey and Connecticut consumers, and to a lesser extent those in Massachusetts and Vermont, paid New York's state impost in the form of higher prices. They subsidized New York's low real estate and personal property taxes. This hidden tax cost New Jersey and Connecticut approximately £30,000 and £50,000 per year, respectively. President Gorham believed that the discontent fostered by this economic domination would "greatly weaken if not destroy the Union." New Jersey's legislature fought back in the only way it could—by resolving not to pay its congressional requisitions until New York gave up its state impost or applied its revenue "for the general purposes of the Union."[124] The pseudonymous author "Gustavus," writing in the *New York Journal*, March 2, 1786, chided his fellow New Yorkers: "That by our own impost we actually lay two states under contributions, and thereby pay our debt with monies which properly belong to the treasuries of Jersey and Connecticut." But most New Yorkers were not embarrassed; they understood the economics of their port and appreciated its benefits. "Let our imposts and advantages be taken from us, shall we not be obliged to lay as heavy taxes as Connecticut, Boston, &c." The bountiful revenue from the port of New York was "a privilege Providence hath endowed us with," and New Yorkers were not about to surrender it to Congress.[125] They hoped that another state would reject the impost, and allow New York to avoid the opprobrium of killing it. That was not to be. All of the other states granted Congress the power to lay the tariff.

National attention focused on the New York legislature in April 1786 as it reconsidered the impost. To some the stakes were high—perhaps the very existence of the union. Some delegates in Congress felt that New York would accept the impost rather than risk the consequences. Clintonians, however, aware of the attention their state was receiving, chose an ingenuous ploy of adopting the impost with certain restrictions that Congress could not accept. New York acceded to the principle that revenue from imports should accrue to Congress for the next twenty-five years to pay the interest and principal on the public debt. But New York would use the mechanism and bureaucracy of the state impost to collect the revenue. Furthermore, the state reserved the right to pay Congress the impost revenue with its paper money.

The Council of Revision accepted the act adopting the impost on May 4, 1786, on which day it was delivered to Congress, now meeting in New York City. Congress appointed a committee to examine the various state actions on the federal impost. On July 27, the committee reported that New York's act "so essentially varies" from Congress' system, that it could not "be considered a compliance."

Not all congressmen wanted to reject New York's adoption of the impost. Melancton Smith, one of New York's delegates to Congress, eloquently argued that most of the states had incorporated "restrictions & limitations" in their ratification acts. According to Smith, under most of the state ratifications, Congress could not "exercise, appoint or controul any judicial power at all—the Courts of the diff. States are only competent, and not accountable or controulable by the U. S." The states, Smith persisted, "generally have not given the powers asked, yet Cong[ress] have determined these Laws are a compliance—a strict compliance they cannot be—it must be meant then that they are a substantial compliance—and so a sub[stantial] comp[liance] is suffi[cient]." With this foundation laid, Smith rhetorically asked: "Is the Law of N. Y. A substantial compl[iance]?" He responded: "That is a subst[antial] compl[iance] which will effect the end Congress have in view," and New York's compliance provided Congress with the revenue it needed.[126]

The Virginia congressional delegation agreed with Smith's logic. James Monroe wrote Clinton that the Virginians wanted to avoid irritating New York. In their judgment, "the best plan" was for Congress to draft an ordinance implementing the impost that would show New York's legislature that the new revenue plan would not be "a system of oppression, but in conformity with the laws and constitution of the state itself." With this assurance, the legislature would be induced "to grant powers in such conformity with the acts of other states as to enable them [i.e., Congress] to carry it into effect." Congress, according to the Virginians, should "proceed with temper in this business . . . to conciliate and gain the confidence of the state and all its citizens."[127]

The majority of Congress, however, disagreed with this conciliatory policy and, on August 11, asked Governor Clinton to call a special session of the legislature to reconsider the impost. Five days later the governor rejected the request, referring to the state's constitutional provision that allowed the governor to call special sessions only on "extraordinary occasions." "I cannot yield a compliance," Clinton explained, "without breaking through one of those checks which the wisdom of our constitution has provided against the abuse of office." This, in Clinton's judgment, was not an extraordinary occasion. On August 23, Congress again debated and rejected New York's ratification of the impost. For a second time, it requested the governor to call an early session, but Clinton, now clearly annoyed, again rejected the request.[128]

Several members of Congress opposed this second request. New York Congressman Melancton Smith unsuccessfully offered a motion opposing a second request to the governor because "it would involve an interference of Congress on a question respecting the construction of the Constitution of that State upon which Congress have by the Confederation no right to decide, will probably lead this house into a dispute with the supreme executive of the State of New York and disgust the Legislature thereof."[129] North Carolina Congressman Timothy Bloodworth thought the request "improper as there is not the least probability of his complying, deeming the measure unwarrantable by the constitution."[130] Massachusetts Congressman Rufus King had a different perspective. Reporting to his merchant colleague, King suggested that "as the lawyers say," Congress was "at issue with New York." King anticipated that Clinton alone among the thirteen state governors would dare "under similar circumstances [to] refuse." But King welcomed Clinton's adamant stance and New York's refusal to alter its act adopting the impost. Without a revenue from the impost, King believed that Congress would be justified in resorting to implied powers to "do every thing in their power for the public Good."[131] Clinton's actions and New York's obstinacy, consequently, would play into the hands of those nationalists who wanted more power for Congress. Other congressmen, such as Stephen Mix Mitchell of Connecticut, hoped that Clinton would see "the Precipice on which the united States as a collective body stand, by reason of withholding the necessary Means for the preservation of our Union."[132]

Historians have often pointed to Clinton's action as a sign of his Antifederalism. Although Clinton certainly did not want to relinquish the state's impost to Congress, he was straightforward and consistent in not calling a special session of the legislature. In reality, by refusing Congress' request for an early session of the legislature in the fall of 1786, Clinton was adhering to a policy he first enunciated when he took office in 1777 and which he restated in January 1786.[133] In Clinton's judgment, he would have violated the state constitution if he had called an early session to reconsider the impost.

When the legislature convened for its regular session in January 1787, the nationalist forces in the assembly were mobilized by a new leader. Alexander Hamilton had been elected to the assembly specifically to fight for the federal impost. Immediately the Hamiltonians tried to censure Clinton for not calling an early session of the legislature. The assembly, however, approved the governor's inaction, 39 to 9. Connecticut Congressman Stephen Mix Mitchell wrote that the assembly, in approving Clinton's action, "step'd as twere out of their way to give Congress a Slap in the face."[134]

On January 13, 1787, Clinton delivered his opening address to the legislature, in which he dutifully—if unenthusiastically—transmitted Congress' request for a reconsideration of the impost. The governor explained that he would "forbear making any remarks on a subject which hath been so repeatedly submitted to the consideration of the legislature, and must be well understood."[135] The assembly submitted the impost to a three-man committee composed of two Hamiltonians and one Clintonian. On February 9, the committee recommended a bill that would meet Congress' standards, but Clintonian assemblymen—described by one partisan as "mere machines" under the control of the governor, amended the bill so that it would still remain unacceptable to Congress. Hamilton delivered a lengthy, impassioned speech in favor of the federal impost that, according to "Rough Carver" was followed by "a contemptuous silence. . . . The members appeared pre-determined, having . . . *made up their minds on the subject*."[136] The assembly then voted 38 to 19 for the amended impost bill—the Clintonian-dominated assembly had succeeded in retaining the impost and its revenue for state use. The assembly's actions, according to Virginia Congressman James Madison, "put a definitive veto on the Impost."[137]

Throughout the controversy over the impost, Governor Clinton kept a low profile. Opposition to the impost came from Abraham Yates in the senate and John Lansing in the assembly, who were attacked as demagogues, pandering to the "little folks." They were also accused, for the love of "power and office," of "daily paying homage to the G———r." As for Clinton, it was "whispered that he also is in secret an anti-impost man." It seemed clear that Clinton had sufficient influence in the assembly to exert his will, and "a distant hint only from" him could have adopted the impost for Congress.[138] A month after the vote, Philip Schuyler charged that the delegates against the impost were led "by promises and the influence" of the governor.[139]

Two years later in the state ratifying convention, Governor Clinton professed that he had uniformly supported an impost for Congress. He confessed, however, that he had strenuously opposed "the manner in which that body proposed to exercise that power. . . . I firmly believed that if it were granted in the form recommended, it would prove unproductive, and would also lead to the establishment of dangerous principles." Clinton favored "granting the revenue" but opposed giving Congress the "power of collection or a controul over our state officers."[140]

The following year, Alexander Hamilton resurrected the debate over the impost as a campaign issue in the hotly contested gubernatorial election of 1789 and accused Clinton of duplicitousness. Hamilton discredited Clinton's statement in the ratifying convention "that he had always been a friend to the impost," but that he could not agree to the power Congress wanted. To oppose a specific plan and profess support for a general principle was sheer "hypocrisy." In reality, however, Hamilton had "unquestionable evidence" that the governor had used his "personal influence" with various legislators to "prejudice them against the granting of the impost." Clinton supposedly warned the legislators that Congress, as a single-house legislature with no effective checks on its power, ought not to be trusted with a revenue independent of state control. Hamilton questioned the propriety of this kind of executive interference with legislators. To him, it appeared "highly exceptionable."[141]

In February 1787, Hamilton, himself, was playing for larger stakes than the federal impost. He realized that New York's legislature under the governor's domination would never approve the impost in a fashion acceptable to Congress. The legislators had, in fact, recently indicated their political orientation when they elected New York's delegation to Congress. North Carolina Congressman William Blount lamented that, despite "the great Choice the state affords of Gentlemen of abilities and who are Candidates," the legislature appointed (except for Attorney General Egbert Benson) "antifederal Peasants."[142] Hamilton did not need to count legislative votes any further—he knew that the federal impost had little chance.

Hamilton, however, decided to take advantage of the inevitable loss of the impost. He used the legislative forum on the impost as a platform on which to advocate a strengthened Congress, a mutual understanding among the states for each other, and a denunciation of those narrow-minded politicians who put state interests above the nation's welfare. In eloquently stating his case, Hamilton had no illusions that he would change any legislator's vote on the impost. What he hoped to do was to draw the battle lines for the future federal-state conflicts, situating himself on the patriotic federal side and the Clintonians on the selfish state side.

The lines that had been drawn fairly clearly over loyalist legislation in 1784 were now being extended on federal-state relations.

By the time the impost question was settled in the legislature, well-organized parties had developed in New York. At first Philip Schuyler served as the acknowledged leader of the aristocrats. Hamilton described his father-in-law as the second most influential man in the state—second only to the governor. Schuyler, however, according to Hamilton, had "more weight in the Legislature than the Governor; but not so much as not to be exposed to the mortification of seeing important measures patronised by him frequently miscarry."[143] By January of 1786, the mantle had shifted to Assemblyman Hamilton.

Party structure and hierarchy were not as clear on the other side. Everyone knew that George Clinton controlled a large number of legislative votes, and that he was the titular head of a party composed of several factions led by different men. The aristocratic Schuylerites—soon to be Hamiltonians—did not want the popular governor as an avowed, personal enemy. Far better to oppose some of the more radical factions led in the assembly by Ephraim Paine, John Lansing, Jr., and "the levellers" Mathew Adgate and Jacob Ford, and in the senate by the irascible Abraham Yates, Jr.[144] Yates served especially well as the aristocrats' whipping boy. According to Hamilton, he "is a man whose ignorance and perverseness are only surpassed by his pertinacity and conceit. He hates all high-flyers, which is the appellation he gives to men of genius."[145]

George Clinton was satisfied to exert his influence behind the scenes and was not eager to be publicly acclaimed as the leader of a political party. He believed that he could be more effective above the fray of partisan politics. Furthermore the majority in the legislature was composed of various elements, some of which were too radical for the governor's taste. By staying publicly aloof, the governor stayed out of the rough and tumble political battles, yet he could usually win support for or kill legislative proposals at will. In fact, Clinton found himself in exactly this position as the state attempted to solve the economic depression of the mid-1780s.

23. A Devastated Economy

The end of the Revolution in New York brought a short period of prosperity followed by a swift deflation that soon deepened into the "bad times" of 1785–1786. These depression years were marked by devastating public and private indebtedness, disorganization of trade, contraction of the circulating currency, and drastically reduced agricultural prices. By 1785 New

Yorkers complained of declining trade, growing inventories of foreign imports in New York City, falling prices, a shortage of a circulating currency, and rising taxes. On November 3, 1785, the New York City Chamber of Commerce complained to the state legislature that "a flourishing and successful commerce has not yet been numbered among the benefits that peace and independence have restored to the state, but that trade, the great spring of agriculture and manufactures . . . is daily on the decline."[146] Distressed New Yorkers demanded some sort of relief. Twice in 1784 the assembly yielded to public demand and passed paper-money proposals, only to have the senate reject them. The bicameral dispute became symbolic of the statewide split over paper money.

Opponents of paper money often challenged the widespread belief that a scarcity of specie existed.[147] Fiscal conservatives such as John Jay believed that the real problem with the economy lay deeper than the mere loss of specie:

> Our Harvest is good, and though the Productions of the Country are plenty, yet they bear a high Cash Price, so that the Complaint of the want of Money in the Country, is less well founded than a Complaint of Distrust and want of Credit between Man and Man would be. For the apprehension of paper money alarms those who have any Thing to lend, while they who have Debts to pay are zealous Advocates for the Measure. Until that matter is decided there will be little Credit, and I sometimes think the less the better.[148]

Jay was partly correct but he failed to realize that credit was tight because of the reduced money supply.[149]

The New York City Chamber of Commerce opposed paper money because it "would not promote the general interest of the State; and that 'till such time as the Public confidence is restored, by a faithful performance of all Contracts Public and Private, it must inevitably depreciate to the Ultimate injury of the Merchants and Inhabitants of this City." It was further resolved that if the legislature did issue paper money, the bills should not be legal tender.[150] Most members of the chamber admitted that a scarcity of specie existed and that the poorer sort were suffering, but they were afraid that paper money would be issued to excess, leading to an unbridled depreciation, such as had happened to Continental currency. To alleviate the distress, petitions submitted to the legislature recommended that the general form of taxation be altered and that the collection of arrears be postponed thus lightening the tax burden on those least able to pay.[151]

Almost daily other suggestions poured forth detailing how the evils of the day might be corrected. One student of history, using the pseudonym

"A Spartan," suggested that New York abolish money and revert to barter. Philip Schuyler lamented that "public credit will be put off to a period which the present race will not see."[152]

Some wealthy New Yorkers felt that relief could be provided by a land bank. Robert R. Livingston maintained that paper money would be "inconsistent with the public good," but that a land bank which loaned specie would be "the true Philosopher's stone that [would] turn all . . . rocks and trees into gold."[153] Livingston's land bank was to be capitalized with specie and improved real estate. Even without the land bank, however, Livingston thought that the state could make a rapid recovery as long as paper money was not issued.[154]

Other influential men who denounced state paper money believed that a private commercial bank was required. By 1784 the Bank of New York had been established, with some of the leading conservatives as stockholders, including such men as Alexander Hamilton and Philip Schuyler, who steadfastly opposed state currency because they believed that it would decrease the bank's profits. The bank aroused intense opposition from the yeomanry because it pooled cash from the state's monied men and refused loans to farmers, even to those who owned substantial quantities of land, while a merchant, "whose property is of the most precarious and delusive nature, may readily procure a fictitious capital to facilitate his importation of foreign merchandize."[155] The only people who benefited from a bank were those who had connections with the institution.

Nationalists had their own economic agenda. In their opinion, America's economic crisis could be solved only by granting Congress the impost, vesting it with the power to regulate commerce, and eradicating the spirit of luxury that existed throughout the country.[156]

As the economic depression deepened, however, the demand for paper money increased. It was easy to find converts to the paper-money cause, because specie was so scarce that even a depreciated paper currency would be of more service than a non-circulating hard currency. Paper-money advocates pointed to New York's colonial experience when paper currency had been a time-honored remedy for economic ills. One such advocate recalled the success of the colonial loan office when New York "felt the invigorating influence of this cheering political sun. May it speedily arise to re-enlighten this western world; and, by diffusing its benign rays throughout our infant empire, quicken the seeds of industry, arts, manufactures, and commerce!"[157] Paper-money advocates rejected the analogy with Continental currency and maintained that "arguments drawn from the abuse of a thing, do not militate against the excellence of the thing itself or its use."[158]

Farmers, artisans, and debtors statewide clamored for paper money. They found it increasingly difficult to meet their obligations and hoped that the government would issue paper money in the form of loans to tide them over until prosperity returned. The universal cry in the Poughkeepsie area was "Cash! Cash! O Cash! why hast thou deserted the standard of Liberty and made poverty and dissipation our distinguishing characteristics?"[159] Many New Yorkers wondered why honest citizens should not be given the opportunity to borrow money at reasonable rates instead of the usurious twenty to fifty percent being offered by the state's monied men.[160]

Ideologues opposed to foreign commerce blamed the merchants for the economic crisis. "Honestus" argued that the state's problems emanated from its unfavorable balance of trade that drew gold and silver out of New York. Merchants were "the bane and pest" of the country. Were it not for these creatures, he suggested, luxuries would not have been imported in such huge volume. Paper money would save the state because imports would diminish when foreign merchants refused to accept New York's currency. As the domestic economy recovered, exports would increase. With greater exports and fewer imports, the circulating specie would expand.[161] To encourage this, "A Citizen of Dutchess County" suggested that the legislature enact laws prohibiting the importation of all foreign articles that might be made among us, and levying heavy duties on all imported luxuries.[162]

The legislative struggle over paper money began in February of 1784, when the assembly passed a bill authorizing £100,000 of paper, but the bill was defeated in the senate. Late in October, the house approved £150,000. The senate again defeated this measure. The following year the lower house, by a vote of 22 to 18, authorized £100,000 in paper. The senate, in mid-April, tenaciously adhered to its hard-money principles and again rejected the assembly's handiwork.[163] By 1786, the senate admitted that a scarcity of specie existed and that yeomen were being ruined by forced sales in which their farms sold for only a fraction of their real value. Despite this admission, the senate still opposed state paper money. The assembly, however, was more resolute than ever.

Early in January 1786, a joint committee was appointed to consider financial matters. Deliberations were "conducted with unusual Harmony."[164] After several meetings, the "prevailing sentiment" favored a paper-money loan office modelled on colonial experience. Furthermore, paper-money adherents on the committee stressed the need for the state to pay public creditors the interest on their securities. Hard-money committeemen warned that New Yorkers would pay their taxes in this newly proposed paper currency, thereby reducing specie revenue enough so that the state would be unable to pay its congressional requisitions. New York would have to break faith with Congress. To prevent this, paper-money committeemen proposed that the state "assume" and "fund" the national debt held by New Yorkers. All national securities would be exchanged for new state securities that would receive interest paid in paper money. The paper currency would be backed by import duties, forced public sales, tax arrears, and other taxes. By accepting paper money for taxes, the state would ensure that the bills would remain buoyant. After consideration, the committee recommended that £200,000 be emitted—one-quarter to pay the interest on the state and the assumed Continental debts and the other three-quarters to be loaned on real estate mortgages.

Acting on the joint committee's recommendation, the assembly appointed a committee on January 21, 1786, consisting of one member from each county, to consider the best method for emitting paper money and for redeeming public securities. On February 23, the committee reported a bill providing for the emission of £200,000. "The grand question" of whether or not the money should be legal tender was put to an initial vote on February 23, when the assembly overwhemingly defeated the tender provision by a vote of 47 to 12. Realizing that a tender provision jeopardized the entire bill, paper-money advocates proposed a compromise, making the currency legal tender only in law suits, thus protecting hard-pressed debtors, but not subjecting the economy to the evils of a full tender clause. The compromise satisfied most assemblymen, and the bill passed on March 6 by a sizeable margin of 43 to 9.

This bill, unlike the three preceding paper-money bills, received the governor's endorsement. Throughout his career, Clinton could best be characterized as a fiscally conservative pragmatist. He tolerated government paper money when absolutely necessary, but he was never comfortable with it. During the war, Clinton strenuously supported it. "To destroy the Credit of our Paper Money," Clinton said, "is to ruin us. . . . To attempt it, is in my Opinion worse than openly to take up Arms against us."[165] He felt more comfortable, however, asking the legislature to levy taxes to conduct the war or retire the state debt. In October 1778, the governor saw that "The only effectual Remedy" for the depreciation of paper money was "reducing the Quantity of circulating Currency, by Taxation." Clinton often repeated his plea for taxes: "no Time can be more proper than the present, for paying off our public Debts by Taxes."[166]

Throughout the war, Clinton relied on the economic advice of conservatives. Chancellor Robert R. Livingston wrote drafts of speeches for the governor and suggested plans "for restoring the Credit of our Money."[167] Early in 1779, Gouverneur Morris, a trusted advisor during the war, urged Clinton to rely on taxes rather than on paper money. He admitted that there were inequities in taxes, but he argued that he could find inequity "in a Tax of any kind." So too could "any man of Genius against any Thing." Morris therefore advised Clinton "For God's Sake tax & leave to a future Period, the equitable adjustment of these things." Immediate fiscal needs should be met by immediate taxes. "To delay . . . is almost madness."[168] The governor lamented the varying advice he received—"every Man is become a financier and of course we have numberless Plans for paying our Debts and restoring the Credit of our Money." The majority of his "advisors," among whom he included "the most sensible," pleaded for continued taxation "until the Credit of our Paper Currency is restored." Those who objected to taxation argued that the paper's credit had sunk too low "to be appreciated by any ordinary Means." Clinton agreed that taxes must be continued.[169]

In 1778, his first full year in office, Clinton supported tax reform that would shift some of the burden onto the wealthy. Tax assessors, elected by the people, were authorized to assess according to "circumstances and other abilities to pay taxes, collectively considered" thereby exposing property to taxation that had never been taxed before. Woodlands and land owned in other counties were now taxed as well for the first time, much to the chagrin of manor lords, who, like Robert R. Livingston, complained about their "Monstrous" new taxes. Margaret Beekman Livingston, the chancellor's mother, prayed to be delivered from "the persecutions of the lower class" and from their tax assessors. When the people's ability to pay became strained, the popularly elected assessors would let up on them.[170] In mid-May 1780, an enraged Chancellor Livingston asked the governor to intervene with the legislature in seeking a reduction in his tax assessment. From a previous level of £3,000, the chancellor's new assessment had tripled to £9,000. Such an increase was unconscionable for a patriot serving his state. Clinton commiserated with the chancellor but wrote that "I have ventured to be silent on the Subject" because "an Application at this Time would at least have been fruitless if not Injurious."[171] Throughout the 1780s, Clinton's pragmatic attitude toward tax collection angered aristocrats who believed that they were being taxed too heavily.

Clinton's fiscal conservativism was also evident in his first peacetime address to the legislature. As soon as practicable, he declared, funds had to be raised to pay the public debt. The prosperity of the state and the honor of government required immediate action. In October 1784, he called for a complete statewide assessment of property so that taxes could be assessed properly "without oppression" thereby preventing "discords and animosities."[172] Although Clinton wanted to make sure that the wealthy bore a larger share of taxes, he was not waging war on property. Quite the contrary. He believed in the sacredness of private property: "Let us give to all protection, encouragement and security, by providing that equal justice be administered, . . . that the recovery of debts be speedy and effectual, [and] that the fulfillment of contracts be enforced."[173] In addressing the legislature on January 16, 1786, the governor again pleaded the cause of the state's public creditors. It was regrettable "that the peculiar circumstances of the state have, hitherto prevented the adoption of more effectual measures for their relief." Justice and public credit demanded immediate action. To assist the legislators, the governor laid before them a complete analysis of the state's public debt. In ending his speech, Clinton stressed "that as the security of property forms one of the strongest bonds of society, too much care cannot be taken to preserve and strengthen it, by a scrupulous adherence to the principles and spirit of our excellent Constitution, and by guarding against an increase of our laws by provisions for partial purposes."[174] It was no easy task for the radical, paper-money forces to win over Clinton; they did it by tying paper money to the program for paying the public creditors.

To gain the governor's endorsement, and thus to assure passage of the bill, several funding proposals were added. The entire state debt was funded, while Continental loan-office certificates and "Barber's Notes" (certificates issued for supplies furnished to the Continental Army) owned by New Yorkers were also assumed by the state. Some people wanted either a complete assumption or a complete separation from the Continental debt. Clinton and the paper-money advocates, however, realized the potency of the partial assumption of the federal debt. The state assumed only twenty-eight percent, or $1,400,000 out of a total federal debt of about $5,000,000 held by New Yorkers. The assumed federal debt was held by approximately half of the state's voters. The unassumed $3,600,000 was owned by several hundred wealthy New Yorkers, most of whom had little sympathy for Clinton.[175] The bill, in essence, made large numbers of federal creditors into state creditors; in the process their economic welfare was tied to the state—not to the Confederation—and earned for the governor their political gratitude.

After the assembly approved the bill, it went to the senate where paper money had always foundered before. On March 29, 1786, the senate proposed twelve amendments—including a prohibition of the assumption of the federal debt. The assembly rejected the amendments, and the senate backed down on all but two rather than killing a fourth paper-money bill. The assembly accepted these two changes, which provided that redeemed bills should be destroyed annually rather than re-loaned and that once £150,000 in principal and interest in specie or paper was collected, anyone could exchange the remaining paper money for specie at the treasury.[176]

Before the bill became law it had one more hurdle—the Council of

Revision. It was here that hard-money men placed their last hope. Within the council there was considerable dispute. John Sloss Hobart, Robert R. Livingston, and Lewis Morris struggled to defeat the bill, while Governor Clinton and Robert Yates favored it. From April 6 to 15, the three opponents presented their reasons for vetoing the bill, but no one veto report received the endorsement of more than two councillors; consequently the bill automatically became law when the council failed to veto it within ten days.

The act authorized £200,000 of paper money—three-quarters earmarked for mortgages on real estate and the remainder to be paid to New York's public creditors as interest on both state and Continental securities. The paper money could be used to pay taxes and other governmental fees. Mortgages had a fourteen-year term at five percent annual interest. According to the plan, no one could receive a loan of more than £300 nor less than £20. The land mortgaged had to be at least twice the value of the loan, while houses used for collateral had to be at least triple the value. All borrowers had to swear that the mortgaged property was free from prior claim. Interest was to be paid annually, while the principal would be paid in ten annual installments beginning in 1791. Counterfeiters faced severe punishment—confiscation of property, life imprisonment at hard labor, and branding on the left cheek with the letter "C."

Supporters of paper money, through perseverance, compromise, and alliance with the governor, had accomplished their task; all that remained was to maintain the integrity of the new currency. Peter Elting, a New York City merchant, expressed the feelings of many: "The Money Bill has past into a Law and [I] am in hopes will meet with auspicious Support in this City. A Resolution of this kind will be moved for [by] the Chamber of Commerce [at] our next meeting."[177] The money's supporters admonished merchants:

> Now that the die is cast, and a paper medium is soon to make its appearance amongst us, the only true policy that can be adopted (to defeat the schemes of wicked and designing men. . .) is for the merchants of this city immediately to unite, and publish to the world their determination to support the new emission by every means in their power. If this be done it can not fail to have a happy tendency.[178]

It was the duty of everyone now to support the money. New York's honor depended upon the money maintaining its value. Only "enemies" of the state would attempt to depreciate the currency.[179] More practically, a failure to support the money would be an economic and political catastrophe with unforeseen consequences.

A major test faced the money even before it began to circulate; the spring 1786 state elections would, in essence, be a referendum on the paper-money program. If paper-money advocates, especially Governor Clinton, were defeated, the whole program of debt assumption and paper money might be repealed. Party heat was high and the elections were conducted with "great exertions."[180] John Jay attempted to explain away the bitterness by stating that "In free States there must and ought to be a little Ferment. When the Public Mind grows languid, and a dead Calm, unmarked by the least Breese of Party, takes Place, the Vigour of a Republick soon becomes lost in general Relaxation."[181] The gubernatorial election provided a real test of the popularity of the governor and his policies. He had been reelected with virtually no opposition in 1780 and 1783, primarily because of the war. Now, after three years of peace, George Clinton would be judged on his own merits.

Clinton's political enemies felt confident in 1785 that they might unseat the governor. Throughout America, political incumbents suffered because of the depression. Philip Schuyler, as the acknowledged leader of the aristocratic party, along with his son-in-law, mobilized their forces during that spring. Hamilton asserted that all who had any property to lose called for a change in the state government.[182] Schuyler, defeated ignominiously in 1783, thought better than to run again. Instead, in the next gubernatorial contest, he assumed the role of king-maker.

On May 30, 1785, Schuyler wrote John Jay, now serving as the Confederation Secretary for Foreign Affairs, trying to convince him to challenge Clinton: "The person, at present in the chair of Government, so evidently strives to maintain his popularity at the expense of good Government, that it has given real concern to many, as well as to myself," both in the northern and southern portions of the state. Schuyler severely criticized the governor's appointees as placemen, but such criticism fell on deaf ears, because Jay had been one of Clinton's closest advisors in choosing officeholders.[183] Schuyler felt optimistic about the chances of unseating Clinton: "Almost every character of respectability and indeed a great majority of all ranks will support the attempt" to reform the government, but this "cannot be accomplished unless Mr. Clinton is ousted." Only three men in the state, according to Schuyler, stood a chance of defeating the governor—Jay, Robert R. Livingston, and himself. He thought that the chancellor would probably be defeated. Schuyler predicted immodestly that he would overwhelmingly defeat Clinton in the northern counties, but, because he was unknown in the south, he too would lose. Anyway, his health would not allow him to serve as governor. It was up to Jay, whom Schuyler encouraged to announce his candidacy soon because "to succeed in a mission of this kind, time must be improved; every day is important." If Jay refused to oppose Clinton, "it will be needless to attempt a change."[184]

Jay, far less passionately opposed to the governor than was Schuyler, could not be convinced to run the uphill race against Clinton. Jay knew that the governor was still immensely popular. Just two months earlier the ship *Governor Clinton* had been launched at the shipyard to the acclaim of "many thousands of people, and all the beauties of the City." Owned by John Franklin and captained by Christopher Miller, the ship had "excellent accommodations for passengers," as well as facilities for ten to twelve horses in the hold. The "noble vessel," designed for the London trade, symbolized the state's triumphant leader.[185]

On June 10, 1785, Jay thanked Schuyler for the confidence, but decided to continue in the diplomatic service. "If the circumstances of the State were pressing," Jay told Schuyler, "if real disgust and discontent had spread through the country, if a change had in the general opinion become not only advisable but *necessary*, and the good expected from that change depended on me," then he would run.[186] But Clinton still held the people's confidence.

The embittered Schuyler refused to rest as long as Clinton served as governor. He disagreed with Jay's judgment that "matters are not sufficiently ripe to attempt a change at the ensuing Election." Schuyler's desire to unseat the governor was so strong, that he convinced himself that "Clinton grows Every day more unpopular and that another Year will afford a better chance." Others, however, thought the chances of defeating Clinton in 1786 were "certain."[187] After a month of lobbying for Clinton's defeat, Schuyler's optimism disappeared. Although Clinton's support had faded, "yet It is not so rapidly as to Justify us wishing a failure. I am therefore of opinion that we must suffer him another term." Schuyler advised his inner circle of political friends in Albany "that You and All our friends should declare decidedly in favor of Governor Clinton at the next Election."[188] They would oppose radicals in the legislature, particularly Abraham Yates, Jr., in the senate, but they would publicly endorse the governor. The next election would see an all-out effort to defeat Clinton.

The paper money came from the presses late in July 1786. Despite the clamor for the money during the early months of the year, there was no great rush to obtain loans. Uncertainty about the money's value gripped even the strongest supporters of the currency. Would the money depreciate at the very outset? To establish confidence, the governor convinced a number of prominent men publicly to exchange "a considerable amount" of gold and silver coin for paper. The move succeeded; even "the *most Torified Infidel*" had to agree that the paper money began successfully.[189]

The fear of depreciation proved unwarranted. The state's money passed "universally equal with gold and silver, and is catched at with avidity even by strangers."[190] Even fiscally conservative Alexander Hamilton

assured the assembly that "there need be no apprehension of" the paper
currency's future fate. Largely because the scarcity of specie still existed,
the demand for paper money "had not lessened," and the whole populace
seemed satisfied with the currency.[191] Even that staunch French "gold bug,"
Brissot de Warville, visiting America in 1788, admitted that New York's
"finances & its promptness in paying the interest on its debt contribute
greatly toward the stability of its paper money" which "is received in the
markets in payment of commodities at the same rate as coinage."[192]

Paper-money men predicted that the state's domestic and foreign
trade would immediately increase when paper was issued. Beginning in late
1786 and early 1787, American commerce grew rapidly; and, by 1788, New
York had regained much of its prewar commercial vitality. By the end of
1788, New York City, a broken port in 1783, was importing and exporting
more than before the war; and about two-thirds of this trade was carried in
New York ships. By the end of the decade, New York City, along with
Philadelphia, handled more than one-third of the entire country's foreign
commerce, while the revenue obtained from the state impost did much to
stabilize the state's finances.[193] Paper money had played a critical role in
restoring the state's prosperity.

The debt-funding aspect of the paper-money program succeeded beyond anyone's expectations. Paper money coupled with the state's other
revenue was used to purchase large quantities of Continental securities,
replacing them with state securities until, by 1790, the state of New York
owned federal securities worth over $2,880,000 in specie. The interest due
New York on these securities more than equalled the annual requisitions
on the state by Congress. Had this process continued a few more years,
New York, along with some of the other states, would have assumed the
entire domestic federal debt.[194] To a considerable degree, the paper money
made these purchases possible, but New York's funding and assumption
programs also contributed to maintaining the paper money's value.

In compliance with the loan-office act, the state annually destroyed
the bills that were paid into the treasury. In November 1787, £6,000 was
destroyed.[195] By 1800, over two-thirds of the paper money had been
cancelled. The amount in circulation thereafter steadily decreased until in
1832 the loan of 1786 was ordered closed within a year. Less than £1,500
was outstanding. The program designed to meet the fiscal requirements of
Governor Clinton had worked well. New Yorkers appreciated the manner
in which their government combatted the depression of the mid-1780s.
While other states struggled with economic and social dislocations including violence and insurrection, New York's economy improved rapidly and
its government remained popular.

24. Mobocracy

George Clinton's friends considered him a man of the people; his enemies saw him as a demagogue. Despite these images, Clinton refused to tolerate violence when peaceful political alternatives existed for redressing grievances. Even his political opponents had to admit that Clinton had a deep respect for the law. On two occasions the governor took decisive action against violence.

Beginning in the fall of 1786, angry and frightened farmers in Massachusetts protested against their government's refusal to provide debtor relief or paper money. In an attempt to save their farms from foreclosures, the insurgents stopped county courts from sitting. By mid-February 1787, the rebels led by Daniel Shays had been put to flight by the militia and by General Benjamin Lincoln's specially raised army. Thinking that the rebellion had been permanently suppressed, General Lincoln disbanded his troops, but fears soon arose that the Shaysites were regrouping and recruiting in Vermont, New Hampshire, Connecticut, and upstate New York. Massachusetts officials especially worried that New Yorkers might be easily recruited because of their animosity over Massachusetts' claim of ownership of western New York territory. These fears were justified when newspapers reported the warm reception that the Shaysites received in New York, from which "the Rebels are enabled to make predatory excursions" into Massachusetts.[196]

In an attempt to enlist support from the governments of the surrounding states, the Massachusetts legislature on February 4, 1787, declared "that a horrid and unnatural rebellion had been openly and traitorously raised and levied against the said commonwealth, with design to subvert and overthrow the constitution and form of government thereof." Massachusetts Governor James Bowdoin issued a proclamation calling for the arrest of the rebel leaders and requesting, under the extradition provision of the Articles of Confederation, that Governor Clinton assist in apprehending the insurgents. When Clinton received Bowdoin's proclamation, he called on the legislature for its full support. Clinton could "see no objection" to issuing a proclamation and "securing such of the rebels as may fly from justice and take shelter within this State." He hoped that both houses of the legislature would join with him in a concurrent resolution that "would more fully evince the sense of our government on this occasion."[197] On February 20, Philip Schuyler, Clinton's legislative colleague over a decade ago on the eve of the Revolution but now the governor's arch enemy, introduced a resolution supporting the governor's request for a proclamation against the Shaysites. The assembly endorsed the resolution four days later.[198] On February 24, Clinton issued his proclamation requiring all state and local officials to assist in capturing the insurgents and prohibiting New Yorkers from abetting the rebels.[199]

In early March, reports reached New York City that Shays with 1,000 rebels had camped in New York near New Canaan in Columbia County, where they had been welcomed and joined by New York enlistments. The insurgents divided into two parties, crossed the border, and raided Stockbridge, Massachusetts, and the surrounding countryside, where they plundered houses (including that belonging to Congressman Theodore Sedgwick) and took hostages. On March 3, Clinton received a message from General Lincoln expressing confidence in the governor's "disposition . . . to promote order & good Government, & to preserve a perfect Friendship & good Understanding with your neighbours." The general hoped that Clinton would make "the most speedy & effectual exertions" to apprehend the rebels who fled into New York.[200]

Immediately Clinton issued orders readying three Dutchess County militia regiments as well as the entire Columbia County brigade. Clinton himself, accompanied by Adjutant General Nicholas Fish, Attorney General Egbert Benson, Colonel Marinus Willett, and several others left New York City early on March 4 to take personal command of the state forces cooperating with General Lincoln "in apprehending and securing such of the Rebels as shall be found in this State."[201] It was expected that the governor would "soon put an end to the disturbances which Shays and his adherents have fomented."[202]

A writer in the *New York Gazetteer*, March 5, deplored the potential danger of civil war: "This diabolical spirit having been thus driven from that scene of action [Massachusetts], we ought cautiously to beware how we suffer it to receive shelter among us: the air it exists in is contagious—its neighbourhood is infectious—its (even momentary) sufferance would create immediate political putrefication, and spread its baneful influence with a most destructive progress." The *Gazetteer* took heart, however, because of the confidence the state had in Clinton, "a gentleman, who, in addition to all that has impressed us with veneration for his character, is, at the present instant, so vigilantly alive to his duty—so attentively watchful of the peace and harmony of the state (over which he presides with so much honor to himself and advantage to the people) that, in a few hours after the intelligence of a transaction which might immediately endanger our tranquility, he hastened personally to suppress in embryo this daring spirit of vagrant insurrection."

On March 17, Clinton met with General Lincoln in New Lebanon, New York. They crossed the border and spent the night in Pittsfield planning the suppression of the insurgents. The next morning the two leaders went to New Concord, New York, where Clinton's civil and military officers had assembled. Lincoln reported to Governor Bowdoin that "in a masterly, spirited and animated manner," Governor Clinton "stated their duty, respectively, and urged them to a faithful and punctual discharge of it." Clinton said: "By the free constitutions of these states, the people enjoy the right of electing their rulers, and the elections are as frequent as can possibly consist with convenience; they have it therefore fully in their power by the mere exercise of the right of election, to relieve themselves from the operation of laws which they may deem grievous, or in any wise improper, and cannot justify recurring to violence, and involving their country in confusion and bloodshed, in order to produce a change in public measures." Clinton reminded the militiamen of the many occasions during the Revolution when they had proven their patriotism. He expected no less on this occasion.[203]

Although some New Yorkers in Columbia County were sympathetic with the Shaysites, they supported Clinton's proclamation and turned out to welcome the governor on his arrival. Sensing their danger, the rebels withdrew to Vermont and Canada. A grateful General Lincoln told Governor Bowdoin that "The state of New York are perfectly disposed to serve us, and no person is better qualified or better inclined, to execute their friendly intentions, than his Excellency their Governor."[204] Pittsfield's Henry Van Schaack told newly-elected Governor John Hancock in August 1787 that "Governor Clinton's visit to our neighborhood has contributed not a little to the quieting the minds of the people in that part of the state of New York and discouraging our Insurgents that had shelter there."[205]

Historians have often portrayed Clinton as being friendly or sympathetic toward Shays's Rebellion.[206] The only proof put forth for this claim is the alleged tardiness with which Clinton assisted Massachusetts. But this is a misreading of the evidence. Clinton did not offer assistance earlier because the rebellion was a completely internal matter being played out within the borders of Massachusetts. Only when the rebels dispersed across state lines did Massachusetts ask for assistance from its neighbors, and Clinton acted swiftly, strongly, and personally.

Clinton's erstwhile opponent Philip Schuyler interpreted the governor's actions differently. According to Schuyler, Clinton had been given strong powers to suppress the insurgents by an unanimous legislature. Schuyler, however, thought that legislators "were not at all actuated by the same motives." Good will and a regard for the government of Massachusetts actuated his followers, but the governor's supporters, who "invariably oppose every measure that tends to give more energy to the federal head, might, and I think were, led by apprehensions of local consequences." Clinton acted out of fear—fear that Shaysism might spread to the tenants and fear that Shays's Rebellion might enlarge the powers of Congress.[207]

Clinton responded to a different kind of popular uprising in mid-April

1788.[208] For several months some doctors and medical students at the New York City hospital had dug up recently interred corpses to use for dissections. On Sunday, April 13, some boys playing behind the hospital saw a human limb protruding from a window. Word spread quickly and a crowd stormed the hospital. Finding students in the process of dissecting a cadaver while other dismembered bodies lay scattered throughout the room, the angry citizens destroyed the room and captured two medical students. Fortunately Mayor James Duane, Sheriff Marinus Willett, and several others convinced the rioters to turn the students over to city authorities, who placed them in jail for their own protection. The crowd dispersed for the evening.

The following morning, a mob of between 2,000 and 3,000 formed to search the doctors' houses. Governor Clinton, Chancellor Livingston, and Mayor Duane tried to reason with the angry crowd, promising that the laws would be enforced and those responsible for illegal anatomical experiments would be arrested and tried. These assurances satisfied a number of individuals, but many others proceeded to search the houses, but found nothing. In the afternoon, a drunken lynching party attempted to storm the jail and execute the two incarcerated students. Clinton, sensing the danger, called out the militia. At about 3:00, a small group of about eighteen armed militiamen walked unscathed through the mob and occupied the jail. About an hour later, another twelve militiamen tried to enter the jail, but the mob, sensing that the soldiers would not fire on the crowd, surrounded them, seized and destroyed their weapons, and roughed them up. The rioters stormed the jail but could not gain entry. Toward dusk, another group of about forty militia armed with muskets and forty citizens armed with swords, led by George Clinton, John Jay, Baron von Steuben, and other public figures, marched to relieve the militia defending the jail. As they passed by, the mob huzzaed and threw rocks, brickbats, and an assortment of other street debris. Jay was struck in the head and collapsed. Steuben also was felled by a rock between his eyes, and Clinton was hit in the side with a large stone that, fortunately for him, riccocheted off someone else's arm. In the confusion, the militia fired into the crowd, contrary to the governor's order. A second volley soon followed. Three men lay dead on the spot and another died the following day. Many were wounded. The mob and onlookers scattered quickly. The militia stayed the night, the next day, and the following morning. No new violence erupted.

Several people thought that the violence had a sobering effect on Clinton, and that the governor would now support the new Constitution. Victor DuPont, a young Frenchman serving as an aide to the French diplomatic legation, reported, "It was good to see men fighting together for the same cause, Colonel Hamilton, the chief support of the Federalists, and

Governor Clinton, the mortal enemy of all Federalists and of the colonel in particular." The "doctors' riots" did little to change Clinton's perspective. For a brief moment, the governor and Alexander Hamilton—the two wartime friends—were allied again. The rapprochement, however, was short lived. Clinton opposed violence but he still opposed the Constitution.

IV

The New Constitution

25. The Constitutional Convention

Even before the Articles of Confederation were adopted on March 1, 1781, attempts were made to increase the powers of Congress. The social unrest of the mid-1780s precipitated by the postwar economic depression sent shivers through patriots who had fought against the mighty British. Angry and frightened farmers, artisans, and mechanics took to the streets in Exeter, New Hampshire; Sharon, Connecticut; Charles County, Maryland; and Camden, South Carolina. In backcountry Virginia, debtor farmers burned the courthouses and, with them, the tax records. Without tax records, back taxes disappeared. In western Massachusetts bankrupt farmers stopped the county courts from foreclosing on their property because of delinquent taxes.

Reports of the recurring violence filled the press. Also widely reported were accounts of relief efforts undertaken by many of the state governments, especially those dominated by the popularly elected lower houses of assembly, efforts often considered the result of "excessive democracy." Rhode Island, the most glaring example, came to symbolize the danger to personal liberties and private property from a constitutionally elected state government run wild. Throughout January and February 1787, newspapers contained extensive coverage of the armed insurrection in western Massachusetts as well as the governmental radicalism in neighboring Rhode Island epitomized by a bill allegedly introduced in the state's assembly that called for the abolition of all debts and the equal distribution of all property every thirteen years.[1] For most war-weary Americans the specter of revolution and civil war still haunted their memories. George Washington anxiously read the news that arrived daily at Mount Vernon in newspapers and private correspondence. He, like many other Americans, concluded that there were combustibles in every state ready to be ignited by a single spark. A sense of general foreboding spread throughout the country, a fear that America was headed for a second revolutionary crisis. Something had to be done to strengthen the powers of the general government so that it could effectively protect personal liberties and private property against the voracious, uncontrollable appetite of the excessively democratic state governments. A correspondent in the *New York Journal* in October 1786 lamented the "wretchedly defective" "present system of the federal government" and went on ominously to "predict the dreadful scene that must happen in this country, where no prudent man would choose to trust his life, his liberty or his property."[2] The fate of America seemed to hang in the balance between *"rising glory,"* or *"debasing ignominy."*[3]

The economic, social, and political conditions of the Confederation provided a convenient opportunity for an ever-growing number of nationalists who wanted a consolidated central government that would assume many of the responsibilities formerly exercised by the imperial government in London. Nationalists argued that only such a strong central government could avert the crisis, and they heightened the level of fear beyond what conditions justified. Only in a few places—Massachusetts and Rhode Island in particular—was there real danger of anarchy or civil war. In most states, however, the people were led to believe that danger loomed everywhere, though not necessarily within one's own borders. Each state, however, felt vulnerable if a general conflagration began elsewhere.

Most Americans by the mid-1780s believed that the Articles of Confederation should be revised. More concerned about creating a consolidated government that could limit state action than with preventing an unlikely civil war, nationalists actively spread the popular "circular theory of government" scenario: Americans would soon tire of the present anarchy and succumb to the entreaties of a benevolent tyrant who would promise to restore political and economic stability. Within a short time anarchy, in fact, would disappear, but benevolence would soon vanish as well, only to be replaced by despotism. This theory gained converts as creditors felt betrayed by their state governments and as debtors and the unemployed lost faith in the ability of those governments to resolve the economic crisis.

State-oriented politicians such as George Clinton were largely satisfied with the division of power between the Confederation and the state governments. They agreed that some added power had to be given to Congress, but they believed that the principles of the Revolution could best be achieved by state governments directly responsible to the people. The real danger in their eyes emanated from "an innumerable tribe of lawless usurpers, some who have already declared, that 'A *Republican Government, is unfit for a Gentleman to live in.*'"[4]

Politicians such as Clinton also believed that the best way to combat nationalists was to transfer limited amounts of authority to the Confederation government. By transferring powers that could safely be lodged in the central government, perhaps the demand for consolidation could be stemmed. Although there seemed to be near unanimity for a strengthened Congress, no single measure could command the support of all thirteen states. Since Article 13 of the Articles of Confederation required amendments to be ratified by all the state legislatures, no amendments to the Articles were adopted.

Contrary to the interpretations of many historians, George Clinton favored empowering Congress to deal with the postwar British trade restrictions.[5] He took this position both because Congress should have the power and for tactical political reasons in opposition to the nationalists. On May 4, 1784, for example, a mere five days after Congress' request, New York's legislature granted Congress authority for fifteen years to curtail trade with foreign countries that had no commercial treaty with the United States. Clinton agreed with Congress that "The fortune of every citizen is interested" in commerce; "for it is the constant source of wealth and incentive to industry; and the value of our produce and our land must ever rise or fall in proportion to the prosperous or adverse state of trade."[6]

After the enactment of New York's state impost in November 1784, Clinton's support of efforts to defend American commerce intensified. Although merchants generally opposed Clinton, the governor supported efforts to increase commerce because more foreign trade meant more revenue for the state treasury. When Congress realized that its request for a temporary grant of commercial power was insufficient, it proposed on March 28, 1785, a permanent commercial power in the form of an amendment to the Articles of Confederation.[7] One week later, New York adopted this amendment.

Clinton's desire to stimulate commerce explains why New York endorsed Virginia's call on January 21, 1786, for a commercial convention of the states, "for the purpose of framing such regulations of trade as may be judged necessary to promote the general interest." On March 14, Clinton submitted Virginia's proposal to the assembly, which the following day resolved that five commissioners be appointed to attend the convention at Annapolis. Three days later, the senate by a fourteen-to-four margin concurred.[8] On April 20, the assembly appointed Alexander Hamilton, Robert C. Livingston (of the upper manor family), and Leonard Gansevoort as commissioners, expecting the senate to add at least two additional commissioners. On the last day of the session (May 5), the senate added three more commissioners—Robert R. Livingston, James Duane, and Egbert Benson—and the assembly aquiesced. All six men had and would continue to support strengthening the powers of Congress.

The joint legislative resolution provided that a minimum of three commissioners could act as a delegation and required that a formal report be made to the legislature at its next session. The legislature authorized the commissioners "to take into consideration the trade and commerce of the United States, to consider how far an uniform system in their commercial intercourse and regulations, may be necessary to their common interest and permanent harmony."[9] Before any power could be conferred on Congress, however, the report of the convention had to receive the unanimous approval of the state legislatures. Clinton wanted to strengthen Congress in commercial matters; he was willing to send agents unfriendly to him to confer with commissioners from other states. But the governor refused to give carte blanche—the legislature reserved the right to reject any plan that might be detrimental to New York.

Of the six New York commissioners, only Hamilton and Benson attended the Annapolis Convention in September 1786, where they met with commissioners from Delaware, New Jersey, Pennsylvania, and Virginia. The commissioners quickly adopted a report, drafted by Hamilton, that acknowledged the states' poor attendance and the diversity of their commissioners' instructions. Rather than deliberate under these conditions, the report called for a general convention of all the states to meet in Philadelphia the following May to revise the Articles of Confederation. Perhaps in an attempt to legitimize the actions of the two New York delegates, who did not constitute a quorum of the delegation, Robert C. Livingston submitted a voucher for payment as an attending delegate. The state auditor approved the voucher and the treasurer made payment.[10] An examination of Livingston's letterbook for this period, however, indicates that not only did he fail to attend the convention, but he never gave any hint that such a mercantile convention was taking place.[11]

On January 13, 1787, Clinton addressed the opening session of the legislature and delivered a copy of the Annapolis Convention report to the assembly. Ten days later the report and Virginia's act authorizing the appointment of delegates to a convention were submitted to a committee.

On February 15, 1787, the assembly rejected an unconditional ratification of the congressional impost, thus effectively killing the impost. Then, on February 19, without any reference to the Annapolis Convention report, the Hamiltonian forces in the assembly proposed that the state's delegates in Congress be instructed to call for a constitutional convention "for the purpose of revising the Articles of Confederation." The next day, Philip Schuyler led the senate in a ten-to-nine vote endorsing the assembly's resolution. The call for a convention could not have succeeded without support from Clinton's followers. They supported it to demonstrate that they were not entirely antifederal, despite their rejection of the impost. Many Clintonians saw the necessity of strengthening Congress in areas other than granting it an independent source of income. Clintonians also voted for a convention because, as with the Annapolis Convention, they were confident that they could prevent the ratification of any radical proposal.

Philip Schuyler had his own interpretation of why New York called a constitutional convention. He reported that several members of Congress had indicated a preference for the call of a convention to emanate from a state rather than from the ad hoc Annapolis delegates. An opportunity for such a state call arose in the New York legislature after Hamilton's impost speech of February 15. Many delegates voted against the impost because of pressure exerted by the governor. According to Schuyler, some of these delegates felt "ashamed of their conduct and wished an opportunity to make some atonement." Seizing this opportunity, Hamilton and Schuyler's forces introduced the call of a convention in the assembly, which was "violently opposed" by the governor's friends, "but as many of those who are at his beck had committed themselves too far in private conversation, they voted (though perhaps) reluctantly for it."[12]

Despite the legislature's call for a convention, Schuyler was pessimistic about New York's and the country's political future. The Clintonians—whose principles included "a state impost, no direct taxation, keep all power in the hands of the legislature, give none to Congress, which may destroy our influence and cast a shade over that plenitude of power which we now enjoy"—were willing that a constitutional convention meet and propose alterations "conferring additional powers on Congress." Clintonians, however, according to Schuyler, would oppose these amendments as "destructive of liberty, may induce a king, an aristocracy or a despot."[13]

When Congress considered the Annapolis Convention report on February 21, New York congressmen Melancton Smith and Egbert Benson submitted their legislature's call for a convention. Although nationalists in both the assembly and senate had pushed this resolution through to adoption, many congressmen looked upon the proposal with considerable skepticism. A state that less than a week earlier had killed the federal impost now seemed to advocate strengthening Congress. To some congressmen, it appeared as if New York was attempting to scuttle the convention called by the Annapolis commissioners by proposing an alternative to it. (By ignoring any reference to the convention called by the Annapolis commissioners, New York's resolutions seemed to invalidate the election of convention delegates that had already taken place in six states.) Partly because of this skepticism, Congress rejected New York's resolution and based its February 21 call of the Federal Convention on a motion from the Massachusetts delegation.

On February 23, 1787, Clinton sent the legislature the congressional resolution calling the Federal Convention. Three days later, the assembly resolved that five delegates be appointed to the Convention by a joint ballot of both houses of the legislature. On February 27, the senate disagreed, objecting to its inferior status in a joint ballot. The following day, the upper house voted eleven to seven that three delegates be appointed by the two houses voting separately—the manner specified in the state constitution for the election of congressional delegates. Clintonians, on a straight party vote of eleven to seven, supported the reduction in the number of delegates. On the same day, Senator Abraham Yates proposed that the Convention limit its proposals to alterations and amendments "not repugnant to or inconsistent with the constitution of this state." The senate narrowly defeated the hotly contested proposal when two Clintonians, Thomas Tredwell and John Williams, abandoned the radical anti-nationalists and Lieutenant Governor Pierre Van Cortlandt, the president of the senate, cast his vote against it, breaking the nine-to-nine tie. The assembly agreed to the senate's resolution for the separate-house election of three delegates, and accepted March 6 as the date of the election.

On March 6, the assembly voted in open ballotting for Convention delegates. All fifty-two assemblymen voted for state Supreme Court Justice Robert Yates, while Alexander Hamilton received all but three votes (one being his own). The real contest centered on the third delegate—and with it, who would control the delegation. Congressman and Albany Mayor John Lansing, Jr., narrowly defeated New York City Mayor James Duane for the assembly's nomination by a vote of twenty-six to twenty-three. After the senate also nominated Yates, Hamilton, and Lansing, the two houses compared their nominees, adjourned to their separate chambers, and passed resolutions officially appointing the three men.

On April 16, the assembly agreed to Hamilton's motion authorizing the appointment of two additional Convention delegates, but two days later, the senate rejected the enlargement. The governor's party had learned some valuable lessons from the Annapolis Convention. By appointing a three-man delegation and weighting it in their favor, Clintonians could control their delegates' actions. Most knowledgeable politicians of the day understood the uneven balance in New York's delegation as well as who was the real power "behind" the delegation. Hamilton had already established a reputation as a nationalist. Yates and Lansing were pictured as opponents of any serious attempt to strengthen Congress at the expense of state power in general or the New York impost in particular. In letters to fellow Convention delegates George Washington and Edmund Randolph, Virginia Congressman James Madison described Yates and Lansing as "pretty much linked to the antifederal party here, and are likely of course to be a clog on their Colleague." Madison believed that the two Clintonians leaned "too much towards State considerations to be good members of an Assembly which will only be useful in proportion to its superiority to partial views & interests."[14] True to form, Clinton never gave any indication that he wanted to serve in the Convention, although the chief executives from New York's two neighboring states as well as Virginia's Governor Edmund Randolph were elected to the Convention. Clinton was content to orchestrate his delegation's action from ninety miles away in New York City, without taking a more public role in Philadelphia that might require a clear-cut stance on federal-state relations.

Yates and Hamilton first attended the Convention in Philadelphia on May 25, the first day of a quorum. Lansing came a week later on June 2. From the beginning the Clintonian delegates had "forebodings" about the Convention. On May 30, Yates voted in the minority against Hamilton on a motion that called for the Convention to create a "*national* Government." The following day Yates wrote a confidential letter to his uncle, Abraham Yates, then serving in Congress in New York City, in which he indicated that his "forebodings . . . are too much realized." Because of the Convention's secrecy rule, Yates could not relate any of "its business . . . while I remain a sitting member." He was uncertain how long he would remain in Philadelphia, but "in the mean while," he was keeping "an Exact journal of all proceedings." With this letter Yates communicated extremely important and sensitive information back to New York. In all likelihood, there was a pre-arranged strategy to suit various scenarios that might develop in the Convention. Yates's information suggested that nationalist sentiment in the Convention was so prevalent that he and Lansing might abandon the Convention. This would leave New York unrepresented because a minimum of two delegates had to be present for a state to vote in the Convention. Yates realized the explosiveness of his letter. He warned his uncle that "This communication is in the most perfect confidence, in which only one Person besides yourself can participate." His implicit instruction was that the governor must be informed of the Convention's radical actions.[15]

Throughout their stay in the Convention, Yates and Lansing voted with a minority of delegates who favored amending the Articles of Confederation to invest Congress with limited additional powers that would not shift sovereignty away from the states. They usually voted together against Hamilton, who favored the abandonment of the Articles and the creation of a national government. During the climactic debate over the choice of the radical Virginia Plan or the more moderate, state-oriented New Jersey Plan, Lansing argued that the mere consideration of a national government violated the resolution of Congress calling the Convention as well as the delegates' commissions from their state legislatures. New York, he told the Convention, "would never have concurred in sending deputies to the convention, if she had supposed the deliberations were to turn on a consolidation of the States, and a National Government." Furthermore, he warned that the states would never "adopt & ratify a scheme which they had never authorized us to propose and which so far exceeded what they regarded as sufficient." The states, according to Lansing, would "never sacrifice their essential rights to a national government." Both the states and the people wanted Congress strengthened; not a new government.[16]

Hamilton had been strangely silent for over three weeks, partly because he disagreed with both the Virginia and the New Jersey plans under discussion and "partly from his delicate situation with respect to his own State, to whose sentiments as expressed by his Colleagues, he could by no means accede." On June 18, however, Hamilton made up for his silence by expressing his opinion that "no amendment of the confederation could possibly answer the purpose." The delegates, Hamilton suggested, "owed it to our Country, to do on this emergency whatever we should deem essential to its happiness."[17] Concluding his impassioned, five-hour oration, Hamilton "sketched" an outline for a plan of government that called for a bicameral Congress composed of representatives with three-year terms elected by the people and senators with life-time terms selected by electors chosen by the people. Hamilton's single chief executive would also be selected by electors chosen by the people and he too would have life tenure. A supreme court of twelve justices with life tenure would have final judicial authority, and Congress could create inferior courts. All state laws contrary to the constitution or federal laws would be null and void. State governors, according to Hamilton, would be appointed by the president, and they would have veto power over their legislatures.

Hamilton knew that his plan was too radical for the Convention, the state legislatures, or the people. But he believed that there were "evils operating in the States which must soon cure the people of their fondness for democracies." Once the people tired of democracy, they would be more receptive to his ideas. Many of the delegates admired Hamilton's forthrightness and some even agreed with his ideas, but few supported him. Totally frustrated with his minority position within the New York delegation, Hamilton left the Convention at the end of June.

Yates and Lansing also became increasingly convinced of their futility as the Convention proceeded inexorably toward the creation of a consolidated government. Finally, on July 10, they too abandoned the Convention, never to return. Various opinions in private correspondence and in newspapers gave contradictory reasons why the New Yorkers left the

Convention.[18] Luther Martin, a delegate from Maryland, most nearly captured the essence of their abdication: Yates and Lansing "had uniformly opposed the system, and I believe, despairing of getting a proper one brought forward, or of rendering any real service, they returned no more."[19]

When Yates and Lansing left the Convention, New York was unrepresented. Hamilton returned to Philadelphia after the Committee of Detail reported a draft constitution on August 6, but under the rules of the Convention, Hamilton's sole vote was not counted because a minimum of two delegates was required in each state's delegation. Hamilton again left Philadelphia from August 20 to September 2. On September 8, he was appointed to the Committee of Style and signed the Constitution nine days later as the only delegate from New York.

For half a year, Yates and Lansing remained publicly silent about their early departure from the Convention. As the legislative session neared in January 1788, they decided to write an "official" report, allegedly with some pushing from the governor.[20] On December 21, 1787, ten days before the legislature's scheduled meeting, Yates and Lansing wrote the governor, giving their reasons for opposing the Constitution and for their abandonment of the Convention. When the legislature attained a quorum, Clinton delivered the letter, the new Constitution, and the other public documents that he had received since the legislature's last session.

Yates and Lansing justified their departure as a matter of principle. The Convention was in the process of creating "a system of consolidated Government" which was not "in the remotest degree . . . in contemplation of the Legislature of this State." The delegates—New York's in particular—had been commissioned to revise and amend the Articles of Confederation, not "to abrogate" them. Furthermore, the consolidated government proposed by the Convention "must unavoidably, in a short time, be productive of the destruction of the civil liberty of such citizens who could be effectually coerced by it." They were certain that the new Constitution would not "afford that security to equal and permanent liberty, which we wished to make an invariable object of our pursuit." The absentees justified their refusal to return to Philadelphia because the principles of the new Constitution "were so well established . . . that no alteration was to be expected, to conform it to our ideas of expediency and safety. A persuasion that our further attendance would be fruitless and unavailing, rendered us less solicitous to return."[21] The letter caused little sensation—it was expected. Former Virginia Congressman Edward Carrington believed that the letter was "in perfect uniformity with the purpose of their Mission," which was to represent the interests of New York, "a state whose measures have for a Number of Years been uniformly against the federal interests."[22]

26. Attacked by an Old Friend

The public debate over the ratification of the Constitution was part of a much larger debate over the nature of government and how best to preserve liberty. Beginning shortly after the French and Indian War when American colonists objected to Parliament's new interventionist policies, the debate intensified as the sporadic but seemingly inevitable march to independence quickened. When Congress voted independence, it also voted to create a new form of government, and for two years it debated a draft of the Articles of Confederation. The original draft, prepared by John Dickinson, had granted great power to the central government. The Articles ultimately adopted left the states fully sovereign and independent. The central government was given little power—no power to tax or to enforce its will on the states or the people. As the conflict with Britain raged and the Articles of Confederation lay unratified, people in the theaters of war advocated a strengthened central government. Governor Clinton and Alexander Hamilton became two of these Revolutionary nationalists. But with the peace, the governor and many other New Yorkers abandoned the idea of strengthening Congress. The rejection of an unconditional adoption of the federal impost by the assembly in February 1787 catapulted New York into the public debate over a revised federal government.

During the four months the Federal Convention sat in Philadelphia, a coordinated effort was made to prepare the public to accept whatever the Convention proposed. The *Albany Gazette*, June 21, 1787, advocated restrictions on "the prevailing rage of excessive democracy—this fashionable contempt of government." The printer of the future Antifederalist *New York Journal* announced on July 12 that all printers should advocate "the necessity of an immediate *Efficient Foederal Government*," while a writer in the *Journal* on August 16 predicted that America would find "a *new birth to glory and empire*" if the advice of the Convention were heeded.

Very few voices were raised during the first half of 1787 warning Americans of the potential dangers from the Federal Convention.[23] Midway through the Convention, however, the first indication appeared that Americans might not be united in support of the strengthened government expected from the delegates assembled in Philadelphia. Surprisingly that first alarm was signaled not by an opponent of a stronger government, but by Alexander Hamilton, who wrote an anonymous newspaper article attacking Governor Clinton for allegedly making derogatory public statements about the Convention.

The trigger that set off the public debate over the Constitution in New York was the departure of the state's remaining two delegates from the

Convention. On their way home to Albany, Yates and Lansing undoubtedly stopped in New York City to report to Clinton. Yates, believing that the secrecy rule no longer applied to delegates who did not expect to return to Philadelphia, had no qualms about telling the governor of the ominous decisions being made behind the closed doors of the Pennsylvania statehouse.[24] Clinton seems to have regretted his willingness to have New York participate in the Convention, and, apparently, he made some unguarded public statements. In response, Hamilton wrote a scathing attack on the governor that was printed in the *Daily Advertiser* on July 21. The anonymous address reported "that his Excellency Governor Clinton has, in public company, without reserve, reprobated the appointment of the Convention, and predicted a mischievous issue of that measure." Clinton supposedly believed

> That the present confederation is, in itself, equal to the purposes of the union:—That the appointment of a Convention is calculated to impress the people with an idea of evils which do not exist:—That if either nothing should be proposed by the Convention, or if what they should propose should not be agreed to, the one or the other would tend to beget despair in the public mind; and that, in all probability, the result of their deliberations, whatever it might be, would only serve to throw the community into confusion.

Hamilton was appalled by these remarks and he attacked the ideas and Clinton. Universally, he said, Americans had endorsed the Convention, thereby agreeing that the Confederation was not "equal to the purposes of the union." "Material alterations," Hamilton asserted, were required. As proof of the Convention's necessity, Hamilton pointed out that delegates had been appointed by twelve state legislatures for the express purpose of an "abridgement of their own power." In Hamilton's judgment, the Confederation government was "fundamentally defective [and] . . . the very existence of the union [was] in imminent danger."

In defending the appointment of the Convention, Hamilton explained why it—instead of Congress—should be used to propose alterations to the Articles of Confederation. The Convention, Hamilton argued, brought together "the collective wisdom of the union" with the sole purpose of addressing the weaknesses of the Articles. Nothing else would detract the delegates from their assigned purpose; no pre-existing parties or coalitions would thwart their progress. Furthermore, Americans would be less suspicious of proposals to strengthen Congress that emanated from a convention that ceased to exist after it made its recommendations. Hamilton also felt that recommendations from an illustrious Convention would have a better chance to be taken seriously by the people in those states—New York being one of them—where "industrious and wicked pains have been taken by the parties unfriendly to the measures of the union, to discredit and debase the authority and influence of Congress." The states could also send delegates to a convention "who could not have been induced to accept an appointment to Congress"—delegates such as George Washington and Benjamin Franklin.

After defending the Convention, Hamilton attacked Clinton for his public criticisms of that body. Certainly, Hamilton conceded, the governor, as any person, had a right to oppose the appointment of such a Convention. But once the Convention was appointed and entrusted with America's "future fate," the governor should not criticize it publicly. It was, in Hamilton's judgment, "*unwarrantable* and *culpable in any man*, in so serious a posture of our national affairs, to endeavour to prepossess the public mind against the hitherto undetermined and unknown measures" of the Convention. Such conduct by a high public official "argues greater attachment to his *own power* than to the *public good*, and furnishes strong reason to suspect a dangerous predetermination to oppose whatever may tend to diminish the *former*, however it may promote the *latter*." Hamilton concluded by warning New Yorkers to beware of such a man, to "observe him with a jealous eye ... when he sounds the alarm of danger from another quarter."[25]

Hamilton's attack on the governor stunned everyone. Such a bold-faced rebuke was rare in newspapers of the day. Much more common would have been a general statement about high government officials or an allegorical essay in which the governor would have been identified only indirectly. But Hamilton pulled no punches; he went out of his way to attack the most powerful man in the state on the eve of the most important political battle since New York declared its independence. And, although the address was published anonymously, Hamilton made no attempt to hide his authorship. E. Wilder Spaulding correctly characterized Hamilton's address as "a declaration of war on Clinton." And in the process, Hamilton destroyed the myth of universal support for the forthcoming Constitution.

Printed responses to Hamilton's attack on Clinton were slow to appear. During a ten-day recess of the Convention, support for Hamilton appeared in the *Pennsylvania Herald* on August 1. The *Herald* reported "that the anti-fœderal disposition of a great officer" in New York had "seriously alarmed the citizens" by creating "a painful anticipation of anarchy and division." The writer believed that, "at this critical moment," men of influence "should be cautious what opinions they entertain, and what sentiments they deliver."[26]

David Humphreys, who like Hamilton had been an aide-de-camp to Washington, congratulated his friend on his "honest boldness to attack in a public Paper, the Antifederal Dogmas of a great Personage in your State.

Go on & prosper. . . . Were the men of talents & honesty, throughout the Continent, properly combined into one Phalanx, I am confident they would be competent to hew their way thro' all opposition." Men such as Hamilton should work to eradicate the "little jealousies, bickerings, & unworthy sinister views" throughout America to "establish a Government calculated to promote the happiness of Mankind & to make the Revolution a blessing instead of a curse."[27]

Throughout September, Hamilton's attack on Clinton was a major topic in New York newspapers. After reading Hamilton's address in the Lansingburgh (Troy) *Northern Centinel,* one poetic upstater viewed his governor in a different light.

> Since late events his *schemes* disclose,
> That Clinton should *Dan. Shays* oppose.
>   To save *one* state—what was the reason,
> But this—he hop'd, though all unseen,
> HIMSELF to wreck the whole THIRTEEN,
>   Without a *partner in the treason.*[28]

The onslaught against Clinton continued as "Rough Carver," a ploy on Abraham Yates's "Rough Hewer" pen name, denounced the governor as the "thick-skulled and double-hearted Chief" of those "who will coolly oppose every thing which does not bear the marks of *Self.*" "Rough Carver" hoped that Clinton's popularity would decline and "that the same wisdom which dictated the necessity of revising the Federal Government, will impress the citizens with just notions of [replacing Clinton as] governing Head." New Yorkers were told to detest "every idea of servile dependence on ambitious Rulers, who have nothing in view but their own aggrandizement."[29] "An Admirer of Anti-Federal Men" warned New Yorkers not to trust "those men who profess to be fathers of their country, [who are] endeavouring, by mean arts, to detach the affections of the people from every thing which bears the name of *federal.*" Instead, Americans should have confidence in the illustrious delegates to the Federal Convention. Led by George Washington and Benjamin Franklin, the delegates would never propose anything that would tarnish the luster they had gained during the Revolution.[30]

Not until September 6 did the governor's forces respond. "A Republican" prefaced his defense of Clinton by stating "that it would be highly improper, in the first magistrate of a respectable state, to enter the list in a newspaper with an anonymous scribbler; and it cannot but afford pleasure to find, that it has accordingly been treated by him with silent and merited contempt." But, as a private citizen, "A Republican" felt no hesitancy "to unmask the motives" of the governor's detractor.

"A Republican" said that he did not know the governor nor his position on the Convention. He did know that the public was unaware of Clinton's alleged derogatory statements until they were printed in the *Daily Advertiser.* "A Republican" argued that "any citizen of a free state," particularly a public officer such as Clinton who was recognized as "one of the guardians of our liberties," had the right "freely and unreservedly to express his sentiments on public measures however serious the posture of our national affairs may be." In fact, it was the duty of public officers to speak out. The more critical the situation, "the more loudly he is called upon to" issue warnings in the defense of liberty. Any attempt to limit the right of citizens and officeholders to speak out should be considered as "high treason against the majesty of the people."

Turning from defense to offense, "A Republican" attacked the anonymous author who had written against the governor as a member of that "opulent and ambitious" party that "would never rest contented with the equality established by our democratic forms of government." He was part of that

> lordly faction [that] exists in this state, composed of men, possessed of an insatiable thirst for dominion, and who, having forfeited the confidence of their fellow-citizens, and being defeated in their hopes of rising into power, have, for sometime past, employed themselves with unremitted industry, to embarrass every public measure; they reprobate our laws, censure our rulers, and decry our government; thereby to induce the necessity of a change, that they may establish a system more favorable to their aristocratic views.

As the democratic symbol of the revolution in New York, George Clinton stood exposed to attacks from these disgruntled aristocratic politicians. He became "the victim of their keenest resentment." They were "devoted to [his] destruction" and no "calumny, personal scurrility and falsehood" would be spared in their effort to defeat the governor. In concluding, "A Republican" quoted a stanza of poetry to intimate Hamilton's authorship of the anonymous attack on the governor.

> Smit with the love of honor, or the pence,
> O'er-run with wit, and destitute of sense,
> Legions of factious authors throng at once;
> Fool beckons fool, and dunce awakens dunce.
> To Hamilton's the ready lies repair;
> Ne'er was lie made which was not welcome there.
> Thence, on maturer judgment's anvil wrought,
> The polish'd falsehoods into public brought;
> Quick circulating slanders mirth afford,
> And reputation bleeds in ev'ry word.[31]

Another newspaper writer, "Adrastus," also defended Governor Clinton in the *New York Journal* on September 6. First, "Adrastus" lamented that the "management of the press" had fallen "into improper hands. Men of weak minds, and no discernment" had become editors of the "public papers, by which means those vehicles of instruction and entertainment are made the instruments of scandal, calumny, and abuse; the great source of public information is disgraced, and pol[l]uted with personal attacks." "Adrastus" thought that it was obvious from the style who had written the attack on the governor. Readers were warned to "be on their guard against so dangerous a member of society, who, with a smooth tongue and double face, is capable of concealing and executing the worst intentions beneath the mask of sincerity and friendship."

"An Old Soldier" also came to Clinton's defense in the pages of the *Northern Centinel*. From the beginning of the war for independence, Clinton had led New York through difficult times. Everyone knew the governor's record and most agreed that it was "the height of ingratitude to villify a character, which ought to be esteemed, and even revered, for his services." "An Old Soldier" asked his fellow citizens to trust the governor—to "support him in all measures tending to the general good of our country, and let us ever detest those vile incendiaries, who (under British influence) secretly endeavour to sow the seeds of division, discontent and distrust among us. Confidence in our rulers will make us a great and happy people; a want of it will be our ruin."[32] "Rusticus" also lamented the sad situation in the state's newspapers, which had been manipulated "to prepare the minds of the people, implicitly to receive *any form* of government" that the Convention may propose. "It seems ... to be highly criminal, especially at this particular period, for any man to differ in opinion from a certain Aristocratic junto, who appear determined, by their writings, to silence, and traduce every person who will not subscribe to every part of their political creed." The aristocracy, New Yorkers were warned, "would trample on the most sacred rights of the people, without the least reluctance or remorse"; they had convinced themselves "that Heaven hath formed the bulk of mankind, to be mere slaves and vassals, to men of their superior genius, birth, and fortune."[33]

Neither Hamilton nor his political allies were willing to allow the Clintonians to have the last word. "Aristides," appearing in the *Daily Advertiser* on September 10, praised Hamilton as the worthiest man in the state. The governor, on the other hand, "has long been viewed as secretly hostile" to any attempts to strengthen the federal government. Unless the governor came forth publicly and denied the charges levelled against him (which none of his defenders had yet done), "Aristides" believed that the public would be justified "to consider him as openly opposed to any change which the wisdom of the present Convention may recommend." Hamilton had done the state a great service—"impelled from pure principles," he had "warn[ed] the people of impending danger"—he had sounded "a *noble* and *patriotic alarm.*"

"Anti-Defamationis" denounced the "obvious" attempts by "'Aristides' and his colleagues . . . by unjust stigmas and innuendoes to cast an odium on our Governor." If Clinton was convinced that the Convention "was ill-judged, and that much evil instead of good would result from their deliberations," it would be "highly criminal" of him to remain silent. Americans would "never consent to have a constitution crammed down their throats."[34]

Between September 20 and October 18, the now blatantly Antifederal *New York Journal* printed a series of allegorical essays by "Inspector" that savaged Hamilton, who was referred to as "Tom S**t." The young "Tom S**t" was said to be "over-rated" and shallow. He had "palm[ed] himself upon a great and good man" [George Washington] during the Revolution and used his position to gain political connections. In time, however, Washington discovered the truth about the "superficial, self-conceited coxcomb," and Tom was "turned off, and disregarded by his patron."[35] This assertion, and a similar charge by "A Republican," so stung Hamilton that he wrote Washington, asking the general "to controvert" the slur.[36] Washington explicitly denied the charges against Hamilton and stated that Hamilton's departure from his entourage "was altogether the effect of your own choice." But Washington deplored the "political dispute" that had arisen between Hamilton and Clinton. "For both of you," Washington stated, "I have the highest esteem and regard. . . . When the situation of this country calls loudly for unanimity & vigor, it is to be lamented that Gentlemen of talents and character should disagree in their sentiments for promoting the public weal; but unfortunately, this ever has been, and more than probable ever will be the case, in the affairs of man."[37] "Inspector" continued his assault on the Creole (a reference to Hamilton's illegitimate West-Indian birth), whose vanity had now led him to attack the "faithful steward George (who is grown so saucy, as to speak his mind without fearing any body)."[38] Tom's aim was to convince the people to vote the governor out of office, to be replaced by either himself or his "immaculate daddy, Justice Midas" (Philip Schuyler). In either case Hamilton's political career would thrive: "whilst daddy swims, Tom cannot sink."[39]

"Tom S**t" was denounced for his monarchist views put forth in the Convention and for his "over-bearing principles." He desired "to ride on the great horse, in order, that he may have the pleasure of trampling on the croud." He was condemned for accumulating wealth by "pleading for traitors, who purchased his friendship with the spoils of their bleeding country." Sarcastically, though, Hamilton was thanked "for discovering that horrid plot of George Steward, which but for Tom S**t would have remained secret to this day; nay, perhaps it would never have been found out at all, had not Tom's patriotic desire of 'advancing the national interest, and throwing light on political controversy,' led him to unfold the whole conspiracy to the public eye."[40]

Historians have long wondered what motivated Hamilton to attack Clinton in July before the debate over the Constitution had really begun and when nationalists were assiduously trying to create the myth that the nation was united in support of the Federal Convention and whatever it proposed. Those historians who have no satisfactory explanation for Hamilton's actions avoid the issue and, like Spaulding, merely report that the attack occurred. Others, however, such as Linda De Pauw, argue that Hamilton misjudged the situation and blundered terribly in a premature assault on Clinton. De Pauw explicitly states that Hamilton's attack pushed an uncommitted Clinton into an Antifederal position on the new Constitution. To avoid such conjecture, historians need only look to Hamilton's own explanation for his actions.

On September 15, 1787, the New York *Daily Advertiser* published an anonymous essay written by Hamilton in which he defended his denunciation of the governor. Hamilton admitted that he had written the July 21 piece; there was never any attempt to conceal his identity. "To avoid the appearance of ostentation," he did not sign his published address, but he had left his name with the printer "to be disclosed to any person who should apply for it, on the part of the Governor." Consequently, neither the governor nor his friends could honestly argue that the July 21 address was an anonymous piece; everyone knew who had written it.

Hamilton indicated that he had no "wanton disposition to calumniate a meritorious character." His attack on Clinton was "an honorable and open attempt to unmask, what appeared to the writer, the pernicious intrigues of a man, high in office, to preserve power and emolument to himself, at the expence of the Union, the peace, and the happiness of America." Hamilton knew very well that his public attack on Clinton would forever doom their relationship. He also realized the danger of attacking Clinton, but the danger of allowing Clinton free rein was even greater. Hamilton hoped that his early assault would accomplish two ends. First, he wanted to show New Yorkers that the governor "was capable of forming such a predetermination, before, it can be presumed, he had any knowledge of the measures themselves, on which to found his judgment." Any future Antifederal statements by Clinton could thus be discounted as the continued opposition of a man who had pre-judged the actions of the Convention. Second, and probably more important, Hamilton had seized the initiative: Hamilton rather than Clinton had decided when to reveal the governor's position on the Convention and its handiwork. Hamilton's judgment ran as follows: "If his Excellency was predetermined to oppose the measures of the Convention, as his conduct indicates, he would take care himself to propagate his sentiments, in the manner in which it could be done with most effect. This appears to have been his practice. It was therefore proper that the antidote should go along with the poison."[41] Hamilton, in essence, was not going to allow Clinton to play his usual game of sitting on the sidelines and waiting for the most opportune time to strike. Instead, Hamilton chose the time and place for Clinton's Antifederalism to become public knowledge. In denying Clinton his usual course of action, Hamilton was following one of his long-established political tactics: "As a general marches at the head of his troops, so ought wise politicians . . . to march at the head of affairs; insomuch that they ought not to await *the event*, to know what measures to take; but the measures which they have taken ought to produce *the event*."[42] Such an offensive strategy was published in verse in newspapers less than three months before Hamilton's original attack.

> You should in order to accomplish
> Your schemes, and put your foes to non-plus,
> Have first begun, by attacking those
> Who are most likely to oppose
> And thwart your complicated plan;
> These should be silenced to a man.[43]

Hamilton realized that he was playing a dangerous game, but he also knew that the governor had long since abandoned the nationalist cause. For several years, the relationship between Hamilton and Clinton had deteriorated. The two men had met in 1777 when Hamilton served as aide-de-camp to General Washington. Clinton befriended the young colonel and helped to nurse him back to health when he was seriously ill. Hamilton greatly respected Clinton and advised Washington to place him in command of the Continental forces along the Hudson. Their friendship grew as they corresponded about the need to strengthen Congress. But, when Hamilton in 1780 married Elizabeth Schuyler—the daughter of Clinton's erstwhile political opponent—it became inevitable that the two friends would drift apart. Such an alienation began when Congressman Hamilton failed to follow his instructions in representing New York's interests on the western posts controversy in 1783. The following year, the division between Hamilton and Clinton widened over the state's anti-loyalist policies, and again the two men found themselves on opposite sides of the paper-money debate in 1786. But, in all of these controversies, public civility was maintained. Hamilton's newspaper attack on the governor stripped away the veneer of civility left between them and made it clear to everyone in New York that these two men had become bitter political enemies.

27. A Quiet Stance

The Federal Convention ended its four month marathon session on September 17, 1787, as thirty-nine delegates from twelve states approved their new charter. Hamilton alone signed the new Constitution for New York. Four days later, the *Daily Advertiser* printed the Constitution for the first time in New York. On September 24, the public debate in New York began in earnest as the *Daily Advertiser* published an essay advocating the adoption of the Constitution because it would "render us safe and happy at home, and respected abroad." The Constitution would "snatch us from impending ruin" and provide "the substantial basis of liberty, honor and virtue." Dutiful, honest, and well disposed Americans would "cultivate and diffuse . . . a spirit of submission" to the new Constitution, which, although not perfect, was "much more so than the most friendly and sanguine expected."

Many New Yorkers did not agree. Marinus Willett, sheriff of New York City and one of Clinton's inner circle, described the reaction of the opposition. The people, Willett said, had been led to believe "the General Idea that let this thing be what it might, it must be received . . . if it could not be chewed, it must be swallowed." Now, however, the people were astonished at "the of[f]spring of the Convention . . . as a Monster with open mouth and monstrous Teeth ready to devour all before it. . . . Many of those who appeared determined to give it the most hospitable reception have taken up Clubs against it." The Constitution, according to Willett, was "an extraordinary conception . . . that totally departed from" the fundamental principles of the Revolution. "Our world is set afloat and unless this thing is laid we are like to become a wandering Comett."[44]

The initial public response from the Clintonians came quickly in the first of seven essays signed by "Cato" that appeared in the *New York Journal*. Throughout the ratification debate, authorship of this series was attributed to Clinton.[45] Despite the governor's attempt to keep a low profile on the Constitution, at no time did he or his lieutenants disclaim his authorship. Although Clinton's authorship cannot be conclusively determined, it is worthwhile to examine "Cato" because most New Yorkers believed that the governor and the essayist were one and the same.

The first essay in the "Cato" series appeared on September 27.[46] "Cato," repeating a theme common in the governor's ongoing battle with his opponents, called on New Yorkers to be prudent and cautious in considering "this new national government." "If you are negligent or inattentive, the ambitious and despotic will entrap you in their toils, and bind you with the cord of power from which you, and your posterity, may never be freed." Government, "Cato" advised, is the study of "political safety," and the governed must always be vigilant of "the vultures of power." Americans had already demonstrated their valor in obtaining their independence from a mighty enemy. They had established republican governments on the state and federal levels; and, after acknowledging the "defects in the federal system," the state legislatures had quite matter-of-factly sought to address these shortcomings in a federal convention. With alterations now before the public, Americans were on the brink of "a very important crisis" that would affect their lives, property, and reputations. "Cato" warned his readers to "beware how you determine—do not, because you admit that something must be done, adopt any thing—teach the members of that Convention, that you are capable of a supervision of their conduct." If the Constitution were found defective, another convention could consider amendments. The Constitution should be adopted if it were acceptable, but if it were judged to be dangerous, freemen should "reject it with indignation—better to be where you are, for the present, than insecure forever afterwards." Knowing the power of George Washington's name and reputation, "Cato" reminded his readers that, although the new Constitution was recommended by "a man who merits the confidence of the public, . . . that the wisest and best of men err, and their errors, if adopted, may be fatal to the community; therefore, in principles of *politics*, as well as in religious faith, every man ought to think for himself."

A Federalist writing under the pen name "Cæsar," assumed by many to be Alexander Hamilton, responded in the *Daily Advertiser* on October 1.[47] "Cæsar" labeled "Cato" a demagogue who wrote in "the language of distrust . . . to prejudice the public opinion against the New Constitution." Amendments to the Constitution, "Cæsar" argued, were impossible to obtain—"the *door of recommendation is shut, and cannot be opened by the same men.*" The Convention was "*dissolved.*" America would have to choose between a complete acceptance or a total rejection. "Cæsar" wondered whether New Yorkers ought to "wrangle and find fault with that *excellent Whole*, because, perhaps, some of its parts *might have been* more perfect?" In closing, "Cæsar" acknowledged "Cato's" "reverence" for Washington, but with remarkable bluntness he warned opponents of the Constitution that it would be wiser to have Washington freely elected as the first president under the Constitution than as the commander-in-chief of another army to establish the Constitution by force.

Submitting his contributions to the printer every two weeks, the governor's second "Cato" essay appeared in the *New York Journal* on October 11.[48] Before proceeding with an analysis of the Constitution, "Cato" felt obligated to respond to "Cæsar." The Federalist essayist, whom "Cato" easily recognized from "his usual dogmatism," had treated New Yorkers "with passion, insult, and threat. . . . he shuts the door of free deliberation and discussion, and declares, that you must receive this government in manner and form as it is *proffered*," even though he himself admits that it is defective. He charged that "Cæsar" denied the ability of the people to choose their own form of government; "Cæsar" would have "the rich and insolent alone be your rulers." But, according to "Cato," "in democratic republics the people collectively are considered as the sovereign"; they alone decide what kind of government they will live under. The time had now arrived for the people themselves to decide whether to accept "this new political fabric," which was so "essentially and fundamentally distinct and different" from the Articles of Confederation. The new Constitution would eliminate the system of sovereign states "united by a confederated league" and substitute in its place a consolidated national government. "Cato" urged New Yorkers "to behave like sensible freemen—think, speak, act, and assert your opinions and rights" despite the threats of "Cæsar." In closing, "Cato" removed any doubts about his stance on the new Constitution. He promised in his future essays to examine the "new form of national government—compare it with experience and the opinions of the most sensible and approved political authors—and to shew, that its principles, and the exercise of them, will be dangerous to your liberty and happiness."

Within a week, "Cæsar" accused "Cato" of "dirty policy" in appealing to the sovereignty of the people.[49] "Cæsar" believed that the people in general were "very ill qualified to *judge* for themselves what government will best suit their peculiar situations." The science of government, "Cæsar" believed and felt that "Cato" would agree, was "not easily understood." "Cæsar" suggested that the people's role should be to maintain "a tractable and docile disposition . . . while others . . . with the advantage of genius and learning, are constructing the bark that may, by the blessing of Heaven, carry them to the port of rest and happiness." "Cato" and his cohorts, on the other hand, were trying to manipulate the people by frightening them "with ideal bugbears, in order to mould them to their own purposes."[50] "Cæsar" then announced that he would no longer respond to "Cato's" criticisms of the Constitution—he would "leave Cato to the wicked influences of his own heart, in the fullest persuasion that all good men, and good citizens, will combine their influence to establish the fair fabrick of American liberty" by adopting the new Constitution.

In his first frontal assault on the Constitution, "Cato" referred to

Montesquieu's theory that republics could thrive only within small territo-
ries.[51] Whosoever seriously considered "the immense extent of territory
comprehended within the limits of the United States, together with the
variety of its climates, productions, and commerce, the difference of
extent, and number of inhabitants in all; the dissimultude of interest,
morals, and policies, in almost every one" of the states, must conclude as
"an intuitive truth, that a consolidated republican form of government"
cannot succeed in America in preserving "lives, liberty, and estates," the
end for which governments are established.

In his fourth essay, "Cato" criticized the "vague and inexplicit" powers
of the president, which would eventually lead "to the establishment of a
vile and arbitrary aristocracy, or monarchy."[52] Again quoting Montesquieu,
"Cato" advocated a shorter term for the president—preferably no longer
than a year—because his powers were so great. Sensing his own vulnerability on this topic, "Cato" anticipated the inevitable comparison between
the president and New York's governor. He warned his readers to beware of
the Federalists' deception "by a fallacious resemblance between" the Constitution and New York's state government. The governor, "Cato" argued,
was directly elected by the people and had limited powers when compared
to those of the president. Comparing the new federal Constitution with
New York's government was akin to comparing "an Angel of darkness" to
"an Angel of light."

In his fifth essay, "Cato" outlined some of his most serious objections
to the new Constitution.[53] In general, "Cato" deplored the "inexplicitness
[that] seems to pervade the whole political fabric." Government, "Cato"
suggested, should fix "barriers which the ambitious and tyrannically disposed magistrate dare not overleap," but the federal Constitution's "mere
implication was too feeble to restrain the unbridled ambition of a bad man,
or afford security against negligence, cruelty, or any other defect of mind."
"Cato" denied the assertion that the "opinions and manners of the people
of America, are capable to resist and prevent an extension of prerogative or
oppression." Opinions and manners could and probably would change,
especially in a commercial society. Americans needed to be "cautious,
prudent and jealous in politics"; they needed a frame of government that
explicitly protected their "valuable rights."

After these general fears, "Cato" listed more than a dozen specific
objections to the Constitution.[54] He believed that biennial elections
departed from the "safe democratical principles of annual ones." He thought
that the number of representatives was too few and that the principle of
apportioning them among the states was unjust. He also objected to the
equal representation of the states in the senate and the election of senators
by state legislatures. He disliked the combination of the senate and the

president in appointments and treaty-making and the senate's judicial power over impeachment. He feared Congress' power to regulate federal elections, to maintain standing armies and navies, and to send state militias to remote parts of the continent. He decried the continuance of the slave trade and anticipated the abuse of the federal government's taxing powers.

"Cato" offered his readers a final admonition.[55] "Hitherto," he wrote, "we have tied up our rulers in the exercise of their duties by positive restrictions—if the cord has been drawn too tight, loosen it to the necessary extent, but do not entirely unbind them." Governors should be trusted, but never given "unlimited confidence." Throughout history, prudent men had maintained a healthy distrust "against the assaults of tyrants. . . . Preserve this carefully, and no calamity can affect you."

During the public debate over the Constitution in New York, Clinton refused to take a public stand on the new form of government. A week after the Federal Convention adjourned, a correspondent in the *Pennsylvania Herald* predicted that the Constitution would be popular in New York, because "the distinguished person from whom an opposition was predicted, has expressed himself in terms favorable to the plan."[56] Former president of Congress Elias Boudinot, however, was better informed. His sources suggested that "the Governor seems rather to be laying by and not decisive, waiting to see how the wind will blow."[57] Virginia Congressman Edward Carrington reported that Clinton remained silent "wishing, it is suspected, for a miscarriage, but is not confident enough to commit himself in an open opposition."[58] Reiterating his remarks to another correspondent, Carrington suggested that this was politics as usual for the governor, who always guarded "against being committed in a fruitless opposition."[59] Carrington's fellow congressman James Madison held a similar opinion of Clinton. "The Governour's party," Madison wrote Thomas Jefferson, "which has hitherto been the popular & most numerous one, is supposed to be on the opposite side; but considerable reserve is practised, of which he sets the example."[60] Despite this reserve, Madison sensed that Clinton was "a decided adversary."[61]

Within a short time, the governor's opposition to the Constitution was widely reported. John Stevens, Jr., of Hoboken, New Jersey, wrote his father that Clinton and his lieutenants, John Lamb and Marinus Willett, "are openly opposed to it—indeed it is natural," Stevens suggested, "to expect that men in office will set themselves against it."[62] Arthur Lee, an Antifederalist serving on the Confederation's Board of Treasury, wrote John Adams that "the Governor & all his friends are in opposition."[63] On October 17, the *Pennsylvania Herald* reversed its earlier announcement and declared now that Clinton was opposed to the Constitution and that the state's "prevailing politics support the principles of the governor." The Philadelphia *Independent Gazetteer* reported in November that the governor was "active against" the Constitution and would not summon a special session of the legislature to call a ratifying convention.[64] Another Pennsylvania newspaper reported that Clinton "sets his face against the new Constitution" and was working behind the scenes to convince New Jersey not to ratify. According to the report, Clinton had negotiated "thro a person of considerable weight in Jersey" (probably Abraham Clark), to return half of New York's state impost to New Jersey if that state refused to adopt the Constitution.[65] This charge was repeated in the election for U.S. representatives in New Jersey in February 1789. Clark was quoted as saying "that New-York would have made large concessions to this state in consideration of their declining that measure [i.e., ratification]; and that they would not only have given up the impost, but would be willing to refund the amount of the duties by them collected in a state capacity"[66]

By spring 1788, Clinton made little attempt to conceal his Antifederalism. Lewis Morris wrote his son that Federalists in New York were "now in the greatest confusion . . . Our Govr. with his Party gives the new constitution all the opposition in his power."[67] Confederation Secretary at War Henry Knox wrote George Washington that New York Antifederalists "are united under the auspices of the Governor and he is supposed to be immoveable."[68] New Hampshire Congressman Nicholas Gilman wrote that "the Governor of this State acts no longer under Cover but is open and indefatigable in the opposition."[68] Massachusetts Congressman Samuel A. Otis believed that "Clinton and some others have done infinite mischief in this business." Otis felt that the governor was "a mercenary man with daring qualities that will carry him thro everything in pursuit of his own interest & aggrandizement."[70] Offsetting Otis's uncomplimentary description, a correspondent in the Providence *United States Chronicle* was grateful that "there are still patriots left,—who like a constellation will clear the mists, too long suffered to blind the eyes of the honest yeomanry of our country." Clinton was a star in that constellation, who would "long be revered" for his "noble stand . . . against the new Constitution."[71] Abigail Adams Smith, the daughter of John and Abigail Adams, also thought better of Clinton. John Adams, serving as U.S. minister to London, had written Clinton in late March 1788 asking that the governor give his daughter and son-in-law "your Protection and Patronage" as well as "the Friendship of your Family."[72] A grateful daughter wrote her mother that

> We are treated, here, with great politeness, civility, and friendship. We were invited to dine with the Governor, which was a *very particular* favour. He nor his family either visit, or are visited by, any families,

either in public or private life, of this place . . . That he is a man of no decided character, no one who sees him will say. To me he appears one whose conduct and motives of action are not to be seen through upon a slight examination. The part he has taken upon the subject of the new Constitution is much condemned. What are his motives, I do not pretend to judge; but I do not believe that he acts or thinks without some *important* motives . . . The Governor does not conceal his sentiments, but I have not heard that he has given any reasons for them.

According to Abigail Adams Smith, the governor was not the only Antifederalist in the Clinton household. Clinton's second daughter was "as smart and sensible a girl as I ever knew—a zealous politician, and a high anti-Federalist. . . . His family are all politicians."[73]

In line with his previous decision on the impost, the governor did not call a special session of the legislature to consider a state ratifying convention. Instead, on December 3, 1787, Clinton issued a proclamation calling the regular legislative session to meet in Poughkeepsie on January 1, 1788. As usual, an insufficient number of members arrived on time to attain a quorum—not until January 11 were both houses of the legislature ready to begin business.

No one knew exactly what to expect from the legislature. James Madison reported that the legislators were "much divided" on the issue of calling a ratifying convention—the assembly was expected to support a convention, the senate to oppose. New York City Federalist Walter Rutherfurd predicted "warm work" in Poughkeepsie. Exactly what role the governor would play was also uncertain. On Wednesday, January 2, Samuel A. Otis ominously wrote that "Gr. Clinton setts off for Poughkeepsie this morning to put his machinery in motion." Albany lawyer Richard Sill pessimistically reported that Federalists "doubted . . . whether we shall have a Convention called by a Legislative Act, the opposition are determined to make their first stand here."[74] Whatever the outcome in Poughkeepsie, New Yorkers of "every class" realized the momentousness of the occasion. Without a convention to consider the Constitution, some Federalists felt as if "Anarchy stares us in the face."[75]

On January 11, Governor Clinton addressed the legislature. Included among the public documents that he submitted for consideration were the Constitution, the resolutions of the Federal Convention and the Confederation Congress requesting the states to call ratifying conventions, and the letter he had received from Robert Yates and John Lansing, Jr., explaining their opposition to the Constitution and their reasons for leaving the Convention early. Maintaining his usual public impartiality, Clinton told the legislature that "From the nature of my office . . . it would be improper for me to have any other agency in the business than that of laying the papers ... before you for your information."[76] Both houses thanked the governor for his speech and the accompanying documents, which they assured him would "claim our most serious and deliberate consideration."

Almost three weeks elapsed before the assembly considered resolutions to call a ratifying convention. Early in the session, Antifederalists in the senate proposed a bill calling for new oaths of allegiance and of office. The oath of office for legislators was "so framed as that they should Swear never to consent to any Act or thing which had a *tendency* to destroy or *Alter* the present *constitution of the state*." Federalists, led by Philip Schuyler, successfully delayed consideration of the oaths until January 26; when, after a long debate, "the objectional clause" was struck out by a vote of nine to six after Antifederalists "were driven to the necessity of letting the cat out of the bag by indirectly avowing that the Clause was intended to Militate and operate against the proposed new constitution."[77]

Contrary to expectations, there seemed to be no legislative opposition to the call of a convention. Much debate, however, occurred over how the convention would be called and what the convention ought to be authorized to do. Antifederalist assemblymen, led by Cornelius C. Schoonmaker of Ulster County and Samuel Jones of Queens County, proposed that the resolutions calling a convention be prefaced with a preamble indicating that the Federal Convention had exceeded its authority by reporting "a new Constitution" that would "materially alter" New York's constitution and state government "and greatly affect the rights and privileges" of all New Yorkers. Federalists opposed this attempt to stigmatize the new Constitution and advocated that the new form of government should be presented to the people without "the inference ... that the Legislature disapproved of the measures of the Convention." Furthermore, the legislature ought not to consider the merits of the Constitution—"the only question" was whether the Constitution should "be submitted to the people." After considerable debate, the assembly rejected any derogatory statement about the Convention or the Constitution. The assembly also rejected a motion from Samuel Jones to submit the Constitution to a state convention for a "free investigation, discussion, and decision," which was understood to be an attempt "to introduce the Idea of *Amendment*."

The assembly then passed resolutions calling a convention to meet at the courthouse in Poughkeepsie on June 17, 1788. The election of delegates would begin on April 29 and continue until completed, but for no more than five days. For the first time ever, state constitutional property qualifications required for suffrage were suspended, thereby allowing all free adult males to vote for convention delegates. Polling places were to be located in every precinct and town, not merely in the county seats, where they had previously been confined, and voting was to be by secret ballot. At the same time that New Yorkers voted for convention delegates, qualified freemen could also vote for assemblymen and for one-third of the state's senators. The senate approved the assembly's resolutions on February 1, 1788.[78]

28. Electing the Governor

Electioneering began almost immediately after the legislature passed the resolutions calling the state convention. The election campaign took place within a highly developed system of political parties that had evolved steadily in New York after the conclusion of the war. Individuals, who on both the state and county levels became chieftains, served as rallying points for party faithful. On the state level, party leaders (Governor Clinton, Melancton Smith, Samuel Jones, Abraham Yates, Jr., and John Lansing, Jr., in the case of the Antifederalists) caucused while the legislature met. Sometimes state leaders met privately with individual county leaders to discuss the particular needs of the local communities; on other occasions the entire legislative wing of the party met to map out statewide strategy. Loyalty to the party ticket was expected and was usually achieved in those counties where no one party was dominant. But in those counties where one party dominated—such as in Clintonian Ulster County— bickering within the dominant party was commonplace. County party chiefs regularly tried to smooth over disagreements by offering compromise party slates in which towns, regions, or key individuals were ameliorated. More often than not, a consensus ticket evolved, but hard feelings inevitably developed when political egos clashed and local leaders vied for dominance at the county level. Such was the case in Ulster County.

The political struggle over the election of delegates to the state ratifying convention created intense interest among New Yorkers. To Antifederalists, the battle over the Constitution seemed to be another dangerous episode in the Revolutionary struggle for liberty. The old British and loyalist enemies had been defeated, but a new set of aristocrats had surfaced, who sought to curtail the democratic state governments by creating a national government that would be controlled by the elites and that would be supreme over the states. Antifederalists in Ulster County saw the election for convention seats in 1788 as part of a continuing struggle to secure their hard-won rights—a new battle in which George Clinton again would lead them. They would not easily give up "those Liberties for which many of their Friends have bled and Died."[79]

During the first week in March 1788, Antifederalist leaders "disposed to assist in Preserving our Liberty and Property" met together in Poughkeepsie about the upcoming elections. In "a Private consultation," Melancton Smith and Samuel Jones consulted with Peter Van Gaasbeck, a wealthy, thirty-four-year-old merchant and public-securities speculator who recently had assumed the leadership of the Ulster County Antifederalists.[80] The trio "agreed for our mutual Interest" to a well-balanced list of six convention candidates, who represented different precincts in the county. George Clinton's name was included on the nomination ticket.[81]

At the request of Smith and Jones, when Van Gaasbeck left Poughkeepsie, he traveled throughout "the Lower End" of Ulster County mustering support for the agreed-upon slate. Pleased with his reception, Van Gaasbeck reported that "every one assured me to support the List." He arrived back home in Kingston "convinced that we can Carry" the ticket "if care is taken."[82]

Soon, however, Van Gaasbeck realized that although Ulster was strongly Antifederal, the party was far from united. He reported that John Addison and Johannis Snyder, "with a few of their associates . . . had Exerted every nerve by Private Consultations and Meetings" to get themselves elected to the convention. On February 14, a public meeting in Kingston "unanimously disapproved of" the Constitution and elected Addison, Snyder, and Dirck Wynkoop to meet two weeks later with other town and precinct delegates in a general county-wide committee that would nominate convention delegates. The Kingston meeting itself proposed that Addison and Wynkoop be held up in the county meeting as Kingston's convention delegates. Sensing the potential conflict with other Antifederalists, the Kingston meeting advocated that "in a business of such importance to the liberty and property of a free and independent people, we trust that a spirit of alacrity, firmness, and unanimity, will mark the conduct and deliberations of the county of Ulster."[83] Van Gaasbeck, however, was not beguiled by this rhetoric; he believed that Addison and Snyder had "Prepared the Minds of many people" to support their candidacy, thus demonstrating their disloyalty to the party by pursuing their candidacy for the convention after they had not been nominated by the caucusing leaders in Poughkeepsie. Such defiance of the party leadership threatened to divide the county's Antifederal support and might result in the election of one or more Federalists. To counter the challenge to his leadership, Van Gaasbeck mounted a letter-writing campaign in support of the Poughkeepsie ticket, stressing the "great importance that we Unite Heart and Hand" in convention and assembly candidates. He warned his lieutenants that there are men in Ulster "who wish to be in Power and will go to any Lengths to Carry the Point"—men who Van Gaasbeck "would not Chuse to trust with A

Dust of Property—nor Powers."[84] Continuing his efforts to thwart Addison, Van Gaasbeck spread a rumor, reportedly "by good Authority," that Addison had "given it as his Opinion that it will be best to adopt the New Constitution." Van Gaasbeck warned his fellow Ulstermen to "beware of the Disguise," lest New York be deceived into ratifying the Constitution as Massachusetts had been.[85]

Ulster Antifederalists gathered together at New Paltz in early March to nominate candidates for the convention. Other attempts to nominate candidates occurred in New Windsor and Newburgh. The latter seems to have been orchestrated by Federalists. On March 10, Van Gaasbeck was informed that a handful of "person[s] of inferior importance" had met at Newburgh and nominated their own ticket, including three candidates who had been nominated at Poughkeepsie (Governor Clinton, Ebenezer Clark, and John Cantine). Johannis Bruyn, Lucas Elmendorph, and Johannis Snyder were also nominated.[86] These meetings alarmed Van Gaasbeck, whose fears heightened when he heard about events that had occurred in Poughkeepsie after his departure.

After Van Gaasbeck had left Poughkeepsie, Antifederalists from all of the state's counties caucused and agreed to form committees of correspondence to inform each other about "the Combinations and Measures that are pursued to Cajole [the people] out of some of their most inestimable Rights."[87] Furthermore, led by Melancton Smith and Samuel Jones, the remaining Ulster Antifederalists agreed to change the ticket previously molded by Smith, Jones and Van Gaasbeck. To maintain harmony in Ulster, especially in Kingston, John Addison replaced Governor Clinton on the ticket. It was assumed that Ulster was so solidly opposed to the Constitution, that Clinton's popularity would not be needed to elect a unanimously Antifederal delegation; nor should the governor's candidacy be wasted on a "sure" thing. Instead, Smith and Jones recommended that the governor stand for a convention seat from one of the Long Island counties, most likely Kings County.

Although broad public opinion on the Constitution on Long Island was as yet unknown, Smith and Jones knew that the governor had "the highest confidence" of the people of Kings County, who, it was felt, "will not hesitate . . . to make him their choice for a Delegate." If Clinton could be elected from Kings, he would deprive Federalists of at least one convention vote, and maybe two if a second Antifederal candidate could be elected on the governor's coattails. If, however, after testing the political waters, Clinton's chances of victory on Long Island seemed uncertain, the governor would again be added to the Ulster County ticket.[88] Ulster Antifederalists at the caucus were dubious about giving up their favorite son, but they consented to the strategy for the general good of the overall campaign. The governor also agreed and suggested that, if he were added again to the Ulster ticket, he replace his brother James as a candidate. Toward the end of the legislative session, Ulster Assemblyman Cornelius C. Schoonmaker, second only to Van Gaasbeck in the county party hierarchy, informed the governor "that many of the principal people in Kingston" had expressed their opposition to Addison's candidacy. The governor, however, hesitated about being put back on the Ulster ticket as a replacement for Addison. Clinton did not wish to give the impression that he and his brother were joined in "partyship" against Addison.[89]

Van Gaasbeck was not happy with the procedure used to develop this new strategy or with the strategy itself. Explaining his apprehensions in a letter to Schoonmaker, Van Gaasbeck strenuously opposed the creation of a committee of correspondence. Perhaps his objection stemmed from a sense that he was losing political control to the committee, but he based his opposition on other grounds. Van Gaasbeck particularly objected to Johannis Snyder serving on the committee of correspondence, because Snyder was suspected of being a Federalist sympathizer. According to Van Gaasbeck, Federalists of the town of Hurley had held a meeting at Kingston that supported the Newburgh ticket, which included Snyder. After the Hurley meeting, which Snyder attended, Addison and Snyder had "frequent Private interviews" aiming to replace some of the original Poughkeepsie candidates with themselves.

Van Gaasbeck also adamantly opposed the deletion of the governor from the Ulster ticket. The people of Ulster, Van Gaasbeck informed Schoonmaker, had been assured that the governor's candidacy in Ulster "was firmly fixed." Dropping Clinton from the ticket would enourage "many People" to become "Cool and many will suspect a design or Trick is intended. This," Schoonmaker was told, "is very easy to imprint on the Minds of the more Ignorant People." Christopher Tappen, the governor's brother-in-law, agreed with Van Gaasbeck. It was their "Candid opinion for the Good of the Cause to support our first List, agreed on at Poughkeepsie." Any deviation from that list could only assist "the federal Interest . . . as to divide our Representation and who knows perhaps may put in one or two Real federals—or such as ought not to be trusted as much—as an open and avowed fedarlist." To forestall this potential loss, Van Gaasbeck and Tappen encouraged Schoonmaker to write to Melancton Smith in New York City "or some other Good Character of our determination and Press them to drop the Governor in that Quarter."[90]

On April 3, Schoonmaker sent Van Gaasbeck a copy of a letter from New York City, describing the bleak state of Antifederalist affairs in that area of the state. Schoonmaker now saw the benefit of the governor's candidacy in Ulster, and he informed every precinct that Clinton would stand as a candidate from Ulster.[91] The next day, Schoonmaker again wrote Van Gaasbeck, expressing regret over the appointment of committees of correspondence. Everyone at the Poughkeepsie caucus believed that Snyder was reliable, and that his membership on the committee was necessary "to satisfy and Unite the good people of Kingston." But, if Snyder was in truth a Federalist, he would soon be discovered and isolated.

Schoonmaker also reiterated his support of the original Poughkeepsie ticket, but advised Van Gaasbeck not to let his "Zeal" for the first slate blur his political vision. Yes, the original ticket should be restored "if there should be any danger of division taking place amongst us, or that by the Change we would have Reason to suspect that a Man would be Elected that was not decidedly against the New Constitution." But Schoonmaker could also support a ticket without the governor, if Clinton could assuredly be elected from Kings, and if Van Gaasbeck could find a suitable candidate in Kingston to replace Addison. Such an alternative would "strengthen the General cause, thereby to gain in Numbers in the Convention." If, however, Van Gaasbeck felt adamant about the governor's candidacy in Ulster, Schoonmaker would "do every thing" in his power to support the original ticket.[92]

Schoonmaker believed that Ulster County contained few Federalists "and most of them very Weak ones too." He felt there would be little danger in fixing upon an entirely new slate of Antifederal candidates "if we will only exert ourselves"; therefore, why, he asked, "should we be afraid for the change of one name only, however important to the List," especially if Clinton's election in Kings County might gain an additional Antifederal seat in the convention? Reluctantly Schoonmaker told Van Gaasbeck that he would "not write to New York to stop the Election of the Governor in Kings," because he thought it best that Clinton "should be elected there." If Ulstermen wanted Clinton as their candidate, so be it—"it will promote the cause if he should be Elected even in both the Counties."[92]

Reflecting on Van Gaasbeck's reasoning, Schoonmaker experienced a change of heart. On April 7, three days after his previous letter, Schoonmaker wrote Van Gaasbeck that he had written to Samuel Jones that Ulster would "not *hazard* the Election of the Governor in Kings County, for fear that the fedral Machinations in the City of New York may probably disconcert our plans and the Elections of the Governor be lost, and that we were determined that he shall be Voted in this County" even if he were held up for election in Kings. Schoonmaker also warned Jones that Snyder, though a member of the Antifederalist committee of correspondence, was not to be trusted with "any Confidential Communications." Schoonmaker also told Van Gaasbeck that Addison had no support in Montgomery and Walkill precincts.[94]

When Melancton Smith returned to New York City, he immediately set about to determine whether the governor could be elected in Kings County. Coincidentally, about the same time that Schoonmaker decided that the governor must be run in Ulster, Smith and other New York City Antifederalists determined "that it will not be prudent to hazard his election" in Kings; the governor should be placed in nomination for Ulster County. Smith, however, told Schoonmaker that New York City Antifederalists had decided to nominate Clinton because "we . . . are not without hopes that we may Succeed for we find our Strength here greater than we expected, and I have no doubt but many of the Opposite party will vote for him notwithstanding he differs in Sentiments with them." Despite the New York City nomination, Smith continued to urge Clinton's nomination in Ulster, "for he had better be chosen in two places, than not to be elected at all."[95]

As the election approached, Van Gaasbeck became increasingly worried about the disunity of Ulster's Antifederalists, especially in Kingston. At "a Meeting of a Number of the Good Citizens of the Corporation of Kingston," Van Gaasbeck and three others were appointed a committee to circularize a new slate that had the unanimous approval of the meeting. George Clinton headed the ticket, which included Cornelius C. Schoonmaker, Dirck Wynkoop, James Clinton, Ebenezer Clark, and John Cantine. John Addison's name was conspicuously absent. The committee recommended the six candidates "as men of Probity, firmness and Stability of approved Political Characters and who have at Heart the real Happiness and Interest of your Country." Kingstonians were urged to unite "in a matter which Involves so great a trust."[96]

"A Dutchess County Anti-Federalist" also sensed the danger in neighboring Ulster. He admonished voters to go to the polls on election day. Too often over the past several years, Ulstermen living within a mile or even within a hundred yards of the polls had not voted. Ulstermen were told to examine the new Constitution; "read it with an eye of criticism, examine the powers which are given and the rights which are reserved (if there are any)." The end of American government, they were told, was political liberty. If the federal Constitution contained liberty, it should be adopted; but if liberty was not to be found, voters should "reject it." In any case, Ulstermen were advised to choose delegates to the convention who "are gentlemen of the same opinion with yourselves." Seemingly referring to Addison and Snyder, voters were told to "Avoid men of fluctuating sentiments in politics. The weathercock of party-spirit, ambition and self-interest, ought not in such a situation as this, to be trusted."[97]

A countywide committee with representatives from ten precincts met on March 28 and nominated six Antifederalist candidates. "A Dutchess

County Anti-Federalist" advised Ulstermen to lay aside their petty squabbles and support this ticket. Again tacitly condemning Addison and Snyder—neither of whom had been nominated—the "Dutchess County Anti-Federalist" charged that "He that would sacrifice the union of his party, or endanger the success of a good cause for the gratification of his personal resentment, is unworthy not only of the confidence, but even of the attention of the public." Federalists, it was said, were trying to divide Antifederalists—"their aim is to divide, and by industriously feeding the little discontents, and fomenting the divisions among the Antifederalists; they mean to lessen the number of votes necessary to carry the Election—and by uniting, bring in characters of the same sentiments in politics with themselves." To combat these Federalist machinations, Antifederalists were encouraged to act "with a spirit of union and discernment." It was "the evident aim" of Federalists to divide Antifederalists into factions; it was "the evident interest" of Antifederalists "to remain united."[98]

The admonition for unity had its effect—Antifederalists elected all six of the candidates nominated at New Paltz on March 28. Governor Clinton received the largest number of votes (1,372), closely followed by Ebenezer Clark and John Cantine with 1,356 and 1,339 votes, respectively. Dirck Wynkoop received 1,055 votes, Cornelius Schoonmaker 1,045, and the governor's brother James garnered 905 votes. Three Federalists received 68, 35, and 29 votes. Ulster County had elected its favorite son to the state convention at the head of a united Antifederalist delegation.[99]

The governor did not fare as well in New York City. From the very beginning, everyone knew that the city would support the new Constitution staunchly. Antifederalists hoped, however, that they might elect one or two of the city's nine convention delegates. With the governor heading their slate, New York City Antifederalists maintained a glimmer of hope that the people's respect and admiration for Clinton would translate into votes at the polls.

As the election approached, nearly "all the Loose Chat" centered on the Constitution.[100] Both parties nominated slates of candidates. Federalists put forth an impressive ticket headed by Confederation Secretary for Foreign Affairs John Jay, Chancellor Livingston, state Chief Justice Richard Morris, Mayor James Duane, and newly elected Congressman Alexander Hamilton. Other candidates were Judge John Sloss Hobart, lawyer Richard Harison, and merchants Nicholas Low and Isaac Roosevelt. Clinton headed the Antifederalist slate, which also included Collector of Customs John Lamb, alderman and former sheriff Marinus Willett, merchant-lawyer Melancton Smith, merchant and Assemblyman William Denning, and lawyer Aaron Burr. As election day neared, the city filled with anticipation. Samuel B. Webb, a merchant, captured the excitement in a letter to his fiance: "This week we expect much noise and bustle thro: the City, with Electioneering, and *May-Day* moveing, we shall be in complete confusion." Referring to the doctors' riots two weeks earlier, Webb hoped that there would be "no more Mobing." He had been "beat and bruised" so severely that he had been "confined to his room for four days." Webb, a strong Federalist, sensed the futility of city Antifederalists, predicting that they would garner less than twenty percent of the vote.[101] "The Governor & his party will probably meet with a great mortification, the great body of Cityzens are much displeased with his political sentiments and Conduct."[102]

Added to the ongoing public debate over the virtues and vices of the new Constitution, the personalities of the candidates became an issue. Antifederalists charged that too many of the Federalist candidates were wealthy lawyers who intended to establish an aristocratic government. Too many of these Federalist candidates already held public office in New York or at the federal level. Federalists countered by examining the Antifederalist candidates. Governor Clinton, "the Head of their Party," was "a man of *large* Property;—that he is among the *wealthiest* men of the State;—and that he has acquired almost the whole of his property in his present station." Furthermore, after "all the pother" about lawyers, Federalists reminded the public that "the Governor is himself a Lawyer. He was bred a Lawyer, and practiced as a Lawyer before the revolution called him into a different situation." Of greater importance than wealth or occupation, Federalists argued, was whether men supported or opposed the Constitution out of principle or out of self-interest. The governor and his party seemed to be motivated primarily by their fear of losing power under a new federal government.[103]

On Tuesday, April 29, the first of a maximum of five voting days, the polls opened at 10:00 A.M. By 6:00 that evening, almost 1,500 votes had been cast for the Federalist ticket.[104] On this first day of ballotting, Antifederalists circulated a new ticket folded in such a way as to appear to be the original Federalist ticket. In reality, however, the bogus ballot placed the governor's name at the head of the Federalist candidates. Alexander Hamilton, writing as "One of Yourselves," warned New Yorkers to beware of this counterfeit. During the first three days of the elections— April 29 to May 1—New Yorkers "laid aside their usual business, and paid their whole attention to the important business before them." According to Samuel Webb, "all was conducted with perfect order and regularity, it was not a *contested Election*, the friends to an Energetic Foedral Government were so unanimous, that no danger was to be apprehended." Webb reported that "a small attempt was made by the Governors expireing party, in the first day, after which we heard no more of them." Out of 3,000 votes,

Webb estimated that Antifederalists would receive only 200.[105] As the polls closed, Antifederalists visibly showed their defeat. Morgan Lewis felt that "If we may venture to infer the Issue of the Business from the Spirits of the two Parties, the Odds would be an hundred to one in favor of an Adoption by New York, for the Federalists may be distinguished by their smiling Countenances and Disappointment and Despair hangs heavy on the Brows of the Anties."[106] The governor must have felt a double loss. Not only had he been soundly trounced, but Marinus Willett, one of Clinton's closest aides, was reported to have "become a Proselyte, declaring it must be right since it appears to be the sense of a vast Majority."[107]

When the ballots were counted, Federalists in New York City had reason to celebrate. A total of 2,836 ballots had been cast. John Jay received the highest number of votes (2,735), followed by Chief Justice Morris (2,716). Hamilton, Hobart, and Livingston each received 2,713 votes; while Nicholas Low received the least support among the Federalist candidates with 2,651 ballots. Clinton, referred to as the "champion of opposition," led the Antifederalist candidates with a mere 134 votes.[108] Marinus Willett got 108 votes and William Denning 102. No other Antifederalist received more than thirty votes.

After the five days of ballotting, no one knew whether Federalists or Antifederalists had won a majority of seats in the June convention. Only in a handful of the state's thirteen counties were poll watchers able to determine which side had won. The uncertainty over the election lasted for another month, because the state election law of 1787 provided that the ballots had to be sealed in county ballot boxes for four weeks after the election had begun. Not until May 27 were county supervisors authorized to count the votes and report the results, after which they were supposed to destroy the ballots and election records. When the returns were counted, nine of the thirteen counties were solidly in the Antifederalist camp. Of the sixty-five delegates, Federalists elected only nineteen to their opponents' forty-six. This lopsided victory came about for several reasons, not the least of which was a well coordinated effort by Antifederalists led by the New York City Federal Republican Committee and its counterpart in Albany coupled with party strife among Federalists in various counties.

Several explanations have been suggested to explain the divisions over the Constitution: north vs. south, aristocrat vs. democrat, tory vs. whig, debtor vs. creditor, and states rights vs. nationalism. Although all of these elements were present in New York politics, no one conflict explains the election of convention delegates. There was, however, one overarching issue that seemed to tie all of these contests together—the personality, policies, and programs of George Clinton. To a significant extent, the campaign for convention seats revolved around the governor's leadership since the end of the Revolution. Were New Yorkers satisfied with their lot? Did they believe that their governor was doing a good job, or did they want to take power away from Clinton's administration and lodge it in the national government proposed by the new Constitution? New Yorkers overwhelmingly cast their vote of approval in favor of the governor in this referendum between Clintonian-dominated New York and the Hamiltonian concept of a national government. One New York City correspondent lamented that "The *Helmsman* leads a majority by the nose just as he pleases."[109] Another correspondent suggested that the governor "is at the head of the opposition, and it is believed that if he would say *yea*, nineteen twentieths of the anti-federalists would say so too. If it be so, the opposition in this state, though apparently formidable, is in fact involved in one man."[110] John Vaughan, a Philadelphia merchant, wrote John Dickinson that Clinton's opposition is the only formidable one," while Chancellor Livingston told the Marquis de Lafayette that "the governor headed the opposition with all the weight arising from his office."[111] Whatever direction Clinton would take, "New York follows of course."[112] A worried Alexander Hamilton, sensing the defeat of the Federalists at the polls, wrote James Madison about the gravity of the situation. Clinton's "influence and artifice were too strong to be eradicated in time to give a decisive turn to the elections." "As Clinton is truly the leader of his party, and is inflexibly obstinate, [Hamilton] count[ed] little on overcoming opposition by reason." New York Federalists' only chance rested on nine states ratifying the Constitution, thereby shaking "the firmness" of Clinton's "followers" and working a change in the sentiments of the people. Although pessimistic, Hamilton promised Madison that "We shall leave nothing undone to cultivate a favorable disposition in the citizens at large."[113]

29. The State Convention

On Saturday morning, June 14, 1788, around 11:00, Governor Clinton and several other Antifederalist delegates left New York without fanfare aboard a Poughkeepsie sloop "determined not to adopt (without previous amendments) tho all the others should." City officials had offered to send off the governor with a ceremonial salute from the Battery, but Clinton, anticipating that his farewell might be dwarfed by the Federalist delegations' ceremonial departure, would not accept the gesture. Seven hours later, Mayor Duane, Judge Hobart, and other Federalist delegates started their trek up the Hudson, cheered on by the "loud acclamations" of "a great concourse of citizens" and saluted by thirteen discharges of cannon from the Battery.[114]

On the eve of the convention, Federalists were deeply worried, while Antifederalists were confident about what would happen in Poughkeepsie. Eight of the required nine states had already ratified the Constitution. Virginia's convention had been in session for two weeks and the second session of New Hampshire's convention would convene the day after New York's convention opened. New Hampshire was expected to ratify the Constitution; Virginia's decision was uncertain. New York City merchant Richard Platt wrote pessimistically to his friend Winthrop Sargent, then serving as secretary of the Northwest Territory: "Clinton is at the head of Antifoederalists, who are upwards of 40 & the Foederalists only 19. . . . in point of Opposition & Rascallity," New York could be compared only to Rhode Island, whose legislature had refused to send delegates to the Federal Convention, had repeatedly defeated the call of a state ratifying convention, and had held a statewide referendum in which the Constitution was overwhelmingly defeated. Platt reported that it was expected that the New York convention would "adjourn to a distant period, not having spirit enough to reject" the Constitution.[115]

Alexander Hamilton expressed his concerns to Gouverneur Morris. "Violence rather than moderation is to be looked for from the opposite party. Obstinacy seems the prevailing trait in the character of its leader. The language is, that if all the other states adopt, this is to persist in refusing the constitution. It is reduced to a certainty that Clinton has in several conversations declared the UNION unnecessary." Hamilton appears to have had a spy in Clinton's inner circle, because he told Morris that his information had come "through channels which do not permit a public use to be made of it."[116]

Congressional delegate Abraham Yates, although comfortable with the Antifederalist majority, was wary about the "steps the Federals mean to take." Referring to the "Common Conversation," Yates reported that Federalists hoped, because of their superior oratorical skills, to convince Antifederalists "either to adopt or to adjourn." After so many states had ratified the Constitution, Federalists believed that their opponents "will not *dare* to Reject it which they suppose an adoption with previous amendments would in its Effect be." Yates predicted that the Federalist strategy would backfire, as Antifederalists led by the governor strongly supported the adoption of amendments before they were willing to ratify the new Constitution. In fact, Clinton and other Antifederalists leaders from throughout the state had met in New York City and prepared a list of proposed amendments. A manuscript copy of the list was given to Abraham Yates; after making "some additions," he had copies printed as a two-page broadside. The day before the convention met, Yates sent fifty copies to Poughkeepsie, ten to Albany, and he kept six with him in New York City.

Yates felt confident that Clinton and the other Antifederalists would require the adoption of these amendments as a condition before they would ratify the Constitution.[117]

Sixty-one of the sixty-five delegates attended the opening session of the convention at the Dutchess County courthouse at noon on Monday, June 17. Governor Clinton was unanimously elected president and other procedural matters were handled before adjourning. The next morning, the convention adopted rules, read the Constitution and the resolutions of the Federal Convention and the Confederation Congress submitting the Constitution to the states, and ordered these documents printed for the members. Antifederalist John Lansing of Albany then moved that the convention sit the next day as a committee of the whole to discuss the Constitution. That night, Federalists expressed their wish that Chief Justice Richard Morris be named chairman of the committee of the whole; but, the following morning, Antifederalists nominated Albany County Judge Henry Oothoudt, and Federalists, to avoid a test of strength, "acquiesced without opposition."[118]

After the Constitution and other documents were read in the committee of the whole, Chancellor Livingston delivered the first speech, an hour-long oration delivered in a voice so low that it was hard to hear amid the stirrings of the crowded courthouse. Livingston expounded on the deficiencies of the Articles of Confederation and condemned New York's inflexible policy on the federal impost. He warned the delegates of the dangers New York faced outside the Union. Surrounded by enemies—New Jersey, Connecticut, Vermont, the British in Canada, and Indians—New York could not survive as an independent state. In concluding, the chancellor moved that the Constitution be discussed by paragraphs and that no votes be taken on the Constitution or any parts of it until the whole had been discussed. Antifederalists agreed to the motion with the proviso that amendments to the Constitution could be proposed and debated at any time.

The vote on Livingston's motion was critical, because it assured Federalists that the convention would stay in session for three to four weeks. Some Antifederalists both in and out of the convention were displeased. John Lansing feared "some Injury from a long delay," while David Gelston in New York City was sorry that the convention did not adjourn "immediately after reading *the Constitution*."[119] Abraham G. Lansing felt that Antifederalists "will eventually be injured by delays, notwithstanding the decided majority," because "our Country Friends with whom it is now the Busy Season" would soon want to leave Poughkeepsie to tend to their farms.[120] Robert Yates, however, explained the Antifederalist thinking on Livingston's motion:

> Our Convention . . . yielded to a Proposal made by our Opponents to discuss the Constitution in a Committee of the whole, without putting a Question on any Part, provided that in the course of this Discussion, we should suggest the Amendments or Explications, which we deemed necessary to the exceptionable Parts—Fully relying on the Steadiness of our Friends, we see no Danger in this Mode and we came into it to prevent the Opposition from charging us with Precipitation . . . We have . . . the fullest Reliance that neither Sophistry Fear or Influence will effect any Change.[120]

Hamilton, on the other hand, wrote James Madison that the vote on Livingston's motion suggested that "a full discussion will take place, which will keep us together at least a fortnight."[122]

On June 20, John Lansing responded to the chancellor. The Confederation Congress needed only a few more powers to serve the country's needs adequately. Fears of a dissolving union did not justify the adoption of a completely new Constitution. Lansing abhorred the dismemberment of the union, but such an event was preferable to submitting "to any measures, which may involve in its consequences the loss of civil liberty." Melancton Smith echoed Lansing's sentiments, saying that "he was disposed to make every reasonable concession, and indeed to sacrifice every thing for a Union, except the liberties of his country."

Governor Clinton addressed the convention for the first time on June 21. After reiterating some of the objections already expressed about the small number of federal representatives, he concluded by stating that the United States was a vast territory and that the states were dissimilar— "Their habits, their productions, their resources, and their political and commercial regulations are as different as those of any nation on earth." Hamilton attacked the governor's inference "that no general free government can suit" the states, insinuating that this diversity-of-interest argument "has been a favorite theme with those who are disposed for a division of our empire." Hamilton agreed "that the local interests of the states are in some degree various; and that there is some difference in their habits and manners." But on broad important matters, "from New Hampshire to Georgia, the people of America are as uniform in their interests and manners, as those of any established in Europe." Furthermore, Hamilton argued that the general laws to be enacted by Congress under the Constitution would reconcile the differences among the states "till they embrace each other, and assume the same complexion." Clinton was aghast at the "unjust and unnatural colouring" given to his comments. He assured the convention "that the dissolution of the Union is, of all events, the remotest from my wishes." Hamilton, the governor argued, wished "for a consolidated—I wish for a federal republic. The object of both of us is a firm energetic government: and we may both have the good of our country in view; though we disagree as to the means of procuring it."

By the end of the first week of the convention, Federalists perceived that "a considerable Majority" of the delegates wanted amendments previous to New York's adoption of the Constitution. Federalists thought that Clinton and a few other leaders "would, if they could find Support, go further; and hazard Every thing rather than agree to any System which tended to a Consolidation of our Governments." Despite the large majority of Antifederalists, the general feeling was that "there is not the least Probability" that the convention would reject the Constitution outright, because many Antifederalists had "avowed themselves Friends to the Union." Although united in their desire for amendments, Antifederalists seemed divided over how best to obtain them. Some Antifederalists supported an adjournment "without coming to any Decision"; others supported ratification with either conditional or recommendatory amendments.[123]

On June 24 news arrived in Poughkeepsie by express rider that New Hampshire had ratified the Constitution. Although expected, no one knew how this news would affect Antifederalist unity. Clinton confidently reported to Abraham Yates that "The Antis are Firm & I hope and believe will remain so to the End."[124] DeWitt Clinton echoed his uncle: "The Republican Members are . . . united as one man."[125] Leaving Poughkeepsie on June 28, Federalist Samuel B. Webb sadly reported that the convention remained overwhelmingly Antifederalist. Despite being bested in the debates, Clinton, Robert Yates, Melancton Smith, and John Lansing led "their party & have their troops (a set of ignorant Dutchman) under perfect command." The Antifederalist leaders felt so confident that, according to Webb, "they begin to grow abusive."[126] Sarcastically, Antifederalists congratulated their opponents on New Hampshire's ratification, which would allow the adopting states to implement the new Constitution "without interfering in the politics of the State of New York."[127]

On June 27, Clinton expressed his own personal philosophy of what government was best suited for America. He reiterated his statement made a week earlier that Federalists and Antifederalists both supported the establishment of "a strong energetic federal government" based on the "principles of republicanism." While they "agreed in the terms," Clinton acknowledged that "we differed essentially in the principles."[128]

When Clinton spoke of "a strong energetic federal government," he meant a government that was "best calculated to preserve the peace and safety of the union, and at the same time to secure the *freedom and independence of the States*." When he spoke of a republican government, he meant "a *government* where *the will of the people* expressed by themselves as representatives *is the law,* and in the present compound government where part of the powers originate from the people in their moral capacity and part from the States in their political capacity." According to Clinton "the will of the component parts expressed in the general government ought to be the law, and that the security of the States and the liberties of the people might depend in having this will fully and fairly expressed in the public councils. These," Clinton explained, "are the true principles of a free representative government—if they are not, the election of representatives is mere matter of form, and the government is not a government of the people or states but of the few who exercise the powers of it—it may indeed be called a republic for the idea is vague and indefinite and may include an arbitrary aristocracy." After all, Clinton said, even the British government had been described as a free republic "by some writers."[129]

Clinton then labeled as "specious and plausible" the Federalist emphasis on the sovereignty of the people and the separation of powers among the legislative, executive, and judicial branches of the proposed government.[130] Federalists concentrated on these seemingly important matters merely to divert attention away "from the true point of inquiry, to wit, whether the powers of this government are well defined and limitted to the proper objects." He denied the Federalists' assertion that the new government had only "expressly or impliedly granted" powers. Clinton pointed to the text of the Constitution itself to show that the new federal government would have unlimited, undefined powers. The protections in the Constitution against the suspension of the writ of habeas corpus, the enactment of bills of attainder and ex post facto laws, "the creation of a nobility and a variety of other restrictions too tedious to mention," proved that Congress would not be limited to delegated powers, but that it would possess dangerous, undefined powers.

Clinton also abhorred the Constitution's concurrent powers—powers possessed simultaneously by both the states and the federal government. Such powers would "endanger the peace and harmony of the union" by creating "the political absurdity of imperium in imperio, so destructive to every idea of good government." Clinton quoted Lord Coke that "*certainty is the mother of quiet.*" In Clinton's judgment it was "unwise and dangerous . . . to suffer the fundamental *compact to rest* upon uncertain *constructions.*" Federalists suggested that in disputed cases, the states would "prevail"; but such a situation, in Clinton's judgment, threatened the very union of the states. He preferred to eliminate every doubt from the Constitution by clarifying federal-state relations in order to "avoid a dangerous and improper interference of State and general Authority." If the general government were confined to its proper objects, the states would have no reason to "combine against" it. Only if "provoked by an undue and wicked [federal] administration," would the people and the states rise to limit the "evil" of the general government. Clinton believed that, unless the new federal government was "so constructed *as to harmonize with the State Governments* and *pursue one common interest,* that the system must fail and end in *ruin.*" The best way to ensure the continuance of republican government was to have "the confidence and attachment of the members of which it is composed." If the states and the federal government had "clashing interests and interfering powers, this confidence and affection will cease and then if any government exists it must be supported by force and the coercion of the sword."[131]

On June 28, Federalists tried to embarass the governor by introducing "a series of official papers, and resolutions of this state, as evidence of the sentiments of the people" during the war. Included among these documents were excerpts from Clinton's speeches in which he called for a strengthened Congress. Discounting all theoretical "speculations and elaborate reasonings," James Duane felt confident that "this evidence will come home: that it will be felt." It would show "that our greatest misfortune originated in the want of such a government, as is now offered to us." These wartime calls for a strengthened government, Duane suggested, would "furnish more effectual arguments, than all that can be said."[132]

Although Clinton did not object to the presentation of these Revolutionary War documents, he decried the limited selection as well as Duane's taking the documents out of their proper contexts. Suffolk County Antifederalist Thomas Tredwell felt that the document-reading exercise was futile because everyone agreed that the Articles of Confederation had to be strengthened. Clinton conceded "that the representations made in them were true. . . . Our severe distresses naturally led us into an opinion, that the confederation was too weak." The governor still felt that way, and he did not now oppose "an energetic government." In fact, Clinton solemnly declared himself "a friend to a strong and efficient government," but the governor warned his fellow delegates to be careful not to "err in this extreme. We may erect a system, that will destroy the liberties of the people."

As an example of how people and politicians overreact to difficult circumstances, Clinton alluded to the attempt in 1780 (at the low point of the Revolution) to give Washington dictatorial powers—a measure the governor strongly opposed despite the wishes of a majority of New Yorkers. Often, Clinton told the convention, a distressed people will "be guilty of the most imprudent and desperate measures." Responding to the document presentation in general, the governor asked: "Because a strong government was wanted during the late war, does it follow, that we should now be obliged to accept of a dangerous one?" For years, Clinton admitted, he had "lamented the feebleness of the confederation," because "its weakness would one day drive the people into an adoption of a constitution dangerous to our liberties." Such was almost the case with the federal impost. Clinton admitted that he had "been uniformly in favour of granting an impost to Congress," but he firmly believed that the last impost proposal would have led "to the establishment of dangerous principles." He was willing to grant Congress import revenues, but he would not give Congress the power to enforce collection of those duties. Clinton told the delegates that people were "too apt to vibrate from one extreme to another." Throughout his career, Clinton said, he had struggled against "the effects of this disposition." He told Federalists that if they could convince him that the new Constitution were safe, he would drop all opposition; but, until that time, he would continue to oppose ratification.[133]

Hamilton responded to Clinton's insinuations about Federalist motives in presenting the wartime documents. The documents were not "brought forward, with a view of shewing an inconsistency in the conduct of some gentlemen," particularly the governor's conduct. Rather, Federalists hoped to show that during times of distress, the Articles of Confederation were totally "defective and rotten." Hamilton agreed with the governor that it was natural for human passions to "flow from one extreme to another." He too denounced the plan for a military dictatorship during the war and reminded delegates that such a plan had "never ripened." The young Federalist leader praised the governor for his support "for a strong federal government" and wished that all the delegates would share that goal. But why, Hamilton asked, has the governor "not given us his ideas of the nature of this government, which is the object of his wishes? Why does he not describe it? We have proposed a system, which we supposed would answer the purposes of strength and safety—The gentleman objects to it, without pointing out the grounds, on which his objections are founded, or showing us a better form." Hamilton then suggested that Antifederalists really did not want a strengthened federal government. The impost, "justly considered as the only means of supporting the union," had been rejected by Clinton and his followers even though it "did not then contemplate a fundamental change in government." Although Hamilton would have liked to believe in the integrity of Antifederalists when they professed an attachment "to a strong united government," he found "it difficult to draw this conclusion from their conduct or their reasonings." Ending his speech, Hamilton, quite out of character, apologized if he had wounded "the feelings of any one who is opposed to me."[134]

For the next few days, the committee of the whole continued its discussion of Article I of the Constitution. Then, sometime before noon

on July 2, word of Virginia's ratification reached the Poughkeepsie convention. Outwardly the news made "no impressions upon the republican
members."[135] In reality, however, Virginia's accession had a profound impact on both Federalists and Antifederalists. Federalists stopped their
delaying tactics, and, in fact, they completely stopped debating. On July 3,
Queens County Antifederalist delegate Nathaniel Lawrence reported that
previously Federalists had "disputed every inch of ground but today they
have quietly suffered us to propose our amendments without a word in
opposition to them." During the first two weeks, the convention discussed
only eight sections of Article I; in the next five days, the convention
finished its discussion of the balance of the Constitution. The extended
debate had served Federalists well. New Yorkers now had to confront the
reality that the Constitution would go into effect and New York would not
be joined by Virginia if it decided not to ratify. Federalists now hoped to
engineer an unconditional ratification with recommendatory amendments
or a recess. Federalists believed that this was possible, despite the huge
Antifederalist majority, because the news from Virginia would have a
sobering effect on their opponents. Spectator Philip Schuyler hoped that
"this event will have a proper influence on the minds of those in the
Convention here who have not resolved to shut their eyes and to steel
their hearts against all conviction." Schuyler sensed "that several of those
in Opposition who came with prejudices created by influence will not
sacrifice their Country to the Obstinacy of certain desperadoes," by whom
he specifically meant George Clinton.[136]

The convention finished its discussion of the Constitution on July 7 at
which time John Lansing proposed that a bill of rights be prefixed to the
Constitution. For the next two days the convention did not meet, as
Antifederalists caucused ostensibly to arrange their proposed amendments.
But John Jay correctly sensed that the "Party begins to divide in their
opinions."[137]

On July 10, John Lansing submitted the Antifederalists' plan. Three
kinds of amendments were proposed: explanatory, conditional, and recommendatory. The explanatory amendments included a bill of rights and
some explanations of unclear portions of the Constitution. The conditional amendments provided that, until a general convention of the states
considered these matters, Congress (1) should not call the state militia to
serve outside New York for longer than six weeks without the consent of
the state legislature, (2) should not regulate federal elections within New
York, or (3) should not collect direct taxes in New York without first
requisitioning the tax from the state legislature. The "numerous and
important" recommendatory amendments should be considered by the
first federal Congress under the Constitution. Federalists attacked the plan

as "a gilded Rejection" that Congress would never accept as a valid
ratification. The governor, joined by Melancton Smith and John Lansing,
defended the plan as "our *Ultimatum*. We go not a Step beyond it." In fact,
many Antifederalists thought the plan had gone too far already.[138]

On July 11, Clinton summarized the Antifederalist position in favor of
a confederation of states in which he emphasized the consolidating nature
of the new Constitution. Quoting Vattel's *Law of Nations*, Clinton argued
that in their sovereign capacities, states are equal no matter what their
sizes. "A dwarf is as much a man as a giant; a small republic is as much *a
sovereign* as the most powerful *kingdom*." Since, according to Clinton,
states, like people, combine together for their *"mutual protection* and the
security of their *equal rights,* . . . the idea of states confederating upon
principles of inequality and destructive of their freedom and independence
is as absurd and unreasonable as it would be to suppose that a man would
take a draught of poison to preserve his life." To ensure "the security of the
rights of the confederating states," a confederacy, in Clinton's judgment,
ought to be based on three premises. (1) Since states are their fundamental
building blocks, "the power of the confederacy *must* originate from and
operate upon *them, and not upon the individuals,* who compose them";
consequently the federal government should "be confined as far as possible
to general extraneous concerns, reserving to the States the exclusive
sovereignty and arrangement of their internal government and concerns."
(2) "*States,* having equal rights to protect, ought *to be equally represented.*"
(3) Because states compose the confederacy and because it is the will of the
states that ought to be expressed in the federal council, the states ought to
have the right to instruct and to recall their representatives to the federal
council. After a fair discussion of the proposed Constitution, it was clear
that the new federal government would violate every one of these premises; and, if adopted, it would ere long destroy the states and "terminate
in a consolidation of the United States into one general government."[139]

The demise of the state governments under the new Constitution was
assured by the broad jurisdiction given to the federal judiciary. In addition
to deciding all cases involving the other branches of government, the
federal judiciary could determine "all cases in law and equity arising under
the Constitution." Therefore, in every case in which a state would argue
for a concurrent power with the general government, the federal judiciary
would decide against the state, and these broadening decisions "will be
engrafted into the original compact." Clinton predicted a steady enlargement of federal power that in turn would extend the jurisdiction of federal
judges. It was "an old established maxim among lawyers that he is a good
judge who enlarges the sphere of the jurisdiction of his Court—a maxim,"
Clinton declared, "that has never failed to have been faithfully pursued."

The governor suggested that "it will not require an extraordinary stretch of legal ingenuity in the judges to extend their power to every conceiveable case and to collect into the sphere of their jurisdiction every judicial power which the States now possess." Using the Preamble to the Constitution, federal judges would find justification to become involved "in every dispute about the powers granted." Clinton asserted "that a good judge would not hesitate to draw this inference especially when supported by the undefined powers" in the necessary and proper clause.[140]

"The undue and extensive powers vested in the general government" would, in Clinton's judgment, so enfeeble the states, that the rights and liberties of the people would be left totally exposed. Consequently, Antifederalists felt it to be their "indispensible duty" to propose "suitable amendments calculated to abridge and limit the powers to general objects." The governor told his fellow Antifederalist delegates that "The evils pointed out in the system are now within our power to remedy—but if we suffer ourselves to be influenced by specious reasoning unsupported by example to an unconditional adoption of an imperfect government, the opportunity will be forever lost, for history does not furnish a single instance of a government once established, voluntarily yielding up its powers to secure the rights and liberties of the people."[141]

During the next two weeks Federalists and Antifederalists proposed various forms of ratification. In mid-July, Clinton made a final attempt to gain Federalist support for a conditional ratification with amendments. He had come to the convention "impressed with an idea that the" Constitution "was unsafe and dangerous to the liberties of the people." But realizing that he, "as all other men are liable to error," Clinton was willing to listen to Federalist arguments "with coolness and candor . . . and to give them their due weight"; therefore, he had avoided taking an active, partisan role in the convention "lest as is too apt to be the case, I might become prejudiced in favor of my own reasoning." Generally when he had spoken, it was to raise an objection that could be responded to by the Constitution's supporters. Clinton told the delegates that he had "listened with candor and attention to every argument that has been offered in support of the system . . . and as far as I have been capable, I have given them their due weight." Had he been convinced that "sufficient security [was] afforded for the existence of the states sovereignty," he "would have cheerfully acquiesced" and would have tried to change the opinion of his Ulster County constituents. But he had not been convinced, therefore he hoped all the delegates would agree to ratify only with conditional amendments. He felt confident that the other states would accept New York's conditional ratification. In public discussions such as the one over the ratification of the Constitution, "political expediency" is usually more important than pure theoretical judgments. He believed "that Congress may without a violation of the Constitution" accept New York's conditional ratification. Since all ten states that had already ratified the Constitution had done so in gross violation of the amendment procedure provided by the Articles of Confederation, Clinton questioned why those states "should hesitate to receive us when only justified in a refusal by refined and subtle distinctions? Would not this be indeed like swallowing a Camel and choking with a gnat?"[142] If Congress rejected New York's conditional ratification, it would be a harbinger of the arbitrariness of the new federal government.

In response to the Federalist argument that New York should ratify the Constitution because it had already had eleven "verdicts in its favor, the Convention at Philadelphia and ten other states," Clinton said that a verdict needed to be unanimous before it counted. In fact, even the strongest Federalists in New York and in other states acknowledged that the Constitution was "dangerously and radically defective." If a conditional ratification were rejected, all the delegates realized that the convention would have no other choice than to reject the Constitution outright. Would such a rejection "promote the peace and harmony of the state?" Clinton pleaded with Federalists to consider what would happen if the convention should reject the Constitution. He alluded to the scare-tactics raised by Federalists themselves—to the dangers New York would be exposed to by its aggressive neighbors—to the potential secession of the southern counties which would leave the state to join the union. Federalists, in fact, had pleaded for conciliation from Antifederalists. Clinton reminded Federalists that New Yorkers were overwhelming opposed to an unconditional ratification of the Constitution. Should the wishes of a majority of New Yorkers be ignored? Was it reasonable to presume that the majority should "yield to [the] minority without the least concessions on the part of the latter." Clinton asserted "that the danger will chiefly be in a deviation from the will of a majority."

The governor then confessed that, although he still opposed the Constitution, he was willing to adopt it with conditional amendments because of his "*strong attachment to the union—*from a spirit of *conciliation* and an *earnest desire* to promote peace and harmony among the Citizens of the states to forward the interest and happiness of whom I am bound by ties uncommonly strong." Clinton concluded by praising the proposal for conditional ratification. "It contains nothing that can give offence or that can prevent its being accepted—its object is barely to prevent the immediate operation of powers the most odious to our Constituents until they can be considered by the people of America to whose decision we declare *our willingness to submit*. There is nothing in the Proposition that can prevent the Government's going into full Operation and having full effect as to all essential National Concerns." The conditional amendments affect only a "few instances" that were of primary concern to many New Yorkers as well as people in other states.[143]

Clinton believed that the proposition to ratify with conditional amendments went "beyond the will of our Constituents." He hoped, however, "that the reasons which have influenced" Antifederalist delegates to support this compromise could be properly explained to them. It was time that Federalists compromise.

Throughout mid-July, both Federalists and Antifederalists considered adjourning without ratifying the Constitution, but some Antifederalists saw real danger in such a move. Late in June, Abraham Yates had warned Clinton and Abraham G. Lansing that Federalists hoped to adjourn the convention so that during the recess the members "will be Seperated and open to their Management" while "the State would be in Continual Convulsion."[144] Lansing agreed with Yates: "If this Measure should take place, all the Exertions we have made and the anxiety we have experienced for the Liberty of our Country will end in nothing." An adjournment would leave Antifederalists

> without any prospects of Success. The Baneful Manor Interest will be exerted to obtain Instructions to the Delegates, and the poor deluded well meaning Yeominery of our Country, not having it in their power to follow the dictates of their own Consciences, will be compelled to sign these Instructions to keep well with their Masters. Our Friends in the City, and Numbers in the County—will decline signing counter Instructions, by the Meaneauvers of the Federalists who will hold out every Circumstance they can to alarm and Intimidate.[144]

Antifederalists outside the convention encouraged their delegates to persevere to a conclusion, even if that meant ratifying the Constitution with merely recommendatory amendments.

While prospects for ratification by the convention brightened, Antifederalists outside the convention looked for a scapegoat. Melancton Smith loomed as a primary candidate. The self-proclaimed manager of the convention, Smith was "charged with some improper steps," which "if it is True, he has injured the Cause of our Country more than any Federalist."[146]

Antifederalists on July 23 moved that New York should ratify the Constitution "upon condition" that certain amendments be accepted. Samuel Jones followed with a motion that the words "upon condition" be replaced by the words "in full confidence." Melancton Smith supported the change, thoroughly convinced that New York must come into the union and that only through New York's presence in the first federal Congress could proper amendments be adopted. Conditional ratification,

Smith argued, "must now be abandoned as fallacious, for if persisted in, it would certainly prove in the event, only a dreadful deception to those who were serious for joining the Union."[147]

Although Clinton remained committed to conditional ratification, a dozen other Antifederalists, including such staunch party men as Dutchess County delegates Gilbert Livingston and Judge Zephaniah Platt, joined with Jones and Smith in reluctantly supporting ratification. Jones's motion passed 31 to 29. On July 25, the committee of the whole approved a form of ratification by a vote of 31 to 28 and unanimously resolved that a circular letter be sent to the states "pressing in the most earnest manner, the necessity of a general convention to take into their consideration the amendments to the Constitution, proposed by the several State Conventions." The following day, July 26 (the governor's forty-ninth birthday), the convention accepted the committee of the whole's report to ratify the Constitution with recommendatory amendments by a vote of 30 to 27, and then unanimously adopted a circular letter to the states calling for a second constitutional convention.

How did such a dramatic reversal occur? How did a convention dominated by a two-to-one majority of Antifederalists come to ratify the Constitution without restrictions? And what was George Clinton's role in this reversal?

Although Antifederalists came to Poughkeepsie with a large majority, they never were a united party with a single end in sight. As state after state ratified the Constitution, Antifederalists in other states became less vocal in their opposition; and the adoptions by New Hampshire and then Virginia drastically changed the perspective of New York Antifederalists. Hamilton reported, "Our arguments confound, but do not convince— Some of the leaders however appear to me to be convinced *by circumstances*."[148] The Constitution was going to go into effect despite New York's actions, and Virginia, the last great state to promise resistance, had now joined the Federalist fold. The only question left was what New York's relationship to the new federal government would be. Completely surrounded by ratifying states, New York could not hope to form a middle confederacy. By staying out of the union, New York City would lose the federal capital and the state would be deprived of much of the revenue from its impost once the federal government enacted trade barriers against an independent New York. Furthermore, civil commotions were anticipated as rumors of a secession of the southern counties loomed.[149] Finally, the difficult task of amending the Constitution seemed most obtainable with New York in the union and represented in Congress, where the state's Antifederalists could cooperate with like-minded representatives from other states. All of these factors convinced the convention's Antifederalist leadership that ratification, however distasteful, was the most palatable policy to pursue.

In all of the convention maneuverings, no delegate seemed more important than Melancton Smith. On June 28, Smith wrote his friend Nathan Dane, a Massachusetts delegate to Congress, expressing his concerns. Smith wanted "to support the party with whom I am connected as far as is consistent with propriety—But, I know, my great object is to procure such amendments in this government as to prevent its attaining the ends, for which it appears to me, and to you calculated."[150]

Dane responded to Smith on July 3. If New York failed to ratify the Constitution, Dane predicted either civil war within New York or between the ratifying and non-ratifying states. Such violence would end in "a system more despotic than the old one we lay aside, or the one we are adopting." "Our object," Dane wrote, "is to improve the plan proposed: to strengthen and secure its democratic features; to add checks and guards to it; to secure equal liberty by proper Stipulations to prevent any undue exercise of power, and to establish beyond the power of faction to alter, a genuine federal republic. To effect this great and desirable object the peace of the Country must be preserved, candor cherished, information extended and the doors of accommodation constantly kept open."[151]

Dane told Smith that Antifederalists should propose amendments in the first federal Congress. "For any state now to stand out and oppose" would be counter-productive. The failure of New York to ratify would harm "the federal republicans or men who wish to cement the union of the states on republican principles." Dane still retained his original Antifederalist attitude toward the Constitution, but he saw "no impropriety in urging" New York to ratify. "Men in all the states who wish to establish a free, equal and efficient government to the exclusion of anarchy, corruption, faction, and oppression ought in my opinion to unite in their exertions in making the best of the Constitution now established."[152]

Massachusetts Antifederalist Samuel Osgood, serving in New York City on the Confederation Board of Treasury, gave similar advice to Smith and Samuel Jones. New York Antifederalists had accomplished all of their goals; the country seemed totally committed to constitutional amendments. In fact, according to Osgood, "the Danger of not obtaining Amendments such as we would wish for, will in my Opinion be greatly enhanced by the Absence of New York."[153] Melancton Smith completely agreed with Dane and Osgood. But Smith realized that he faced a divided party: "Time and patience is necesary to bring our party to accord, which I ardently wish."[154]

Other Antifederalists went through the same soul-searching metamorphosis as Smith. Dutchess County Judge Zephaniah Platt voted for unconditional ratification "not from a conviction that the Constitution was a good one or that the Liberties of men were well Secured. No—I voted for it as a Choice of evils in our own present Situation." Platt knew that the Constitution "Must and would now go into operation. The only Chance remaining was to get a Convention as Soon as possible to take up our Amendments & those of other States while the Spirit of Liberty is yet alive." The convention, according to Platt, "Endeavoured to consider all Sides of the question & their probable consequence—on the whole [we] desided on what we Suposed was for the Intrest and peace of our State under present Circumstances."[155]

George Clinton played the key role in the New York convention. According to Federalist Abraham Bancker of Richmond County, had Clinton not opposed the Constitution so strenuously, the convention would have adopted it a month earlier. Hamilton believed that Clinton's obstinacy stemmed from his desire "to establish *Clintonism* on the basis of *Antifoederalism*."[156]

Although less active on the floor of the convention than Melancton Smith and John Lansing, Clinton played a pivotal role throughout. As president, Clinton served as a symbol both of the state of New York and as the *de facto* leader of New York Antifederalists. Every day, as he presided at the beginning and end of the sessions, his presence reminded the delegates—both Federalists and Antifederalists—of New York's role in the Confederation and of the overwhelming majority that Antifederalists had in the convention. For many delegates and for spectators in the gallery, George Clinton was an impressive figure. James Kent, a young Dutchess County lawyer destined to become state chancellor, was deeply moved by "the simplicity and unpretending good sense of Clinton." Though strongly opposed to the governor's Antifederalism, Kent "became favorably struck with the dignity with which he presided, and with his unassuming and modest pretensions as a speaker. It was impossible not to feel respect for such a man, and for a young person not to be somewhat over-awed in his presence, when it was apparent in all his actions and deportment that he possessed great decision of character and a stern inflexibility of purpose."[157]

By the end of the convention, Clinton's attitude toward the Constitution remained unchanged, but he too yielded to the reality of the circumstances. Clinton took a moderate position on Samuel Jones's July 23 amendment to change the wording of the ratification document from "upon condition" to "in full confidence." Although he refused to vote in favor of the amendment, he gave a clear signal to Antifederalists that they were released from their commitment to him. Clinton announced "that whatever his opinion might be, he stood there as a representative of the County of Ulster; that he should therefore pursue what he believed to be the sense of that County, and vote for the conditional adoption."[158] What Clinton said was that Antifederalists, no matter what they felt personally, ought to vote the will of their constituents. If their constituents now supported unconditional ratification, Antifederalist delegates ought to support Jones's amendment. With this statement, the governor virtually assured that enough Antifederalists would alter their votes so that the Constitution would be adopted with recommendatory amendments.

Historians have not recognized this subtle, but important shift. Federalists did realize the change, but refused to give the governor any credit for obtaining the state's ratification. Just the opposite. Hamilton took the position—one swallowed whole by historians—that Clinton retained an obstinate anti-federal position from the end of the Revolution through the end of the convention. Federalists later attempted to ruin Clinton's political career by painting him as an enemy of the new federal government. In reality, however, Clinton used the same political tactics that had served him so well for so long. He allowed Melancton Smith and Samuel Jones to take the outward lead. Both men resided in strongly Federalist districts and might avert political ruin by their more moderate stances, while also serving the interests of the state and the union.

Although Clinton would not coerce his fellow Antifederalists into a continued opposition, he decided for several reasons to maintain his own dissent. Clinton realized that an unconditional ratification of the Constitution would disillusion and infuriate many New York Antifederalists. They had become convinced that the Constitution was dangerous, and they had won an overwhelming majority of convention seats. To lose the struggle over the Constitution in the convention would be difficult to understand—it would certainly look as if ratifying Antifederalist delegates had betrayed their trust. But George Clinton would remain true. Only by continuing as the leader of the opposition to the end could he serve as the unifying force in reconstituting the disunited party in the spring statewide elections. He would stand for a fifth term as governor, and he would fight for amendments to the Constitution.

Clinton's stance would catapult him into the leadership of Antifederalists nationwide. Armed with the convention's circular letter calling for a second constitutional convention, he would mobilize Antifederalists throughout the country in the continuing struggle to adopt amendments to the Constitution. It would be important to have a firm, dedicated believer leading this struggle.

Finally, Clinton saw his political star rising on the national scene. As the country's most popular Antifederalist, Clinton sensed that he might make the perfect vice presidential candidate. A majority of all Americans seemed to support some amendments to the Constitution. Surely Clinton would be attractive to these people. And a Clinton candidacy might appeal to Federalists as well. Their support for him might be perceived as an olive branch extended to Antifederalists—an indication that Federalists could be trusted to consider appropriate amendments to the Constitution. Surely Washington would support the election of his old comrade in arms. Once elected, Vice President Clinton could advise Washington, support constitutional amendments as he presided over the first United States Senate, and perhaps be heir apparent when Washington decided to retire to Mount Vernon. Clinton's posture of consistent Antifederalism throughout the struggle, while freeing his forces to support unconditional ratification, placed him in a position to ask for the support of his Antifederalist constituency throughout the state and to seek the vice presidency with a hope of Federalist support.

Convention Federalists probably never approached Clinton with anything resembling a deal. There was no place in Schuyler and Hamilton's party for George Clinton. Federalist support for Clinton in the 1789 gubernatorial election would mean three more years of the yeoman governor—a thought Federalists could not bear—a situation they could not abet. Therefore, despite the Federalists' awareness that the surest way for the New York convention to adopt the Constitution would be to win over the governor, no overtures were made to him. All parties agreed that, had Clinton—for whatever reason—come to support an unconditional ratification, the New York convention would have adopted the Constitution much earlier and with near unanimity.[159] But neither Clinton nor Federalists would alter their positions. Until the end, the "Pharoah" of New York remained "unrelenting."[160]

On July 26, with Clinton presiding, the New York convention ratified the Constitution with recommendatory amendments, with a prefatory statement of what rights New Yorkers believed were reserved to the people, and with a circular letter addressed to the states calling for a second constitutional convention. Governor Clinton told the delegates that he would do everything in his power "to maintain the public peace" and to put the new "system *into operation*." Eight months later during the bitter gubernatorial election, Hamilton referred to Clinton's final convention speeches, saying that the governor "seemed carefully to confine his assurances to a mere *official compliance*." The governor would in "official transactions *conform* to the constitution, but that he should think it expedient to keep alive the spirit of opposition in the people, until the *amendments proposed*, or another convention . . . could be obtained."[161]

In his last official act as convention president, Clinton signed a letter to the president of Congress officially transmitting the convention's form of ratification. As a conciliatory gesture, the governor entrusted his letter and the form of ratification to Hamilton's care.[162] Perhaps the two strong-willed adversaries could reestablish their wartime friendship. The governor, at least, seemed willing to mend the broken friendship and perhaps the old political relationship as well. Soon Hamilton's attitude would be clear to everyone.

30. A Second General Convention

In order to ratify the Constitution, Federalists in the New York convention unanimously agreed to support a call for a second constitutional convention that would propose amendments to the new Constitution, as provided for in Article V. On July 26, the last day in its session, the New York convention adopted a circular letter to the states calling for such a general convention. Other state ratifying conventions had called for amendments to the Constitution, but none had called upon the other states for direct action in endorsing a second general convention. It was the price demanded by Antifederalists and a potentially costly gamble by Federalists.

The New York circular letter was a remarkable document. After a mature consideration of the Constitution, the letter stated, a majority of delegates found several articles "so exceptionable . . . that nothing but the fullest Confidence of obtaining a revision of them by a General Convention, and an invincible Reluctance to separating from our Sister States, could have prevailed upon a sufficient Number to ratify it, without stipulating for previous Amendments." All of New York's delegates united in the belief that amendments were necessary before a majority of New Yorkers would give their "Approbation and Support" to the new compact. The apprehensions of the American people would disappear only when the first federal Congress, upon the request of two-thirds of the states, called a constitutional convention to propose necessary amendments. Only by this action would "the Confidence and Good-Will of the great Body of the People" become attached to the new federal government.

The New York delegates denied that their call was motivated by narrow, local interests. "Motives of mutual Affection and Conciliation" guided them. How else could the convention's actions be viewed—ratifying a Constitution that two-thirds of delegates viewed as dangerous. The New York delegates asked the various state governors to lay the circular letter before their legislatures. The governors were encouraged to use their influence to promote "national Harmony and good Government" by supporting the call for a second convention.[163]

George Clinton returned to New York City a popular man. Rumors had spread throughout the southern counties as the convention met. What would happen if New York rejected the Constitution? Of course the federal capital would have to leave New York, but would the southern counties secede from the state? If so, would the rest of the state attempt to stop the secession with force? The danger was so pitched that reports spread about Federalists holding Mrs. Clinton hostage in New York City and not allowing her to join her husband in Poughkeepsie.[164] The young Frenchman Victor du Pont reported other rumors in the city that the governor would "be placed at the head of all the Antifederalists as Washington was the head of the Whigs and stir up a civil war." More likely, however, du Pont thought that militant Federalists would seize the governor and some of his friends when they returned home and "smear them with tar, roll them in feathers, and finally walk them through the streets." This "charming English custom," would have amused du Pont, because "it spills no blood, it hurts no one, and it brings men strongly to their senses."[165] Another Frenchman, St. Jean de Crevecoeur, expressed the hope of many Federalists when he suggested that the state would turn in favor of the Constitution, and then "down goes the Idol of the People, that tool of Popularity . . . our Governour I mean."[166] Samuel B. Webb predicted that the southern district would secede from the state if the convention rejected the Constitution and that Clinton's life would not be safe in New York City.[167] But when news arrived in the city that the convention had adopted the Constitution, the mood toward the governor slowly changed. Initially, for example, at midnight on July 26, an angry, Federalist-inspired mob paraded by the governor's house and played the Rogue's March and then racked the print shop of Antifederalist Thomas Greenleaf. Within days, however, Clinton was warmly received when he arrived home and all expected that he would be reelected governor the following spring.[168] A correspondent in the New York Packet, July 25, 1788, observed "that this is a favorable period for restoring harmony and union to this State. By burying the spirit of party—obliterating from the mind past animosities and adopting the proposed Constitution; we may rise like the Phoenix from her ashes, to greater glory and honor."

This euphoric reaction to New York's ratification lasted briefly. By the end of September 1788, over forty newspapers throughout the country had printed the convention's circular letter. Rather than a simple broadside circular, the New York convention sent its request in the form of a letter signed by its president, George Clinton. Soon the circular was commonly referred to as "Governor Clinton's Circular Letter." As such, the letter served two purposes. In addition to its ostensible purpose of encouraging the states to request a convention to amend the Constitution, the circular letter also thrust Clinton's name before the country as the champion of amendments. Such nationwide recognition would be valuable when the country voted for the first president and vice president.

Many Federalists throughout the country believed that their New

York counterparts had given up too much to gain their state's ratification. James Madison felt that the circular letter was "certainly a matter of as much regret, as the unanimity with which it passed is matter of surprise." The letter had "a most pestilent tendency," and Madison soon came to agree with many other Federalists "that the circumstances involved in the ratification of New York will prove more injurious than a rejection would have done." A rejection by New York would have worried well-meaning Antifederalists and raised the ire of New York's neighbors. In all likelihood, another New York convention would have hastily reconsidered and ratified the Constitution.[169]

Madison found that New York's circular letter was received everywhere, and especially in Virginia, "as the signal for united exertions in pursuit of early amendments." Governor Edmund Randolph, a fence sitter who had sided with Federalists in the Virginia ratifying convention, continued to walk the political rail as he endorsed Clinton's letter. "It will give contentment to many, who are now dissatisfied." Randolph felt that it was not too early for such a call "because it will only incorporate the theory of the people with the theory of the convention; and each of these theories is entitled to equal respect." Randolph feared that too many amendments might enervate the Constitution, "but if such be the will of America, who can withstand it?" Randolph planned to submit the circular letter to his legislature with his endorsement, but with the advice that no instructions be given to the future conventioneers who should be left "perfectly free."[170] By mid-September, Madison's fears persisted as he found "that all the mischief apprehended from Clinton's Circular Letter in Virginia will be verified. The Antifederalists lay hold of it with eagerness as the harbinger of a second convention."[171] George Washington was told that the circular "seems to be the standard, to which the various minoritys will repair, & if they succeed in bringing quickly into action the objects of that letr., new and serious difficultys must arise, which will cross & may destroy the govt. in its infancy."[172]

From its initial publication, Clinton's circular letter received stinging attacks in the Federalist press. "The *impertinent* letter" was denounced for its "*impudent*" call for a convention. Those who proposed immediate amendments secretly wanted to "annihilate the Constitution, and throw the United States not only back again into anarchy, but introduce poverty, misery, bloodshed and slavery into every state in the Union."[173] Soon Federalists, especially those in New York, concentrated their attacks on Clinton personally. If Clinton's integrity could be impugned, so too would the movement for a second constitutional convention. Why follow self-serving state politicians when the Constitution had been adopted by eleven of the thirteen states? Give the Constitution a chance, they argued.

In fact, Federalists now seized the initiative and supported amendments—but amendments that experience would dictate were necessary. Soon this argument won adherents, and only the Virginia legislature joined with New York's in calling for a second constitutional convention.

At first glance, the strategy behind the New York circular letter appears to have failed. Instead of the necessary eight states, only two states called for a general convention. Actually, however, the letter was anything but a failure. It spread the word throughout the country that there was substantial support for amendments and that if Congress did not provide them there would be pressure for a second constitutional convention. This stimulated James Madison to defuse this nationwide demand for amendments by proposing constitutional amendments in the first federal Congress. Madison eschewed the structural amendments thought so important by many Antifederalists—amendments that would have changed the very nature of the new government under the Constitution. Instead, Madison presented only amendments that protected the rights of individuals against the tyranny of government. These kinds of amendments were not opposed vehemently by Federalists, who generally felt that such rights-protecting amendments, although unnecessary, were harmless. Many Antifederalists believed that Madison was throwing "a tub to the whale"—creating a diversion. By giving Antifederalists a few amendments protecting rights, most people would forget the structural amendments that would change the fundamental relationship between the federal and state governments.[174] If the circular letter failed to achieve these amendments, it did inspire Madison to propose the Bill of Rights. In this sense, the circular letter was a glorious success, far greater than its authors understood at the time.

Finally, the Federalist assault on Clinton created suspicion in the minds of many people throughout the country. Was Clinton really this wild-eyed radical who had failed to defeat the Constitution in his state convention but now sought to destroy it surreptitiously by amendments? This raised enough doubts to jeopardize Clinton's intended run for the vice presidency.

31. An Antifederalist Vice President

George Washington was the unanimous choice of Americans to become the first president under the Constitution. In contrast to the unanimous support for Washington, no consensus existed on a candidate for vice president. Massachusetts Federalists had promised their support to Governor John Hancock in exchange for his efforts in getting his state's convention to ratify the Constitution. But Federalist support for Hancock, luke-

warm at best, evaporated when the demagogic governor persisted in advocating amendments and even made political moves aimed at capturing the
presidency through the vagaries of the electoral college. At least four other
Massachusetts Federalists were suggested for vice president: John Adams,
James Bowdoin, Henry Knox, and Nathaniel Gorham. But no one stood
out as the frontrunner. A couple of other states suggested favorite sons for
the position, but George Clinton was the logical candidate for many—and
the target for others.

The first reports of support for Clinton as vice president outside New
York came from Virginia. Federalist Edward Carrington wrote to James
Madison alerting him that Patrick Henry was "putting in agitation the
name of Clinton for Vice Presidt. which takes well with the Anti's—
indeed it is more than probable he will receive a Majority amongst the
Electors to be chosen." William Grayson, soon to be elected one of
Virginia's first two federal senators, was said to be "warm in such an
election."[175] Worried about the prospects of a New York–Virginia coalition
that might elect Clinton, Madison wrote to Alexander Hamilton about his
fears. Hamilton tried to ease the Virginian's concerns: "I cannot . . .
believe that the plan will succeed. Nor indeed do I think that Clinton
would be disposed to exchange his present appointment for that office or to
risk his popularity by holding both." Despite these assurances, Hamilton
wrote that the Antifederalists' attempt to elect Clinton as vice president
"merits attention and ought not to be neglected as chimerical or impracticable."[176]

Federalist fears about Clinton's candidacy were well founded.
Antifederalists mounted a coordinated effort in support of the governor,
while Federalists, especially Hamilton, needed to go to extraordinary
lengths to defeat Clinton. Everyone realized the importance of this election. Washington let it be known that, although he did not want to serve
as president, he would accept the position with an understanding that he
would not serve a complete term. Furthermore, the death of the president
was always possible (and in fact Washington barely escaped death early in
both of his terms). In case of retirement or death, Federalists wanted a
strong supporter of the Constitution and a vigorous opponent of amendments serving as vice president. Alternately, Antifederalists realized that
an early ascendancy to the presidency by an advocate for amendments to
the Constitution could play an important role in shaping the new form of
government and in safeguarding the country's liberties. Therefore, the vice
presidency was no trivial matter—the incumbent could determine the
future constitutional development of America.

On October 30, 1788, a group of Clinton's New York City supporters
met at Fraunces' Tavern to form the Federal Republican Committee.

Chaired by Marinus Willett, the committee consisted of Melancton Smith, Samuel Jones, John Lamb, David Gelston, Charles Tillinghast, and other advocates of constitutional amendments. In mid-November, the committee addressed a circular to sympathetic politicians in other states advocating the election as vice president of "a person who will be zealously engaged in promoting such amendments to the new Constitution as will render the Liberties of the Country secure under it." The circular indicated that the New York committee had corresponded with Virginia Antifederalists "who are united in sentiment with us" and who intend to vote for Clinton as vice president. The committee expected that all of the New York electors would vote for Clinton as well. If the recipients of the circular would join Virginia and New York, it would be "highly probable . . . that Governor Clinton will be elected." Such an election would be of monumental importance because of "the influence that the Vice President will have in the administration of the new Government." The committee did not need to persuade its correspondents about Clinton's "talents or sentiments. . . . Both are well known throughout the union." Correspondents were encouraged to "take such measures to communicate the matter to the Electors of your State as your prudence may direct."[177]

On December 13, the partisan Philadelphia *Federal Gazette* warned its readers that the Antifederalist "party have also agreed to run governor Clinton, of New-York, for vice president." Such a measure was "dishonorable to their authors, and inimical to the glory, happiness, and safety of our country." Newspaper printers throughout the country were asked to reprint this warning so "that the people at large may be apprised of this last shift of the opposers of the constitution, to destroy it in *embryo*."[178] A week later, the *Federal Gazette* continued its attack on Clinton's candidacy. "His talents are as contemptible as his principles. He possesses neither dignity nor understanding fit for that important station. After inflaming the state of New-York by false jealousies, he now calls for a new convention, to *quiet the minds of the people*." A man like John Adams, John Rutledge of South Carolina, or Connecticut Governor Samuel Huntington would make a far superior vice president.

Federalists all over the United States worried about Clinton's candidacy. James Madison wrote Thomas Jefferson that "The enemies to the Government, at the head & the most inveterate, of whom, is Mr. Henry are laying a train for the election of Governour Clinton."[179] Edward Carrington reported that Virginia Antifederalists were making "a determined push" to elect Clinton, and that Patrick Henry would "extend this measure into South Carolina & Georgia, where there will doubtless be some to favor it upon principles of Antifederalism."[180] Determined "to make the best effort within my power for counteracting so wicked a purpose," Carrington decided to run against "a Clintonian" candidate as a presidential elector.[181] Carrington also wrote to his Federalist correspondents around the country encouraging them to unite against Clinton by "concentering the Federal votes" on a single candidate. If one candidate could not be agreed upon, Federalists should "place their votes where they will be most likely to stand against Clinton."[182] Support for Clinton surfaced elsewhere. St. Jean de Crevecoeur, French consul in New York City and a fervent anti-Clintonian, reported that all of New York and backcountry Pennsylvania "will unite" for Clinton; while a correspondent in the Baltimore *Maryland Gazette* warned that Richard Henry Lee and Clinton would be supported as president and vice president by "the violent anties in the back counties of Pennsylvania."[183]

As the election of the presidential electors neared, Federalists seized upon a new tactic in their struggle to defeat Clinton. Suggestions arose throughout the country that Antifederalists supported Patrick Henry for president and Clinton for vice president. It would have been incredulous to charge that Clinton wanted to supplant Washington as president, but Patrick Henry was a different story. Federalists portrayed Henry as trying to cheat Washington out of the presidency, and Clinton was Henry's choice to serve at his side.[184] Clinton, thus, was guilty by association. Worried Federalists urged the Southern States to unite behind Adams as vice president, "otherwise governor Clinton will be the man. A *division* among the federalists in the choice of this great officer, will give the most votes to Clinton." Should different Federalists be put in nomination for the vice presidency, "CLINTON of New-York may *creep* in," but if Federalists acted "with unanimity, CLINTON'S chance of being appointed vice-president, will be as bad as PADDY HENRY'S prospect of being chosen president."[185] "A Marylander" warned his state's voters against electing even an equivocating presidential elector, "lest he should vote for Mr. *Patrick Henry* as president, and *Governor Clinton* as vice-president, and against the great and good *General Washington*, who is the only man of continental popularity enough to please all the states."[186] Three days later "A Marylander" continued his assault upon Clinton.

> *Governor Clinton*, the most powerful and inveterate anti on the continent, is wished for as vice-president by his party; he is continually enflaming his own state against the fœderal government and trying to bring about a new general convention, which would dissolve the union, as the members from the different states would come to it, shackled with local and contradictory instructions—if he should be chosen, and succeed to the presidency, in case of the death or resignation of the saviour of his country, it might be attended with the most fatal consequences— The way to prevent such a mishap, as far as in *us* lies, is to appoint no

elector of his political principles, which precaution is additionally necessary, as no one man is generally fixed on by the concurrent voice of all
America as vice-president, and yet a large majority wish the office to be
held by a staunch federalist.[187]

A correspondent in Litchfield, Connecticut, abhorred the possible election of Henry and Clinton—"From such an election, may the good Lord
deliver us."[188]

Occasionally support for Clinton appeared in newspapers. "A Real
Federalist," written by Charles Tillinghast, sketched "the *real* character of
Governor Clinton." He demonstrated "that few persons in the union have
better pretensions to the dignified office of VICE-PRESIDENT." When Clinton
first entered public life in opposition to Parliament's policies, he emerged
as "a decided supporter of the rights of the people." While a state legislator,
"he was the most active and powerful opposer of the arbitrary designs of the
[colonial] Governors." As a delegate to the Second Continental Congress,
Clinton "discharged the duties of his appointment with the abilities of an
experienced and disinterested statesman, and the zeal of a true patriot; and,
as a general, he united the talents of a soldier, with the temper and
disposition of a friend to the civil liberties of his country." While serving as
wartime governor, Clinton was "prudent and intrepid" as he "frequently
took the command of the militia to oppose the progress of the enemy." But,
most important, "to the friends of just government," Clinton continued "a
GENUINE REPUBLICAN, and a strenuous advocate of the rights of the people."
If elected, there was every reason to believe that he would "constantly
study to promote the true interests and welfare of the community."[189] "A
Friend to Good Government" refuted these accolades, suggesting that
Clinton's "military reputation, tho' older, . . . will outlive his civil." But
America was now at peace and needed a peacetime executive. John Adams
was a far better candidate. Clinton's civil tenure proved him to be
"unentitled" to the office of vice president. Throughout the ratification
debate, the governor had charged that the Constitution would give the
federal government too much power while depleting the rights of the states
and individuals. This was the "delicious poison" that Clinton offered
America. In reality, however, it was "more the effect of a blinded ambition,
than of love for the community."[190]

To combat Clinton's candidacy, Hamilton developed a multifaceted
strategy. By the end of November 1788, Hamilton decided to endorse John
Adams for vice president. Hamilton did not particularly care for Adams
and he knew that Adams was not an admirer of George Washington. But
Hamilton saw two advantages in Adams—he supported the Constitution
and preferred to delay consideration of amendments until experience
dictated them. Furthermore, if Adams were not elected vice president,

"two worse things will be likely to happen": Adams would be nominated to an important federal office for which he would be ill suited or he would become a malcontent, perhaps encouraging Antifederalists in their drive for amendments. With Adams designated as his vice presidential candidate, Hamilton wrote to Federalists throughout the country encouraging them to elect presidential electors opposed to Clinton and favorable to Adams. Hamilton realized a potential danger in this plan. Unless Clinton remained a viable candidate, Adams might accidentally receive more votes than Washington. Yet, if Hamilton softened his opposition to Clinton's candidacy, the governor might receive more electoral votes than Adams. Hamilton decided to attack the seemingly greater danger—a Clintonian vice presidency. Hamilton's anti-Clinton strategy concentrated on the governor's base of support by trying to deny Clinton the votes of New York's presidential electors.

Presidential electors, according to the Constitution, were to be chosen in a manner to be decided by each state legislature. On September 13, 1788, the Confederation Congress adopted an ordinance calling the first federal elections under the Constitution. The ordinance provided that the states elect their presidential electors on January 7, that the electors meet somewhere in their home states and cast their ballots on February 4, and that the ballots be counted in Congress when it assembled on March 4, 1789.

On October 13, 1788, Governor Clinton issued a proclamation calling the legislature into special session on December 8. Purposefully, the governor had waited exactly a month after the Confederation Congress had passed its election ordinance before summoning the legislature. By not convening until the second week in December, direct election of the electors by the people became impossible: there was not enough time for the candidates to campaign, hold the usual five-day election, and wait the necessary four weeks to open the ballots as required by the election law of 1787. Clinton did not want a popular election in which Federalists would use George Washington as a weapon by arguing that a vote for Federalist presidential electors would be a vote for the former commander-in-chief and a vote for Antifederalist electors would be a slap in Washington's face. Furthermore, many grass-roots New York Antifederalists had been disillusioned by the actions of their large majority in the state convention. Antifederalists leaders wondered whether they could control a statewide election for presidential electors or would they leave the field to Federalists to elect whomever they wanted? It was far better, Clinton thought, to keep the choice of presidential electors in the legislature where Antifederalists controlled the assembly and Federalists had only a slim majority in the senate.

On December 11 the governor addressed a joint session of the legislature in the assembly chambers. Clinton told the legislators that he had convened them so that he "might have a seasonable opportunity of laying before" them the proceedings of the state convention and Congress' election ordinance. Instead of transmitting the official documents without comment, as was his usual practice, the governor called attention to the amendments proposed by the convention. A declaration of rights, he said, had been inserted in the certificate of ratification "in order to remove doubtful constructions, and to guard against an undue and improper administration." Furthermore, the convention had ratified the Constitution "on the express confidence, that the exercise of different powers would be suspended, until it should undergo a revision by a General Convention of the States." To that end, the state convention had sent a circular letter "to our Sister States" urging them to call for a second general convention. Quoting the convention's circular letter, "that no Government, however constructed, can operate well, unless it possesses the confidence and good will of the great body of the people," Clinton expressed his belief that the legislators would "engage your best endeavors for effecting a measure so earnestly recommended by the Convention, and anxiously desired by your Constituents."[191]

On December 23, the Antifederalist assembly responded warmly to Clinton's address, acknowledging that the governor had been correct to call the legislature into special session. The assemblymen assured Clinton that they would "pursue, with an ardor and perseverance adequate to the importance of the object, every measure which will tend to induce a speedy revision of the General System of Government, by a new Convention," which was the only way to allay the apprehensions of a majority of New Yorkers.[192]

The Federalist senate appointed a three-man committee to respond to the governor's speech. Chaired by Antifederalist Abraham Yates, Jr., the committee's other two members were Federalists, John Lawrence and Philip Schuyler, who took this opportunity to tweak the governor. Schuyler was particularly pleased when, on December 24, Yates reported the committee's response to Clinton's speech. The report praised the new Constitution "as a great and most desireable blessing" that would rescue America from the chaos of the Confederation. It said that Clinton's call of the special legislative session was "fully justified," but questioned why the governor had waited so long. Had the governor acted sooner, the legislature would have called a general election so that "the suffrages of the People at large" would have chosen the state's presidential electors. The report also lukewarmly endorsed the state convention's call of a second general convention to amend the Constitution.

As soon as the draft report was read, Yates proposed a substitute that deleted any criticism of the Confederation, removing the censure on Clinton for his delay in calling the special session, and strongly endorsed as "our first business" the call of a second constitutional convention. After considerable debate, the senate rejected Yates's substitute response by a ten-to-eight vote. Antifederalist Thomas Tredwell then moved to delete the rebuke of the governor for his tardiness in calling the legislature into special session. Again the governor's forces lost, but this time by an even wider margin (twelve to six) as some Antifederalists also thought the governor disingenuous or negligent. Tredwell called for deletion of two other objectionable paragraphs, both of which the Federalists rejected.[193]

Clinton was not about to accept this critical response to his speech. Refusing to debate the merits of the Constitution or the call for amendments, Clinton believed that he had discharged his duty "by faithfully communicating the sentiments and wishes of the Convention, which, it is to be presumed, are consonant to the will of our Constituents." As to the timeliness of his proclamation, Clinton regretted that it had been "impracticable" to assemble the legislature "at so early a period as to have afforded time to have made and carried into effect the arrangements necessary for appointing electors, in the manner which it seems you would have preferred." The governor was "persuaded" that the senate would choose the method "most nearly to approach an election by the People"—election by a joint ballot of both houses of the legislature.[194] Such a method guaranteed the election of eight Antifederalist electors who would cast their ballots for Washington and Clinton.

Federalists were irate with the governor's response. Ten weeks later, in the heat of the gubernatorial election, Alexander Hamilton, writing as "H. G.," attacked Clinton's "very ungracious and exceptionable" speech that betrayed the governor's "secret hostility" to the new federal government. Clinton's "procrastination . . . wore the aspect of *slight and neglect* at least. . . . *Neglects* and *slights* calculated to lessen the opinion of the importance of a thing and bring it into discredit," Hamilton suggested, "are often the most successful weapons by which it can be attacked." By depriving the legislature the opportunity of giving the people the choice of presidential electors, "H. G." charged "that the Governor *undertook to think* for the legislature."

"H. G." criticized Clinton for his "petulant and indecent reply" to the senate's "very gentle" intimation that it had wanted an earlier session. The governor also was censured for making "himself a party on the side of the assembly, in the controversy between the two houses." Hamilton charged that Clinton's preference for a joint ballot was executive interference that only exacerbated the tension between the two houses, and made the assembly more obstinate and the senate more irritable. "This species of interference in a question between the two branches of the legislature was very unbecoming in the Chief Magistrate—and bespoke much more the intemperate partizan than the temperate arbiter of differences prejudicial to the state."[195]

Although outnumbered in the assembly, Hamilton hoped that Federalists could use their slim majority in the senate and the schism among Antifederalists caused by the split at Poughkeepsie to advantage. Two weeks before the legislature met, Hamilton told Madison "that if matters are well managed we may procure a majority for some pretty equal compromise."[196] Hamilton's strategy called for Federalists in the senate to hold out for a plan that would guarantee them at least half of the presidential electors. Four Federalist electors would neutralize Clinton's New York power base and virtually ensure the election of Adams as vice president.

When the legislature considered the method of electing senators and presidential electors the fundamental split appeared immediately: the assembly called for the election by joint ballot of the two houses; the senate would not submit to such a combined vote that guaranteed the election of Antifederalist senators and electors. The senate demanded a concurrent election in which both houses were equal. Both houses suggested derivative plans, but neither house would submit to the other. Although the debate ostensibly focussed on the constitutional issue of the relationship between the two houses, everyone realized that the legislature was involved in a simple battle of power politics. As the January 7 deadline passed, the legislature found itself hopelessly divided and immobilized. The legislators continued to seek a solution to the impasse, but found none. New York did not vote in the first presidential election.

Historians have criticized Antifederalists for their obstinacy in refusing to concede to Federalists' demands for a compromise that would give each side four presidential electors.[197] In fact, such a "compromise" would have contradicted the long-standing practice of the legislature to vote by joint ballot. In reality, there was no real prospect for compromise. Federalists did not want one. They knew that their demand for half the electoral votes was impossible. In early January 1789, Hamilton went to Albany to coordinate Federalists efforts in the senate.[198] Three weeks later, about a week before the presidential electors were scheduled to cast their ballots, Hamilton confided to a friend that Antifederalists still hoped to make an appointment, but that he "discourage[d] it with the Fœderalists."[199] Throughout the whole legislative controversy, Hamilton encouraged Federalists to hold fast. The least that Hamilton was willing to accept was a four-to-four split of presidential electors. But he preferred that no electors be appointed, because Clinton would get no votes from New York. Hamilton not only wanted to defeat Clinton's vice presidential bid, he wanted to embarrass the governor and discredit Antifederalists by depriving them of as many votes as possible. The Federalists' lack of real concern for constitutional issues became apparent in the next legislature when they controlled both houses. Instead of standing up for its constitutional right of equality, the senate agreed to a joint-ballot election of both senators and future presidential electors.

With no support from New York, Clinton's vice presidential candidacy collapsed. Nationwide, Antifederalists abandoned Clinton and voted for either a favorite son or for Adams, the obvious victor. Hamilton rightly understood that "Men are fond of going with the stream."[200] On February 4 the electors chosen in January voted unanimously for George Washington and gave thirty-four votes to John Adams. Clinton got only three votes, all from Virginia. Antifederalists' disappointment with Clinton's defeat was expressed best by Joshua Atherton of New Hampshire:

> To have rendered any Service to so distinguished a Patriot and Ornament of his Country as Governor Clinton—To have put it more in the power of his great Abilities to secure to the United States Freedom and Happiness—To have placed him as one of the principal Directors of the Scene in so interesting a period; would indeed have been rendering a Service highly honourable to myself, and of the utmost Importance to our tottering Country.[201]

32. A Fifth Term

Once the presidential electors cast their ballots, New Yorkers turned their attention to the spring gubernatorial election. Federalists had denied Clinton the vice presidency, but Antifederalism was still a potent threat and George Clinton was still a leader to be feared. David Ramsay of South Carolina felt that Antifederalists in the first federal Congress would "meet with a powerful support from govr. Clinton & his Adherents. Perhaps the government may not be strong eno' to resist their combined machinations."[202] Alexander Hamilton and Philip Schuyler needed no such fears to rouse them—they would do all in their power "to kill the governor politically."[203] In the spring gubernatorial election, they led a vicious, demagogic campaign to smear the governor. According to the Comte de Moustier, the French minister to the United States and a Federalist sympathizer, "The cause of Antifederalists has become personal to the governor and to his supporters; there is now no argument, except for the man. . . . Never before," Moustier reported, "has there been seen in the United States more activity, animosity, and hate than seen there today to return this odious officer to the multitude."[204] Antifederalist Abraham Yates, Jr., also saw the election as a plebiscite on Governor Clinton, but not on Clinton alone. As occurred three years before when the gubernatorial election was viewed as a popular referendum on Clinton's paper-money policy, so the election of 1789 would be a referendum on Antifederalism and amendments to the Constitution.[205] Because of this, the state election of 1789 had much broader implications than who would preside over New York for the next three years.

Federalists' desires to see Clinton removed from office often ignored the political realities. A report from New York City published in the Boston *Herald of Freedom*, December 22, 1788, expressed the hope that if Clinton were defeated for federal office and then for governor, he would be forced to "retire to the humble vale of obscurity—to the no small chagrin of his party and dependents." Chancellor Livingston was more realistic about the situation. Although esteem for Clinton had fallen, Livingston believed that the governor was unbeatable. Yet, he too harbored an unrealistic hope: perhaps Clinton would not seek reelection because "office with all its emoluments loses many of its charms when it is not attended with the respect & favor of the people."[206] Crevecoeur also saw the governor's popularity decreasing daily, particularly "among his Warmest Partisans." Despite their confidence in his abilities and "the righteousness of their Cause," Antifederalists throughout the state saw Clinton as "less Infallible" and the Constitution as "less obnoxious."[207] Perhaps indeed the governor was vulnerable. Massachusetts Federalist Samuel A. Otis, in New York City lobbying for a clerkship in the new federal Congress, thought otherwise. In January 1789, Otis observed that Clinton's influence "seems to encrease."[208]

For their first task, Hamilton and Schuyler had to find a serious opponent. No paucity of Federalist candidates existed. Chief Justice Richard Morris had considerable influence in New York City and was nominated formally at a public meeting in mid-February.[209] Supporters announced his nomination in the New York *Daily Advertiser*, February 12, with the sincere hope that he would receive the "Support of his fellow Citizens in every part of the State."[210] Merchant Isaac Roosevelt also had support in New York City, while Attorney General Egbert Benson boasted a broad appeal throughout the state. It was clear to many observers, however, that none of these men stood "any chance of success" against Clinton.[211]

Tired of being Clinton's lieutenant governor for twelve years, Federalist Pierre Van Cortlandt took the advice of "friends from several Counties" and publicly announced his candidacy.[212] Despite Schuyler's request that he withdraw, Van Cortlandt persisted, thinking "himself too far engaged to recede." Schuyler hated to alienate or embarrass the lieutenant governor, but he realized "that every division among the Federalists must be attended with the utmost danger."[213]

On February 11, a public meeting in New York City, organized by

Alexander Hamilton, unanimously nominated Antifederalist Supreme Court Justice Robert Yates as its candidate for governor. Although Yates had opposed Hamilton in the Constitutional Convention and had left that body early, he was an excellent choice. Yes, Yates had voted against an unamended Constitution in the Poughkeepsie convention; but since the state convention Yates had expressed his willingness to support the Constitution. He seemed to have "no personal revenge to gratify, no opponents to oppress, no partisans to provide for, nor any promises for personal purposes to be performed at the public expence." Crevecoeur characterized Yates as the only Antifederalist "who Can be listen'd to with Some patience; all the rest being Illiterate & Ignorant."[214] The "tranquility and prosperity of the State," Hamilton concluded, required "a change in the person of the chief magistrate."[215] Above all, Yates had one trait that attracted him to Federalists—he might win. Coupling the large Federalist majorities in the southern counties and in the city of Albany with Yates's Antifederalist following in the northern counties, Hamilton and Schuyler believed that they had found a coalition-building candidate who could defeat Clinton.

While Hamilton acted in New York City, Schuyler moved in Albany. A meeting of delegates from various districts of Albany, Columbia, and Montgomery counties assembled in Lansingburgh on Tuesday, February 10, and nominated Yates as governor. Two weeks later, a committee wrote to Yates telling him that he was the one candidate "in whom all parties ought to concur, from a wish to heal those unhappy divisions which have subsisted in our country." Yates's nomination "was best adapted to promote the dignity and interest of the public." The committee promised its support, and asked Yates to "signify to the public a disposition to serve with cheerfulness, should you be elected to that important station." The following day, Yates responded that if "honored with this important trust, I shall endeavor to discharge it with uprightness and fidelity."[216]

In addition to nominating Yates, the New York City meeting named Hamilton chairman of a thirteen-man committee of correspondence to enlist support for Yates in other counties. Serving with Hamilton on the committee was Aaron Burr, a close political friend of Yates.[217] On February 16, Hamilton wrote Van Cortlandt informing him that the New York City meeting had nominated him to run as lieutenant governor along with Yates. Hamilton understood Van Cortlandt's frustration, but asked him "to yield to the exigency of the case and withdraw" from the competition so that Federalists could achieve their ultimate goal—"the removal of the present governor."[218]

Two days later, Hamilton began the arduous campaign against Clinton by writing to county committees throughout the state soliciting support for Yates and Van Cortlandt.[219] In the beginning of his letter, Hamilton veiled his opposition to Clinton as he sketched the qualifications necessary for the state's executive officers. New Yorkers were advised to commit affairs of state to "disinterested, discreet and temperate rulers . . . at a period when the heats of party are to be assuaged, discordant opinions reconciled, and all the inconveniences attending changes in national government provided against." If these were not sufficient reasons to turn out Clinton, Hamilton encouraged the people to unite behind "men who will neither be seduced by interest, nor impelled by passion into designs or measures, which may justly forfeit the confidence or friendship of the other members of the great national society." Additionally, the new governor "should be free from all temptation wantonly to perplex or embarrass the national Government, whether that temptation should arise from a preference of partial confederacies, from a spirit of competition with the national rulers for personal pre-eminence, from an impatience of the restraints of national authority, from the fear of a diminution of power and emoluments, from resentment or mortification, proceeding from disappointment, or from any other cause whatsoever." "Power and opportunity," Hamilton warned, should be kept "from those, whom we have reason to believe may be predisposed to employ them in a manner, calculated to alienate the friendship and confidence of our sister States." The governor "should be a man of moderation, sincerely disposed to heal, not to widen those divisions, to promote conciliation, not dissension, to allay, not excite the fermentation of party-spirit, and to restore that cordial good will and mutual confidence which ought to subsist among a people bound to each other by all the ties that connect members of the same society."

Throughout the state, communities either endorsed candidates or elected delegates to attend countywide meetings that endorsed gubernatorial and federal and state legislative candidates. The contending parties had reports of these endorsements printed in the state's newspapers to convince the public that their candidates held the greater appeal. When one gubernatorial candidate was nominated in a county, the other candidate's supporters in that county would hold a nominating session. Sometimes only a handful of freeholders attended, sometimes most of the nominators failed to meet the state's constitutional requirements to vote for governor, and sometimes totally fictitious meetings were reported.[220] Occasionally violence threatened to break out at meetings, but nothing more than newspaper exchanges resulted. On February 24, freemen from Orange and Ulster counties assembled at Ward's Bridge, where the Constitution had been burned publicly a year earlier, and ordered that Hamilton's letters as chairman of the New York City committee of correspondence "be thrown under the table" as a sign of disdain.[221] Three weeks later freemen in Chester, Orange County, repeated the gesture against Hamilton's "scurrility."[222] On March 4, Ulster freemen in New Windsor "publicly burnt," New York City's nominating proceedings on "an elevated pole." The offending proceedings were "esteemed no better than a libel against our present Governor, and the proposing of Judge Yates for that office only a party scheme."[223]

Federalists objected to the report of "a numerous and respectable meeting of Freeholders and Farmers of Kings county" that met on February 13 at Flatbush and unanimously nominated the governor for reelection. On February 17, an inhabitant of Kings appeared in the New York *Daily Advertiser* and denigrated the meeting as "only a partial and interested one, made up chiefly" of placemen or potential appointees. The gathering had "the appearance of a stolen meeting and sent abroad with a *brazen* countenance." The next day, "A Spectator at the Meeting" asserted that the meeting was attended by the judges of the court of common pleas, the high sheriff, the county clerk and some other civil magistrates, the supervisors, all of the field officers and some of the commissioned officers of the county militia, every person that had represented Kings in the state legislature since the Revolution (except for the present members who were attending the legislature in Albany), and a number of respectable freeholders and inhabitants. Despite the Federalist charges, "A Spectator" insisted that the meeting was broadly representative of Kings.[224] The Federalist critic acknowledged the attendance of all those specified by "A Spectator," but still charged that the meeting was "partial and interested." Refining his argument, however, the Federalist critic said that he intended that his charges apply not to those attending the meeting, but only to those who called it.[225] Despite Clinton's support in Kings, a correspondent reported "that *both parties* are now uniting to honor the hon. R. Yates" for governor.[226]

The Federalist gubernatorial campaign took on an ugly, negative character. Orchestrated by Hamilton in New York City, the campaign avoided any serious examination of Yates's position. The only Federalist argument in support of Yates was that he was a cordial man who, although he had opposed the Constitution, could now unite the opposing parties. Instead of praising their candidate, Federalists doggedly attacked the governor's entire career. Hamilton, who had railed for years against demagogues, now sank to new lows in vituperation.[227] For Hamilton, the campaign became a moral—almost a religious—crusade to save the new Constitution. Anything was justified to rid the state and country of George Clinton, the most dangerous man in America.

Hamilton used two public vehicles to attack the governor. First, he wrote and published several letters as chairman of the New York City committee of correspondence. He also published a number of anonymous campaign pieces, including broadsides under the signature "One of Yourselves," and a scathing, malicious series of letters signed "H. G." The unusually vicious attacks on the governor attracted broad public notice. Federalists argued that "Never was any thing read with more avidity and with greater success—The necessity of a change is almost in every bodys mouth."[228] Antifederalists suggested that "the torrent of scurrility which has been poured out" against the governor "argues a want of every manly generous principle, and would make an inhabitant of Billingsgate blush."[229]

Hamilton's sixteen "H. G." letters appeared in the New York *Daily Advertiser* from March 11 through April 15, 1789. A derivative piece—a lengthy, five-column biographical essay, probably also written by Hamilton—appeared in the Hartford *Connecticut Courant* on March 30.[230] Many of the arguments and innuendoes in the biography appear in "H. G." letters printed both before and after March 30. This biography was probably sent to Jeremiah Wadsworth, a wealthy Hartford merchant and one of Hamilton's frequent correspondents, for publication in the *Courant* because of its circulation in upstate New York. Given Connecticut's hatred of Clinton and New York's state impost, this seemed an effective way to get Hamilton's message to the people of northern New York.

In the first five letters, "H. G." denigrated the governor's early career. Reluctantly admitting that Clinton deserved some credit for his role both before and during the war, "H. G." argued that the "cunning," "artful," and obstinate Clinton acted more out of self-interest than patriotism. Acknowledging that Clinton was "a man of courage," Hamilton downplayed the governor's military prowess by reminding readers that only once did Clinton actually see combat when he commanded the Highlands forts and, "after a feeble and unskillful defence, . . . the governor made a well-timed retreat" while the greater part of the garrison was captured.[231] After the war, "H. G." charged, Clinton's administration lost whatever merit it had achieved in fighting the British. "All that succeeds, is either negative, or mischievous." "H. G." could "not recollect a single measure of public utility since the peace, for which the state is indebted to its Chief Magistrate." Clinton, himself, sowed the seeds of partisan politics when he combined with those "restless and turbulent spirits, impatient of constraint, averse to all power or superiority, which they do not themselves enjoy." The governor "formed a plan of building up his own popularity" by siding with anti-loyalist forces in New York City and pursuing a policy of persecution—not "in the shape of mobs and riots, but of *law*." This attachment bode ill for the state because "the transition from demagogues to despots, is neither difficult nor uncommon."[232]

In his last ten letters, "H. G." concentrated on Clinton's anti-federal policies since the peace. Despite acknowledging the weaknesses of the Articles of Confederation, the governor had opposed every attempt to strengthen Congress. In fact, he had gone out of his way to treat Congress and the individual state delegates "in a contemptuous manner." Clinton opposed the appointment of the Federal Convention, "prejudged and condemned the new constitution before it was framed," opposed it "with unreasonable obstinacy" when it appeared, and continued his opposition even after the state convention ratified the new form of government.[233] How could such *regular* and *undeviating* opposition" be explained? After observing both the governor's "secret and public proceedings," "H. G." concluded that Clinton wanted to erect "a system of STATE POWER unconnected with, and in subversion of the union."[234] Therefore, "H. G." considered it as his "sacred duty" to his country to do everything in his power to unseat the traitorous governor.[235]

Other Federalists joined the attack against Clinton. The governor had violated one of the first maxims of republican government by not voluntarily giving up office and returning to the people. Antifederalists in the state convention had criticized the reeligibility of the president and had proposed an amendment providing "that no person shall be eligible to the office of president of the U.S. a *third time.*" Frequent rotation in office, it was said, "was most compatible with the safety and the genius of republican government."[236] "An Amendment Man" from Schenectady suggested that at least Clinton's backers ought to "have the appearance of consistency."[237] In his April 7 letter to the state's electors, Hamilton wrote that his committee had no objection in principle to the reeligibility of the president or the governor. Perhaps, however, it would be wise to observe a rotation in office in practice rather than embodying it in constitutions. In that way, the people would not be deprived of the services of a particular man during an emergency, but it would "be very prudent in them to make changes from time to time, when no public exigencies call for particular men, merely to guard against the danger of a too long continuance in office."[238]

The governor was also accused of filling offices with his dependents and that he abused his privilege in the council of appointment by assuming the sole power of nomination. When, at the last legislative session, it appeared as if the council would not approve his nominations, Clinton avoided the other councillors and no appointments were made.

Clinton was also charged with being parsimonious to a fault. The legislature provided the governor with a generous annual salary of £1,500 to defray the entertaining expenses necessary to maintain the dignity of the state. Governor Clinton did no entertaining. Members of Congress, foreign diplomats, and visiting dignitaries were all ignored much to the detriment of the state, but to the lucrative advantage of the governor. Clinton allegedly "accumulated a very large and opulent estate" from his office. He entered office as a man of the people, but had now distanced himself from them with his large fortune. Only when this issue became a matter of public debate did the avaricious governor ask the legislature to reduce his salary by £300.[239]

Of paramount importance, argued his critics, Clinton should be defeated because he had abandoned the rightful role of the governor. No longer was he the even-handed executive attending to the interest of the state. He had used his office to gain "a dangerous influence and attachment." He had "devoted himself to a party, and not to the whole, and has carried that spirit into his administration in such a manner as greatly to discolour and dishonor it."[240] Like overturning a boat by putting too much weight on one side, Clinton had upset the balance of government. "Instead of acting as the common father of his constituents," he joined a party and meant "to overturn the government and liberties of the people."[241] "An Independent Elector," charging that Clinton himself was "the leader of a powerful party, which takes its tone from him," demanded that this partisanship must be stopped. "Every good man must be willing to use every exertion in his power to destroy the fatal seeds of discord by destroying the plant which produces them."[242] The voters were asked to support Judge Yates—"a man of popular and amiable manners—without property—of the same decided sentiments with the present governor as to the new constitution, but withal a man of impartiality and moderation."[243] Only with the defeat of Clinton, argued the critics, would confidence be restored in government.[244] Federalists did not attack Clinton's ideology, which was virtually identical to Yates's, but his virulent partisanship which they portrayed as extreme and dangerous.

Antifederalists felt confident that Clinton could weather the scurrilous Federalist storm. Victory over such slanderous attacks would only add luster to Clinton "both as chief magistrate and citizen."[245] According to an Albany correspondent, Governor Clinton was "one of the best public characters on the continent." Federalists used "every artifice, scheme and project" to turn the people away from him "because he is still a whig, a republican, a friend to the liberties of the common people, and a professed enemy to aristocracy, which he and all writers upon the subject justly declare to be the most oppressive kind of government upon earth." Federalists opposed Clinton because he supported amendments to the new Constitution. It would be dangerous "to dismiss from the helm a pilot of experience, skill, courage and integrity, at a time when the political horizon lowers so heavily." New Yorkers were warned not to make any important change in their state government at a time when the cold water thrown on the proposed amendments by Federalists "will prove like oil to the fire of discontent already kindled throughout this continent by the very defective and dangerous" new Constitution.[246]

The governor was attacked not because he had formed "great connections, but large ones." Clinton's supporters readily admitted that he had connections "with the great body, not with the great folks of the community." He had earned the attachment of the people by consulting "the honor, interest and dignity of the state."[247] The proud and aristocratic families of New York opposed Clinton out of ambition, envy, revenge and resentment—not out of patriotism. Their pride was hurt because "an obscure *Plebeian*" had been delivered instead of born, was descended from forgotten, not ancient ancestors. If New Yorkers wanted "to avoid the evils of *family despotism*," they should vote for the "man without the influence of connections; without a train of obsequious tenants." The people's ranks ought not to be divided if yeomen wanted "a firm barrier against the boundless ambition of *Patrician* families." If Clinton were defeated, all state offices, honors, and emoluments would be monopolized by "uncles, cousins, and nephews . . . they would be on the body politic like warts on the natural body."[248]

The governor's supporters defended his parsimony as a republican virtue of frugality. There was no proof that he had amassed a fortune of £30,000. But if the governor had attained a financial independence, he had come by his fortune honestly. "The *magistrate* stands *unimpeached*, and the *man unstained*." Clinton's supporters suggested that his haughty and aristocratic opponents, on the other hand, had come by their wealth— huge fortunes far, far greater than the governor's—"by flagitious strokes of *embezzlement* and *peculation*." And as for the charges against the governor for his refusal to entertain governmental officials, Clintonian supporters asked the frugal farmers of New York if they would support a tax on their land "to support the pantry of the chief magistrate?"[249]

Clinton's long tenure in office was defended with homely analogies understandable to New Yorkers. Would a farmer fire an effective overseer after three years of honest service? Should an able and experienced pilot be dismissed from his post at a time when dangerous storms threatened? The framers of the state constitution, it was argued, believed that the governor should be eligible for reelection and should be reelected if the people were satisfied with his performance. Clinton's long tenure was also defended by using arguments put forth a year earlier by "Publius" in defending the reeligibility of the president of the United States. "Publius'" defense of the president's exclusive power to nominate officeholders was also used to justify Clinton's exercise of that authority in the council of appointment. Hamilton's "*professional versatility*" as a politician, it was suggested, gave him the "ability to advocate any side of a question, and make 'the worse appear the better cause.'"[250]

Clinton's friends charged that Federalists despised the governor because he had steadily opposed those parts of the new Constitution "which he esteemed to be destructive of the rights and sovereignty of the state government (which it was peculiarly his duty as chief magistrate to support) and of the rights and liberties of the people, to which he has ever shewn himself an invariable friend." But, now with the new federal government about to commence, Clinton and his supporters gave assurances to the people that they would not continue their opposition to the Constitution or "throw obstructions in the way of its fair and free operations." They would, however, continue to pursue "all proper measures for obtaining the necessary alterations and amendments with an ardor and perseverance not to be diverted."[251] His advocates extolled Clinton's ideology—his posture as a friend to the people—and vigorously denied the charge of excessive partisanship.

Clinton's supporters characterized Robert Yates as a pawn, a wretched tool of faction and the cat's paw of a few designing men who hoped that Yates would draw moderate Antifederalists away from the governor. "A Freeholder of the Southern District" pitied Yates, whose "silly ambitions . . . led him into the snares of his enemies." He was "the mere *puppet* of the *shew,* moved by *interested, characters,* who will enjoy all the profits of this *political farce,* but must despise and ridicule the *dupe* of the *plot.*" Antifederalists portrayed Yates as a traitor possessed of no "political *integrity . . . a deserter,*" a political Benedict Arnold, a Judas. If, by chance, Yates should defeat Clinton, Federalists would cast him off at the next elections so that the "F——r and the S-n, and others" will divide the fishes and loaves.[252]

As the election neared "both parties appear[ed] sanguine as to their success."[253] An Antifederalist correspondent wrote to a friend in Philadelphia that "We have squabbles without end; but the grand one is for the choice of governor—and all opposition to Governor Clinton's re-election is now folly and idleness, for he will be again chosen in spite of all his noisy and clamourous opposers."[254] Long Island Antifederalist David Gelston predicted that Clinton would be reelected by 1,500 votes, but the Albany Republican Committee was less confident as it encouraged Clinton's supporters to turnout the vote.

> Our opponents are very industrious in all parts of the County—and we do all we can to counteract their Measures and advance the Reelection of Governor Clinton—Dont be assured gentlemen—pray exert yourselves and let *every man* who has a legal Vote come to the Poll—and keep open your Polls in every Town until every republican Vote has been given—our Cause depends on Exertions—The Accounts we have from Montgomery & Washington [counties] are favorable—but we must not let our Prospects of Success relax our Labor & Perseverance until the Business is accomplished.[255]

Federalist Kiliaen Van Rensselaer was optimistic in Columbia County. "A Change in Administration is the cry in Claverack and its neighborhood— Col. H. has taken a very active part in favour of Judge Yates from which circumstance much is expected—I believe old Clinton the *sinner* will get *ousted.*"[256] Margaret Beekman Livingston, the chancellor's mother, was not as confident. She was disappointed that the chancellor planned to sit out this election on the sideline, especially since "your not being here may give C____ the Majority."[257] A correspondent in the *Goshen Repository*, April 28, thought it peremptory for any person to predict who would be elected governor. He was happy that the election finally had come. It was needless to waste any more time, ink, or paper on the debate, "for too much has been already spent." No matter what the result, he hoped "to see peace and unanimity reign throughout the state."

As the campaign came to a close, Federalists benefitted from the beginning of the new federal government. Congress, scheduled to meet in New York City on March 4, straggled into the city, and the two houses formed quorums during the first week in April. The electoral votes were counted and Washington and Adams were announced winners. After a triumphal week-long procession from Mount Vernon, Washington arrived in New York on April 23, and his inauguration took place a week later. The ceremony took place while the polls for the state elections were open. Federalists wrapped themselves in the glories of the Constitution, the new federal government, and the image of Washington as the father of his country. A vote for Clinton would endanger this new beginning; a vote for Clinton would guarantee the departure of the federal capital.

Clinton also took advantage of Washington's arrival. The two old friends had not seen each other since the commander-in-chief's departure from New York City in November 1783. They both looked forward to reminiscencing with each other about the Revolution and discussing their mutual land investment. As Washington stepped off the specially-built presidential barge that carried him from New Jersey to New York, Governor Clinton was the first to welcome him to the federal capital. To the chagrin of Hamilton and other Federalists, the president elect spent his first evening in New York dining with the governor. Throughout the next week as the election approached, Washington went out of his way to be seen with the governor. It could well be interpreted as an informal, but tacit endorsement.

The election started on April 28, a clear sunny day on which the temperature warmed to only fifty degrees.[258] Because the newspaper "war" had been filled with "rage and animosity," New York City Mayor James Duane "predicted a warm and heated Election" in which some rioting might occur. His fears, however, proved "groundless" as an "unusual good humour was displayed at every Poll," "as if no man had interested himself in the Contest."[259] The election was close enough so that no one could predict who had won before the canvassers reported on June 4. Two weeks before that report, Philip Schuyler wrote to his son-in-law, anticipating victory for Yates if Federalists had taken the southern district by 300 votes—perhaps even if they managed to break even. Rumors also spread that some polls had been incorrectly taken in Westchester and Orange counties thereby invalidating many of the ballots. Federalists took this as a favorable sign because Clinton was expected to win Orange County by a larger number of votes than Yates was expected to win in Westchester.[260]

When the canvassers reported the outcome of the election in New York City on June 4, Federalists had carried the assembly, capturing almost two-thirds of the sixty-five seats. They also retained control of the senate by a majority of two.[261] But by a margin of only 429 votes (6,391 to 5,962) Clinton had won reelection.[262] Yates amassed substantial majorities in the City and County of New York and in Albany County, but the governor won Queens, Orange, Washington, Clinton, and Ulster counties by large margins. Almost 1,000 votes were invalidated in Westchester and Orange counties because the ballots had been taken separately for governor, lieutenant governor, and state senator. The missing votes, however, did not affect the outcome.[263]

Federalists were amazed at their landslide victory in the assembly. But Clinton had managed to eke out a victory. Shortly after the election results were announced, Virginia Senator William Grayson reported on the campaign:

> There has been a most severe attack upon Governor Clinton: He has been slandered and abused in all the public newspapers for these five months by men of the first weight and abilities in the state. Almost all the gentlemen, as well as all the merchants & mechanics, combined together to turn him out of his office: he has had nothing to depend on but his own integrity & the integrity of an honest yeomanry, who supported him agt all his enemies. . . . As this gentleman is the great palladium of republicanism in this state, you may guess at the situation of anti-ism here, as he did not carry the election by more than 5 or 600.[264]

Despite the Federalist victory in the legislature, Hamilton felt cheated because he had lost what he most wanted. In the personal battle between the governor and Hamilton, Clinton had prevailed. On June 5, the governor and his supporters celebrated at Fraunces' Tavern. Thirteen toasts were drunk and saluted individually by cannon. The first three toasts honored the United States, the new president, and the federal government—"may energy and liberty ever be its distinguishing features." Other toasts honored American women and the heroes who had "gallantly fought and died in defence of American liberty." The kings of France, Spain, Prussia, and Sweden, and the government of The Netherlands were honored, as were "the republican interest and independent electors of this State." The final toast saluted "the State of New-York," which was safe for another three years under the direction of Governor George Clinton.[265]

Courtesy of the Temporary State Commission on the Restoration of the Capitol, Albany, New York.

V

A State Republican Leader

33. Rebuilding a Majority

The year following the Antifederalists' landslide victory in the elections to the state ratifying convention had not been a good one for George Clinton. He had sensed a growing rift between his party and the people. Clinton's leadership over the party had weakened. Despite an overwhelming majority in the state ratifying convention, Clinton had been unable to block an unconditional ratification of the new federal Constitution. With a large majority in the 1788 assembly, the Clintonians failed to elect even one U.S. senator and could not appoint presidential electors who would have given Clinton a chance to be elected vice president. The spring elections in 1789 were nearly calamitous: Federalists kept their slim majority in the state senate, gained a two-thirds majority in the assembly, elected half of the state's six representatives to Congress, and almost defeated the governor himself. Only the personal popularity of Clinton prevented his defeat. It had been a disastrous turnabout for Clinton, who three years earlier had controlled both houses of the legislature and had been reelected without opposition. In 1790, Federalists swept to even more impressive victories in the congressional elections. The governor realized that the momentum at both the state and national levels had shifted dramatically in favor of Hamilton's Federalists; the governor determined to form a new coalition that would reverse the recent losses and could propel him into a successful bid for the vice presidency in 1792.

Clinton's effort to reconstitute a winning coalition began before the end of the spring 1789 elections. The governor showed proper deference to the new federal government by honoring President Washington and by taking an oath to support the federal Constitution.[1] George Washington also assisted his old friend. When the president-elect arrived in New York

City for his inauguration, he chose to spend his first evening in town with the governor. Clinton appeared regularly with Washington on ceremonial occasions and the two men often visited with each other. Washington even invited Clinton to join him on a trip to Providence and Newport in August 1790 to celebrate Rhode Island's ratification of the Constitution. The governor's moderate actions and the president's friendship assisted Clinton in shedding his image of the uncompromising Antifederalist. In Baltimore, George Lux wrote that "I am also happy to learn, that Governour Clinton has abandoned his virulent opposition to the New Government, & become moderate & dispassionate."[2]

After the results of the 1789 elections were announced, Clinton immediately called a special session of the legislature to appoint U.S. senators. Knowing that Federalists controlled both houses and that they could appoint whomever they wanted, Clinton attempted to entice Federalist Rufus King into his camp by offering the newly elected assemblyman his support for the federal senate. King listened politely to Clinton's overtures, accepted his support, but gave no assurances that he would abandon Hamilton.[3] The governor also courted Robert R. Livingston, who, instead of backing Yates as was expected, had remained strangely aloof during the recent gubernatorial election.[4] When, on the advice of Hamilton, President Washington overlooked the Livingstons in making federal appointments, the chancellor responded receptively to Clinton's overtures.

Clinton effectively used his patronage to rebuild his coaltion. Working within the accepted limits of partisanship, the governor moved Hamiltonian officeholders from one position to another and filled vacancies with either wavering supporters or potential allies. To replace Attorney General Egbert Benson, who was elected to the U.S. House of Representatives, Clinton nominated state recorder Richard Varick, a prominent Federalist. The recorder's position was given to Clintonian faithful Samuel Jones, who was being wooed by Hamilton and would soon join the Federalists. When Federalist New York City Mayor James Duane was appointed a U.S. district judge, Clinton nominated Varick for the vacancy, and extended an open hand to Aaron Burr by offering him the position of state attorney general, which Varick had vacated. Although Clinton, like Hamilton, distrusted Burr, and although Burr had supported Yates in the spring elections, Clinton wanted to add Burr's growing following to the new Republican coalition—a coalition now based as much on national as on state issues. When Burr was elected U.S. senator in 1791, Clinton filled the attorney general vacancy with Morgan Lewis, the chancellor's brother-in-law. When Chief Justice Richard Morris resigned in 1790, Clinton replaced him with Associate Justice Robert Yates, thus healing the wound that had seriously injured Antifederalists the year before. The governor successfully fought to fill Yates's vacancy with party stalwart John Lansing. Lansing's position of mayor of Albany was given to Abraham Yates, Jr., the 66-year-old Antifederalist curmudgeon who in 1790 had decided wisely not to seek another term in the state senate. The governor also attempted to work with U.S. Secretary of State Thomas Jefferson and Virginia Senator James Monroe in publicly criticizing Hamilton's new economic program for the country and in vocally supporting the French revolutionaries and the numerous republican societies that began springing up throughout the state. To assist him in his political rejuvenation, the governor appointed his nephew DeWitt Clinton as his personal secretary. The young Clinton steadily grew in stature and increasingly became more influential with his uncle.

Clinton tried to avoid any action that might cost him votes. When in 1790 abolitionists pressed for the gradual emancipation of slave children, the governor and his party's newspapers took a decidedly neutral stance. In the mid-1780s, Clinton had encouraged limited measures that responded to the revolutionary rhetoric of liberty and equality, and he even served as vice president of the state's abolitionist society for one year. The Clintonian-dominated legislature had prohibited the slave trade and eased restrictions on manumissions, while, however, also strengthening the slave codes. But neither Clinton nor other Antifederalist leaders wanted to threaten or alienate the nearly 8,500 New York families (many of them in Ulster County) that owned 21,000 slaves. Consequently, Cornelius Schoonmaker, the Ulster County Clintonian lieutenant, led the successful opposition to the gradual emancipation bill in January 1790.[5]

By January 1791, Clinton was ready to put his new coalition into action. The target would be U.S. Senator Philip Schuyler, who had drawn a two-year term in the senatorial lottery that staggered the terms of the first federal senators into two, four, and six-year terms. Schuyler expected to be reelected by the Federalist-controlled New York legislature. But a hushed dissatisfaction with Schuyler permeated the legislature. Livingston expressed concern for the state's honor as Schuyler, Hamilton's son-in-law, was being too strongly "led by the Treasury." Furthermore, many state legislators objected to the secret sessions of the U.S. senate, which smacked of "high-toned" Federalism. Lastly, contrary to a law passed the preceding year prohibiting dual officeholding, Schuyler refused to resign his state senate seat and he continued to sit on the council of appointment, where he regularly voted against Clinton's nominations. Federalist James Kent believed that, despite these arguments against Schuyler, the issue "will be in some measure a question of northern & southern Interests."[6]

Clinton and Livingston agreed that Aaron Burr would be the best compromise candidate to strike against Schuyler. To achieve their goal, all the Clintonians would have to remain united, a handful of Federalists would have to be enlisted, and other Federalists would have to agree to absent themselves from the proceedings. For several months preceding the session and into the first weeks of the meeting, Livingston, Clinton, Burr, and their followers delicately managed the secret campaign. Later Robert Troup told Hamilton of the incredible "twistings, combinations and ma-neuvers." With a new council of appointment available, the governor could offer political appointments to those who joined in opposing Schuyler. Using such a potent weapon deftly, "many who were Federalists were sucked into his Excellency's vortex, [and] the Chancellor's family became one of the principal satellites of this noxious planet."[7]

In the assembly, Schuyler was defeated by a vote of 32 to 27, after which Burr was elected. The senate then voted to elect Burr by a vote of fourteen to four, with six Federalist senators absent. Clinton was ecstatic, reporting to James Monroe that "the removal of one of our Senators affords some Evidence of a declension of Influence of a certain faction."[8] The governor had struck back successfully at Hamilton and Schuyler; the chancellor also got his revenge; while Burr's ambition had just been given a major boost.

From Philadelphia, Morgan Lewis wrote to his brother-in-law, asking about Schuyler's ouster. He told Livingston that there was a "Report of a Coalition between you and the Governor." Lewis confessed that "the Thing was both unwished for, and unexpected by me. Unwished, because I am persuaded nothing beneficial either to the public or yourself will result from the Change; unexpected, because the very last Time I heard you speak on the Subject you declared for Schuyler." Admitting that he was "a Novice in politics," Lewis felt that Livingston's actions were dictated, not "by sound Policy," but by "Resentment." Yes, Lewis admitted, Hamilton and the Federalists had snubbed the Livingstons, because of the chancellor's opposition to the secretary of the treasury's proposed program. But once Hamilton's plan was enacted, Lewis had "Reason to believe" that all such opposition to the Livingstons would end. Lewis hoped that "the Change" in New York politics "may turn out to Advantage, tho' I have not the least Expectation it will." He warned his brother-in-law to beware of Burr: "If you have the same Opinion of Mr. Burr that many have, you will not rely much on his friendship. . . . 'tis a pretty prevalent Idea, that he is a Man who makes every Thing subservient to his private Views."[9]

Three days later, Livingston responded to Lewis. "What you say is reported of a coalition between me & the Govr. is so far true as it related to a union of interest in opposing Schuyler's election & confounded if carried beyond that object. I feel myself too independent to draw with any party farther than I think the public Interest may require." Livingston expressed regret that Lewis opposed the coalition "as inconsistent with the public good & my present interest. The first I should consider a matter of moment; the latter as of very little consequence." The chancellor suggested that he had "no expectation from favor at court" and that he was "totally indifferent about it." He, however, was upset about the "pains . . . taken to prejudice me in the president's opinion by men whom I have never injured & who professed a friendship for me." In a wonderfully illuminating paragraph, crossed out in his draft, Livingston laid bare his motives. The chancellor thoroughly objected to the opposition to an appointment of Edward Livingston "merely because he was my brother. It will not be thought strange then that I too shd. be able to distinguish between my political enemies & my private friends—Schuyler's conduct has been equally unequivocal. Without feeling any personal resentment to either it was certainly proper, 1st to lessen the power of my *political enemies* to injure my friends & second to convince them that I know how to make an adequate return in kind for political injuries, tho' offered by private friends."[10]

As far as Burr's character, Livingston told Lewis, "I make no comparisons between Burr & Genl. Schuyler. They are both men of understanding." According to the chancellor, however, the state would gain by Schuyler's removal because "in the public estimation, [he] leads the delegation & is supposed to be led by the treasury. This Idea is not very honourable to the state and they begin to think that it has not been very promotive of their Interest."[11]

Federalists in New York were stunned by "the fruit of the Chancellor's coalition with the Governor." This "coalition of interests from different principles" brought fear to the Hamiltonians.[12] Hamilton was warned about the "drooping party," the "broken party," and the "utter destruction."[13] Schuyler expressed less anxiety, preferring instead to focus on revenge. He told his son that "the day will come when I shall be able to retaliate on Mr. Clinton and his tools."[14] The land scandal of 1791 soon gave Schuyler his opportunity.

Land was one of the most important measures of power in colonial and revolutionary New York. Colonial governors had granted huge tracts to a handful of aristocrats. Landlords leased their property to tenants who stayed attached to the land generation after generation. The policy of confiscating loyalist property during and after the Revolution emphasized two goals: a source of revenue and the wider distribution of land to a growing yeomanry. These policies were institutionalized in 1784 when the legislature established a land office commission, consisting of the governor, lieutenant governor, speaker of the assembly, secretary of state, attor-

ney general, treasurer, and auditor. The heavy burden on the commission
forced the legislature to authorize any three commissioners excluding the
governor to make grants. During the late 1780s, however, land sales slowed
to a trickle, amounting to only $3,000 in 1789. To counteract this stagna-
tion, the legislature in March 1791 authorized the land commissioners to
"sell and dispose of any of the waste and unappropriated lands in this state
in such parcels on such terms and in such manner as they shall judge most
conducive to the interests of the state."[15]

The commissioners took the legislature at its word and embarked on
the most ambitious land-grant binge in New York's history. Between May
and September 1791, the commission sifted through 201 applications,
eventually approving thirty-five grants transferring 5,542,170 acres for
$1,030,433, most of which was payable in installments. A handful of small
grants totalling less than ten percent of the acreage went to personal
friends of the governor—2,000 acres to Melancton Smith, 6,000 to Marinus
Willett (with Smith), 1,000 to James Clinton, and 3,000 to John McKesson.
Some party faithful and a few new recruits received grants between 25,000
and 80,000 acres. Some of the Federalist senators who had absented
themselves from the state legislature when Burr was elected to the U.S.
senate were rewarded with handsome grants, the largest to Nicholas
Roosevelt (shared with John Roosevelt) amounting to 500,000 acres.
Understandably, many Federalist applicants were rejected, but the largest
grants also went to Federalist speculators, including a 3,635,200 acre grant
to Alexander McComb (in combination with Federalists William Constable and Daniel McCormick) for eight cents an acre with no money
down. One-sixth of the payment was due in a year and the balance in five
annual installments.

By April 1792 Federalists led by Philip Schuyler seized upon the land
grants as the primary issue in the gubernatorial election. They charged
Clinton with making lavish grants to his political cronies. Privately,
however, Schuyler and other Federalist leaders worried that Clinton's
public generosity might win him friends among prominent Federalist
speculators. Moreover, Clinton's land policies seemed to be accomplishing
his two primary aims. The state's income from land sales skyrocketed to
$256,000 in 1791 and to $559,500 the following year. With this kind of
revenue, the governor could pursue his popular public works plan of roads
and canals without having to levy land taxes. Such a policy spelled
political defeat for Federalists; consequently, they emphasized the governor's
part in the seemingly corrupt land sales. No proof, however, ever surfaced
that Clinton expected or received any personal gain from the land grants.
After the 1792 gubernatorial elections, Clinton released affidavits he had
solicited from Macomb and his two associates stating that the governor

had no financial interest in their grant. Macomb even went further in discrediting Clinton's opponents by divulging that Schuyler, Hamilton, Henry Knox, and other Federalists had been his secret partners in the huge one thousand square-mile Ten Towns purchase in 1787. During the contest between Clinton and Burr for the vice presidential nomination in 1792, Hamilton privately vindicated the governor by describing him as a man of "probity" though "of narrow and perverse politics."[16] Later, in November 1793, a jury vindicated Clinton when it decided in his favor in a $50,000 libel suit brought by the governor against Judge William Cooper. The jury, after deliberating an hour and a half, awarded Clinton damages of $1,000.[17]

34. Reacting to Hamilton's Plan

George Clinton's fifth term as governor coincided with the first federal Congress' implementation of the new Constitution. Although Congress met in New York City, Governor Clinton made few public statements on the measures under its consideration. Believing "it improper to do more," Clinton "touched lightly on our National Affairs."[18]

Perhaps the most controversial legislation considered by the first Congress was the secretary of the treasury's economic plan for the country. Hamilton's plan had both an economic and a political side to it. Economically, Clintonians understood and were sympathetic with most of Hamilton's program, especially where it benefited New York. Politically, however, Clintonians publicly condemned the waves of speculation that preceded and followed the enactment of the plan as well as the consolidation of government implicit in the proposals. Privately, Clintonians disliked the fact that the people who profited the most from the economic plan were their political opponents. But, to a great extent, Hamilton's economic proposals were mirror images of Clintonian economics.

Clinton's economic program rested on a foundation of revenue derived from a state tariff and land sales, both payable in state and federal securities as well as specie. Clinton was committed to paying the state debt and assuming part of the federal debt held by New Yorkers through a system of interest-bearing state securities; providing credit to farmers and others through a state land bank funded with paper money; granting bounties to selected manufactures and agricultural commodities; and tying the state together with a broad system of internal improvements. Hamilton's plan had similar components. Clinton's programs were implemented in a partisan fashion, benefiting mostly the governor's political supporters, with as little benefit as possible accruing to opponents. An important objective of Clinton's plan was to attach the interests of federal and state creditors to New York. Hamilton hoped to transfer the allegiance of these creditors to the federal government. In a sense, the governor must have felt justified seeing familiar economic proposals emanate from the secretary of the treasury—proposals that Hamilton and his party had opposed at the state level half a decade earlier.

The Constitution provided that the new federal government was still liable for all debts contracted by the United States before the adoption of the new Constitution. The domestic federal debt amounted to about $32 million, which Hamilton proposed to fund with interest-bearing federal securities. Empowered to levy a federal tariff, excise taxes, and other direct taxes, and endowed with a huge federal domain, the central government had enough revenue to support the credit of its new "paper money." In principle, Clintonians generally supported this federal plan to finance the country's debt, which really replicated the state funding plan of 1786. Economically, the state benefited from funding. New York was the single largest benficiary of the federal funding program. Throughout the Confederation years, New York had accepted federal securities for purchases of land and for payments of the state impost. Through these payments, New York accumulated about $2.9 million worth of federal debt, which when funded netted the state over $70,000 annually in interest payments.

Politically, Clintonians had mixed emotions. Individual New Yorkers owned about $2.65 million worth of federal securities. New York City was known as the center of speculation in both federal and state securities. Clintonians roundly condemned this kind of speculation, which their political opponents dominated. George Clinton worried that "the Aristocratic Faction among us supported by a host of Stock Jobbers [. . .] amassed great Wealth & consequently power."[19] Clintonians believed that speculation in government securities reduced the amount of money available for more traditional investments and loans to farmers, merchants, and manufacturers. Robert R. Livingston complained to his sister that "The only evill here is that money continues as scarce as ever & that no property or credit can raise a shilling. This is principally owing to the rise of our funds & the spirit of stock Jobing which has invaded all ranks of people."[20]

Federalists in New York were the primary beneficiaries of Hamilton's funding system. A mere 250 New Yorkers owned almost $2.5 million of federal securities. Philip Schuyler received $67,000 in funded securities; William Constable much more. Other Federalists including such federal officeholders as James Duane, Gouverneur Morris, William Duer, Rufus King, and Richard Harison made sizeable profits—fortunes in some cases— off their investments. Sometimes these speculators benefited from inside information. Clintonians also profited from the funding system, although not on the same scale. George Clinton received at least $1,288 in funded securities; James Clinton perhaps $6,895, and John Lansing $7,311.

Clintonians saw the financial benefit of bringing this large amount of capital into the state. They did not support Madison's plan of discriminating between the original owners of the securities and the nominal holders. All the funded securities, they believed, should remain with the actual holders. Their only qualms were that their opponents would profit so exorbitantly. The Clintonian economic package had cleverly provided that those federal securities most owned by anti-Clintonians would not be assumed by the state. No such qualifier appeared in the federal funding act.

Clintonians were less clear on Hamilton's plan to have the federal government assume the revolutionary war debts of the states, under which the state of New York stood to receive $1.2 million. Some states were scheduled to receive much more; for instance, both Massachusetts and South Carolina claimed $5 million, while some states were entitled to as little as $200,000. Clintonians weighed the net benefit of having the federal government assume its state debt against the increased federal taxes New Yorkers would have to pay to assume the debts of all of the states.

One part of the assumption program dealt with the settlement of revolutionary war accounts between the states and the federal government. After a preliminary accounting, it appeared that there were six debtor states and seven creditors. The six debtors owed the federal government a total of $3.5 million. New York's share of that debt stood at a whopping $2 million. Two creditor states each had balances due them of $1.25 million. As a sweetener for debtor states, an unwritten understanding was reached that their obligations would be forgiven if the assumption program were adopted.

The assumption program also had a speculator side. New York speculators (mainly Federalists) had purchased huge quantities of securities from other states for a pittance. Seventy-eight New Yorkers owned $2,717,754 in other states' securities. If the federal government assumed the state debts, these speculators would make huge profits; if assumption failed, much of this alienated state debt would be worthless. Those New Yorkers who owned their own state's securities were ambivalent, because they knew that their state had the will and the means to fund its own debt. They would gladly receive payment from either the state or the federal government.

Clintonians objected to the assumption program's tendency to create a consolidated federal government. In 1786, Clintonians had succeeded in attaching the interests of most federal securities owners to the state. Hamilton's plan not only reestablished the bond between federal securities holders and the central government; but, if assumption passed, state securities owners would also look toward the federal government. Because Clintonians equated "the twin bastards of consolidation and assumption,"[21] their three representatives in Congress voted against assumption,

while the state's three Federalist representatives and two senators supported the program.

Clintonians were also ambivalent over chartering a national bank.
Many Clintonians, including the governor, were distrustful of banks, partly
because they were dominated by their political opponents. Being primarily
farmers, Clintonians also opposed commercial banks, such as the Bank of
New York, because they believed that these banks tied up capital and
usually made loans only to merchants for short periods of time at high
interest rates. The governor also viewed the creation of the Bank of the
United States as an example of the federal government's expansion through
a broad interpretation of the Constitution. This use of "implied powers,"
precisely what Antifederalists had warned against, threatened a continued
consolidation of power in the federal vortex. But Clintonians also saw a
positive aspect to the bank.

In 1784 Alexander Hamilton led a group of merchants and other
investors in establishing the Bank of New York. The legislature, however,
refused to grant the new institution a charter. Most New Yorkers with
primary interests in agriculture feared that the bank would concentrate
capital in the mercantile community. Robert R. Livingston actively lobbied for a land bank that would make longer-term loans based on real-
estate collateral. In 1790 the legislature again refused to grant a charter to
the bank.

When Hamilton proposed that a national bank be chartered by Congress and established in Philadelphia, the attitude of most New Yorkers
changed toward their bank. The legislature now readily granted the Bank
of New York a charter. Federalist Assemblyman James Watson commented
on the changed opinion. "The Governor and his adherents are as eager for
it as they have formerly been against it."[22] Now, rather than viewing the
Bank of New York as a threat, Clintonians saw it as a counterbalance to the
anticipated national bank. Federalist Assemblyman James Kent suggested
that "It is as requisite to have a State Bank to control the influence of a
National Bank as of a State government to control the influence of the
general government." The creation of a national bank had transformed
people who were "in general opposed to the thing in the abstract" into
advocates of a competing state bank.[23]

Clintonians also saw both banks as investment opportunities for the
state. In 1792, a legislative committee enunciated a principle that had
already been implemented: the state should regularly convert its surplus
revenue "into productive capital." This kind of investment would help
supplant the loss of revenue from the state tariff. In granting the charter to
the Bank of New York, the legislature reserved an option to buy one
hundred shares of stock worth $50,000, an option exercised in 1792. When

the Bank of the United States was chartered, the legislature voted unanimously to buy 190 shares. Within a year the state owned 152 shares purchased for $60,000.

Generally, historians have viewed George Clinton and his party as political radicals and economic reactionaries fearful of the modern state and capitalism. To a great extent, however, Clinton's economic and fiscal pragmatism at the state level anticipated Hamilton's plans on the federal level. Although Clinton objected to the political ramifications of Hamilton's program, the governor had few reservations about the economics behind it. What he intended was for New York to benefit from such a plan.

35. Campaigning in '92

The 1792 gubernatorial election provided the first real test for the new Republican coalition that Clinton had forged since his narrow reelection three years earlier. The Clintonian coalition would be put to its stiffest test because Robert Yates, the expected Federalist candidate, had been elevated to chief justice and the governor was saddled with the opprobrium of the Macomb land scandal. Clinton's difficulties were heightened by the wave of Federalist New Englanders who had flooded into western New York, particularly into Montgomery and western Albany counties. Federalists had also made significant inroads in the governor's home county, where Peter Van Gaasbeck had bolted from the Clintonians and was now an ardent Burrite.[24]

Moss Kent, a young lawyer, wrote to his brother James expressing the feelings in Otsego County. The gubernatorial election began "to be very generally talk'd of." Judge Yates was the obvious candidate to re-challenge Clinton. Being "very inquisitive," Kent talked with many people and the concensus seemed to be that Yates would "very generally prevail in the Northern part of the State," and that unless the governor had "encreased prodigiously in Popularity in the southern District since the last Election," Yates would be elected "by a Large Majority." Kent knew that his prediction would please his brother "unless you are grown very lukewarm or are sucked into the Vortex of C____n's Influence."[25]

As the campaigning was about to begin in early February, Federalist leaders were shocked when Robert Yates told them privately that he would not run. The governor's salary, Yates said, was too low for him to make ends meet—a strange argument to make after Federalists had asserted in the 1789 campaign that Clinton had grown wealthy on his salary. In reality, however, Yates refused to run because of pressure from Senator Burr, who had designs on the office himself. Burr and his supporters hoped that he might be able to poll a majority vote from disgruntled Clintonians and Federalists who opposed Hamilton's economic policies for the country. But, by this time, the Federalist and Clintonian leadership had determined that the talented and appealing Burr was not a man to be trusted. Sensing Burr's growing statewide support, some Federalists approached the senator seeking commitments that he would not oppose Hamilton's economic proposals. Burr, who had generally sided with Republicans in the senate and who seemed to favor the French Revolution, responded ambiguously, saying that he had "an entire confidence in the wisdom & integrity" of Hamilton's plan and he felt "a real personal friendship" for the secretary.[26]

Schuyler and Hamilton, however, refused to back Burr. Unless a viable candidate could be found to force Burr out of the contest, Schuyler and Hamilton would probably have "to promote the interest of the Old Incumbent, which might be considered a dereliction of sentiment."[27] A third candidate joining Burr and Clinton would guarantee the latter's reelection. Schuyler and Hamilton approached Chancellor Livingston, Stephen Van Rensselaer, and John Jay, now chief justice of the United States. Each, showing the proper sense of aloofness, refused the overture. For a while Schuyler and Hamilton were determined to support Clinton against the ambitious and unpredictable Burr.[28] A caucus of northern legislators met in New York City on February 10 and "almost unanimously agreed to nominate" Jay as governor and Stephen Van Rensselaer as lieutenant governor. Jay's "Character & popularity," it was said, "will ensure his Election."[29] As Van Rensselaer and his followers prepared to declare his candidacy, Jay surprised everyone by stating his willingness to accept the nomination with the stipulation that he would not campaign personally.[30]

Wealthy and aristocratic, Jay was well known throughout the state and his honesty was legendary. Schuyler had unsuccessfully implored Jay to run against Clinton in 1786. Six years later, Schuyler and Hamilton believed that Jay was a candidate they could trust, a candidate they did not have to justify, and a candidate who could probably defeat the incumbent. With Jay and Clinton in the race, Burr slowed his politicking and eventually let it be known that he was no longer a candidate. In some counties, such as Dutchess, Burr never had much support and was quickly abandoned in favor of the more popular Jay.[31] In other counties, such as Ulster, Burr's supporters very grudgingly relented. Peter Van Gaasbeck informed Burr on March 28 that only after receiving specific orders from his agents to desist was it with the greatest reluctance we agreed to relinquish You as our Candidate for Governor." Some Ulster Burrites shifted their support to Jay; and, despite his abolitionist sentiments, which alienated the county's slaveowners, Van Gaasbeck predicted that Jay might eke out a slim majority in Ulster. Burr, however, could have won 75 to 80 percent of the vote.

With Jay and Clinton battling, Van Gaasbeck predicted "the warmest and most spirited Election that ever has been in Ulster." He described the Clintonians "as active as the Bee in June, without great Prospects."[32] After dropping out of the race, Burr sat on the sidelines without endorsing either candidate.

The contest between the two old wartime allies was close from beginning to end. Many New Yorkers shared the sentiments of the old Kinderhook loyalist Peter Van Schaack who felt himself more "warmly Interested" in this election than any previous one.[33] James Kent predicted that "a serious Contest lies between Jay & Clinton." Kent privately felt that Jay's victory would be a "very great & signal Blessing" that would restore "halcyon Days" to the state. Such was Jay's "independent condition, such his Knowledge & experience—such his Talents—Integrity of Heart, that if Providence should but grant his Success, we may rationally expect a sudden Death to the little Intrigues of families & Party, & on their ruins to arise an administration of rectitude & Firmness."[34] Despite this strong endorsement, Kent could not determine "how far Mr. Jay will be supported" in Dutchess County. The county sheriff strongly endorsed Jay and first judge Zephaniah Platt would also support him "if he thought" Jay "could be successful." According to Kent, Platt esteemed "no man on earth" more than Jay.[35] On the eve of the elections, Henry Remsen wrote Thomas Jefferson:

> I cannot yet judge whether Govr. Clinton or Mr. Jay will be elected. Their advocates are respectively very zealous and sanguine. The great sale of land to Macomb has lessened Govr. Clinton's interest among the farmers in the upper part of the state, where he was formerly very popular; but in this city and indeed in the whole southern district of which this city is only a small part, he will have a decided majority of votes.[36]

James Clinton felt confident that his brother would be reelected "if the Governor's friends will turn out and give their Votes as those Against him will spare no pains."[37]

Clinton's coalition with the lower-manor Livingstons held firm. The chancellor, who had not actively opposed Clinton in 1789, was described as "a firm tho . . . not a *powerful* Clintonian." He and his relatives (including Brockholst Livingston, Jay's brother-in-law), much to the chagrin of Federalists, took an active part in the campaign.[38]

Clinton also received solid support from the upper manor Livingstons, who were feuding with their lower manor relatives. John Livingston, who had been defeated for Congress in 1790 by the Schuyler candidate, wanted to run for the state senate, and felt that he needed the backing of the

Clintonians. John Livingston also sought the governor's assistance in releasing a large land grant that Clinton had held up because of the Indian title to the tract. On his way to Albany in November 1791, Clinton breakfasted with Livingston, and on his return trip the governor "staid & supped" with the land-hungry manor lord. Clinton was still uncertain of the Indian title, but he did not close the door entirely. He suggested that John Livingston should consult the law to see if the land office "was inhibited from selling it." "Perhaps," wrote John to his brother Walter, "the approaching Election may do as much for us in this business as any thing whatever." John told his brother to check the law secretly so that no one else would bid for the tract. The governor had given his word "to keep it to himself." In any case, John Livingston wanted to settle the matter before the election; he did not want the governor to use the tract to "play off & on."[39]

Early in the gubernatorial race, Schuyler's aides approached John Livingston seeking support for Jay. The upper manor grand jury declared with only one objection that they would support Robert Yates, but if the old judge declined to run, "Clinton was the Man and that they wou'd support him with all their influence agst every other person." The time was right for the upper manor Livingstons to sound out Clinton again. "Perhaps," John Livingston wrote in mid-February, "it wou'd be well to push the Land business at this moment. Perhaps Herry [Henry Livingston] cou'd ask Clinton in a way that wou'd not give offence, but not to pledge himself in such a way as Clinton can have any hold on him." Clinton might also be persuaded to take Walter Livingston as his lieutenant governor, in which case John would have "no objections to support him to the utmost." Within a month John Livingston and all but one of his brothers were supporting Clinton, and Peter R. Livingston, the maverick, predicted a Clintonian victory in Columbia County.[40] John readily admitted that he was "clearly" in the governor's interest. Reiterating the family squabble, John told his brother Walter that "was not the Chancellor in his favor I shou'd be very warm for Clinton."[41] The old loyalist Peter Van Schaack was sickened by the "forced and unnatural coalition. . . . People cannot be brought to believe that there is not some concealed Quid pro Quo in this bargain."[42] Shortly after Clinton's reelection, John Livingston and his brothers received the land grants they had sought. But even without the land grant, John Livingston might have supported Clinton. Schuyler and Stephen Van Rensselaer had opposed the upper manor Livingstons in various economic and political contests. It was time to return the favor— "I love to Retalliate," John told Walter Livingston, "and no better opportunity can offer."[43]

The most significant problem faced by John Jay in the campaign was

his abolitionist sentiments. John C. Wynkoop, a former Clintonian lieutenant in Kingston, believed that the chief justice would "not have many
Votes from the *Dutch Inhabitants*" of Ulster County, because "a great
majority" of them "possess *many Slaves*, and as Mr. Jay is President of the
Society for the abolition of Slavery, they will probably vote against him for
that reason alone." Wynkoop regretted the prejudice of his fellow Ulstermen
and believed that Jay's sentiments were "founded on the eternal Law of
Nature and Nature's God."[44] Former Staten Island assemblyman Joshua
Mersereau expected the election to be "Very *Tight*. Mr. Jays being one of
the Emancipation Committee opperates much against him with our Old
Copper heads."[45] John C. Dongan warned Jay that his opponents "descend
to the lowest subterfuges of craft and chicane, to mislead the ignorant and
unwary. . . . It is said that it is your desire to rob every Dutchman of the
property he possesses most dear to his heart, his slaves."[46]

Jay decided to meet this opposition straightforwardly by declaring that
"every man of every color and description has a natural right to freedom."
He believed that emancipation should be accomplished "in such a way as
may be consistent with the justice due to them, with the justice due to
their master, and with the regard due to the actual state of society. These
considerations unite in convincing me that the abolition of slavery must
necessarily be gradual."[47] Jay defended the New York Abolition Society
and his association with it, which he had severed when he became chief
justice of the United States. He explained that the Society tried "to
promote by virtuous means the extension of the blessings of liberty, to
protect a poor and friendless race of men, their wives and children from the
snares and violence of men-stealers, to provide instruction for children
who were destitute of the means of education, and who, instead of pernicious, will now become useful members of society."[48]

Although opposition to Jay's abolitionist sentiments also thrived in
Columbia County, Peter Van Schaack held out some hope that a change
was imminent.

> The manumission business is here as with you made an Engine of to
> tarnish the Illustrious Character of Mr. Jay; but I trust its pernicious
> effect will in a great measure be defeated. People are already coming to
> their senses and feel the Impropriety of opposing a man so unimpeach-
> able upon grounds so Questionable at least, if not wicked. They consider
> that if it *should really* be true that they have not an absolute right to
> Convert a part of God's rational Creatures into Brutes, It would add to
> the Iniquity of the Practice if they were to Oppose a man who holds a
> doctrine so full of Philanthropy, even if it should in this Instance be
> misapplied.[49]

Federalist writer "Tammany" suggested that Jay did not advocate emanci-

pation "without the consent of the proprietors, or an adequate compensation. Slavery," Jay allegedly believed, "is indeed odious, and the practice of
it in a free country, much to be lamented; but as the laws of society have
tolerated the practice, it is but reasonable, that the abolition should be
effected in such a way, as not to interfere with the regard that is due to
private property."[50] A reported dialogue between two farmers in Wallkill in
Ulster County brought the worst kind of bigotry out into the open. "You
know," farmer Abraham said, "he is for making the negroes free, and let
them stay amongst us, that they may mix their blood with white people's
blood, and so to make the whole country bastards and out-laws." Farmer
David responded. "As for Mr. Jay's making the negroes free, they said it
should not cost our treasury a penny, and that the owners of them would
have '*a full compensation*,' for that as negroes were generally thieves, idlers
and squanderers of their masters' property, it would be proper to set them
free and discharge them; and for farmers to do their own work, and take
care that every thing was safe and in its place; for that farmers generally
smoaked too much, took too much leisure, and trusted too much to their
negroes, and this was a loss to them and the state, in a few years, which
amounted to more than the negroes were worth. Hence, sir, you see how a
full compensation may be had."[51]

   Van Schaack and other Federalists eventually responded to the criticism of Jay's abolitionism by asking Clinton to disclose his own sentiments
on slavery. If Clinton believed that slavery was wrong, "it would be more
heroick tho' to his own disadvantage to assent to the truth, than to rest
under the Veil of concealment & mistery."[52] As the election neared, Van
Schaack reported "that the Manumission Business dies away People growing ashamed of such an Objection against a Character in all other Respects
so distinguish'd and Unexceptionable."[53] John C. Wynkoop also reported
that Ulstermen had softened their attitude toward Jay, thinking that his
abolitionism was "*an amiable Error*." More important, however, was the
discovery "that *Clinton* is *at least* as much for *manumitting* the Slaves as his
Competitor." Federalists found that, when the legislature in 1785 passed a
gradual-emancipation bill that "made some odious Distinctions between
the Blacks when freed and the Whites, such as *disqualifying* the former from
being *Electors* etc.," the governor opposed the bill in the council of revision
"because the Blacks would not . . . be entitled *to all the* Priviledges of
Freemen." Accordingly, the bill was defeated. This information, Wynkoop
reported, "has an amazing Weight here, and if properly enforced will have
the same with your Dutch Friends."[54]

   Clintonians also represented Jay as a national political figure with
little understanding of state problems, who had allowed himself "to be
made the momentary whirligig of a restless combination." Jay should

realize that he would be much more effective as chief justice than as governor.[55]

Federalists again made an issue of Clinton's long tenure. The Federalist committee of New York City granted that Clinton had served the state well in the past, but that did not mean that he should be reelected in perpetuity. "One would suppose that our State was totally Barren of Merit, and that there was no Person except himself Qualified to Execute the Office of Governor. It would seem that he possessed some NOSTRUM unknown to any other Person to cure all Diseases incident to the Body Politick and that without the benefit of his great Experience; it might Infallibly perish and suffer a premature death." If, because of his experience, Clinton was the only man for the job now, "the Argument will be much stronger at the Next and every future Election." Why, Federalists asked, should elections be held? New Yorkers should "waive the Formality of Voting and . . . let Mr. C. remain in office for Life."[56] Federalists argued that it was "improper to give any man (whatever may be his character or conduct) a perpetuity in the chief magistracy." Voters were reminded of the old republican principle that "frequent change in government" was necessary to guard against influence, corruption, and faction. "All tyrannies in the world," they were told, "have been the effects of *power* usurped, or *continued* too long in the hands of one man, or set of men. . . . Is it then not high time for the citizens of this state to arouse from their lethargy?— '*Slavery is ever preceded by sleep.*'"[57] Clintonians reminded voters that Jay had "warmly opposed" a rotation-in-office clause in the state constitution and that the framers of the federal Constitution, which Jay had supported, also had refused to limit the number of terms a president could serve.[58]

The governor's "unreasonable opposition" to the Constitution was also resurrected. Despite his efforts to convince the public to the contrary, Federalists suggested that "a considerable share" of the governor's Antifederal "Leaven still remains."[59] Despite the apologies of the governor's supporters for his conduct in 1788, New Yorkers were told to be wary of Clinton's "*Conversion.*" Better to trust "the approved Believer" [Jay] than the "Proselyte" who had not demonstrated "the sincerity of the Conversion."[60]

Federalists, led by Philip Schuyler, again assailed Clinton for the previous year's land sales. Shortly before the end of the session, Schuyler proposed that the assembly censure the governor for the sale of "extravagant large tracts" that were "incompatible with the spirit of the government and the true interests of the people." Schuyler hoped that the legislators, "impatient to return to their homes," would refuse to consider the matter, "which would have afforded a fertile topic for slander, and given reason to suppose that the Governor's friends stifled an enquiry into his conduct."[61] But the Clintonian assembly rejected Schuyler's censure resolution in favor of another that criticized the previous land policy for having failed to bring in revenue. The assembly acknowledged that the land office had been given wide latitude and declared that the commissioners had exercised their authority responsibly. Defeated in the legislature, Schuyler continued his attack in the newspapers in a series of vicious articles signed "Decius" which repeatedly accused Clinton of violating his republican principles in order to profit personally from the huge land sales to his friends. "Decius" made these charges so close to the election that Clintonians did not have time to respond to them. Instead, Clintonians continued their attack on Hamilton's national economic policies and attempted to link the secretary of the treasury to the economic panic of 1792 and to the scandal involving his assistant William Duer. Duer had been arrested for embezzlement and imprisoned on March 29, while others in his circle, fearing arrest, fled the city. A mob of four to five hundred people converged on the jail seeking revenge on the man who had swindled many of them. The financial collapse and economic dislocation immediately felt in New York City played into Clinton's hands. Hamilton was told that "The Bank Mania rages violently in this City, & it is made an engine to help the Governors re-election."[62] Charges of land fraud against the Clintonians paled next to the alleged corruption of Federalist insiders. Federalists knew that the scandal had cost them what they hoped would be a landslide victory in New York City; they hoped that the rest of the state would not become as emotionally involved in the unfolding financial morass.

In a more positive vein, "Cato" stated the character traits necessary for an effective governor. "He must possess political integrity; the love of the people at heart; he must be generous; brave; well versed in the military art; not reserved; accessible to by every member in the community, and ready in communicating those things wherein the true interest of the state consists." "Cato" asked, "Does Governor Clinton possess" these traits? He answered: "Those who have been with him in the cabinet, in the field, and in the social walk of private life, will and can best answer the queries, in the affirmative." The governor's opponents might sneer at the thought that he was generous, but "Cato" advised them to call on the state treasurer who would show them the large reimbursements made to Clinton "since the peace, for money loaned to the state, by him, during the war, when pinched by cruel necessity, and when there was no eye to pity or hand to help. Would Mr. Jay have done this?"[63] Furthermore the governor had already "publicly renounced all claims on the United States for his military services."[64]

Clintonians argued that Clinton was the right man for the job in 1777 and that he was still the best man for the post in 1792. The governor stood on his record—victory in war and prosperity in peace. The state's laws had been revised and codified, boundaries had been fixed peacefully, and the population had nearly doubled. The state debt had been funded; commerce, agriculture, and the mechanical arts flourished, and ample public appropriations had been made for schools, roads, and canals. All of this had been accomplished under Clinton without recourse to state taxes. In fact, the state treasury had amassed an enormous surplus from land sales, the state impost, interest from the paper-money loans of 1786, and licensing fees. By coupling wise investments of this "immense property in money" with frugal expenditures, the administration could assure the people of New York that direct taxes would not need to be levied. New York was the most prosperous state in the union, so much so "that emigrants are continually flocking in from other states and nations, to share our advantages."[65] The governor's supporters satirized his opponents who ascribed to Clinton "all the improper measures of the government, and to allow him no merit for the good. The absurd maxim of the English law, that the King can do no wrong, is, by them, as absurdly reversed, that the Governor can do nothing right."[66]

Yes, Clintonians admitted that the governor had opposed the Constitution in 1788 "because he conceived it would subvert the foundations of equal liberty." Now, however, Clinton equally supported the state and federal governments. His "conciliating deportment, in acquiescing with the general government, and his attachment to our state constitution, must surely have weight with the reflecting mind."[67] Delegates from nine of Dutchess County's twelve towns thought that Clinton's Antifederalism was a strength. During the debate over the ratification of the Constitution, Federalists and Antifederalists alike believed "that the state governments would be the most substantial securities against any mal administration of the federal government, and the great barriers against its encroachments." Now, the first encroachments began to appear—the assumption of state debts and the establishment of a monopolistic bank. People needed to elect governors and lieutenant governors who would defend the states—not join with the federal government to weaken them. Jay's career had been intimately connected with the federal government, and Stephen Van Rensselaer had familial connections—his father-in-law General Schuyler had "participated in its counsels, and his brother-in-law, Mr. Hamilton, is the great pivot, on which every measure in that government turns." Both Jay and Van Rensselaer also owed their nominations to Schuyler and Hamilton. Clinton and Van Cortlandt, on the other hand, "have no kind of connection with, or relation to the federal government; but from a long series of services in the state government have acquired an attachment to the interest, and a sympathy in the feelings of the state, that will not easily be eraced from their minds." It was not good policy to "change for change sake" and thus "blend the two governments together, by placing the same connection at the head of each, and thereby throw down the barriers which the nature of our governments, and the constitution has erected against the inroads of arbitrary power."[68]

Others argued that Clinton's leadership was especially needed now. In November 1791 federal troops and Kentucky militia had been annihilated on the Ohio frontier, and a general Indian war appeared imminent. Who would New Yorkers want to lead them should "this unfortunate crisis happen—the governor who was known "for his judicious, active, and brave exertions" or Mr. Jay who had "never exhibited any proofs of military ardor or skill.".?[69] With "the black storm" gathering in the west and "the scalping knife and the tomahawk suspended over our heads," New Yorkers were advised that this was "the most improper time to divest ourselves of a Military Governor."[70]

A correspondent in the *Goshen Repository* explained to the voters the choices they had:

> . . . it is said, that Mr. Jay has been from the beginning of the contest with Great-Britain, a firm and decided patriot; so has Mr. Clinton; that Mr. Jay has represented this state in Congress; so has Mr. Clinton; that Mr. Jay has negotiated with our enemies and assisted in bringing about a peace; so has Mr. Clinton, only their negotiations were carried out in a different manner, the one negotiated with the pen, the other with the sword; which of the two had the most merit, and influence in procuring peace, I leave you to determine. Mr. Jay presided in Congress, Mr. Clinton in Fort Montgomery, Mr. Jay assisted in forming our state constitution; Mr. Clinton has supported it ever since.[71]

As the election neared, reports and speculation varied. Rumors spread that Clinton was about to resign. The governor assured his supporters that such stories were unfounded. "I am certain I never gave the least Intimation of the Kind to any Person—I should have considered it as a Disertion of my Friends without consulting them and I have reason to believe they would not have consented to it." Clinton was more confident of success than before the 1789 election.[72] An extract of a letter from Ulster County reported that parties were "very busy," but that Clinton seemed to have a ten-to-one majority, while Dutchess and Orange were also strongly in favor of "the old governor."[73] On the other hand, Jay's supporters grew increasingly confident. Peter Van Schaack reported that he had "the greatest reason to believe that Mr. Jay's Cause gains Ground in every part of the State." "Good Sense, publick Spirit and Independence of mind," he felt, would prevail "notwithstanding the Effects of *Influence*."[74] An anonymous letter writer from Orange thought that his county's freeholders were "inclined for a change in the administration of affairs," believing that Clinton's "abilities in the cabinet are not so splendid or exalted as they were in the field." Furthermore, the chancellor's "indefatigable endeavors, to promote the re-election of his Excellency . . . have not met with that success expected." An "extract of a letter from a character of respectability in Columbia county, dated April 14," said that Clinton's "coalition with the Livingston family has, in these parts, done him no good."[75] The campaign got "hotter daily," and "bets, to a high amount, have been laid upon the success of the two candidates." People expected a close contest.[76]

36. A Tarnished Victory

During the four-week interim between the election and the counting of the ballots, Federalists believed that Jay had won. Clintonians in the northern part of the state were said to be "lowspirited and have done betting." Robert Troup, Hamilton's occasional law partner and now clerk of the U.S. district court, assured Jay that he would "be carried by a Majority that, under all circumstances, will be deemed honorable to you." In New York City, Clintonian leaders were "extremely uneasy."[77] Clinton himself and the Livingstons seemed "driven to despair."[78] In Philadelphia, the federal capital, Thomas Jefferson reported that Philip Schuyler offered to take wagers up to five hundred guineas at three-to-one odds that Jay would be elected. No one else in the capital felt so sure about Jay's victory.[79] Reports seemed to indicate that the only way Clinton could be reelected would be through political machinations. In reporting the news of Governor Clinton's reelection, James Kent lamented that though this event "would have been melancholy if it had been the voice of the People, yet [it] is rendered deeply afflicting from the consideration that it takes place in violation of Law & Justice."[80]

The election began on April 24 and the polls stayed open five days. Under the provisions of the 1787 election act, voters were to cast paper ballots folded over "so as to conceal the writing thereon." When the polls closed, each local inspector was to seal the ballot box and deliver it to the county sheriff. The sheriff, in turn, was to place all of the sealed boxes from his county in a large box which he was required to deliver to the secretary of state's office, where they all remained unopened until the last Tuesday in May. A committee of twelve canvassers (six assemblymen and six senators, each elected by their respective houses) counted the ballots, determined whether any ballots should be disallowed, and announced the victorious candidates. Disallowances were not unusual. In the 1786 elections, in which Clinton ran unopposed, more than half of the ballots were thrown out because of irregularities. The decision of the canvassers was final, and the law provided that the ballots be destroyed immediately after the results were announced.

After the polls closed, the governor wrote a letter to his brother James giving him an assessment of how the election went. The detail indicates that the governor was intimately acquainted with what was going on in the state and was an active participant in election strategizing. Clinton told his brother that

> both Parties are sanguine of a Majority—by the best Calculation I can form I will have a Majority of 500 in the Southern district—It would have been greater if West Chester had turned out agreeable to our Expectations—in Dutchess I am led to conclude there will be a small Majority agt me—my Opponents say 200; but they also say very positively that there will be a Majority of 150 at least agt me in Ulster—Of this you can best Judge—Nothing conclusive can be drawn from our Accounts to the North of Dutchess we generally believe that Columbia Saratoga & Washington stand well. The latter however not equal to our Expectations but the former far exceeding them—All however is yet uncertain & I presume will remain so until the Canvassing is over.

Knowing the danger from Peter Van Gaasbeck in Ulster County, the governor requested that his brother make sure "that the Poll Lists in the Towns where I have a Majority are sent in due Time to the Sheriff & delivered to him in the Presence of credible Witness."[81]

When the canvassers met on May 29, they and party leaders realized that the gubernatorial election was extremely close and that irregularities had been reported in a number of counties. The legitimacy of the votes of three entire counties—Otsego, Tioga, and Clinton—was questioned because of the manner in which the ballots were delivered to the secretary of state. Tioga County's sheriff deputized Benjamin Hovey to carry the ballots to New York. Along the three-hundred mile trip, Hovey became ill and entrusted the ballots to his clerk. In Clinton County, the sheriff also deputized a courier, but failed to provide written authorization.

Even before the canvassers met, there seemed to be a general presumption that the results of the election hinged on whether or not the Otsego ballots would be disallowed. The county was run with an iron hand by Judge William Cooper, "the Bashaw of Otsego." Cooper's hand-picked man, Richard R. Smith, had informed the council of appointment in January that he would not seek another appointment as sheriff after his commission expired on February 18. On March 30, the council appointed Benjamin Gilbert as Smith's successor. Gilbert's commission was given to Senator Stephen Van Rensselaer on April 13. Van Rensselaer gave the commission to Cooper, but for some unknown reason, Gilbert did not receive the commission until May 11. Smith continued to serve as sheriff throughout the gubernatorial elections, even though he had been elected an Otsego town supervisor during the first week in April—an office that could not legally be held by the sheriff. Smith placed the precinct ballot boxes in one large, sealed box and in a separate bundle of ballots labeled "The votes of the town of Cherry-Valley." He then deputized a courier to deliver them to New York City.

More than a week before the canvassers convened, Robert Troup informed Jay of the Clintonians' machinations. "Clinton and his worthy adherents (the Livingstons) seem now to be driven to despair. All their hopes of success rest upon setting aside votes for you; their particular object at present is the votes of Otsego County which are pretty unanimous for you and which, from the last information we have, will yield a majority of upwards of 600 for you." The Clintonian effort to disallow the Otsego votes "upon a mere law quibble are really characteristic of these virtuous protectors of the rights of the people, of the enemies of aristocracy, and the declaimers against ministerial influence."[82]

The governor, the chancellor, and other key advisors held a meeting to determine their strategy. Troup reported that later "Brockholst went about almost like a madman vociferating against the legality of the return of the Otsego votes and roundly asserting that there was not a Lawyer out of this State that would give an opinion that the votes were legally returned." Rummaging through their law books, Brockholst and Edward Livingston searched for "a stratagem" to use with the canvassers.[83]

Party leaders from both sides sought legal opinions from in-state and out-of-state lawyers. The canvassers, meeting in New York City, felt uneasy about their situation. Canvasser Thomas Tillotson wrote to the chancellor, his brother-in-law, to ask for advice. "Our fate will be unpleasant, turn which ever way it may. If we decide in favor of Clinton, it is ascribed to partiality; if for Jay it will be ascribed to our being duped by the multiplicity of their Law opinions etc. So that we have a Sylla & a Caribdis to steer our course through."[84] Seeking advice from wherever they could, the canvassers asked the state's federal senators—Rufus King and Aaron Burr—for their opinions. The senators conferred for almost two days and departed in disagreement. King wanted to count the ballots in all three ballot boxes, while Burr favored accepting the Clinton County ballots but rejecting the Tioga and Otsego returns. (Both men recommended disallowing the Cherry Valley ballots, which had not been sealed in the sheriff's box, but had been put in an accompanying envelope.) Because they disagreed, Burr preferred that he and King should remain silent; but when King insisted on presenting his written opinion, Burr felt compelled to submit his.

Burr was criticized for his position. "A Freeman" in the *Poughkeepsie*

Journal reminded his readers that Burr was "the same gentleman who was bro't forward as a candidate for Governor last winter, and who shortly after declined when the advocates for a change almost unanimously turned their eyes from him, and fixed on Mr. Jay." The author questioned how much Burr's opinion was influenced by these events. "Columbianus" defended Burr in the *New York Journal* on August 11, 1792. To bolster his position, Burr solicited legal opinions substantiating his opinion. Robert Troup characterized Burr's opinion as "a most pitiful one, and will damn his reputation as a lawyer. ... We all consider Burr's opinion as such a shameful prostitution of his talents, and as so decisive a proof of the real infamy of his character, that we are determined to rip him up. We have long been wishing to see him upon paper, and we are now gratified with the most favorable showing he could have made."[85]

Trying to salvage some support among his Federalist backers, Burr wrote Jacob Delamater of Ulster County. "I shall never fail to recollect" the support from Ulster for the gubernatorial nomination. Burr expressed his regret that his opinion assisted Clinton—Peter Van Gaasbeck's sworn enemy—and explained that he had taken no part in the election. "Had I been so inclined, I have no doubt but I could, in various parts of the state, have essentially injured Mr. Jay's interest; but I made no attempt of the kind." Burr asserted that his legal opinion was proper—it had nothing to do with any attempt to curry favor from Governor Clinton. "It would, indeed, be the extreme of weakness in me to expect friendship from Mr. Clinton. I have too many reasons to believe that he regards me with jealousy and malevolence. Still, this alone ought not to have induced me to refuse my advice to the canvassers. Some pretend, indeed, but none can believe, that I am prejudiced in his favor. I have not even seen or spoken to him since January last."[86]

Burr was convinced that Federalists had their eyes on broader political gains than the mere election of Jay. Consequently, it was important to persuade the people that the canvassers' decision was just. "This persuasion must principally be wrought by the authority of great Names, (for it cannot be expected that the public will reason on law points)."[87] Thus, on November 14, Burr published a pamphlet entitled *An Impartial Statement of the Controversy, Respecting the Decision of the Late Committee of Canvassers— Containing, The Opinions of Edmund Randolph, Esq. Attorney General of the United States, and Several Other Eminent Law Characters.* Federalists responded with their own pamphlet anthology of lawyers' opinion—*An Appendix to the Impartial Statement of the Controversy Respecting the Decision of the Late Committee of Canvassers.*

Eleven of the state's twelve canvassers began deliberations on June 1.

Clintonians dominated because, although the senate selected three Clintonians and three Federalists, the assembly chose six Clintonians, including Pierre Van Cortlandt, Jr., the son of Clinton's running mate.

On June 9, eight Federalist lawyers printed their opinion of the Otsego case with their names affixed in the New York *Daily Advertiser.* The short opinion ended with a challenge to Clintonian lawyers "to come forward with their case and argue the legality of our opinion." The publication "threw the city into a greater ferment and increased the indignation against the attempt to reject the votes." Clintonian lawyers "went about the city to and from the place of canvassing like mad men."[88] On June 12, the canvassers on a straight party vote decided that all of the votes from the three counties should be disallowed and burned without first counting them. George Clinton and Pierre Van Cortlandt were declared elected.[89] The general presumption was that Governor Clinton had won a majority of the votes in the two small counties of Tioga and Clinton; but that Jay had won a much larger majority of votes from populous Otsego. With the loss of the Otsego votes, most people presumed that Jay lost the election.

An analysis of the official returns suggests that Clinton still attracted voters in the yeoman-dominated counties of Long Island (Queens, Kings, and Suffolk); Dutchess, Orange, and Ulster along the Hudson; and Washington and Clinton in the north. The governor also made significant inroads in the City and County of New York and in Columbia. Three years earlier, Clinton had received only 385 votes in the City and County of New York against Yates's 833. In 1792 the upper manor in Columbia County gave Clinton a victory of 270 to 5 despite his loss to Yates in 1789 by a margin of 313 to 3; the lower manor of Clermont shifted from a Yates majority of 43 to 29 to a Clinton majority of 71 to 2. The coalition with the Livingstons had paid off, while the Duer financial scandal probably won support for Clinton in the area close to New York City.

Jay's strength lay in the traditional Federalist areas in the Hudson River Valley. All of the cities (New York, Albany, Kingston, and Hudson) except Poughkeepsie supported Jay. The Schuyler–Van Rensselaer tenantries also overwhelmingly backed Jay: Rensselaerville (296–15), Stephentown (214–8), and Watervliet (421–31). In addition Federalists made significant gains in some yeoman counties, especially in Ulster because of the efforts of Peter Van Gaasbeck. In 1789 Clinton won his home county by a whopping 1,039 to 206, but Jay narrowed that five-to-one margin to less than three-to-two (947 to 654). Jay also won every frontier county except Tioga. Many of the frontier settlers had emigrated from New England, where Clinton was disliked because of his Vermont policy. Furthermore, all frontier inhabitants looked to the federal government for protection from

Indian depradations. Jay's largest margin occurred in Otsego where he had
between 550 and 800 votes compared to only 150 for Clinton.

COUNTY VOTES FOR GOVERNOR, 1792

County	Clinton	Jay
Suffolk	481	228
Queens	532	288
Kings	244	92
New York	603	739
Orange	551	80
Dutchess	751	945
Westchester	347	824
Richmond	106	4
Ulster	947	654
Columbia	1,303	717
Rensselaer	404	717
Washington	758	471
Saratoga	405	461
Albany	444	1,178
Montgomery	306	424
Herkimer	247	401
Ontario	28	92
Totals	8,457	8,315

Clintonians gave three reasons for Jay's large turnout: pressure on
tenants from the manor lords, the many new voters who had recently
emigrated from New England, and the large number of non-qualified
voters whom Federalist voting officials allowed—even encouraged or intimidated—to vote. Although these reasons all had some validity, it also
seems likely that many former Clinton supporters felt it was time for a
change. They found the democratic arguments of Federalists persuasive—
such as rotation in office, the aristocracy of the Livingstons, and the
scandalous land sales to Clinton's friends.

Sarah Jay, daughter of the late New Jersey Governor William
Livingston, wrote her husband about the efforts to defeat him. "Oh, how
the name of Livingston to be disgraced! Brockholst, Edward, William S.,
Maturin, etc., are to be of the number. Those shameless men, blinded by
malice, ambition, and interest, have conducted themselves with such
indecency during the election, and daily since the canvassing of the votes,
as to open the eyes of every one respecting their views in their opposition

to you." Mrs. Jay condemned the canvassers for giving the people a governor rather than allowing the people the choice themselves. She described the scene in New York City after the canvassers' announcement. "The dejection, uneasiness and dissatisfaction that prevails, casts the darkest Odium upon our shameless Governor." Commiserating with her husband, Mrs. Jay wrote, "Much rather would I lose a crown as you have lost the Office contended for, than gain an empire upon the terms Governor Clinton steals into his."[90] Upon hearing the news of the canvass, Jay wrote his wife that "The reflection that the majority of the Electors were for me is a pleasing one; that injustice has taken place does not surprise me, and I hope will not affect you very sensibly. . . . it shall neither discompose my temper, nor postpone my sleep. A few years more will put us all in the dust; and it will then be of more importance to me to have governed *myself* than to have governed the *State*."[91]

The decision of the Clintonian-dominated canvassers to reject the Otsego County ballots was one of the most controversial and criticized events in George Clinton's political career. Although the decision allowed Clinton to retain the governorship for three more years, it also turned Clinton into somewhat of a caretaker during this term, ruined his chances for the vice presidency later in the year, and virtually forced the governor into retirement in 1795. For a time, it also created a constitutional quagmire in which the state was "eaten up with a tedious and stormy political campaign" unmatched since the tumultuous days that led to independence.[92]

The day after the canvassers' decision was announced, a correspondent in the *New York Journal* expressed the hope that "As the election is now over, that party spirit will subside, and the genial streams of wonted friendship reassume their course; that no ill omened asservations may be heard, but that a general and respectful acquiescence be afforded to this *dernier* and interesting decision." Federalists, however, were in no mood to acquiesce. Robert Troup wrote Jay that "If we tamely submit to this flagrant attack upon our rights we deserve to be hewers of wood and drawers of water to the abandoned despots who claim to be our masters."[93]

Almost immediately Federalist leaders in New York City caucused to plan their strategy. A Federalist committee in Red Hook, Dutchess County, wrote to Peter Van Schaack in Kinderhook, Columbia County, to coordinate activities. "The shamefull conduct of the Canvassers has placed the government of this State in a situation little Short of Anarchy." Word spread about forthcoming Federalist meetings in New York City "to concert measures to overset this business by an appeal to the Legislature or a Convention to amend and alter the Constitution, or in some way or other to compel Governor Clinton to quit the Chair of Chief Magistrate." Much could be expected if Federalists throughout New York would cooperate. "The friends of Mr. Jay are unanimous in this County and rather prefer extreem measures than to submit any longer to an administration so hostile to their wishes and degrading to the Dignity of the State."[94]

On hearing the news about the canvassers, Federalists in Kingston marched to Bogardus' Inn where they drank thirteen toasts accompanied with a discharge of cannon. The first toast was to "John Jay (Governor) by the voice of the people." The electors of Otsego were encouraged to "act like freemen, and display a spirit ever ready to assert their privilege." Finally, the opposers of Jay were called upon to acknowledge his dignity and agree to "the absolute necessity of a change in the chief magistracy." The procession left the inn and traveled to the hotel which was appropriately illuminated for the occasion. The gathering spent the evening condemning the canvassers and proclaiming "Mr. Jay is governor by the free suffrages of the people."[95]

On June 18, New York City Federalists held a meeting in the large room in City Hall to protest "the dangerous attack made upon the constitution of this state, by the majority" of the canvassers. Overflowing the room, the meeting adjourned to the open street in front of Trinity Church, where it passed eight resolutions stating "that any attempt to defeat or impair the exercise and operation of the right of suffrage, is a violation of the fundamental principles of the constitution, and an invasion of the sovereignty of the people." The action of the majority of the canvassers was "unwarranted by the constitution; contrary to law, and a dangerous violation of the sacred right of suffrage." The destruction of the right to vote in one county, Federalists asserted, tended "to destroy the rights of the electors in every other part of the state"; consequently "the conduct of the majority" of the canvassers "merits not only the censure, but likewise the indignation of every citizen who values the blessings of liberty." The meeting chose a forty-one-man committee of correspondence that was instructed to communicate with other county committees in petitioning the legislature "for a redress of the injury which has been done to the rights of the people." The committee's circular called upon "the Free and Independent Electors of the several Counties in the State of New-York" to unite in their struggle against the majority of the canvassers, who "upon the most frivolous pretences, has given a stab to the freedom of our country." The circular called for "temperate and firm" action that would "lead to measures which are constitutional. . . . To be silent or inactive, would argue a want of regard for the constitution of our country, and a disposition ready to wear the fetters of despotism without a struggle." It was not the personal cause of one candidate that should be championed, "but the cause of freedom and the constitution that is concerned" because "the right of suffrage, that inestimable privilege, by which alone you participate in the government of your country, is totally annihilated."[96]

A week after the Federalist meeting, Robert Troup, one of the committee of forty-one, sent the circular to Peter Van Gaasbeck. "Whatever the tools of Clinton may say to the contrary, you may rest assured that a more respectable meeting never was had in this City." "More than a majority of the merchants and mechanics" were united in the cause, which "is daily growing more popular & our strength is consequently encreasing." The Federalist intentions were explained. "The Legislature we hope & expect will interfere & compel another election." To strengthen the impact on the legislature, Troup urged Van Gaasbeck that "there be as great an unanimity in the state as possible & let us shew our enemies and the world that we are freemen who know our rights and have spirit to maintain them." Ulster Federalists should call a meeting and appoint a committee "to express your sense of the common injury. . . . Every nerve should be strained to open the eyes of the blind followers of Clinton & convince them that his sole aim is power—not the public good." Troop asked Van Gaasbeck to distribute the New York City circular "far & wide," have it printed in the *Goshen Repository*, and "make an impression upon Orange County" because New York City Federalists "have few friends or acquaintances there." Troup also suggested that Federalists in Ulster and other counties appoint committees to join the city's "for the purpose of forming a convention to present our memorial to the Legislature & to attend both houses daily till the business is determined." Troup assured Van Gaasbeck "that in this City we are as firm as a rock & that we are determined to have redress—A more flagitious & criminal attack I believe was never made upon the rights of a free people & if we tamely submit to it we deserve the Yoke which has been made for us." Van Gaasbeck was encouraged not to be "negligent in your quarter. Many of Clinton's reflecting & sober-minded friends have deserted him and are well wishers now to us & our measures." Yes, there was danger. "Great pains have been taken here to terrify us—but these threats & maneuvres have only cemented our union the more closely & increased our spirit—Stick by us & we will by you—We need not be ashamed of our cause—It is that of our Constitution & the rights of Mankind."[97]

One hundred and fifty electors from eleven of Dutchess County's twelve towns met on the Fourth of July in the town of Clinton, where they unanimously endorsed the New York City circular and vowed "to unite with their fellow citizens in all such measures as shall be consistent with peace and good order, and with the laws and constitution of this state, to obtain a redress." They also condemned the majority of the state assembly for electing a totally partisan list of canvassers, all six of whom were announced supporters of the incumbent, including Pierre Van Cortlandt, Jr., son of one of the candidates for lieutenant governor.[98]

By the end of June 1792, Chief Justice Jay had finished his eastern circuit in Vermont and was on way home. As he travelled southward down the Hudson, he was feted at every stop as the elected governor of the people. In Lansingburgh, referring to Jay as "the man of their choice," the freemen thanked him for his service during and after the war. They regretted "the palpable prostitution of those principles of virtue, patrio-tism, and duty, which has been displayed by a majority of the canvassing committee, in the wanton violation of our most sacred and inestimable privileges, in arbitrarily disenfranchising whole towns and counties of their suffrages. . . . we trust the sacred flame of liberty is not so far extinguished in the bosoms of Americans as tamely to submit to wear the shackles of slavery, without at least a struggle to shake them off." In response, Jay suggested that "The people of the State know the value of their rights, and there is reason to hope that the efforts of every virtuous citizen to assert and secure them will be no less distinguished by temper and moderation than by constancy and zeal."[99] On July 2, the freemen of Albany told Jay that he would have been elected by hundreds of votes had not the canvassers "in direct violation of law, justice, precedent, and the most essential principles of our constitution" disallowed the votes of several whole counties. They would "wait with a firm and cool deliberation for Legislative interposition to afford or procure redress," but if redress were not forthcoming, "the people must then proceed to determine, whether a Chief Magistrate is to be elected by their voice, or by a Committee, the majority of whom were selected and named by a party." After thanking the freemen for their best wishes, Jay expressed the hope "that the important question you mention may be brought to a decision with all that mature reflection as well as manly constancy which its connection with the rights of freemen demands; with all that temper which self-respect requires; and with all that regard to conciliation, benevolence, and good neighbourhood which patriotism prescribes."[100]

Federalists were amazed at the public reaction against Clinton. What would normally have been viewed "as treason or sedition at other times, is daily proclaimed in every street. We hear talk of a governor *de facto* and governor *de jure*; of one, who for the sake of peace, in one part of the state, is barely *permitted* to hold, by non-resistance; of another, who in other parts of the state, is received with all the *honor* of the magistrate elect." In short, the community was reverting to "first principles" and would demand a convention if the legislature failed to offer redress.[101]

On July 10, Jay returned to New York City to a hero's welcome. Greeted at the outskirts of city, he was escorted in by citizens on horseback and in carriages. When he reached the two-mile post, Jay was surrounded by a huge throng on foot. As the procession approached the town, church bells rang, cannon saluted, and the people shouted "Jay & Liberty."[102] Banners proclaimed "John Jay, Governor by the Voice of the People." Before going to his house, Jay's procession took "care to make a circuit & pass before the Governor's Door." In front of his own house, Jay tried to address the people but the loud and repeated applause made it impossible for him to be heard. On July 13 an official welcoming committee told Jay that it was unexpected that he should be cheated out of the governorship "by the machinations of a few interested and designing men." The freemen of the state would seek redress, and, although they respected the law, they respected themselves and their rights more. "The cause in which we are engaged being the cause of the people we trust that it cannot fail of success." Jay, sensitive to the growing prospect of hostilities, cautioned against precipitately recurring "to violence and commotion."

Federalists were not united in how best to resolve the crisis. Alexander Hamilton worried that "Some folks are talking of Conventions and the Bayonet." He felt the situation warranted "neither a resort to first principles nor to violence." Nothing should be done to reverse the decision "by any means not known to the Constitution or Laws." Hamilton reminded his friends that "the opposers of Clinton are the real friends to order & good Government; and that it will ill become them to give an example of the contrary." For a convention to reverse the canvassers' decision, he felt, would be similar to a legislature reversing the judgment of a court. Such a precedent might appeal to Federalists today, Hamilton warned, "but tomorrow we may rue its abuse." Hamilton equally opposed any alterations to the state constitution by a convention. "Such weapons are not to be played with. Even the friends of good government in their present mood may fancy alterations desireable which would be the reverse." Once started, he cautioned, a ferment "may not be allayed when you wish it."[103] Yet Hamilton saw the benefit of keeping "the public indignation" alive if it could be kept "within proper bounds." A month later, he felt that "Men's minds are too much unsettled every where at the present juncture. Let us endeavour to settle them & not to set them more afloat." Perhaps an amendment to the election law and an impeachment of some of the canvassers "who have given proofs of *premeditated* partiality" would be sufficient.[104]

Robert Troup tried to set Hamilton at ease. Yes, Federalists had been cheated and they had to make a proper show of it. He explained to Hamilton "that allowance should be made for the keen anguish we suffer from the wound we have received. But Troup realized that redress was impossible. His aim all along was "to make a strong impression upon the public mind of the deep corruption of Clinton & his party and thus to render him odious." In this, Federalists had succeeded without blowing "the political ship" off course.[105]

Clintonians were unsure of what response to offer. Chancellor Livingston expressed the feelings of many of Clinton's new supporters. "I find the determination of the canvassers occasions much uneasiness. I confess I could have wished that all the votes had been counted whatever might have been the event. The idea of Jay's being injured will contribute much to his popularity." Second-guessing the whole 1792 campaign, the chancellor felt that from the beginning Clinton "was sacrificing the interests of his party to his personal interests even tho' he should get in which I supposed he would by a small majority." Clinton should have refused the nomination, just as Yates had done. Clinton then could have chosen his successor "& quited the government with reputation."[106] Once elected, however, the chancellor felt that Clinton owed it to his supporters not to resign or campaign for the vice presidency. The chancellor therefore would support Adams' reelection.[107]

Federalist William Wilcocks suggested that Clinton would have gained eternal fame had he, like Washington, retired at the end of the war or after the close election of 1789. Wilcocks told the governor that it still was not too late. If he were "a free agent," Clinton should resign and give "the state a fair chance" at another election. But it was supposed, Wilcocks said, "that you are so compleatly fettered by a party, some of whom have made the most deadly sacrifices for your support, that you cannot forsake them: Nay! Some of your new made friends have declared, 'that if you should dare, even to think of a resignation, they would cut your throat!'" Wilcocks, however, hoped that at the ensuing legislative session Clinton would assert a firmness of character and "embrace that last and *proper* opportunity of renouncing the supreme authority." Clinton, it was suggested, would "do what is right in his own eyes" rather than pursue the interests of a selfish, little political junto that had little "real affection or regard, either to his person or administration."[108] Another correspondent in the *New York Daily Gazette*, knowing the governor's "spirit and independence," felt confident that Clinton would not accept the appointment, thus opening the door for a new election in which the voters would "alter or confirm" the canvassers' choice.[109] Other Federalists agreed that Clinton wanted to resign, but his close friends and the Livingstons would "not permit him to,"[110] while still others, such as Ebenezer Foote, Peter Van Gaasbeck's Ulster lieutenant, insisted that "Clinton must quit the chair or blood must and will be shed."[111] Rufus King, however, believed that there was plenty of fight left in the old incumbent: "Mr. Clinton is in fact Governor, and though he may not be free from anxieties & Doubts, he will not willingly relinquish the Office—the majority, and a very great one are now against him—should he persist, and the sword be drawn, he must go to the wall." King worried that New York's succession problems might be a harbinger of problems at the federal level in finding a replacement for Washington.[112]

In Philadelphia, Thomas Jefferson lamented the whole political morass. It seemed impossible "to defend Clinton as a just or disinterested man if he does not decline the office." Such a clamor would not help the national ticket if Clinton should become the Republican candidate for vice president later in the year. Clinton's embarrassment would hurt "the cause of republicanism"; and, asked Jefferson, for what purpose? "To draw over the Antifederalists, who are not numerous enough to be worth drawing over."[113] James Madison felt that Clinton should resign if he felt that Jay had received a majority of legally cast ballots. But, if this were not the case, the governor should "be restrained by respect for his party if not by a love of power" to retain his position.[114]

Old-line Clintonians ridiculed this talk of resignation. "The question should be abstracted from all personalities, and should be discussed on its legal and constitutional merits. A resignation at this moment would be attributed to their menaces, and his fears." But George Clinton had steeled his nerve on the battlefield; he would not be "alarmed by the vapouring language of verbose attorneys, and pusillanimous patriots." "A public character does not belong to himself, but was the property of legal electors in this state, they value him not from a *personal idolatry,* but from republican principles: They wish to employ his talents and virtues in support of our equal rights, as electors, against the ambitious designs of *one* family." The people of New York would not let *"the father of their country"* resign.[115]

Like other Clintonian leaders, Morgan Lewis tried to discover Federalists' plans. When Jay was still in Albany, Lewis received secret reports that Jay and his supporters were "adopting Measures subversive of the State Government." The outline of the plan called for an application to the legislature to call a convention that would amend the state constitution. Among other changes, Federalists wanted to abolish the council of appointment—one of Clinton's major sources of power. If the legislature refused to call a convention, Federalists would call one "by their own Authority," which would set "the Constitution & government on float" and would annihilate all state offices. According to Lewis, Jay "is either the Author of this Opinion or certainly sanctions it." Federalists, Lewis fretted, "are extremely industrious in establishing Committees every where" and would continue to gain ground "unless something be done to counteract them." Judge John Lansing suggested that addresses to the governor be circulated throughout the state to be signed by every man who supported Clinton. This would warn Federalists that their subversive activities had been discovered and would "operate as an Association to defeat them."

Immediate action was needed, but "In whatever we do," Lewis counselled, "let us manifest a Spirit of Temperance & firmness." Finally, Lewis reported that Federalists at Kinderhook, following the sentiments of Peter Van Schaack, "are loud for Monarchy, and say we never shall be happy 'till we adopt the British Constitution."[116]

Edward Livingston also thought it advisable for Republicans—now synonymous with Clintonians in New York—to counteract Federalists, who relentlessly pursued "every measure that can tend to disturb the tranquillity of the State." By mid-July, newspapers throughout the state had reprinted the New York City Federalist circular several times, and Livingston noted that New York City newspapers were now "filled with resolves from the Country, every succeeding one being more violent & seditious than the former." If Republicans failed to act, Federalists would succeed in having a convention called, "for tho' they can not intimidate the Governor, they may possibly operate on the fears of the Legislature. Legislators felt that a convention would "be infinitely more desireable than the unconstitutional Step of a New Election ordered by the Legislature." Everyone knew that Clinton would "never yield his Seat to any man chosen under such a law."[117]

Action was needed to intimidate Federalists as well "as to bolster Republican spirits." Some Clintonians had become disillusioned with their defensiveness. A frustrated Marinus Willett challenged anti-Clintonian William Wilcocks to a duel. (No one was injured.)[118] Republican leaders finally "determined to give some System to their Operations." A meeting was called for July 16 at which resolutions would be passed supporting the decision of the canvassers and the laws and constitution of the state, "and also reprobating the Conduct of a Chief Justice of the U.S. who suffers himself to be placed at the head of a faction & supports measures tending to destroy the Peace of the State." An address would also be made to Clinton and he would be feted at a public dinner. At first Edward Livingston opposed these plans, but he soon realized that they were "absolutely necessary." Republican inactivity had "been ascribed to fear and a consciousness of wrong." Furthermore, "considering the Part our family has taken, Jay's Success will be the signal for every indignity if not Violent oppression that an unforgiving temper can devise."[119]

The Republican meeting assembled at Corre's Hotel in New York City on Monday evening, July 16. Those in attendance expressed their concern about "a dangerous party" forming within the state "under the plausible pretext" of seeking legislative redress to the canvassers' decision. In reality, however, the "real object" of this "angry and disappointed faction" was "to disgust the people against the government, and to subvert" the state constitution. The meeting declared that George Clinton was the "constitutionally and lawfully" elected governor for the next three years. The canvassers had correctly decided the issue of the Otsego ballots because most of the votes had been "obtained by undue influence" and were "illegally returned." To have counted these tainted ballots would have violated "the right of suffrage in other parts of the state," where "a large and decided majority of the qualified and unbiassed electors" favored the reelection of George Clinton.

Because the election law provided that the canvassers' decision was final and also provided for punishment for corrupt canvassers, the Republican meeting charged that any attempt to have the legislature set aside the election could only be viewed as an attempt to "introduce anarchy and confusion in the state, in place of that order, peace, and tranquillity which it now so happily enjoys." The meeting singled out John Jay himself for special attention: "That whenever any man (however dignified his station) whose eminent duty it is to preserve the public peace from inordinate ambition, or any other sinister motive, places himself at the head of a party, whose measures tend to a subversion of the government and constitution of their country, he ought to forfeit the esteem of every worthy member of society." The meeting articulated these themes in a circular addressed to "the Friends of Liberty and Good Order, in the State of New-York" which were repeated in Republican newspaper essays published during the next six months.[120] "A Patriot" saw things differently, asserting that it was the election law that violated the state constitution. Clintonians had made the constitution a "shuttle cock of party . . . a common prostitute . . . debauched and diseased to suit different occasions." Freemen should stand up "to this first (perhaps fatal) stroke at the root of the tree of liberty" before they lost the appellation of "*republican citizens.*"[121]

A committee appointed by the meeting congratulated Clinton on his reelection and hoped that his "fortitude, patriotism, and perseverance"— so prevalent during "the most perilous times—would continue to defend the state's constitution and laws. The good and honest people of New York were determined to unite with him "in preserving the peace we now so happily enjoy, and in defending a constitution so well calculated to preserve that tranquillity from violation."

Responding to the address, the governor felt confident that his opponents would end their disruptions "as soon as they shall be found inconsistent with good order, and a regard to the constitution and laws, under which we have the happiness to live." Knowing that some of his supporters wanted Federalists tried for sedition, and perhaps aware of the meeting's circular that called on the courts to do their duty concerning seditious libels, Clinton expressed his own thoughts on the freedom of political expression: "In this enlightened period, when the rights of man are so well understood, and the blessings of liberty and peace so highly prized, a spirit of free enquiry should not only be permitted, but encouraged upon every question in which the constitutional privileges of the people may be concerned. While the discussion is conducted with temper, and by an appeal to the reason, not to the passions of our fellow citizens, those who have done right need not fear the investigation; a good cause will ever find its best and firmest support in its own merit." Clinton felt certain that his supporters would continue "such temperate measures, as will . . . satisfy the public that you are actuated by principle and a sincere regard for the welfare of your country." He also assured his followers "that inclination, as well as duty, will ever prompt me to co-operate with my fellow citizens, in every legal and necessary measure to maintain inviolate the constitution and tranquility of the state."[122] The governor was assuring his supporters and alerting his opponents that he would not resign and that he would use force if need be to stay in office.

Throughout the six months before the legislature convened, Republicans postured as supporters of law and order and protectors of the state constitution. They held meetings throughout the state in which Clinton's election was acknowledged, and they suggested that Federalist meetings "were only composed of the very violent members of a disappointed faction."[123] Federalist leaders were individually castigated: John Jay for encouraging violence and sedition;[124] Stephen Van Rensselaer for serving as a biased election inspector;[125] William Cooper and Peter Van Gaasbeck for heavy-handed electioneering in their counties; and Philip Schuyler for his coordination of anti-Clinton activities.[126]

By mid-October 1792, Jay's supporters in the southern part of the state acknowledged that Clinton could not be deposed. In other parts of the state, however, the crisis intensified as the legislative session approached. Assemblyman Silas Talbot reported "that our State is convulst to its very senter." Frustrated Federalists realized that the Clintonians held small majorities in both houses of the legislature, and that they seemed intent "to go to all Lengths to keep Mr. Clinton in office."[127] As more legal opinions from out-of-state lawyers drifted in, it became apparent that the legislature could not reverse the canvassers' decision "without doing violence to the constitution—or, in other words, effecting a revolution." Those Federalists who wanted political peace and who sought to ruin Clinton's reputation were pleased; others felt betrayed by the system. "Republicanism and despotism were synonymous terms—with this only difference, that the former, signified a plurality of tyrants, the latter, but one."[128] The young lawyer Moss Kent, counsel to William Cooper, "was satisfied as to the constitutional right of the Legislature to interfere & redress the Violence that has been committed on the right of Suffrage."[129]

Cooper himself railed against any "shameful compromise," vowing never to submit to the canvassers' decision. Deputies, he said, should be elected and go en masse to city hall daily until the legislature called a convention.[130]

When the legislature convened, "party spirit kindled up to a perfect flame."[131] Republicans had a small but firm majority, so that there was never any likelihood that the election would be put aside or that a convention would be sanctioned. Instead, the assembly held lengthy hearings into the canvassers' decision, which "after a full and fair examination," ended on January 18, 1793, when the assembly resolved that there appeared to be no evidence that the majority of canvassers "have been guilty of any mal or corrupt conduct in the execution of the trust reposed in them by law."

By the time the assembly finished its hearings, the public's interest in the disputed election had waned. Newspapers were now filled with accounts of the debates in Congress and the dramatic events unfolding in Europe. Federalists had failed to get John Jay elected governor, but they succeeded in a number of areas. Governor Clinton's reputation had been tarnished badly, thus diminishing his authority to rule. The bank controversy and the speculation scandal had all but disappeared from the public's attention. Nationally, New York's disputed election helped reelect John Adams as vice president in 1792. With these significant political gains, New York Federalists eagerly looked forward to the spring legislative elections in 1793.

Courtesy of the State Historical Society of Wisconsin.

VI

A National Republican

37. A Second Attempt at the Vice Presidency

Almost from the day that George Clinton was defeated for the vice presidency in January 1789, Federalists worried that he would mount another campaign for that office. The bitter and prolonged dispute by Federalists over the canvassing of votes in the governor's race in the spring of 1792 was at least partly aimed at lessening Clinton's vice presidential chances later in the year. Alexander Hamilton explained to New York Senator Rufus King that "Clinton & his party should be placed in a just light before the people, and that a spirit of dissatisfaction within proper bounds should be kept alive; and this for National purposes, as well as from a detestation of their principles and conduct."[1] As early as June, Hamilton told Vice President John Adams "that Mr. Clinton is to be your Competitor at the next election." Appealing to Adams's ego, the secretary of the treasury said that he felt Clinton "could not have succeeded in any event, but the issue of his late election will not help his cause."[2] But a month later, Pennsylvania Federalists were so fearful that Clinton would defeat Adams, that, according to Republican observers, they encouraged their own governor, Thomas Mifflin, to run for the vice presidency.[3]

In September one of the first newspaper pieces appeared on behalf of Clinton's vice presidential campaign. "A Citizen of the United States" believed that there could be no doubt but that the illustrious Washington would be continued in his "important and honorable station," but "the independent citizens of these United States" would determine "whether true republicanism shall prevail and flourish, or the seeds of aristocracy be permitted to take deep root in this soil of freedom." The writer insinuated that John Adams was a tyrant "anxious to overthrow the glorious fabric of freedom, and erect on its ruins that deformed monster, *Aristocracy*." Several vice presidential candidates seemed plausible to the author: Adams, Clinton, Jay, Mifflin, James Madison, and Governor John Hancock of Massachusetts. From among these candidates, "A Citizen" recommended that voters single out the one "man most likely to maintain the *republican* interest" and "the greatest enemy to monarchy." Obviously George Clinton was that man. Avoid the man "who is favorable to European systems, and place, in the second office of your government, one favorable to Independence, Liberty, and the Rights of Man."[4]

"Columbus" seconded these opinions:[5] "The supporters of tottering monarchy, and the friends of different *orders* in the nation, would certainly wish" to elect an aristocrat such as Adams. But "Columbus" felt confident that "the friends of liberty will rally round the altar of freedom, and disappoint the expectations of their enemies." Republicans should unite behind Hancock, Madison, or Clinton, "or else the foes of a free government will undoubtedly succeed in choosing one friendly to their own schemes." The tree of liberty needed to "be pruned of the poisonous twigs that at present spring up and retard its growth, or it will wither and decay." In a not so subtle reference to the revolution in France, the essayist encouraged freemen to "Lop off every unfruitful branch, and root out of the soil of freedom all the noxious weeds of aristocracy. Attend to the voice of the fair goddess, Independence, who once called upon you in a loud voice; but now gently whispers, that Liberty is in danger."

By mid-September, New York Federalists had another concern. Aaron Burr let it be known that he would accept a Republican nomination for the vice presidency. New-Haven lawyer Pierpont Edwards, Burr's uncle, made "interest" for him in Connecticut; as did Benjamin Rush, John Nicholson, and Alexander J. Dallas in Pennsylvania. Dallas, a Philadelphia attorney and secretary of the commonwealth, came to New York with promises of support for Burr's candidacy; while Rush encouraged Burr to contact Samuel Adams and the new Republican "Association in Boston." Rush told Burr that "your friends every where look to you to take an active part in removing the monarchical rubbish of our government. It is time to *speak out*—or we are undone."[6] Burr himself traveled to Philadelphia to solidify his support.[7] Although some Federalist leaders by this time were confident that Adams would be reelected, they feared that if Jefferson backed Burr, Adams's margin of victory might be reduced so severely that he would "decline the Office." Other Federalists thought that Burr would be a stronger candidate than Clinton and might even defeat Adams. With Adams defeated, Republicans would attack Hamilton's economic policies.[8]

Burr's supporters in Philadelphia and New York City sounded out Madison and James Monroe to determine whether Southern Republicans would be willing to switch candidates. In a joint letter, Melancton Smith and Marinus Willett, two of Clinton's closest friends and political advisors, informed the Virginians that New York Republicans "unanimously" agreed with their colleagues nationwide on the importance of unseating Adams. Smith and Willett felt that Republicans should unite behind a single candidate. In New York, Clinton and Burr were the only candidates being considered. Based upon "their characters, their years, and their habits of life," Smith and Willett preferred Burr to Clinton. Any hesitancy on their part was removed, they said, by two factors. First, Clinton had told them in "repeated conversations," both together and apart, that he did "not wish to be a candidate," explicitly stating that Republicans should "unite in some other person." Second, they believed that the office of governor of New York was of more importance to Republicans than the vice presidency. With a great deal of difficulty, Clinton had won another three-year term. His supporters did not like the idea that he would abandon them in favor of the vice presidency. If Clinton were elected vice president, the governorship would become vacant; and, although Burr could probably be elected to replace Clinton, it seemed "highly improper to hazard another election at this juncture."

Smith and Willett anticipated the argument that Southern Republicans were committed to Clinton. They stressed that Clinton had done no campaigning in either the north or the south, and that Southerners supported the principles of Republicanism, not the fortunes of one particular man—especially if that one man did not want to be a candidate. Furthermore, Burr, unlike Clinton, had supporters in Pennsylvania, New Jersey, and New England.

Smith and Willett emphasized their affection for both Clinton and Burr. They should not be considered "Competitors." The governor's friends were Burr's friends. They had conversed together and agreed on their candidate. But if the Virginians felt Clinton would be a stronger candidate, New York Republicans would unite behind him.[9]

At the same time, Philadelphia Republican John Nicholson, the state comptroller general and one of a few former Antifederalists who had statewide connections, wrote Madison on Burr's behalf. Clinton had been the first choice, but the controversy over his reelection as governor coupled with his own wish not to run convinced Pennsylvania Republicans to support Burr. If Virginia wanted Clinton, however, Pennsylvanians would unite behind him as their candidate; for, although Clinton wanted to defer to Burr, the governor did "not Absolutely refuse to serve if elected."[10]

Monroe received Smith and Willett's letter by courier at his home in Fredericksburg; Madison received a copy at his home, Montpelier. Both men were embarrassed. They had already started their campaign for Clinton in the South and had already received commitments of support.[11] They believed that Clinton was the better candidate. His principles were known, and he had a long record of public service. To unseat Adams would be difficult and unpleasant, and probably could not be accomplished with a political novice such as Burr. The Virginians agreed to cushion their rejection of Burr by telling Nicholson and the New Yorkers that their candidate was too young and inexperienced to run against the old patriot Adams.[12]

Burr's candidacy particularly alarmed Alexander Hamilton. He suspected that it might be "a diversion in favour of Mr. Clinton" or that Burr and Clinton together could be a diversion for Jefferson. Even worse, Hamilton despised the thought of Burr's election. The secretary of the treasury believed that it was "a religious duty to oppose" Burr's career, and he felt obliged to abandon his policy of not interfering in elections while he served in the cabinet. He wrote to Federalists in states south of New York, while Rufus King warned friends in New England of Burr's machinations, advising them "to resist the present design."

Hamilton believed that Clinton was "a man of narrow and perverse politics, and as well under the former as under the present Government, he has been steadily since the termination of the war with Great Britain opposed to national principles." But Clinton was "a man of property, and, in private life," a man "of probity." Burr, on the other hand, was "unprincipled both as a public and private man. . . . In fact, I take it, he is for or against nothing, but as it suits his interest or ambition. He is determined, as I conceive, to make his way to be the head of the popular party and to climb per *fas et nefas* to the highest honors of the state; and as much higher as circumstances may permit." Hamilton felt that Burr's object was "to play the game of confusion. . . . In a word, if we have an embryo-Caesar in the United States 'tis Burr." Ironically, Hamilton found himself supporting Clinton as the Republican candidate to oppose Adams.[13]

A week after writing to Madison and Monroe, Melancton Smith traveled to Philadelphia to coordinate plans for Burr's candidacy. In a letter introducing Smith to Nicholson, Burr referred to the New York envoy "as the representative of the republicans of this State and the Man of the first Influence in that Interest—The most entire Confidence may be placed in him as to Men and Measures." Any plans agreed on by Nicholson and Smith would be favorably received by Burr and his supporters.

On October 16, Republican leaders from at least New York, Pennsylvania, Virginia, South Carolina, and perhaps Georgia caucused in Philadelphia and concluded "*finally & definitively* . . . to exert every endeavor for Mr: Clinton, & to drop all thoughts of Mr: Burr." This meeting was supervised by John Beckley, the clerk of the U.S. House of Representatives and a leading Republican political operative.[14] Although no evidence indicates that Jefferson attended the meeting, he was in Philadelphia at the time and was almost certainly kept well informed of the proceedings by Beckley. Because of the broad representation at this meeting, it might well be viewed as the birth of a national Republican party organization. John Adams later referred to these kinds of coordinated efforts as "the pure Spirit of Clintonian Cabal [and] of Virginia Artifices."[15] When the meeting ended, Smith asked Beckley to inform Madison and Monroe that New York's Republicans would unfailingly support Clinton. Smith even made plans to travel to Massachusetts, Rhode Island, and Connecticut to win support for the governor.

By the time Smith returned to New York, and before Madison and Monroe's response arrived, Burr had dropped out of the race. On October 2 the governor adroitly cast the deciding vote in the council of appointment naming Burr to a new associate justiceship on the state supreme court.[16] (Later, in December, Burr turned down the appointment, preferring instead to stay in the U.S. Senate and perhaps run for governor if Clinton were elected vice president.) Madison and Monroe felt justified in their decision when Beckley informed them in mid-October that estimates indicated that Clinton would defeat Adams by a vote of 63 to 56, while Burr himself had given assurances "that he would cheerfully support the measure of removing Mr. A____ & lend every aid in his power to Clinton's election."[17]

Much of the support for Clinton's candidacy over Adams was less an endorsement of Clinton than a reaction against Adams. In referring to the election of Virginia's presidential electors, John Dawson commented on "the friends to Mr. Clinton," but immediately corrected himself by saying "or rather the opponents to Mr. Adams."[18] Nationwide, Republicans preferred Jefferson to Clinton; but, because the Constitution prohibited presidential electors from casting both of their ballots for candidates from their home states, and because Virginia's twenty-one presidential electors were committed to Washington, Jefferson seemed unelectable.

Although Clinton's supporters had successfully staved off the challenge from Burr, they were unsuccessful at keeping their own state coalition intact. The chancellor, piqued at what he perceived to be Clinton's insufficient appreciation for the Livingstons' support during the gubernatorial election, decided to sit out the vice presidential campaign. Edward Livingston pleaded with his brother to abandon Clermont and assist Clinton in his race for the vice presidency. The chancellor was indifferent, explaining that "as you advance in life you will be more and more convinced that great obligations are seldom repaid." He would remain on the manor and "if the choice is to fall upon a man I like better, I will support him, if not the little weight I have will be thrown into A's scale."[19] John

Armstrong, the chancellor's brother-in-law, also abandoned Clinton, ridiculing the governor's southern supporters: "Are not the Antis a little humbled at the issue of the election for Vice President? Clinton's *democratical* support is completely ridiculous to be seen. I even now see his southern Advocates penning maxims upon republican equality and the rights of men with one hand, and with the other, lashing scores of poor devils [i. e., slaves] before them, to the iniquitous task of the day. But inconsistency is an ingredient in antifederalism as well as in all other vices."[20]

On November 20, the Republican-controlled New York legislature elected twelve presidential electors. Each house voted separately, but both elected the same "*staunchest friends to true republicanism.*"

By the end of November, it was clear that there were only two vice presidential candidates: Adams and Clinton. Southern Federalists circulated rumors that Clinton opposed the projected move of the federal capital to the banks of the Potomac, while Southern Republicans denounced Adams's support of titles and his stand on the apportionment bill which seemed to favor the Northern States.[21] In a Richmond newspaper, Governor Clinton was praised as "a republican both in principle and practice," while Adams was reprobated for "his love of . . . hereditary monarchy, and hereditary and selfish aristocracy."[22] Electors of the vice president were admonished to vote "in favour of a man whose principles are congenial with the constitution—for it should not be forgotten that you are choosing a *legislator* and a *judge*, as well as a member, and *eventually*, the head of the *executive* department." Governor Clinton seemed to be the best choice for the position. He "stands as high as any friend to a *pure republic*" as well as being "a vigorous executive."[23] In Halifax, N.C., the town's only newspaper drew attention to the two-man vice-presidential race, suggesting that Adams's philosophy of government was unclear because he hid behind the secrecy of the U.S. Senate, but that Clinton had "been long distinguished as a man of talents and patriotism."[24] North Carolinians seemed to want a change in the vice presidency, and "they unanimously speak of Gov. Clinton as the man."[25] A South Carolinia correspondent hoped that his fellow citizens could "get the better of a little state pride, and a prepossession in favour of some one of our own Dons" and support "that distinguished patriot Governor Clinton."[26] Nationwide, Republicans argued that Adams had proven himself friendly to a government of king, lords, and commons, while Federalists again raised the spectre of Clinton's Antifederalism. Republican correspondent "Lucius" asked from which candidate did Americans have the most to fear? Adams's political philosophy had changed while he was stationed abroad—he had become an aristocrat. Clinton's philosophy remained the same—he had always been a republican. "His maxim has been, to keep the government, in all its departments, essentially connected with the people." Furthermore, many of Clinton's objections to the Constitution had been eliminated with the adoption of the Bill of Rights in December 1791. In fact, the Constitution "must be deemed, in all its parts, as nearly correspondent with his own theory." "Lucius" asserted that the gulf between Federalists and Antifederalists during the debate over the ratification of the Constitution "was a narrow one." This "trifling" disagreement had virtually disappeared with the passage of the amendments; consequently there was no danger "of a vibration back" to the weak government of the Confederation, "for in truth, no person wishes it." The danger lay "in the opposite direction"; "antirepublicanism, and not antifederalism is now most to be guarded against."[27]

Federalist William Wilcocks disputed Clinton's political conversion and the Republican claim "that the spirit of antifederalism is extinct." Such transformations were as likely as "a whale on horse-back. . . . Sophistry may gratify the appetites of some political gudgeons; but facts are stubborn things, and speak louder than words."[28] Referring to the dispute over his reelection as governor, Wilcocks declared that it was preposterous to believe that Clinton, "who holds the first office in a state in open contempt and violation of a Constitution he pretends to respect," would "be faithful as Vice President in the support of the Constitution he abhors."[29] Massachusetts Congressman Fisher Ames reported that "The *antis* have joined to set up Clinton against John Adams. They seem to wish he may have the singular chance to mar two constitutions."[30]

On December 5, 1792, the presidential electors cast their ballots, reelecting Washington and Adams. Clinton received fifty electoral votes to Adams's seventy-seven. The governor was unanimously supported by the electors of New York, Virginia, North Carolina, and Georgia. He received only one of Pennsylvania's fifteen votes, and Burr received one of South Carolina's eight votes. Jefferson received the four Kentucky electoral votes despite earlier assurances from Congressman John Brown that they were committed to Clinton.[31] All of the other electors voted for Adams.

Republicans had not expected to fare well in New England. But Clinton did even worse than anticipated. Beckley had estimated an Adams margin of 27 to 12. New Hampshire and Connecticut were each expected to provide two votes for Clinton, and Vermont and Rhode Island were each expected to cast their four votes for Clinton. None of these votes materialized. Clinton himself speculated on why he failed to receive any New England votes. Surely, he felt, that Rhode Island Governor Arthur Fenner would cast an electoral vote for him. Clinton had "always considered [Fenner] as a Republican," but the Rhode Islander voted for Adams.

Clinton rationalized that Fenner "was Ignorant of my being in Nomina-tion." But the governor also realized "that local Considerations will in many Instances controul the Opinions of those who might otherwise be disposed to be favourable to the Republican Candidates,"[32] and local conditions had changed dramatically after Rhode Island ratified the Con-stitution in May 1790.

Clinton's candidacy faced monumental logistical difficulties. Presi-dential electors were elected in mid-to late-fall and were required to cast their ballots on December 5. To inform all of these electors that Clinton was the designated Republican candidate was nearly impossible. In Vir-ginia, the day before the electors voted, Richmond merchant Robert Gamble complained that "too little pains has been taken by Gentlemen in Congress and others in Office at the seat of Government to inform Such as either are Electors or who could influence those who are. All seem to depend on Vague rumors. Prejudice and Caprice must direct."[33] Virginia elector Archibald Stuart confirmed the lack of coordinated effort on Clinton's behalf. On the day after the ballotting, Stuart reported that all of the electors agreed that Adams should be replaced. Only one of the electors had received information about Clinton's nomination. That infor-mation was shared with the other electors assembled together in Rich-mond. Some of the electors, including Stuart, preferred candidates other than Clinton or Adams "had there been hopes of success." But since Clinton was the only candidate capable of defeating Adams, "necessity therefore in some degree contributed to our Unanimity." Even after all of the Virginia electors voted for Clinton, Stuart had pangs of remorse. "Tho I disapproved of Mr. A.s political Creed yet . . . I felt gre[a]t reluctance in voteing against him." Jefferson had previously told Stuart that Adams was honest and wise and everyone remembered the "essential services to our Country" that Adams had rendered "at a critical period." Stuart also felt that "the desertion of old servants was a blemish in the Character of Republics but on the Other hand I conceive it dangerous and inconsistent to retain in so important an Office however worthy in other respects a man not entirely devoted to the republican Cause."[34]

On hearing the results of the election, a relieved Hamilton wrote Jay that "The success of the Vice President is as great a source of satisfaction as that of Mr. Clinton would have been of mortification & pain to me." Hamilton would have preferred to believe that Antifederalism had disap-peared, but he still worried that Clinton and his followers were not to be trusted.[35]

38. The Decision to Retire

George Clinton's sixth term as governor was his most difficult. For the first six months after the canvass of votes, he was scorned as illegitimately holding the office. When opposition to his governorship finally subsided, he was narrowly defeated for the vice presidency, and his party lost seven of ten seats in the January 1793 congressional elections, including Clinton's home district of Ulster–Orange. (In 1791, Federalists had won four of six seats.)

Knowing that Federalists would be difficult to defeat in the spring 1793 legislative elections, Clinton attempted to mend the damage to his tenuous coalition. Preferring to enlist support through rewards rather than through fear of retribution, the governor appointed Morgan Lewis, the chancellor's brother-in-law, to the post on the supreme court that Burr had declined. Lewis' position as state attorney general was filled by Nathaniel Lawrence, who had been recommended for the position the year before by Burr and Melancton Smith when Burr vacated it to become a U.S. senator. Despite a robust state economy, Clinton realized that he needed all the support he could muster for his uncertain political future. Despite Clinton's efforts in the 1793 legislative elections, his Federalist opponents captured majorities in both the assembly and senate. Added to these political ailments, the governor's health suffered, as recurring bouts of rheumatism became more severe and persisting. It appeared as if the fifty-three-year-old governor's political career was nearing an end. But, in certain ways, this last term would be satisfying as Clinton culminated a quarter century of public service.

Beginning in 1789, New York's newspapers were filled with accounts of the French Revolution. As the conflict broadened into a European and then a world war, Federalists supported Great Britain and Republicans backed America's old ally France. New York Republicans saw the French Revolution as an offspring of the American Revolution in which "the sacred rights of mankind" were wrested from "the arbitrary will and licentious ambition of weak and wicked men."[36] Just as Americans had thrown off the yoke of oppression from their king and his aristocratic minions, it was time for the French people to do the same. Republican essayists argued that Americans should learn from their French cousins that aristocrats—that is, Federalists—should have no place in government.

George Clinton's sympathies unquestionably lay with the French, both because his ideas were ideologically compatible with the republicanism first espoused in Revolutionary France, and because of his dislike for Great Britain. He remembered the long years of fighting, the slaughter on the frontier, and the British occupation of the Northwest forts that per-sisted—an occupation that kept frontier land values down, deprived New Yorkers of the lucrative fur trade, and contributed to British influence over the powerful Indian tribes of the north.[37] But the French Revolution put America and George Clinton in an awkward position. For several years the European naval war threatened neutral American shipping. The French used American ports to bring in captures and to refit warships and priva-teers. Such allowances evoked bitter objections from the British.

When the French revolutionaries executed the king and queen and established a republic, foreign affairs became a prominent issue in New York politics. Political divisions within America solidified, and virtually no one was neutral in spirit; but neutrality was the only option Clinton saw in his public role as governor. On January 7, 1794, ten weeks before President Washington proclaimed America's policy of neutrality, Clinton told the New York legislature that "the preservation of our neutrality inviolate became an object of the first magnitude, and has commanded the attention of the general as well as of the particular governments." In trying to maintain neutrality, which Clinton believed "so essential to the present happiness and future prosperity of our country," the governor frequently found himself called upon by the federal government to curb the belliger-ent activities of France, Great Britain, and their American supporters.[38] On May 9, 1793, two weeks after the publication of Washington's Neutral-ity Proclamation, Clinton issued his own proclamation of neutrality be-cause New York "as a constituent member of the Union" should follow "the disposition of the United States." As part of the proclamation, Clinton instructed port officials—all of whom were federal officials—to inform him of "the arrival, situation, and time destined for the departure of all ships of war, or other armed or prize vessels belonging to any of the Belligerent powers."[39] On several occasions the governor seized French prizes in port that had been armed, equipped, and manned with French and American seamen—such as the British sloop *Polly* (renamed *The Republican*) and the brigantine *Catherine*—and turned them over to federal authorities for violating America's neutrality.[40]

Other New York officials led by Chancellor Livingston did little to hide their pro-French feelings. In fact, through secret political maneuverings and anonymously written newspaper articles, they strongly encouraged America's entry into the war. But the governor's neutrality was praised by Washington, by British diplomats in America, and by those New Yorkers who felt unprepared to go to war. On August 8, 1793, a public meeting held in front of Trinity Church in New York City praised the president for his "wise and well timed measure" advocating neutrality. The meeting also praised Governor Clinton "for his prompt and decided support of the system of neutrality and peace, enjoined by" Washington's proclamation.[41] A week later, Clinton thanked the citizens for their support, "as the approbation of a free and enlightened people is the most honorable and pleasing reward that can be conferred upon their public officers." Perhaps referring to earlier charges that his Antifederalism made him hostile to the federal government, Clinton said that "the firm determination of the citizens to support the government of our country, in the exercise of its important functions, must reflect honor upon their patriotism and good sense."[42] When Washington asked Hamilton to draft an appropriate response to the New Yorkers, he pointed out that it would be "good policy to make proper mention" of Clinton's "promptness & [the] efficacy" of his aid. Reluctantly, Hamilton fulfilled the president's request, and on August 18 Washington sent his reply thanking the New Yorkers for their support. In closing, the president took the "opportunity of publicly . . . acknowledging the prompt and decided co-operation of the Governor of New York towards the support of the neutrality of our country." It was "a pleasing evidence of a spirit of concert for the general good, happily calculated to harmonize and invigorate all the parts of our political system."[43]

On August 8, 1793, Edmund Charles Genet, the French minister to the United States, arrived in New York City. Republicans supported the controversial envoy; Federalists led by Rufus King and Chief Justice Jay opposed him, spreading a report that Genet had threatened to appeal directly to the American people for a change in Washington's policy. Republicans led by Chancellor Livingston denied this report, but Jay and King publicly admitted that they were the source of the report, which, they declared, was true. Republican support for Genet cooled throughout the country as Federalists posed a contest between Genet and Washington. New York Republicans, however, stuck with Genet. They accused Federalists of manufacturing false allegations against the minister.

Governor Clinton warmly welcomed Genet and often appeared with him at public ceremonies at which toasts were offered to the president, the governor, and the revolutionaries of France. At a gala celebration of the tenth anniversary of the British evacuation of New York City on November 25, 1793, Genet publicly saluted the governor as "a true friend to the cause on which the fate of our two countries depend." America and France, Genet suggested, were bound together a decade earlier and now as despots in Europe and in the United States "honor our principles with an implacable hatred." The governor had "rendered to the [French] Republic, and to all the French in these states in general, all the good offices" in his power. Accordingly, Genet assured Clinton that his name was as dear to Frenchmen as it was to Americans. The governor thanked Genet for his "very friendly sentiments," praised "the peaceable and orderly behaviour" of French soldiers and sailors in New York, and expressed the continuing gratitude of America for France's "generous aid in our arduous struggles for Liberty and Independence." The American citizen, Clinton said, "blessed with Peace and happiness, cannot but feel a warm interest in your prosperity."[44]

At one reception hosted by Clinton, Genet met the governor's twenty-year-old daughter Cornelia. It was love at first sight for both of them. Cornelia, a romantic republican, was attracted to the thirty-year-old Genet even before she met him. She pictured him as the great defender of the rights of mankind patriotically fighting America's old enemy. The meeting confirmed her passionate feelings for the flamboyant Frenchman. Genet too became enamored with the governor's free-spirited daughter, and in September rechristened the French privateer *La Petite Democrat* as *Cornelia*. Rumors circulated about the romance, and by fall the couple secretly became engaged. Some Federalists hoped that the marriage would take place because they expected that Genet's obnoxiousness would "in a Year or two, have a favorable influence on the Politics of this State."[45] The marriage, however, was delayed when Hamiltonians spread rumors that Genet already had a wife and two children in France. The ambassador's amorous attention to Cornelia was thus attributed to a desire to ingratiate himself with the governor "for the sake of gaining anti-federal Interest."[46] Told about the engagement, the governor refused to give his permission for the wedding until Genet's marital status was clarified. At about this time, a change in government occurred in France and Genet was recalled, in all likelihood to face execution. In November 1794, after Washington granted Genet asylum and the rumors of a previous wife were refuted, Genet and Cornelia were married at the governor's house with Clinton's blessing. Cornelia brought with her a dowry of £2,000.

Clinton had endorsed the President's neutrality policy not only because of his great respect for Washington but also because he knew that New York was ill-prepared to fight. In his address to the legislature on January 7, 1794, Clinton asked for state appropriations for fortifications for New York City and the frontier and for arms and artillery for the militia. Although he hoped that America might avoid involvement in the war, he viewed New York's situation as "critical." Consequently, "it might be imputed to me as a want of duty, were I to omit reminding you of the naked and exposed condition of our principal sea port, and urging the necessity of immediately providing for its defence. To prevent insult and invasion, we must ever be prepared to punish the one and repel the other." He asked legislators who felt that matters of defense appertained "exclusively to the general government" to understand the seriousness of the situation. Constitutional quibbles should be set aside when the safety of the state was endangered.[47]

The governor also reminded the legislature of the continued British presence in the Northwest posts. Again he acknowledged that this aggression was a federal matter, but pointed out that settlers and land-grant holders had recently complained that their property had "been taken from them within our territory under authority derived from the British government." This news forbade the governor from "observing a silence on this head."[48]

The governor then commented on the weakness of the militia. According to the Constitution, Congress was charged with organizing and arming the militia, and the federal militia act mandated that every citizen was responsible for providing his arms and other accoutrements. According to Clinton, however, "many of our citizens, especially those on the frontiers," were unable to arm themselves. Because the militia was the state's only defense against foreign invasion and domestic insurrection, "too early attention cannot be bestowed to the arming and accoutering of them." To assist in implementing "the plan adopted by the general government," Clinton asked the state legislature to provide for the arming of those citizens "incapable of doing it themselves." Three weeks later, the governor informed the legislature that the state's military stores were exhausted and the artillery was in bad order. "The necessity of provision before the hour of danger is evident."[49]

The Federalist-dominated assembly discussed Clinton's requests but failed to pass any appropriations because the legislators felt that such action would be a step toward war with Great Britain. Clinton condemned the "very learned debates" in the assembly over the constitutional niceties of which level of government should construct fortifications. But the decidedly Federalist assembly had "it in view as far as possible to manifest their contempt for the state government—and to place the governor in the light of a mere inferior deputed to obey the orders of the United States."[50] Even Clinton's request for funds to equip the militia foundered in the assembly. But, during the second week of March 1794, reports arrived in Philadelphia that the British had seized another ninety-three American ships that were being detained at Jamaica and that more than 200 ships (among them the schooner *Governor Clinton* held at New Providence) were held captive in the Caribbean.[51] New York newspapers reported that the British were "fitting up a Prison Ship for Americans" in Jamaica and that upon their arrival prisoners were "stripped of every thing, even of their necessary clothing."[52] These reports brought back vivid memories of the horrid conditions endured by American prisoners during the Revolution. Federalists now agreed that American ports and harbors should be put in "a respectable state of defence, capable of placing us as a nation, above the fear of injury, or the apprehension of insult."[53] Even Hamilton recommended to Washington that the country ought to be in a respectable

military posture, because "war may come upon us, whether we choose it or
not and because to be in a condition to defend ourselves and annoy any
who may attack us will be the best method of securing our peace."[54] The
citizens of New York, it was reported, would "cheerfully submit to any tax
. . . which in the wisdom of their representatives may appear necessary to
defray the expence attending the support of our independence as a nation,
the honor of our flag, and the dignity of our country and government."[55]
The legislature, however, still dallied over fortifications on constitutional
principles and argued that America was in no imminent danger. Assemblymen representing interior districts safe from naval attack objected to the
cost. Finally the legislature passed an appropriation of $75,000 to equip the
militia and purchase artillery.

On March 20, New York City Republicans petitioned the legislature
for state funds to augment the meager federal appropriations for fortifications of "the defenceless" condition of the port and city of New York. The
petitioners hoped to avoid the general war that was devastating Europe,
but acknowledged that America was "already in a state of actual warfare
with a barbarous nation. . . . The honor and dignity of the State, as well as
that of the United States" required action.[56]

A week later, New York City newspapers announced that Lord
Dorchester had conducted secret meetings with the seven Indian villages
of Lower Canada. In his published address dated February 10, 1794,
Dorchester told the tribes that Americans had violated the Canadian
border established in 1783 and that he anticipated war between Great
Britain and the United States by the end of the year. Because Indian
representatives planned to visit New York to sell land, Dorchester was
willing to give them passports so they might return if war broke out.
Dorchester, however, advised the Indians that he would never countenance their sale of land to New York. Because Americans had violated the
peace treaty, that treaty no longer bound British forces.[57] This British
incitement greatly agitated the legislature, which immediately appropri-
ated £30,000 (not the £40,000 requested by the governor) for the construction and repair of forts on Governor's Island and on the frontier.

Throughout the spring of 1794, George Clinton led a volunteer
movement among New York City artisans to assist with the construction of
the fort on Governor's Island. Boats carrying between fifty and a hundred
men left daily as laborers and professionals donated a day's work in the
defense of their city. As the spring legislative elections neared, the governor spent more and more of his time on the island.

Republicans profited from the war scare at the polls as Federalist
majorities in both houses of the legislature were significantly reduced.
Republicans regained control of Ulster and almost achieved voting parity

in New York City. No longer would Federalists command a large majority in the state's largest city. Federalists also faltered in the congressional elections. In 1792 Federalist candidates had been elected in seven of the state's ten districts. Two years later Republican candidates won six seats. This gradual realignment in state politics, although accentuated by the fear of war, was taking place in response to the great national issues that divided Federalists and Republicans.

As Republican election prospects brightened, Federalists launched a major offensive against one source of Clinton's power. The ensuing controversy that developed over the council of appointment in 1794 greatly contributed to Clinton's decision to retire in 1795. The state constitution provided that the council be composed of the governor and a senator from each of the state's four senatorial districts selected annually by the assembly. Councillors were ineligible for consecutive terms, and the governor had only a casting vote in case of a tie.[58] Although not specifically stated in the constitution, the governor exercised sole power to nominate candidates. The council of appointment filled all state offices for which the constitution did not specifically provide an alternative method of election. The council selected the chancellor, the supreme court justices, the attorney general, the recorder, the surveyor general, the mayors of cities, and all county sheriffs, clerks, judges, coroners, auctioneers, and other minor officials. Conservatives in 1777 had hoped to use the council to control local government, which in turn would have an important impact on the kinds of people elected at the state level. However, they did not count on George Clinton being elected governor for six consecutive terms.

Throughout his first five terms, Clinton dominated the council of appointment, but he exercised restraint in his appointments.[59] Officeholders who performed well could count on being reappointed annually. Certain offices seemingly were earmarked for anti-Clintonians—the mayor of New York, the attorney general, and the recorder were often political leaders from New York City and therefore opponents of the governor. After the Revolution, the governor's critics held three of the state's leading judicial positions (Chancellor Robert R. Livingston, Chief Justice Richard Morris, and Associate Justice John Sloss Hobart), the attorney generalship (Egbert Benson and then Richard Varick), the recorder (Richard Varick), and the mayor of New York (James Duane).

Only occasionally did opponents complain about Clinton's excessive patronage. An embittered Philip Schuyler tried to convince John Jay to run against Clinton in 1786 by complaining about the governor's appointments. "Not only the lowest but the most unworthy characters are countenanced by him, and through his influence placed in office of trust; a great part of the magistracy of this [Albany] and the adjacent western and northern counties are wretches that would disgrace the most despicable of all governments,—these serve his turn. He abets a faction ... which wishes to destroy both public and private credit, and whose whole aim is to rise into importance on the ruin of others."[60] In commenting on Clinton's appointment of judges, Brockholst Livingston "repeated a saying of the Governor's ... 'that he considered Abilities in a Judge not so Essential as Republican principles.' "[61]

Alexander Hamilton used Clinton's patronage against him in both the debate over the ratification of the Constitution and the 1789 gubernatorial election. For the first time Federalists argued that the governor should not possess the sole power to nominate candidates, but that he should share this authority with other members of the council of appointment. Such arguments were overtly political and no one took them seriously. After all, the governor's casting vote could only be explained in the context of his exclusive power to nominate. Little came of these Federalists complaints at that time because of Clinton's political strength.

After his controversial reelection in 1792 and his defeat for the vice presidency, Clinton became vulnerable. Anticipating a victory at the spring legislative elections, Federalists acted quickly when the legislature met in November 1792 to elect presidential electors. Federalists, through "the intrigues and address of the old Albany Sachem" (Philip Schuyler), turned out in force for the opening session. Immediately after the governor addressed a joint session, the assembly returned to its own chamber where Federalists used their temporary majority status to elect a new council of appointment. Such a quick election violated "the established custom" that called for the council to be elected later in the term after the outgoing council had served a full year. Schuyler and three other senators (Reuben Hopkins, Selah Strong, and Zina Hitchcock) were elected to the council; a Clintonian described Strong and Hitchcock as having "a proper mixture of ignorance and obstinacy to answer the purposes of the Sachem."[62]

Refusing to call the new council together for a meeting, Clinton met with the old council, which did not make any new appointments. Schuyler and the other new councillors petitioned the governor to convene them, but Clinton ignored their request. The governor, however, felt uneasy about making appointments because of a 1784 precedent of an early council.[63]

Schuyler was particularly concerned about the council of appointment because it was apparent that a new supreme court justiceship was about to be created. Aaron Burr had turned down an appointment to the court; and, although both Clintonians and anti-Clintonians wanted another justiceship, the governor refused to nominate anyone throughout 1793. He did not care for the Republican choice (Peter W. Yates) and would not nominate someone acceptable to the Federalist majority of the council.

After the spring elections of 1793, Federalists held comfortable majorities in both houses of the legislature. On the first day of the new session in January 1794, the assembly again elected a Schuyler-dominated council of appointment. At its first meeting, a Federalist councillor nominated Egbert Benson as associate justice of the supreme court. Despite Clinton's objection to this nomination as unconstitutional, the other councillors voted to confirm the appointment, and Benson took office. The council then went on a rampage. It nominated and confirmed new officers who unseated incumbents, and it created many new county judgeships and justices of the peace. Clinton's tradition of restraint and of limited partisanship was replaced by an unrestrained partisanship in appointments. Ulster County Federalists informed Peter Van Gaasbeck that the council was "properly disposed to grant anything and everything to our friends."[64]

Throughout the council's session, the governor tacitly objected to its actions by refusing to sign the minutes of its proceedings. On March 27, 1794, the last day of the legislative session, Clinton formally protested "in the most explicit and unreserved manner against" what he labeled new procedures that were "repugnant" to the principles of the state constitution, lest his "silence on the subject should be construed to sanction a precedent detracting from the executive's powers and injurious to the interests of the state." He objected to the displacement of many officers "without a hearing or any adequate cause assigned." The constitution neither explicitly nor implicitly authorized the council to increase the number of offices. That power fell within the governor's purview as the supreme executive officer of the state. Clinton argued that although the constitution provided that all officers without a fixed term should serve "during the pleasure of the council," this was not to be construed as "a capricious arbitrary pleasure but a sound rational discretion to be exercised for the promotion of the public good." The council's new policy "renders the constitution unsafe and its administration unstable and whenever parties exist, may tend to deprive men of their offices because they have too much independence of spirit to support measures which they suppose injurious to the community and may induce others from an undue attachment to office to sacrifice their integrity to improper considerations."[65]

On October 3, 1794, Schuyler and his two Federalist colleagues defended the council's actions in a lengthy rebuttal. If the council had violated the constitution, they charged that Clinton had "been most culpably deficient in his duty" by not protesting earlier in the sesssion. The three Federalists admitted that the number of offices had been increased and officeholders had been removed without hearings or cause being shown. They argued, however, that these actions were constitutional and that the council itself had done similar things in the past.[66] The Federalist-dominated legislature ignored the governor's protest.

When John Jay became governor in 1795, he immediately asked the legislature for a declaratory act interpretating the procedures to be followed in the council. Such a bill was introduced, but on February 3, 1796, the assembly resolved that such "a declaratory act defining the powers of the Council of Appointment, or prescribing the manner in which they shall be exercised would be inexpedient."[67]

Throughout his two terms, Governor Jay maintained his exclusive right of nomination. The Federalist-controlled council acquiesced. When Republicans led by DeWitt Clinton regained control of the council in 1801, they advocated the right of the council alone to make nominations. Governor Jay repeated his request for a declaratory act, which was again denied. (George Clinton, now in the assembly, voted against such a declaratory act because the legislature, in his judgment, should not determine the constitutional relationship between the executive and the members of the council.) Jay also requested a ruling from the chancellor and the state supreme court, but Chancellor Livingston and Chief Justice Lansing—both Republicans—refused to offer opinions. The legislature turned the matter over to a constitutional convention empowered to investigate only the total number of state senators and assemblymen and the method of making nominations in the council. Meeting in October 1801, three months after George Clinton began to serve his final term as governor, the convention, presided over by Aaron Burr but under the direction of DeWitt Clinton, ruled that council members as well as the governor could make nominations. The spoils era in New York politics, begun by Federalists in 1794, was now to be carried to its extreme.

Federalist legislators also used Clinton's own Republican principles to tweak the governor and weaken his authority. On January 11, 1794, the assembly voted to shorten the governor's magnificent title from "His Excellency George Clinton, Esquire, the Governor-General and Commander-in-Chief of all the militia, and Admiral of the Navy of the State of New-York" to "His Excellency George Clinton, Esquire, Governor of the State of New-York." Continuing the assault on titles, two days later, Federalist William Wilcocks moved to eliminate all "lengthy titles or terms of pre-eminence, and distinctions not known and warranted by the constitution" as unnecessary and "inconsistent with the plainness and real dignity of republican manners." The chief magistrate of the state should be called simply "The Governor of the State of New-York," and the term "honorable" should be eliminated in referring to state officeholders and governmental institutions, such as the council of appointment, the council of revision, the supreme court, and the senate.[68] The assembly postponed consideration of Wilcocks' motion. During the last week of the session, Federalists attempted to embarrass the Republican governor further by suggesting that he held his clerkship of Ulster County "by virtue of a Commission from the King of Great Britain; which commission ordained, *that he hold his office as long as he should well and faithfully perform the duties thereof.*"[69]

By 1794, New York Republicans worried about the future of their party. With Clinton's popularity in decline and his powers substantially reduced, and his health impaired, they realized that he might retire in 1795. Most people expected that Federalists would again nominate Chief Justice Jay. Although Jay had been sent to Great Britain to negotiate a treaty, Federalists expected his candidacy "to carry with great ease if Clinton is his opponent." Some New Yorkers thought that Alexander Hamilton had designs on the governorship. Among Republicans, Aaron Burr had already started campaigning for the nomination and Robert Yates intended again "to try his strength." For a while, Chancellor Livingston thought he too might be a candidate.[70]

All of this posturing transmuted from theory to reality when, on January 22, 1795, Clinton announced his intention to retire. In his farewell address "to the Freeholders of the State of New-York," given in plenty of time so that the field would be open for others to seek nomination, Clinton said that he had been thinking about retirement "for a considerable time." After nearly thirty years of continuous public service, his failing health and the duties owed to his family required a withdrawal "from a station never solicited by me, which I accepted with diffidence, and from which I shall retire with pleasure." He summarized his political philosophy succinctly: "It has been my invariable object to promote and cherish the republican system of government, as well as from a sense of duty as from a full conviction that it is the only one calculated for the happiness and dignity of man."[71] Agreeing with the Democratic Society of New York, the governor hoped "for an union of sentiment throughout the nation, on the *real principles of the constitution, and original intention of the revolution.*"[72]

Clinton readily admitted that he had made mistakes; he hoped that his successors, "with intentions equally pure, and with the same object in view, may be more successful." The governor concluded by expressing "the warmest emotions of a grateful heart for the repeated and signal proofs of your confidence and affection, and for the efficient aid and support rendered to my administration, as well in the perilous and gloomy scenes of the revolution as in the auspicious period of peace and national prosperity."[73]

As Clinton prepared to leave office, he looked back with pride on his years of service. He had led his state throughout the Revolution and after, in war and peace. Although ill and unable to appear in person to deliver his final address to the opening session of the legislature in Albany in January 1795, Clinton proudly referred to the prosperity and stability of New York. "In a ready obedience to the laws, in the prevalence of public tranquillity, in the advancement of our population and settlements, and in the growing interests of general improvement, we find abundant and multiplied sources of private happiness and national felicity." The fortifications approved the previous spring were "in great forwardness," but the continuing war in Europe and the unstable condition on the frontier required greater exertions. The governor also asked the legislature to consider a revision of the criminal code to bring punishments more in line with "the mild genius of our constitution" rather than the "cruelty of despotic governments." Clinton wanted hard labor and confinement substituted for the death penalty for most crimes. He also asked that a public-school system be established so that all children, not only those of the wealthy, could obtain an education. These humanitarian proposals were only the last in a string of social programs and internal improvements that Clinton had proposed and the legislature had adopted during his last two terms. His proposals included fair treatment of Indians; the improvement and construction of roads, bridges, canals, courthouses, and jails; the drainage of marshlands; aid to Columbia University and the academies; and loans and bounties for farmers and manufactures.

During the 1770s, Governor Clinton led the state in securing independence; during the 1780s he helped achieve economic recovery; and during the 1790s, Clinton tried to improve the living conditions of all New Yorkers. In 1792 he reported that the state's revenue would exceed its ordinary expenses. The legislature should manage this surplus responsibly in a program of internal improvements, assistance to individuals, and wise investments. Clinton hoped that his enviable record of no direct taxation could be maintained. In fact, rather than taxing the people, his administration wanted to offer economic assistance to them by reestablishing a system of government loans to private individuals, using land as collateral (in essence, a continuation of the 1786 loan office).[74] Through this use of the state's capital, Clinton suggested, "the necessities of individuals may be supplied, the settlement of the country advanced, and the interests of agriculture and commerce promoted."

Although content with the state's progress, he was uncertain what the future held for New York. The Federalist ticket of John Jay and Stephen Van Rensselaer had defeated the Republican ticket of Robert Yates and William Floyd. How the state would fare under Federalist rule was as uncertain as how New York would fare without George Clinton. Like

George Washington at Newburgh in 1783, Clinton could justly say that he had grown old in the service of his state. Now for the first time in thirty years, Clinton would become a private citizen.

39. A Short Retirement

George Clinton looked forward to his retirement from public office. During his last two gubernatorial elections, in 1789 and 1792, Clinton himself had been the crucial issue. He did not like the limelight. Nor did he like being shunted aside, as happened after the spring 1793 elections when Federalists won control of the state legislature. Clinton preferred to let others take the lead in the political process, to hang back until the end, when he could tip the balance one way or the other. Since his role in state politics had become unpalatable, especially with his growing health problems, retirement was to be a real blessing. Clinton even found it easy to turn down a formal Republican application to stand for the vice presidency in 1796.[75]

For the next five years, Clinton devoted himself to personal business. As his health improved, he spent more time with his real-estate investments. Throughout his career Clinton's frugality had been criticized as penuriousness. While governor, Clinton lived a simple, unpretentious life. His one passion, however, was investing in real estate. His investments were similar to George Washington's. Both men avoided huge land speculations that might endanger their solvency, and they also avoided speculation in government securities, partly for philosophical reasons and partly to avoid any semblance of impropriety with their public roles. Generally, Clinton's business activities included making personal loans, buying mortgages, and purchasing relatively small parcels of prime land close to established towns or town lots or houses. When buying farms, Clinton looked for good quality soil, a proper proportion of meadow, a pleasant location, a durable stream, an orchard, and the condition of any buildings.[76] These purchases were often made in partnership with others. Usually Clinton would sell a portion of these investments within a few years, recouping his initial investment. He would retain or rent the balance of the holding in anticipation of larger gains. Land sales would usually be made on relatively easy terms—a down payment of one dollar per acre with the balance and interest due in five or six annual payments. Clinton felt that this procedure rendered "the sale of [the] whole safe & compleat."[77] Because of this conservative approach, Clinton never faced the kind of financial catastrophe that was so common in the late 1790s.

Like Washington, Clinton was dispassionate when it came to business

dealings. If someone owed him a debt—whether political friend or opponent—Clinton expected to be paid. He often would encourage his debtors
to pay with strangely friendly letters. He never would stoop "to animadvert,"
but matter-of-factly would inform his correspondent that he intended to
sue. In one such letter, Clinton wrote Judge Zephaniah Platt, a long-time
friend and political ally: "I shall only barely observe that should I unfortunately be involved in Litigation with an old & esteemed Friend I shall have
the Consolation to reflect that the whole Tenor of my Conduct and
particularly the unreserved Communication I made to you of the Measures
I was pursuing were well calculated to have prevented it, and that if those
marks of Confidence had been reciprocated, it never should have happened."[78] The governor felt no remorse at foreclosure—just the opposite.
Clinton believed that his investments served a public purpose and that
those who defaulted on their obligations to him also disserved the public
interest. He believed that he was forced to pursue legal means to ensure the
sanctity of the contract that his debtor had failed to uphold.

Although he was concerned that his children might be left with "a
disagreeable Inheritance,"[79] more importantly, land and property represented freemanship in New York. Clinton could never hope to possess the
vast amounts of land owned by the wealthy patroons, but he felt that he
and his investments played a key role in expanding settlement along the
New York frontier. He saw his investments as helping to enlarge the
number of yeoman freeholders throughout the state. These were the kinds
of people who would preserve republicanism against the oppression of
aristocracy. Those who failed to make good in their dealings with him
represented a flaw in the effort to spread republicanism throughout the
state. Because of this, Clinton felt little personal animosity toward his
destitute debtors. He did feel, instead, that they let themselves, him, and
the whole revolutionary movement down.

In 1790 Clinton sold his New Windsor farm along with its saw and
grist mills, which he had rented out since 1777. It now brought him
£1,500. In 1805 he sold half of his Greenwich Village estate to John Jacob
Astor for $75,000. Clinton and the entrepreneurial German, who had
immigrated to America in 1784, entered into a partnership that called for
laying out streets and neighborhoods and the sale of individual lots.
Confusion set in, however, when the legislature did its own survey and
established an alternative system of subdivisions. The plan became extremely profitable, but not before George Clinton died intestate, leaving
his children an estate valued at about a quarter million dollars.

These kinds of financial ventures made retirement interesting for
Clinton. He also enjoyed his family, particularly the grandchildren. Daughter
Cornelia and Edmund Genêt had moved to the Albany area to be close to

her parents during the governor's last year in office. When the Clintons moved permanently to their farm in Greenwich, the Genêts purchased a farm in Jamaica, Long Island. Often Clinton and his wife would visit their children or have them come to the Greenwich farm. But in late 1799 Clinton's life changed dramatically when his wife Cornelia became fatally ill. Suffering from fever and coughs, she seemed to make some improvement so that her doctor gave the family "flattering Hopes of her Recovery."[80] After lingering for several months, her condition worsened and both Clinton and his daughter Cornelia sensed the inevitable. On March 15, 1800, Cornelia Clinton died, leaving her husband of thirty years alone.

Shortly after Cornelia's death, Aaron Burr appealed to George Clinton to come out of retirement. Burr realized that Thomas Jefferson's election as president in 1800 probably depended on New York's electoral vote. New York's presidential electors were chosen by a joint ballot of the legislature. Much, therefore, depended upon the outcome of the assembly election for New York County. With the rest of the state about evenly divided between Federalists and Republicans, control of the legislature would be determined in New York City.[81]

To ensure the election of Republican assemblymen from New York City, Burr decided on an ingenious plan that united the three wings of the Republican party—the Livingstons, the Burrites, and the Clintonians. Burr waited until Federalists nominated their twelve candidates (all rather nondescript),[82] and then, shortly before the election, announced a slate of prominent Republican candidates. Burr carefully chose the individuals to lead the Republican ticket: Revolutionary War hero Horatio Gates, Judge Brockholst Livingston, and George Clinton. Unfortunately for Burr, all three men refused to stand for election. In an atmosphere of complete secrecy, Burr convinced Livingston to be a candidate if Gates and Clinton also ran. When informed of Livingston's decision, Gates agreed to run, but Clinton remained adamant against serving. Clinton refused the nomination because of ill health and his unwillingness to leave his children so soon after the death of their mother.

Only after three intense sessions with Burr and his chief advisors did Clinton half-heartedly allow his name to be put in nomination. According to Clinton, on the evening that the Republican nomination committee was to meet "to make their final Arrangement," he was asked to attend a meeting at Burr's house. When he arrived, Clinton realized that the meeting's sole purpose was to convince him to run for the assembly. Despite his persistent refusal, Burr and his associates "were extremely importunate declaring that the Success of the Election woud depend upon my Name being on the Ticket and that on this woud also depend the Fate of the Presidential Election." Clinton argued that the election was about

principles—not men. In an effort to excuse himself, Clinton said that he
was disappointed with Jefferson. He and others worked hard against John
Adams and in favor of Jefferson in the 1796 presidential election. But
when Jefferson was elected vice president, he betrayed his supporters by
praising the new Federalist president in his inaugural address to the United
States Senate. Clinton considered Jefferson's speech "as a public contradiction of the Objections offered by his Friends against Mr. Adams's
Election and as a high Censure of their Conduct." With this sour taste still
in Clinton's mouth, Burr and his colleagues could not expect "so great a
sacrifice." The Burrites persisted. One of them told Clinton "that the
public had a Right to command the services of any Citizen." Clinton
"admitted the Truth of the Assertion, but added that they had mine as long
as personal Services could reasonably be required and if I shoud be nominated I certainly woud have a right to appeal to the public by assigning my
Reasons for an Exemption from this duty." The committee implored him
one last time, warning that if he persisted in his determination not to run,
no nomination would be made. Faced with this ultimatum, Clinton agreed
that the committee "might pursue their own Measures and I would be
silent on the occasion."[83] As recalled by one of Burr's lieutenants, Clinton
"never consented to stand, but pledged himself to Colonel Burr and the
committee that he would publish nothing in the newspapers, reserving to
himself the right (which he subsequently exercised) of stating in conversation that his name was used without his authority or permission."[84]

On April 15, 1800, about forty Republicans met at Brockholst
Livingston's house, where they agreed on their candidates and the strategy
for announcing them. On April 16, the newspapers announced that a
nominating meeting would convene the following evening. The meeting
assembled on schedule, at which a nominating committee was appointed.
Half an hour later the committee announced the pre-arranged Republican
ticket led by Clinton, Gates and Livingston.

Burr and his lieutenants took precautions to assure a fair election.
Party observers were stationed at each poll to make sure that no Federalist
intimidation occurred. Burr himself stayed at the poll in the seventh ward
for ten consecutive hours on the last day of the election. When the polls
closed, enough votes had been counted by the poll watchers to determine
that the entire Republican ticket had been elected by a margin of about
500 votes. Ecstatic New York Republicans celebrated and sent word to
their friends in Congress. To many it portended a victory for Jefferson in
the presidential election later in the year. Alexander Hamilton and the
Federalists despaired.

Hamilton had one last hope of preventing a Republican presidential
victory. He and Philip Schuyler each wrote to Governor John Jay request-

ing a special session of the old legislature, which would be asked to alter the method of selecting presidential electors. Instead of being chosen by the new legislature, which would be controlled by Republicans, Hamilton recommended the passage of a law providing for the popular election of presidential electors in districts. This change would guarantee the election of some Federalist presidential electors. Hamilton realized that what he recommended was of dubious propriety, so he asked the usually constitutionally scrupulous Jay to appreciate the country's desperate situation:

> I am aware that there are weighty objections to the measure; but the reasons for it appear to me to outweigh the objections. And in times like these in which we live, it will not do to be overscrupulous. It is easy to sacrifice the substantial interests of society by a strict adherence to ordinary rules.
>
> In observing this, I shall not be supposed to mean that any thing ought to be done which integrity will forbid—but merely that the scruples of delicacy and propriety, as relative to a common course of things, ought to yield to the extraordinary nature of the crisis. They ought not to hinder the taking of a *legal* and *constitutional* step, to prevent an *Atheist* in Religion, and a *Fanatic* in politics from getting possession of the helm of the State.[85]

Appalled by the suggestion, Jay rejected it out-of-hand as he scribbled across the bottom of Hamilton's letter: "Proposing a measure for party purposes which it would not become me to adopt."

The general presumption in early 1800 was that Jefferson would be the Republican candidate for president later in the year. With Republicans in control of the New York legislature, Jefferson's election seemed likely. But little thought had been given to a vice presidential candidate, except that the candidate should come from a large, northern state, preferably either New York or Massachusetts. Elbridge Gerry was the logical candidate from Massachusetts as he might be able to entice some of his state's electoral votes away from John Adams. New York, however, seemed a more likely state from which to choose a running mate.[86]

As soon as word arrived of the Republican victory in New York City, party leaders in Congress assigned Albert Gallatin the task of communicating with New York leaders about a vice presidential candidate. On May 5, Gallatin received a letter from Matthew Livingston Davis suggesting that New York should provide the vice presidential candidate and that only three men could be considered—Robert R. Livingston, George Clinton, and Aaron Burr. Davis informed Gallatin that Clinton "seems averse to public life, & is desirous of retiring from all its cares & toils," while a number of serious objections to the chancellor were apparent. (Livingston's inconsistency and aristocratic air haunted him and he was becoming deaf.)[87] Davis urged Burr as "the most eligible character," suggesting to Gallatin that, if Jefferson selected Burr as his choice for vice president, "it would awaken so much of the zeal and pride of our friends in this State, as to secure us a Republican Governor at the next election" in April 1801, thus guaranteeing the continued support of New York in future presidential elections. But if Burr were passed over for the nomination, "many of us will experience much chagrine & disappointment"—a veiled threat that Burrites in the New York assembly might fail to vote for Republican presidential electors.

Gallatin asked his father-in-law, Commodore James Nicholson, to discuss the vice presidency with the two New York principals. Nicholson traveled to New York and met first with Clinton, telling him "that our republican Friends in Congress were united in Opinion" that he should be Jefferson's vice president. Clinton was unwilling to run for the vice presidency, citing his increased personal responsibilities because of his wife's recent death, his own ill health, and his advancing age. He also felt that his having run for the assembly for the express purpose of electing Republican presidential electors could appear self-serving if he turned out to be the vice presidential candidate.[88] Clinton told Nicholson that he had agreed to serve in the assembly only because of "the peculiar and unhappy condition of our public affairs and the pressing importunity of His friends." In the assembly, Clinton looked forward to selecting presidential electors who would vote for Jefferson. Furthermore, Clinton argued that if he were nominated for the vice presidency, he would be required by tradition not to campaign. If someone else were nominated vice president, Clinton would "use every exertion in my Power" to elect Jefferson.[89] The former governor then recommended Chancellor Livingston, Burr, and John Langdon of New Hampshire as likely vice presidential candidates. Nicholson, however, did not give up easily. He "pressed" Clinton "with great earnestness," suggesting that Jefferson's election might hinge on Clinton's candidacy. Clinton could not believe that this would be the case, but he consented to let his name be put into nomination "without any Contradiction on my part." He wanted it understood, however, that if elected, he "should be at liberty to resign without giving umbrage to our friends."

Nicholson drafted a letter to Gallatin outlining the former governor's position. He showed the draft to Clinton who approved it. Nicholson then visited Burr and showed him the draft. Burr was outraged. He would not be put in a position where Southern Republican leaders again would choose between him and a partially committed George Clinton. Eight years earlier he had allowed such a choice, and the Virginians supported Clinton; Burr would not give them the luxury of such a choice again. He did not trust them to make the right choice. Instead, he would give up the possibility of being vice president and run for governor in 1801—"he would not give up the certainty of being elected Govr. to the uncertainty of being chosen V.P." With this ultimatum, Burr left the room. Two of Burr's agitated advisors joined Nicholson, who showed them his draft letter. They were adamant that for the good of the country Burr should be the vice presidential candidate. The advisors left to talk with Burr. The three men returned, and Burr reluctantly consented to be considered for the nomination.

Because Nicholson felt that Clinton would not accept the office, he altered his letter to Gallatin, writing that Clinton had given "an unqualified declension" while Burr was willing to serve. Burr read the revision and gave his approval. After he sent the letter, Nicholson informed Clinton of the revision. The former governor showed no dissatisfaction, and, according to Nicholson, Clinton believed that Burr was "the most Suitable person & perhaps the only Man" for the job. Clinton was, in fact, "happy in having thus got rid of the Business."[90]

40. Another Term as Governor

An air of optimism enveloped Republicans as the new legislature assembled in Albany in November 1800. They controlled the legislature and with it the council of appointment. It appeared that Thomas Jefferson would soon be elected president of the United States and that Aaron Burr would be his vice president. Burr's influence in the new administration would be strong, guaranteeing federal jobs for party stalwarts. On the state level, Republicans expected to consolidate their legislative strength at the upcoming spring elections. DeWitt Clinton, the dynamic nephew of the former governor, was now leading the state Republican party and he too, through the council of appointment, was expected to provide positions for the party faithful. The only missing piece was a gubernatorial candidate. Burr had been expected to run, but his nomination as vice president eliminated him. Republican leaders had sounded out George Clinton in September, but it was "positively asserted" that he had refused to come out of retirement. Rumors circulated that state Chief Justice John Lansing would be nominated.[91] Republican legislators came to Albany in November 1800, knowing that they needed a candidate who could win a statewide election limited to the £100 freeholders. When a healthy, rested George Clinton arrived in Albany, support for Lansing evaporated. Republican legislators wanted Clinton to be their candidate.

After the legislature adjourned on the evening of November 8, 1800, a Republican caucus met and nominated George Clinton for his seventh term as governor. Clinton again expressed the desire not to serve, but party leaders convinced him to accept the nomination on condition that, if elected, he could resign at any time during his three-year term if the job became too onerous. The nomination, however, was not to be announced formally until late February—the usual beginning of the gubernatorial campaign. Because Clinton was afforded the opportunity to withdraw, the caucus decided not to select a candidate immediately for lieutenant governor. Not until February 26, at the Adams's Hotel in New York City, was Clinton endorsed publicly, along with the nominee for lieutenant-governor, Jeremiah Van Rensselaer.[92]

Still uncertain about another three-year term, Clinton reluctantly accepted the nomination. Only nine days before, Burr's hopes to win the presidency had crashed, when the House of Representatives voted on the thirty-sixth ballot to elect Thomas Jefferson president. DeWitt Clinton probably convinced his uncle to run as a means of forestalling Burr from making a desperate effort to salvage his career by seeking the governorship.

The end of the presidential election of 1800 further convinced both Clintons that Burr was untrustworthy. When Jefferson and Burr each received the same number of electoral votes for the presidency, Burr assured George Clinton that he had no intention of seeking the election in the House of Representatives.[93] Despite these assurances, Burr's forces strenuously advocated his right to the presidency. On February 17, however, Burr's presidential challenge ended when the House elected Jefferson. Burr had gambled everything and lost. He knew that his influence in the new administration would be negligible. Perhaps his career could be salvaged by resigning the vice presidency and seeking the governorship of his home state. But an ambitious DeWitt Clinton saw the danger to his own career if Burr were allowed back as the Republican gubernatorial candidate. DeWitt convinced his uncle that only he could thwart Burr's candidacy and all the dangers inherent in a Burr governorship. Three years later, anticipating his retirement from public office and realizing that Burr was no longer a likely threat, George Clinton wrote to his nephew.

> You are sensible that it was with great reluctance I consented to be held up as a Candidate for the Office I now hold or to enter again into public Life in any Station whatever. . . . The Reasons which then influenced me no longer exist. The Object is happily accomplished and whether my Services have contributed to its success or not is immaterial. The Cause of Republicanism is now so well established as not to require any new sacrafice on my part.[94]

For several months it had been assumed that John Jay would forego an attempt at a third term as governor. Federalists readily admitted that Jay probably could not win reelection. "His manly and inflexible virtue have at length wasted his popularity—Justice cannot long remain popular—She cannot long protect herself."[95] Finally, according to the Republican press, Governor Jay "publicly declined the honor of a defeat by Gov. Clinton, whose election again, in April next, we consider as certain."[96] For a time, Federalists put forth the idea that they would "yield the Contest as not to set up an Opposition Candidate," but, by early January, Federalists in New York City and Albany announced the nomination of Stephen Van Rensselaer (the incumbent lieutenant governor and Philip Schuyler's son-in-law) and James Watson as their candidates to run on a platform of "UNION, GOOD GOVERNMENT AND RATIONAL LIBERTY."[97]

The 1801 election campaign was mild compared with Clinton's two previous gubernatorial elections. The personalities and economic perspectives of the candidates were key issues. A committee of Albany Republicans told New Yorkers that they were living in extraordinary times. While a European war raged, Americans too were embroiled in a war—"a war of principles—a war between equal and unequal rights, between Republicanism and Monarchy, between Liberty and Tyranny." America's contest had started twenty-five years earlier and it continued unabated. British armies had been expelled from our country, but they left behind their mantle of "unequal privileges," which Federalists had made their own.[98]

The committee recommended that the freeholders should vote for the one candidate

> bred in the school of Liberty; the one who has felt the evils of Tyranny and abhors them; the one who has in the most dangerous times shewn himself the Friend of his Country and the bold assertor of her rights— The one hated by Tyrants in '76, and dreaded by the sons of corruption still; he should be the one who has proved himself prudent in Council, and who knows the value of the earnings of industry. In the venerable CLINTON you see all these qualities combined, you see in him all that freemen can wish, or Tyrants abhor.[99]

Freemen were urged to compare Clinton's eighteen tax-free years as governor with his successor's record. The committee believed that Stephen Van Rensselaer was a fine young man, but too inexperienced for such a responsible position. While Clinton had fought the battles for his country's liberty, "Mr. Van Rensselaer was dandling on the lap of his nurse."

Anticipating the old charge of Clinton's Antifederalism, the committee readily admitted that the former governor felt that the new Constitution had not sufficiently guarded against oppression; yet the committee affirmed "that he has always been friendly to a national government" and that his objections to the Constitution were removed when the amendments were adopted in 1791. Even before the amendments were proposed, however, he abided by the wishes of the state ratifying convention and "uniformly and faithfully supported" the new Constitution.[100]

Federalists claimed that the Constitution and the Washington and Adams administrations were responsible for the country's robust economy. Most Republicans in New York and elsewhere had followed "their file-leader" in violently opposing the Constitution. Clinton's election now would jeopardize New York's prosperity.[101]

Federalists conceded Clinton's heroism during the Revolution. His "memorable defence" of the Highlands and other "honorable, praise-worthy and hazardous enterprizes, to deliver oppressed America from British thraldom, will hold a place in the grateful remembrance of his countrymen." But surely such honor for Clinton did not make Van Rensselaer's youthfulness during the Revolution "a crime." Furthermore, Van Rensselaer, in fact, had experience. When, they asked, does a person arrive "at the age of manhood?" As an unsuccessful candidate for lieuten-ant governor in 1792, Van Rensselaer had been criticized for being too young. He was now nearly forty, they said (actually he was thirty-six), and he had already served ten years in the state senate, the last six as its presiding officer. During these last six years as lieutenant governor, Van Rensselaer had demonstrated a "natural force of prudence and good sense, joined to a consummate impartiality, candor and generosity of spirit." He was a disinterested, moderate man, who could serve as a compromise candidate. Wasn't such a candidate preferable "to one whose views are all obstinately fixed, who has one set of interests to pursue?" Mr. Van Rensselaer was "a bigot to no system."[102]

Another Federalist correspondent satirized the age question.

> But say the friends of Clinton, Mr. Van Rensselaer is a "Young Man." This must, indeed, be conceded, if Mr. Clinton's age is the standard of mental maturity. The truth, however, is, that Mr. Van Rensselaer is in the vigor of manhood, about 40 years old, and that Mr. Clinton is in the *decrepitude of age*. Six years ago he declined a re-election on account of his advanced years and increasing infirmities. We should be very glad to be informed by what rule it is, that Mr. Clinton renews his age, and bodily and mental faculties, and becomes more fitted to perform the duties of an office, which six years ago, he declined on account of his incapacity—and whether it is the same rule by which Mr. Van Rensselaer grows younger, and less qualified for his situation.[103]

Federalists in Rensselaerville did not take the age issue so lightly. The charge that Van Rensselaer was dandled on the lap of his nurse while Clinton was fighting America's battles was labeled "false and malicious and intended to insult Mr. Van Rensselaer, for which the freeholders of this town . . . feel a just resentment." Such "malicious, illiberal and unjust" charges were "intended to mislead, and to create unfounded suspicions and a seditious spirit in the minds of the people of this State, which must be reprobated and condemned by every honest American citizen who is a friend to the constitution, the laws, and the true interests of his country."[104] Other Federalists hinted that Clinton agreed to run for governor with the clear understanding that he would "discharge the office *in propria persona*, or by proxy." If elected, Clinton would hold the title but someone else would be "*de facto*, our chief magistrate." Perhaps Clinton's son-in-law, Genêt, would be the power behind the throne or perhaps Clinton's "two sons" on the council of appointment—DeWitt Clinton and Ambrose Spencer—would be given the opportunity to display their "cruelty."[105]

Republicans proudly recalled that their candidate had for eighteen years avoided direct taxes. They charged that after Governor Clinton turned over a healthy state treasury to his successor, the new Federalist administration levied direct taxes almost immediately. If Van Rensselaer were elected governor, he too would raise taxes.[106] Clinton, on the other hand, not only would repeal Federalist taxes, but supporters in some areas of the state even implied that Clinton would refund the taxes that had been paid under Jay's tenure. Republicans tried to convince voters that the choice was simple. As Republican campaign workers went from house to house, they told "each voter that this election is a contest between the Rich and the Poor—that Governor Clinton is the friend of the poor, and will be supported by every poor man in the state—that Mr. Van Rensselaer is a rich man, and a friend to the rich men."[107]

Federalists resurrected many of their old charges against Clinton. The land scandal of a decade earlier was revived and expanded as Clinton was accused of corruptly obtaining extensive land holdings when he was governor and a member of the land-office commission. Clinton was accused of being "the *richest man* in the Union."[108] He had entered public service with "very moderate possessions, and when he *left it*, had amassed a princely fortune."[109]

Albany Federalists attempted to link Clinton with the radicalism of the French Revolution. "The rapid stride of Democracy and Jacobinism throughout most parts of the Union is truly alarming, and calls for a union of sentiment in those good Citizens who possess correct political sentiments in making a firm and decided stand against the many-headed Monster which threatens destruction to our Country's best interests." The election of Van Rensselaer and Watson would allow the state "to be ranked with those in favor of Order and good Government"; Clinton's election would "form a link in the chain of Democracy and Disorganization."[110]

Perhaps the most severe censure was reserved, however, for two non-candidates. The day before the election began, Alexander Hamilton was said to be supporting the Federalist candidates by "harranguing the citizens of New-York, in different Wards, in his usual style of imprecation and abuse against the character of the venerable Clinton." The correspondent felt that it might have been more discreet of Hamilton to remain "obscure and inactive," "having been detected in his illicit amours with his lovely Maria, on whose supposed chastity rested the happiness of her husband and family."[111]

Once Clinton was nominated, Burr decided to use all of his influence to defeat Van Rensselaer. With his bridges burned in Jefferson's administration, Burr hoped to reestablish a home base with his old Republican coalition in New York. Hamilton severely criticized this "active personal" involvement by the vice president, but expected nothing less from Burr than "that he will in every event continue to play the Jacobin Game."[112]

As the election approached, Republicans sensed victory. They eagerly bet on Clinton's election, giving two-to-one odds. Federalists, on the other hand, although trying to exude optimism, were reluctant to give such odds.[113] Aware that Van Rensselaer's candidacy was in trouble, Hamilton tried to goad Clinton into a public debate with Van Rensselaer, but the former governor never gave such a proposal serious consideration.[114]

Some Federalists convinced themselves that Van Rensselaer would sweep to an easy victory. In Kingston Federalist Congressman Barent Gardenier predicted that the patroon would carry Ulster County by between one and two hundred votes.[115] Other Federalists were not as confident. Francis Crawford felt that Ulster would cast 1,600 votes in the gubernatorial election, only 400 of which could be counted on for Van Rensselaer. But Crawford hoped that Federalists would not give up without a fight. "It has been vainly boasted that the Sun of Federalism was about to Set and that we were about to die, but Surely we are not dead yet and if it must be so let it not be without a Struggle—let us pray as Sampson did on a former Occation that we may be avenged on Our political enemies once more and that those men who are Stigmatizing us with the Name of Tory and every other Opprobrious Epithet might be Once more Disappointed."[116]

Despite a prediction by New York City Federalists that their city's £100-freeholders would defeat Clinton by a majority of 400 votes, the former governor carried Manhattan by 176 votes.[117] Republicans were elated. For the first time in a gubernatorial election, Federalists had failed to carry their stronghold—a turning point in New York politics.

Statewide, Clinton won by a landslide 4,000 votes. Van Rensselaer carried only his home counties of Albany and Rensselaer, Greene County in the middle district, and the frontier counties of Oneida, Ontario, and Chenango, where Federalists had strong landed interests and where substantial numbers of New Englanders had settled. Clinton carried everything else.[118] Although Federalists made some gains in upstate towns, such as Troy and Utica, Republicans more than offset that with their strong showings in the south. A realignment of state politics had begun.

On May 17, 1801, President Jefferson congratulated Clinton on his election. The president confided that he had trouble making some of the federal appointments in New York and in some neighboring states. He confessed that of all the duties of an executive, making appointments was "the most difficult & most irksome." Jefferson explained that he was disposed "to make as few changes in office as possible, to endeavor to restore harmony by avoiding everything harsh, and to remove only for malconduct." The governor entirely agreed with this policy. The president believed that some federal officers needed to be changed in New York and that most of Vice President Burr's recommendations were unacceptable. Unacquainted as Jefferson was with New York politics, he told Clinton that "there is no one whose opinion would command with me greater respect than yours, if you would be so good as to advise me."[119] Three years later, Clinton wrote Jefferson about his distaste for filling offices. "The prevailing Itch for Office threatens much Danger from the discord which compe[ti]tions always occasion; besides everyone of this numerous & sordid Tribe of Office Hunters has in his own Opinion, a strong Claim to the favour of Government either for what he has done, said or Thought— They cannot & ought not all be gratified and disappointment will put an end to their patriotism."[120]

This was Jefferson's first overture to preserve the vital Virginia–New York connection after Burr's duplicitous actions. Contrary to the advice of Albert Gallatin, who felt that Burr was too powerful in New York to be ousted by the Clintonians and the Livingstons, the president shunted Burr aside and prepared to reestablish the political bond that he and Clinton shared in 1792.[121] DeWitt Clinton and Chancellor Livingston worked hard to solidify their control over the Republican party in New York; President Jefferson worked with Governor Clinton to isolate Burr at both the federal and state levels.

George Clinton took office for his final gubernatorial term on July 1, 1801. To a great extent, Federalists' predictions of a proxy executive materialized. Much of the governor's authority had dissipated when he lost the exclusive power to nominate officers in the council of appointment. The vigorous DeWitt Clinton, aided by his brother-in-law Ambrose Spencer, became the real power in New York politics. Their uncle strongly disapproved of the ruthless way they exercised their authority in the council of appointment. To cement the Livingston–Clinton coalition, Edward Livingston was appointed mayor of New York City, Morgan Lewis chief justice, Brockholst Livingston a judge of the supreme court, and Thomas Tillotson secretary of state. Many other Livingstons replaced Federalist officeholders or filled entirely new positions. The governor considered such blatantly partisan patronage as an abuse of power, and he protested on the council minutes, often refusing to sign the most obnoxious proceedings. Although Clinton also got a number of appointments for people recommended by Burr,[122] for the most part, he could do little to stem his nephew's growing power. Despite their disagreement on appointment policies, the two men remained close. On the federal level, President Jefferson appointed Chancellor Livingston as U.S. minister to France, which left the leadership of the coalition solely to DeWitt Clinton. The governor accepted this new arrangement, acknowledging to DeWitt that "Business is done with Reluctance in your Absence."[123]

A year after George Clinton took office, DeWitt Clinton mounted a full-scale attack on Burr in the press. In mid-July A View of the Political Conduct of Aaron Burr, Esquire was published, questioning Burr's political orthodoxy and ambition. Burr's friends responded with A Full Exposition of the Clintonian Faction, in which George Clinton's Revolutionary war record and his service as governor were paid proper respect, while DeWitt Clinton was criticized severely. DeWitt's seizure of power was "one of those instances, where vice is descended from virtue, and vicious inconsistency from prudent resolution." Unfortunately, "the honesty of an uncle" did not "flow in the veins of a nephew."[124] The Full Exposition acknowledged that George Clinton and Burr were not friends—they were temperamentally unsuited for each other. It suggested that Clinton, opposing Burr's vice presidential aspirations in 1800, had recommended John Langdon of New Hampshire and had confided to friends at the time, that he himself would run to deprive Burr of the candidacy, as distasteful as that might be.[125]

The most spirited of the Burrite assaults on the Livingston–Clinton coalition was a pamphlet entitled An Examination of the Various Charges Exhibited Against Aaron Burr . . . and a Development of the Characters and Views of His Political Opponents, written by William P. Van Ness under the pseudonym "Aristides." Unlike earlier Burrite tracts, "Aristides" did not spare George Clinton. Ever since 1788, Van Ness charged, Clinton's popularity had declined. "He has never been the idol of the party, which his unblushing eulogists wish the world to believe." Now, in the twilight of his career, he allowed himself to dwindle "into the mere instrument of an ambitious relative, and his mercenary adherents; that a paltry and contemptible faction, alike destitute of talents and of worth, are sheltering themselves under his name, availing themselves of the imbecility of his age, and converting him into a convenient tool, through whom they may dispose of the honors and offices of the state for their own profit and aggrandizement."[126]

According to Van Ness, Clinton had never forgiven Burr for his 1789 gubernatorial challenge. The governor should have realized that Burr was the only serious vice presidential candidate in 1800, and that Jefferson had made inquiries into Clinton's candidacy only out of respect for an old man's feelings. "Aristides" then charged that at a meeting at Burr's house in the spring of 1800, Clinton had contemptuously referred to Jefferson as "an accommodating trimmer, who would change with the times and bend to circumstances for the purposes of personal promotion." Clinton reportedly said "explicitly that he had long entertained an unfavorable opinion of Mr. Jefferson's talents as a statesman and his firmness as a republican. . . . Impressed with these sentiments," Clinton could not with propriety "acquiesce in the elevation of a man destitute of the qualifications essential to the good administration of the government; and added other expressions too vulgar" to be repeated in print. Clinton assured the assembled company that he "would act with pleasure and with vigor" should Burr be nominated "the candidate for the presidential chair." According to "Aristides," Burr anticipated "the evil consequences that at that critical moment would result from such conduct in Governor Clinton" and "insisted before he left the house, that he should promise his friends to desist from using such language, previous to or during the election. This was very reluctantly complied with on the part of Mr. Clinton."[127]

The governor was outraged and described these charges as lies "worse than Billingsgate."[128] Politicians in New York and Washington watched this dispute and wondered "whether silence, lawsuits, or duels are to grow out of it."[129] Clinton could not allow such accusations to stand unanswered. He defended himself in a lengthy letter to his nephew and brought suits against the author and the publisher, both of whom by mid-1804 agreed to print complete retractions if the suits were dismissed. The governor asked James Nicholson to prepare a memorandum describing his role in selecting the vice presidential candidate in 1800. Finally, three days before Christmas, a troubled Clinton wrote to the president, denouncing the "scurrilous Pamphlet" and denying the "accommodating trimmer" statement as "a base and dishonorable Misrepresentation." The governor hoped that such scurrility would not affect their "private Friendship." Clinton regretted that his "Zeal for the public Interest" had brought him "on that Occasion into bad Company without suspecting that I was under the Roof of a corrupt Intriguer surrounded by his worthless Minions."[130] On the last day of 1803, Jefferson responded.

> I received last night your favor of the 22d, written on the occasion of the libellous pamphlet lately published with you. I began to read it, but the dulness of the first page made me give up the reading for a dip into here and there a passage, till I came to what respected myself. The falsehood of that gave me a test for the rest of the work, and considering it always useless to read lies, I threw it by. As to yourself, be assured no contradiction was necessary. The uniform tenor of a man's life furnishes better evidence of what he has said or done on any particular occasion

than the word of an enemy and of an enemy too who shows that he prefers the use of falsehoods which suit him to truths which do not. Little squibs in certain papers had long ago apprized me of a design to sow tares between particular republican characters, but to divide those by lying tales whom truths cannot divide, is the hackneyed policy of the gossips of every society.[131]

Clinton responded that he was "highly gratified by the generous and very friendly Sentiments."[132]

Governor Clinton also revealed to Jefferson his intention to retire again. At present, he told Jefferson, New York Republicans were "able to effect any good Thing we please to undertake and as it is uncertain how long this may be the Case it will be wise in us to embrace this favourable Juncture to fill the important Office I now hold with some suitable Character not so far advanced in years and enjoying a better share of health. . . . Prudential considerations however forbid publishing this determination at present." The governor knew that his friends, "who overrate my Services & personal influence," would oppose such a retirement, but he hoped that they would "acquiesce."[133] Already informed of the governor's plans by DeWitt Clinton, Jefferson started to think about the old governor as a running mate.

Burr had failed in his effort to disrupt the Virginia–New York alliance led by Jefferson and Clinton. The Republican administrations in Albany and Washington continued to work closely together throughout Jefferson's first term, and soon the two leaders would combine their efforts in the next presidential election. Burr, on the other hand, was discredited in Washington and New York. According to Clinton, "the very expression of his Friendship wou'd tend to exite Jealousy against the Object of it."[134] John Armstrong hoped that Republicans would unite with "an unbroken vote" against Burr in the upcoming gubernatorial election. Such a vote would not only "disappoint" Burr—"it prostrates him and his ambition forever and will besides be a useful admonition to future Schismatics."[135]

With Burr eliminated from the Republican coalition in New York and the chancellor serving abroad in France, DeWitt Clinton consolidated his power. Elected a U.S. senator in 1802, he resigned his seat to become mayor of New York City from where he could more effectively orchestrate Republican politics. The mayorial appointment was made by the council of appointment, but the governor told the senator that "his Appointment coming from the Council without any ostensible Agency of mine will be most elligible & honorable."[136]

The governor realized the proper limits in which a party leader could exercise his prerogative. Unfortunately, Ambrose Spencer, the Clinton leader during DeWitt's absence, had overstepped his authority in the selection of a senator to replace DeWitt. "It is to be regretted that the Republicans divided in the Choice of a Senator. It has certainly created some coolness between them." In commenting on Ambrose's behavior, the governor outlined the correct way—his way—of conducting business. Ambrose had pushed too hard for his candidate, rather than covertly influencing the right people at the right time to obtain the desired results. The governor did "not believe that our Friend Spencer conducted properly & wisely on the Occasion—He took too active a Part in the Business considering his Situation which excited disgust & Jealousy that Injured his Friend" and cost him the election. Clinton told DeWitt that "I esteem Spencer & feel myself disposed to do every proper Thing to serve him, but he is an impetuous politician & stands in need of a confidential Friend of more moderation to advise & controul him."[137]

As the business of administering the government grew onerous and as the Livingston faction became alienated from the Clintonians, the aging governor relied more heavily than ever on his nephew.[138] Clinton maintained a steady correspondence with his nephew when DeWitt was in Washington or in New York City. "I have too much to do and too little help to be a punctual or even an intelligible correspondent," but he promised to write as often as possible "if you will promise to burn my Letters as soon as read."[139] Fortunately, DeWitt did not comply with his uncle's instructions. In September 1803 the governor asked DeWitt to draft his annual address to the legislature. "Your knowledge of the present Situation of our Affairs will furnish you with Material and from my former Communications you will be able to collect my Sentiments on the different Subjects." The elder statesman confessed that, after writing speeches for so many years, he "found it extremely difficult to draft one for the last Session, without committing Plagiarism." With an "Outline from you," Clinton felt that it would "be easy for me to make such Additions & Alterations in it as Circumstances may require."[140]

The governor's policies changed little in his seventh term. He asked for and received appropriations for strengthening the militia, and he continued his decade-long pursuit of additional fortifications for New York City. Unfortunately, the cost-cutting Jefferson administration failed to provide adequate funds for defense and matters were made worse when New York's treasurer embezzled funds earmarked for fortifying the port. Despite his best efforts, the governor realized that New York City Federalists "will endeavour to acquire popularity by exclaiming against the defenceless situation of the Port of New York and the Conduct of the Administration as well of the General as State Governments in suspending Measures for fortifying it—This will be a popular Theme especially at a Moment when there is some *small* Appearance of War however remote."[141]

Each year the state's financial condition improved. During the first year of his term, Clinton asked that the assessment of taxes be "more equal and just, collections more speedy and operative, and both less expensive." By the time Clinton left office, the state tax was abandoned. The governor still advocated internal improvements, especially turnpikes and the removal of navigational impediments on the Hudson below Albany. He was pleased to announce that even though the state's population had increased dramatically, crime had decreased in the last three years. He attributed this phenomenon to the new, more humane, criminal code. Although the support he previously advocated for public education had not worked satisfactorily, he continued to press for a new experiment in this area. No new plan was implemented, but the legislature did establish a fund that would support such a program in the future.

During his last year as governor, Clinton again faced the difficult issue of banks. Over the governor's opposition, Alexander Hamilton had successfully launched the Bank of New York in 1784 without a state charter. Clinton moderated his anti-banking attitude when the Washington administration advocated the establishment of the Bank of the United States. The governor saw the new bank as an investment opportunity for New York's surplus funds as well as a counterbalance to Hamilton's bank. Soon Republicans led by Aaron Burr and Brockholst Livingston established a bank in New York City (the Manhattan Bank) and Federalists created another bank in Albany. Clinton, however, remained skeptical. Banks consolidated capital, making the business of obtaining loans more centralized. Those merchants, artisans, farmers, or speculators who had the appropriate connections—all too often political connections—were able to secure loans on the most favorable terms. Furthermore, financial centralization could easily be channeled into political favoritism. The wealthy would band together and signal the demise of republicanism. Because of this, the governor viewed banks, despite their obvious benefits, as potentially destructive forces.

In February 1803 two proposals for banks came before the legislature—one from a group of Albany Republicans and the other from a consortium of New York City Federalists. The governor viewed the Albany plan sympathetically because Albany's lone, Federalist-controlled bank was "very unaccommodating. . . . instead of serving commercial purposes on a liberal Scale [it] is a powerful Engine in the Hands of an over bearing party to serve political purposes." The proposed bank was "intended to emancipate the republicans." "Effectual measures" were devised to keep control of the bank in Republican hands. Unsure of the plan's outcome, Clinton told his nephew that "It will meet with all the Opposition that Federalizm can muster against it."[142]

The second proposal, presented as a petition to the legislature in early February by John Swartwout, called for the chartering of a new Exchange Bank in New York City. Despite the public advocacy by Swartwout, an acknowledged Republican who had been appointed marshal of New York by President Jefferson, it was clear that Hamilton was the primary force behind the proposal. As an inducement to grant the charter, Swartwout offered the state the Cayuga Bridge. The bank would lease the bridge for ten years at an annual fee of $2,500 and would keep up the repairs. If the state did not care to assume control of the bridge, the consortium offered a one-time cash payment of $40,000.[143] Swartwout also offered to "connect" the two proposed banks with Albany serving as the principal location and New York City as the branch. The Albanians decidely rejected the combination.[144]

While a grand committee of the assembly considered the proposal, Swartwout gathered support from all but one of the New York City assemblymen—Republicans as well as Federalists—and from "unsuspecting Friends" who had been duped into signing the petition. The governor also lobbied legislators, warning that the chartering of this ill-conceived bank would be "the death Warrant of Republicanism." Aware of the governor's hostility, Swartwout visited Clinton and "opined his views with considerable Freedom." The governor treated Swartwout with "Civility," reiterated his "disposition to serve the Cause of Republicanism by every proper Means," and reminded the lobbyist "of my uniform opposition to Banks as great Evils in a Republic."[145]

The assembly committee, by a vote of 17 to 9, reported against the Exchange Bank proposal as "inexpedient and unnecessary." The assembly accepted the committee's report and refused to grant a charter. Alternatively, the state senate quickly approved the Albany bank proposal and the assembly concurred. Sympathizing with their Albany friends, Republican legislators "generally believe this Institution to be necessary to emancipate the Albanians who are certainly now in a steep Thraldom too great for them to resist without some Aid." The governor remained skeptical not only about the bank, but also about the Albany Republicans. "For my own Part, I do not believe that any Aid we can give them will make them very useful to the Cause of Republicanism. They are too mercenary and Selfish to make considerable Exertions where their immediate personal Interest is not to be promoted by them."[146] Six months later, Clinton had become thoroughly disenchanted with the Albany bank. The governor felt that the increase in banks had ended. "I have always considered them great Evils and altho it has in some Instances been found expedient to counteract their Mischievous Influence by increasing them, This expedient I trust is put an End to by the interested & selfish Conduct of some of our Friends who originated the State Bank last Winter. They forfeited the Confidence of the Legislature & will not again be able to deceive them with the false show of Patriotism."[147]

Foreign affairs became an issue in Clinton's final term as governor. Throughout his many years as governor, Clinton avoided involvement in matters that he felt were strictly of national concern. In 1803, however, Clinton altered that stance and persuaded the legislature to censure the actions of Spanish authorities in New Orleans, while offering strong support to the Jefferson administration.

In 1783 the Treaty of Peace gave the United States the right to navigate the Mississippi River and to deposit goods in New Orleans as they were transshipped off flatboats onto ocean-going vessels. In 1784 the Spanish government, which was not a party to the peace treaty, disallowed these provisions, opening a decade-long diplomatic standoff. In 1795 Spain and America settled their differences in the Pinckney Treaty (or Treaty of San Lorenzo), which, among other things, granted Americans the right of deposit in New Orleans. But in mid-October 1802, the acting intendant of Louisiana announced that Spain would soon revoke the right of deposit in New Orleans. Enraged westerners threatened to take action as President Jefferson attempted to sort out the complicated diplomatic problem. The administration had received hints that Spain had secretly agreed to retrocede the Louisiana Territory back to France. War seemed possible with Spain or perhaps even with the old ally France. Jefferson sought to strengthen his diplomatic leverage by secretly soliciting resolutions of support from various state legislatures.

Governor Clinton realized the importance to New York of the revocation of the right of deposit in New Orleans. In 1802 more than 250 American vessels carried exports out of the port of New Orleans. New York City dominated this commerce. It was clear that Jefferson was seeking a replacement for Vice President Burr for the 1804 election. Clinton felt that he would make an excellent replacement, assuring the continuation of the New York–Virginia coalition.

As New York's January 1803 legislative session approached, the governor prepared his opening speech uncertain what he should say about the pending crisis in New Orleans. A day before delivering his address, Clinton received an informative letter from Senator DeWitt Clinton in Washington outlining the actions of the Spanish authorities in New Orleans and predicting injuries to New York's commerce, "the magnitude of which is at present beyond calculation." The governor was told that Maryland's legislature had already "passed spirited resolutions upon the subject . . . which will probably be followed by the other states." But Federalists were trying to use the crisis to their advantage. By filling the country's newspapers with inflammatory articles, Federalists "hoped to produce a war immediately with a view to embarrass our financial arrangements and overthrow the administration." The senator advised his uncle to bring the matter to the attention of the legislature. Resolutions supporting the administration would "confound these insidious attempts" of Federalists by stifling the immediate demand for war. The senator assured the governor "that this measure will be very acceptable to the republican interests of the Union" (i.e., the President).[148]

On January 26, Governor Clinton addressed the opening session of the legislature. He reported that the public tranquility remained undisturbed and the prosperity of the state continued, but he regretted the "unwarrantable conduct of the Spanish Intendant at New Orleans, calculated to deprive the people of the United States of the free navigation of the Mississippi." The governor assured the legislature that "there is every reason to believe that the wise and temperate measures adopted by the President will remove all cause of complaint. Should this not be the case and a more vigorous course become proper and necessary, I feel confident it will be pursued, and that this state, which so eminently exerted itself in the establishment of American Independence, will display equal firmness and patriotism in vindicating our national rights from whatever quarter they may be assailed."[149]

The next day, the governor sent a copy of his speech to his nephew. Clinton wrote that even before DeWitt's letter arrived, he had felt it would be appropriate to bring up the Mississippi business; but, not until he received DeWitt's information was he "possessed of knowledge of the Transaction sufficiently correct to enable me to venture to do it." The governor felt that the subject had been properly introduced and he expected that his sentiments would "be reiterated by the Senate and Assembly in their Answer and Address." He suggested that if it should "be thought useful, . . . they woud adopt Resolutions similar to those of Maryland." In any case, copies of the senate's and assembly's responses would be sent to the senator in Washington.[150]

Fearing that he might have misunderstood his nephew's veiled suggestions, the governor stated that "I have always avoided interfering with Affairs appertaining exclusively to the General Government and you will observe in the present Instance (if it can come under that Denomination) I have used a considerable degree of Controll in the manner of introducing it." Should any doubts arise in Washington that the governor had overstepped himself, Clinton asked his nephew "to explain to our Friends the reasons which induced it" (i.e., DeWitt's letter). The governor suggested that DeWitt inform Jefferson of the entire matter, even if no questions arose about it.[151]

On January 28 the senate delivered its response to the governor's speech, which included a lukewarm statement on the Mississippi crisis. The senate believed "that all cause of complaint will probably be removed by wise and temperate measures on the part of the Executive of the United States."[152] The governor forwarded a copy of the senate's response to his nephew apologizing for its temperateness. It was "intended to be better than it is. The fault is in the draftsman in not Expressing as fully & unequivocally as he ought to have done the Sense of a large Majority of this House on the Mississippi Business. It seems there was no body capable to correct it who had confidence enough to do it." The governor felt that the assembly's response would "be more explicit and of better Composition."[153]

On February 3 the assembly justified the governor's confidence. After condemning the Spanish transgression "on the rights of a free people, who consider national honor above all price, the assemblymen expressed their determination "to support" the national honor "at every hazard."[154] The governor expected that this response would "please" his nephew and "meet the Ideas of our Republican Friends at Washington." No other resolutions seemed necessary.[155] The governor continued to support Jefferson's foreign policy, praising the purchase of the Louisiana Territory and advocating a continuation of the neutrality policy toward European belligerents.

Clinton was satisfied that the republicanism he had championed over a lifetime was bringing prosperity and happiness to the people of New York. His philosophy of a strong, but limited, government was working well. "Our fellow citizens, attached to our happy constitution from a conviction that it is wisely calculated, under Divine Providence, to ensure all the essential benefits of civil society, without any unnecessary abridgment of their natural rights, generally manifest a disposition to pay a due obedience to the laws, which they justly consider as the expression of their own will, and to give to government that genuine energy and support which are only to be derived from their confidence and affection."[156] In the closing paragraph of his last annual message to the legislature, what he thought would be his "last Speech in political Life,"[157] Clinton reflected "on the many distinguished blessings we enjoy, as well as on the numerous evils incident to other governments, from which we are exempted." Americans in general and New Yorkers in particular had "abundant reason to rejoice that we live in a republic thus highly favored of heaven, and under a social compact from which so many benefits result." These blessings, he felt, "should animate us with exalted sentiments of patriotism, and with a lively zeal to cherish the fundamental principles of our political institutions."[158] Clinton worried, though, that republicanism might have reached "its Zenith and if so we must expect from the natural Course of Things it will in some degree decline." To combat this danger, Clinton realized that the state needed a governor with more vigor—"a Person not so far advanced in Years as I am and enjoying better Health." He readily admitted that "the constant and unremitting Care and Toil which the Duties" of the office require were more than he "could endure for another Term." Influenced by these factors, midway through his term Clinton confidentially told his nephew and a handful of other trusted friends that it was his "intention to decline a Reelection shoud I be proposed as a Candidate."[159] However, he considered that an immediate public announcement would be imprudent—the party leadership could be told at the end of the upcoming legislative session. His friends opposed the decision, but Clinton never changed his mind. He was convinced that they had nothing to fear. If they exerted themselves, they would "succeed with whatever new Candidate they may think proper to nominate." The only danger they needed to guard against was disunity within their ranks. He did not believe that would happen, but wanted it "explicitly understood" that his refusal to accept another nomination was not motivated by the desire to run for the vice presidency. He assured his friends "with great truth and sincerity" that "Retirement and Ease are my Objects and if I may be permitted to enjoy these it will be an acceptable Indulgence."[160]

DeWitt Clinton did not want his uncle to retire from the governorship. Certain that Aaron Burr would make a run at that office, DeWitt knew that his control over state Republicans depended on Burr's defeat. DeWitt wrote to President Jefferson asking that he encourage the old governor to seek another term. George Clinton, Jefferson was told, would surely defeat Burr by a "numerous majority," but the old war horse had informed his nephew of "his intention to decline" a renomination. Since this information was "known to nobody but one or two intimate friends," DeWitt hoped that the governor's "determination" could be changed. A letter from Jefferson "may be of singular service."[161] The president, however, adhering to his announced policy, refused to interfere in state politics. Responding to DeWitt, the president wrote that it would be "a serious misfortune should a change in the administration of your government be hazarded before its present principles be well established through all its parts. Yet, on reflection, you will be sensible that the delicacy of my situation, considering who may be competitors, forbids my intermedling, even so far as to write the letter you suggest. I can, therefore, only brood in silence over my secret wishes."[162]

DeWitt Clinton's worst fears came true when Burr convinced New York Federalists to support him for governor in 1804. No regular Federalist stood a chance of being elected, so Burr persuaded many Federalists that he was the best alternative. A Federalist governor elected in the spring of

1804 might help elect a Federalist president later in the year. Failing this, Federalists believed that a victorious Burr would have a moderating effect on Jefferson, while a hard core of New England Federalists even considered a separate eastern confederacy with New York as its capital. Burr as governor might lead New York out of the old union into a new one.

Aware of these separatist ideas and filled with suspicion and loathing of Burr, Alexander Hamilton did everything he could to thwart his candidacy. Despite Hamilton's strong opposition, however, Federalists in Albany and New York City nominated Burr in late February. When George Clinton and Jeremiah Van Rensselaer refused to accept renomination by the Republican legislative caucus on February 14, 1804, Hamilton feared that Burr would fill the leadership vacuum. But Governor Clinton worked actively against Burr's candidacy, describing the Burrites as "disappointed Office hunters & Men of desperate Fortunes." Clinton's primary concern was not that Burr would move into a position of leadership in the Republican Party, but that he would "receive a pretty powerful Support from the Federalists."[163]

When Hamilton could not get his own party to endorse a regular Federalist, he and his supporters prepared to endorse the moderate Republican candidate, Chancellor John Lansing.[164] Shortly after his nomination, however, Lansing withdrew because the Clintons demanded that he pledge to defer in all matters to DeWitt Clinton and Ambrose Spencer. Lansing also charged that George Clinton had suggested that his nephew be appointed chancellor.[165] When Lansing withdrew, DeWitt Clinton convinced state Chief Justice Morgan Lewis to accept the nomination. Lewis was thought to be malleable because he owed his career to the Clintons. He had been appointed attorney general in 1791, supreme court justice in 1793, and chief justice in 1801. Furthermore, Lewis' opposition to the merchant's bank in early 1803 had been influential and seemed to sever any connections he might have retained with Federalists. "If ever he leaned towards that party, he has now renounced them & cant decently go back."[166] Hamilton agreed that as a body, Federalists "could not be diverted from Mr. Burr to Mr. Lewis, by any efforts of leading characters." Hamilton had favored a Clinton and then a Lansing candidacy against Burr. Both men, he felt, could defeat Burr, but Burr would probably out-poll Lewis.[167]

Three months before the state elections, Clinton wrote to President Jefferson assessing both national and state politics. On the federal level, the governor warned Jefferson to be wary of Burrites who might now support Jefferson's reelection. "I calculate little upon the Return of deserters at this late Hour. Shoud they come back it will be for interested Motives, and tho they may increase our Numbers, they will add nothing to our strength and by deceiving us into a false calculation of our Force, our exertions will be relaxed. If this shoud be the Case, their return will be an Injury." On the state level, Clinton was far more optimistic,[168] but, as the campaign progressed, Clinton's optimism faded. Republicans had not worked as hard as they should have. Federalists joined with "the few Apostates among" the Republicans might succeed in electing Burr because "They are indefatigable & stick at no Trouble or Expence." Fortunately, however, Republicans realized the formidability of their opponents. "This has at length roused our Friends to correspondent Exertions which will I am persuaded ensure Success."[169] As the election neared, Clinton predicted a Republican victory by 4,600 votes. When the votes were counted in the City of Albany and Burr received only a two-vote victory, the governor saw "no Reason to alter my Opinion except to increase the Majority."[170] A week after the elections, Clinton notified the president that early returns indicated that Lewis would be elected by at least 8,000 votes despite the "united and vigorous Exertions of the Federalists in every quarter of the state." New York would also send all but two or three Republicans to Congress.[171] "The Republican interest," according to Henry Rutgers, had emerged victorious over "all the arts & designs of Federalism & Burrism united."[172]

Two months after the spring elections, the embittered Burr challenged Hamilton to their fateful duel. Burr's gubernatorial defeat and the ensuing duel changed New York and national politics forever. On the state level, the two most powerful opponents of the Clinton–Livingston coalition had been removed. Despite this, Clinton regretted Hamilton's death. He reported that those New Yorkers "in the habit of approving duels" saw no need for it. Many in New York saw Burr's actions more as "an assassination than a duel." Although saddened by Hamilton's death, Clinton felt that the state, the Union, and republicanism were safer. He characterized Hamilton as "a great man—a great lawyer—a man of integrity—very ambitious—& was very anxious to effect that ruinous measure, a *consolidation of the States*.[173]

41. The Vice Presidency

Despite George Clinton's protestations to the contrary, he allowed DeWitt to write a letter to Republican congressional leaders indicating that the governor would be available for the vice presidential nomination. Governor Clinton himself did not close the door on a vice presidential nomination. Ending a letter to Jefferson, the old soldier assured the president "that when relieved from Command," he would "return to the Ranks and with unabated Zeal assist in defending the ground we have gained."[174]

Frightened by the electoral crisis of 1800, Congress proposed in December 1803 an amendment providing that electors vote separately for president and vice president. Ratification of this Twelfth Amendment to the Constitution was expected quickly.[175] Consequently, Republican electors could cast all of their ballots for a vice presidential candidate without fear that that candidate would challenge Jefferson if they both received the same number of votes. By allowing Republicans to unite behind one candidate, they would forestall the election of a Federalist vice presidential candidate receiving the total support of Federalist electors. Thus the time looked propitious for Clinton to make a third attempt at the vice presidency.

On February 25, 1804, the Republican congressional caucus (with only the Burrites absent) nominated Clinton for vice president. Clinton received 67 votes, while his nearest challenger, John Breckinridge of Kentucky, received 20 votes. Four other candidates received a total of twenty-one votes. Burr got no votes. Notified of his nomination, Clinton accepted with an apparent relunctance. "I was in hopes that upon my relinquishment of the office I now hold, I would have been permitted to pass the remainder of my Life in ease and retirement, But finding this to be inconsistent with the wishes of my Friends . . . I shall consider it a duty to yield to their Opinion."[176]

At first the old New England animosity toward Clinton surfaced, but a month later Gideon Granger wrote DeWitt Clinton that "all new England was perfectly willing & I believe in favor of the Candidate selected. . . . there is not an eastern man who did not consider his [Clinton's] pretensions Superiour to those of any Citizen in New England."[177] Some murmured against Clinton's "great Age & *Supposed* infirmities," but others thought "that he will prevent disunion among the Republicans better than any other person."[178]

With Jefferson and Clinton running as a ticket, victory was certain. But the Republican margin of victory was greater than expected. When a somber Vice President Burr opened the sealed envelopes on February 13, 1805, Jefferson and Clinton received 162 electoral votes to their opponents' 14. Only Federalist Connecticut, Delaware, and Maryland voted against the Republicans. To many it seemed logical that Jefferson would want George Clinton as his vice president. The Virginia–New York alliance had been decisive in 1800; it was important to perpetuate it. But to others, there seemed something machiavellian in Jefferson's choice. By choosing a sixty-five-year-old vice president, it seemed that Jefferson was setting the stage for the 1808 presidential nomination of his secretary of state, James Madison.

The seven years that George Clinton served as vice president were not happy ones. Washington City was foreign to him.[179] After trips home to

Poughkeepsie, he regularly returned to the federal capital in his own carriage accompanied by one of his daughters and a servant. While in Washington, Clinton and his daughter Maria lived with John Beckley, Jefferson's confidant. After Beckley's death in April 1807, Clinton lived in a number of different boarding houses.[180] As was his custom while governor, Clinton did little entertaining—a fact that did not endear him to society-conscious Washington.

Clinton was ill-prepared to serve the role of a presiding officer over a legislative body. Throughout his entire career he was an executive—a man of action, not a facilitator for others. Although he looked every inch the part with his wavy silver hair, it was hard for him—now in his late sixties—to stay attentive while the Senate's business dragged on. Further, Clinton also suffered by comparison with Burr, who had presided skillfully for four years.

Vice President Clinton presided over the Senate for the first time on Monday, December 16, 1805. His debut, according to Federalist New Hampshire Senator William Plumer, was inauspicious: "He is an old feeble man—he appears altogether unacquainted with our rules—his voice is very weak & feeble—I cannot hear the one half of what he says—he has a clumsey awkward way of putting a question—Preserves little or no order—What a vast difference between him & Aaron Burr! One would think that the *office* was made for Clinton, & not *he* for the office."[181] Plumer hoped that Clinton would improve, but a month later, John Quincy Adams had no better assessment:

> Mr. Clinton is totally ignorant of all the most common forms of proceeding in Senate, and yet by the rules he is to decide every question of order without debate and without appeal. His judgment is neither quick nor strong: so there is no more dependence upon the correctness of his determinations from his understanding than from his experience. As the only duty of a Vice-President, under our Constitution, is to preside in Senate, it ought to be considered what his qualifications for that office are at his election. In this respect a worse choice than Mr. Clinton could scarcely have been made.[182]

Three years later Senator Plumer had not changed his opinion of the vice president. "He is old, feeble & altogether uncapable of the duty of presiding in the Senate. He has no mind—no intellect—no memory—He forgets the question—mistakes it—& not infrequently declares a vote before its taken—& often forgets to do it after it is taken—Takes up new business while a question is depending."[183] But Plumer saw another side of Clinton's personality, part of what had made him a brilliant leader and politician.

> The more I see & know of this man the more highly he rises in my estimation. . . . But there is something venerable in his appearance—

There is that pleasing cheerfulness—that easy access—that flow of good humour—& docile manners, that are so seldom found in men of his age—& which renders him, to me, a very interesting companion. He appears honest.[184]

After he was elected vice president, Clinton played a limited role in New York state politics. The Clinton–Livingston coalition—always tenuous at best—started to unravel during Morgan Lewis' tenure as governor, as he and the council of appointment (dominated by DeWitt Clinton) battled over patronage. Governor Lewis and DeWitt Clinton also disagreed over the chartering of the Federalist Merchants' Bank of New York. By mid-1805 the split between the Livingstons and the Clintons seemed irreconcilable. Clinton stalwart Theodorus Bailey lamented that Governor Lewis "is pursuing with all his address and industry the policy of conciliating his late political enemies, at the expence of the feelings and reputation of his old Friends." Lewis, according to Bailey, "has taken a vast deal of pains to show his hostility to those men who spent much time and money and toiled incessantly to elevate him to his present Dignity & He seems to have forgotten that his new friends . . . were equally industrious & nearly ruined their fortunes to oppose him." Such conduct "not only evinced a base ingratitude to his Friends," but it showed the governor to be "guilty of perfidy & dereliction of political principle." Perhaps, Bailey suggested,"it would be less injurious to say of him that he was always a *Federalist* in Disguise. We have indeed in my estimation been truly unfortunate in his elevation."[185] By the spring of 1806 the old coalition had totally disintegrated as the Livingstons joined Federalists in routing the Clinton Republicans in the legislative elections.

Fearful of their weakened position, some desperate Clinton leaders (with DeWitt Clinton secretly orchestrating the proceedings) "more zealous than prudent" decided to seek a rapprochement with the Burrites. Theodorus Bailey, representing the Clintons, presided over a supper with the Burrites in New York City on February 18, 1806. Toasts were drunk to the renewed coalition, which looked to defeat Governor Lewis, to resurrect Burr's career, and to elect either George or DeWitt Clinton as president in 1808. Most Clinton Republicans, however, objected to such a political alliance. The "ill-judged project . . . produced a storm of serious magnitude."[186] Two days after the "novel interview," James Fairlie warned DeWitt Clinton about the dangers inherent in dealing with the Burrites. In New York City, Fairlie predicted "that where one vote will be obtained by the Union (as it is called) there will be five lost.[187] A week after the attempted rapprochement, a general meeting of hundreds of Republicans assembled in New York City and denounced their leaders' actions by unanimously censuring the supper and Aaron Burr. Fairlie told DeWitt Clinton that "The mass of our friends before the meeting appeared to be much agitated, that a few should attempt to do an act, and one so important too under the Sanction of a great & respectable party without consulting the party at a meeting called previously." Fairlie feared that the meeting might get out of hand, but leaders of the rapprochement were ready to "give up the project . . . and acknowledge that it was indiscreet on their part."[188]

George Clinton wrote from Washington expressing his opposition to the Clinton–Burr coalition. The vice president was heartened to learn that New York Republicans had regained some of their strength; he hoped, however, that it was not because of "the accession of the Burrites." Some Burrites, Clinton suggested, were honest men who had been "misled." These men would have returned to the Clintonians "tho their Leaders had held out." The Burrite leaders could not be trusted—they sought only "their own Interest and the Ambitious Views of their Principal." Clinton told his nephew that the unholy coalition "excited great Alarm among our Friends throughout the Union who speak of it with detestation & Concern and it is next to impossible to give them a satisfactory Explanation of the Business."[189]

The embarrassed Clinton leaders lamely explained away the meeting as accidental, and Bailey apologized for his actions. With all his political acumen, DeWitt Clinton had not yet learned the political fact so well understood by his uncle. "The Republican party is . . . very large, and contains many respected persons." Prudence and discretion were "requisite in all matters that require the Sanction of the Party at large."[190]

By the end of the year, George Clinton's long-held suspicions of Burr had convinced him that the former vice president was involved in "some Criminal Measures" in the West. He felt relieved with the president's proclamation disavowing any of Burr's activities because the former vice president had "induced many to believe he was acting under the Sanction of our Government." Clinton encouraged the president to take "Prompt Measures" to defeat Burr's "Enterprise."[191] Clinton worried that Burr might still be receiving aid from New York Republicans. He advised his nephew to guard against any efforts in New York to assist Burr in "this Treasonable Conspiracy." He did not want either New York or DeWitt to suffer the pain and disgrace of being associated with this despicable traitor. Clinton assured DeWitt "that the Measures taken by the Executive are wise & efficient & that there is nothing to fear from Burr's Conspiracy," which Clinton considered "as already defeated unless he shoud receive Aid beyond any Thing we have reason to suspect."[192] The defeat of Burr's expedition would also herald "the downfall of Quiddism & Federalism . . . for it cannot be doubted that both were in some measure implicated in it at least as far as to wish it a successful issue."[193]

To regain their hold on state government, Clinton Republicans again approached George Clinton about a gubernatorial nomination in 1807. This time the vice president refused adamantly. "It really gives me much Pain," he wrote, "to learn that my Friends have it in Contemplation to hold me up as a Candidate for Governor." Clinton reminded his nephew DeWitt that it was only with "great reluctance" that he agreed to run for governor in 1801, and then only under the express condition that he could resign during his three-year term if he "found the Duties of the Office disagreeable and Burthensome." Despite the onerousness of the job, Clinton completed his term because of the "fear a resignation might be injurious to my Friends & the Cause of Republicanism." Clinton had thought that "this sacrifice at my Time of Life . . . would be the last my Friends would ask of me." The vice president was aware that his supporters might say "that it is only a Transfer from one Public Station to another," but Clinton argued that the vice presidency kept him busy only three to four months a year and required him to travel between New York and Washington, which he found "serviceable" to his health. Clinton asked his nephew to explain his situation so that he would not be forced to make an "absolute refusal" of a nomination.[194] "Sick of the [Lewis] administration," "the Old Republicans" nominated as governor Judge Daniel D. Tompkins of the state supreme court.[195] Tompkins defeated the incumbent Lewis, and Vice President Clinton, writing from Washington, was elated. "It is now perfectly understood here as a struggle between the Old, sound (Whig) republican Party & the Federalists."[196] The vice president felt confident that Republicans would again carry the next presidential election. First, however, they would have to choose a candidate to lead them.

42. An Unsuccessful Bid for the Presidency

By 1807 the national Republican party had become as divided as the New York party. President Jefferson, like Washington before him, tried to avoid the European conflict, but as French and British violations of America's commercial rights increased, Jefferson resorted to drastic measures to preserve American neutrality. His extremely controversial embargo of 1807 seemed to place the burden of American foreign policy on the northern commercial states. The budget-conscious administration also did little to strengthen coastal and frontier defenses. Because of this, northern states suffered most in peace and stood most exposed in case of war. A small group of ardent "Old Republicans" led by John Randolph of Roanoke opposed Jefferson's policy that, to their way of thinking, tended to expand the power of the executive and the authority of the general government. The purchase of the Louisiana Territory, presidential involvement in legislative affairs, the expansion of the federal government's financial activity along with the support for rechartering the Bank of the United States all alienated Randolph and his "Quids." Within this tense climate, the approaching presidential election of 1808 created a conflict among Republicans over who would succeed Jefferson. The three most likely successors seemed to be James Madison, James Monroe, and George Clinton.

Although the president publicly stayed aloof from the political contest, it was obvious that he preferred Madison. As the election neared, the vice president became more disenchanted with the administration's policies, and Jefferson cooled toward Clinton. The president did not consult with Clinton on political appointments in New York or on important foreign-policy matters. On a visit to the federal capital, former Governor Morgan Lewis was warmly greeted at the executive "Palace." Clinton believed that Lewis would be "duly noticed & rewarded" if he used his influence in New York to elect Madison president. The administration also considered dividing New York into two states, thereby weakening it and ensuring "Virginia's perpetual dominion over the states, and perpetual succession to the Presidency."[197]

By February 1808 Clinton believed that war was inevitable "unless we consent to surrender our Independence." It was impossible "to accommodate Matters with one of the Belligerent Groups of Europe so as to stear Clear of War with the other One." Diplomatic negotiations merely delayed the outbreak of hostilities. The negotiations afforded America the opportunity to mobilize, but the president avoided any meaningful armament program. This troubled the New Yorker who had long advocated a strong defensive posture.[198]

Sensing that they trailed Madison, Monroe's supporters suggested a union with Clinton. Because of his age and his position as vice president, Clinton should be nominated for the presidency and Monroe as his running mate. Such a pairing would unite the party nationally and guarantee at least eight to twelve years of Republican domination of the executive branch. Support for a Clinton–Monroe ticket surfaced throughout the country. Congressman Josiah Masters of New York predicted a nomination soon.[199] Even Quid-leader John Randolph endorsed the ticket, although such an endorsement probably did little to improve its chances of success.[200]

Madison's supporters lobbied hard for their candidate. Massachusetts and Virginia members of the House of Representatives were nearly united in their support of Madison with a New England vice presidential candidate, presumably John Langdon.[201] On January 19, 1808, Vermont Senator Stephen Roe Bradley (president of the 1804 congressional caucus) invited all Republican senators and representatives and a few nominal Federalists, such as John Quincy Adams, to a congressional caucus in the Senate chamber on January 23 at which presidential and vice presidential candidates would be chosen. Congressman Masters publicly condemned the proposed meeting, while Virginia Congressman Edwin Gray wrote to Bradley privately denouncing the invitation as an "usurpation of power."[202]

About fifty Republicans boycotted the meeting, while another ten were out of town. Eighty-nine members of Congress attended. Feeling a sense of impropriety because two states (Connecticut and Delaware, neither of which had any Republican members of Congress) were unrepresented, Bradley stepped down as presiding officer and Senator William Branch Giles of Virginia moved that the meeting "re-assemble" as ordinary citizens with Bradley as chair. After this charade, eighty-three delegates voted to nominate Madison as the Republican party's presidential candidate. Clinton and Monroe each received three votes. The caucus overwhelmingly nominated Clinton for a second term as vice president. He received seventy-nine votes to five for John Langdon, three for Henry Dearborn, and one for John Quincy Adams. A few days after the caucus, word arrived that on January 21 a legislative caucus in Virginia had also nominated the secretary of state to be president.

Clinton's supporters refused to sanction the caucus' action. The vice president denied that he had been notified of the meeting. He did not attend, nor was he consulted about being nominated for vice president. The public, he said, should not infer that he accepted the results of the caucus.[203] Clinton told his nephew DeWitt that the Bradley conventioneers "dare not speak to me on the Subject. They find themselves much embarrassed & they shall remain so as long as I can be silent on the subject with propriety."[204] Throughout the entire election, Clinton never formally accepted the vice presidential nomination.

New York Senator Samuel L. Mitchell, who boycotted the caucus because he feared that he "should be blamed for having any thing to do with the business at this time," visited the vice president on the evening after the caucus. According to Mitchell, Clinton considered "himself treated with great disrespect and cruelty by the gentlemen of his own party who acted at the caucus." Mitchell, however, put much of the blame on Clinton himself for having too much "self-complacency."[205] Because Clinton felt so strongly that the nomination was due him, he believed others should feel the same way and that there was no need to lobby for it. After the caucus, Mitchell believed that "there does not appear the remotest probability of his success as President." Even before the caucus, Mitchell held out little hope for Clinton. Mitchell wrote to his wife that Madison and Clinton were the two strongest candidates. "The former gives dinners and makes generous displays to the members. The latter lives snug at his lodgings, and keeps aloof from such captivating exhibitions. The Secretary of State has a wife to aid his pretensions. The Vice-President has nothing of female succor on his side. And in these two respects Mr. M. is going greatly ahead of him. Besides, people object to Mr. Clinton, his advanced age, and his want of diplomatic knowledge and of the foreign relations of the country. Notwithstanding all his integrity, worth, and decision, I do not at present see how we can assure his election to the Presidency."[206]

Even as his chances for the presidency faded, Clinton remained silent. Agreeing with various party leaders about "the critical and alarming situation of our national affairs," the vice president vowed not to be involved in election politicking while Congress was in session.[207] He told his nephew that "At the earnest sollicitation of many Gentlemen whom I consider as the most virtuous & intelligent Friends to the Cause of Republicanism from different parts of the Union, I have withheld a Public Expression of any Sentiments or determination of mine respecting the next G[eneral] Election, and I consider myself bound as well in honor as from a regard to the Cause to Continue to observe Silence on that Subject." This, Clinton admitted, "is a painful task; but believing it to be the last sacrafice that will be asked of me, I shall submit to it." Clinton hoped that his silence might enable Congress to enact legislation that could keep the country out of war or at least prepare America for hostilities. Silence, however, would assist Madison, and his election would be a disaster for both the country and the party. "It is in my Opinion impossible that the Cause of Republicanism can exist much longer under the present visionary Feeble & I might add Corrupt Management of our National Affairs. It is calculated to disgust our best Friends and is fast doing so—The medidated successor will improve upon the example of his Patron to whom he will owe his Election & make our situation still worse if possible."[208]

Clinton and some of his supporters saw a Madisonian conspiracy against them. Six weeks after the caucus, Congressman Masters explained to Edmund Genêt what was happening. Throughout the last session of Congress and through December 1807, Clinton's congressional supporters had attempted "to harmonize and conciliate" with the Jefferson administration. Nothing the Clintonians did, however, could assuage the Madisonians' "hostility and wrath." Madison's Virginia and Massachusetts supporters were "determined to destroy" Clinton; they "prevented every thing, that Looked like union." Clinton and his followers refused to attend or sanction the caucus because they felt that a Madison candidacy would end in the "destruction to our principles & friends."[209] Masters then unconvincingly reported that "Our prospect of success is flattering." A Clinton–Monroe ticket was "safe" in Pennsylvania, New Hampshire, Vermont, and Rhode Island. A majority of Maryland electors was expected. Some chance of success existed in Massachusetts, Georgia, and South Carolina, while three or four votes could be expected from both North

Carolina and Kentucky. The Clintonians would not even give up hope for Virginia. Clinton's supporters had asked the New York legislature to endorse the Clinton–Monroe ticket, which would "give a spring to our friends through the Union."[210] Such an endorsement never came.

Virginia Representative John Randolph mounted a strong campaign among his Quid followers against Madison and in support of a Clinton–Monroe ticket. In mid-February, Randolph reported that Monroe was gaining "ground very fast" in Virginia. Massachusetts Governor Sullivan had formally "declared against" Madison and the Republicans of that state seemed to be divided. Pennsylvania appeared to "be decidedly for the V.P." If anti-Madison presidential electors united behind the Clinton–Monroe ticket, Madison would be defeated. A division among anti-Madison electors would force the election into the House of Representatives, where "Madison is the man."[211] A month later, Randolph's optimism had waned. Madison's opponents in Maryland, particularly in Baltimore, were "unnerved." "It is necessary to *speak*, & *to speak out*, especially those who justly possess the public confidence." Unless the "timid" supporters of the vice president in Maryland and throughout the country exerted themselves, all would be lost.[212]

Because Clinton refused to endorse the caucus' nomination, rumors spread that he had withdrawn from the Republican party. A congressional committee visited Clinton on March 30 seeking a clarification of his position. The vice president gave the committee "a tart, severe, and puzzling reply." The Republican leaders remained "in a quandary" over "what to do with their nomination of him; for as he has not declined to serve his country when duly called upon, he may be considered as much a candidate for the Presidency under another nomination as for the Presidency under this one made by themselves."[213] Clinton steadfastly denied all reports that he had bolted from the Republican party and refused to withdraw as a candidate for president. Somewhat disingenuously, Clinton suggested that he felt "perfectly disinterested as to the Result of the Election, for indeed as it respects myself personally success woud give me more pain than Pleasure. . . . I have never obtruded myself on the Public as a Candidate; it woud be therefore an Absurdity to think of withdrawing my Name from where I have never placed it & thereby promote the Success of a Measure [the caucus] which in my Opinion is destructive of the Vital Principles of Republicanism."[214]

For a while, Federalists considered endorsing Clinton as their presidential candidate. Alarmed at such a prospect, Virginia Federalist John Thierry Danvers wrote a satirical pamphlet attacking Jefferson and the two primary Republican presidential contenders. Madison was pictured as a loathsome, venal politician grasping to retain the cloak of his mentor. Clinton was ridiculed as the "venerable sage" who, "having some years ago retired from public life, under the pressure of years, again revived to all the vigour of youth." The vice president was being manipulated by advisors who could not hope to be elected on their merits alone. Once the congressional caucus endorsed Madison, the Clinton camp decided that it was "necessary to tickle the federalists a little, in order if possible to gain their suffrages as a counterpoise to the weight of his rivals interest. There appeared no more certain way of doing this, than by pretending a most cordial affection for the commercial interest of the nation, and a most brotherly sympathy for the distresses of the merchants."[215]

Danvers hoped that Federalists would not "be cajoled by such bungling artists." If Clinton were indeed elected, Federalists' interests would "be the first that are sacrificed. For a little while perhaps, he may condescend to acknowledge his obligations; but democracy has always been his religion, and he would return, at the moment he could do it with safety, into the bosom of his *mother church*." Danvers warned well-meaning Federalists not "to contemplate any kind of fellowship with the 'venerable sage' and his hungry band." He hoped that the Federalist party "will never descend to become the ladder for Mr. Clinton to mount aloft."[216]

During the third week of August 1808, about twenty-five "respectable men" from New Hampshire, Vermont, Massachusetts, Connecticut, New York, Pennsylvania, Maryland, and South Carolina met secretly in New York City in what has been called America's first national nominating convention. They considered whether they ought to run their own candidates or support Monroe or Clinton. Alarmed at the sectional bias of Madison, New England Federalists were willing, as the lesser of two evils, to unite behind a northern Republican "of practical talents, of energy, of character;—a friend to commerce." Clinton seemed to fit all of their requirements. Massachusetts Federalists George Cabot and Harrison Gray Otis enthusiastically supported him, but the New York and Pennsylvania delegations opposed such an endorsement.[217] When it was determined that the New York Republicans—both "Madisonians and Clintonians"—were "disposed to unite to the abandonment of Clinton," the Federalist meeting decided not to endorse the vice president.[218] It is uncertain that Clinton would have accepted such a Federalist nomination; he might have rejected it as an unholy alliance as he had opposed the conciliatory moves made by his supporters toward the Burrites in 1806. Federalists ultimately nominated Charles Cotesworth Pinckney and Rufus King, although at least one newspaper reported that this secret Federalist meeting had nominated Clinton for president and Pinckney for vice president.[219]

Clintonians mounted a vigorous national newspaper and pamphlet assault on the caucus. Americans were advised to oppose Virginia's pretensions to providing the president perpetually. "This pride has stimulated the people of that state to believe that Virginia geese are all swans."[220] Why not elect the man who stood with Jefferson for four years—the man who was "selected four years ago by the nation, as the most proper person" to succeed Jefferson?

On the other hand, Clintonians charged that from the very first day of Clinton's vice presidency, "a host of unprincipled and disappointed men attempted to seal his political death." He was isolated from President Jefferson—never consulted "nor supplied with the confidential information which was due to his character and his station." The administration's friends tried to devise a mechanism "best fitted to exclude Governor Clinton from the presidency; without generosity or honor, they opened all the sluices of calumny, and endeavoured to sink him in the whirlpool of Virginian aristocracy." Clintonians charged that Madisonians in the congressional caucus nominated Clinton for the vice presidency for purely tactical reasons. His presence would satisfy the "plain republicans." But Madison's plan was to wound Clinton's "feelings and to overload him so much with disgust that he would give up the nomination." Madison's friends used the expectation of a vacant vice presidency "as the golden apple," holding it out to prominent men in every state as the reward they would receive for their support.[221]

As in previous elections, Clinton's advanced age played a major role in his opponents' campaign. Clinton supporters responded that the vice president had served conscientiously and faithfully as president of the Senate—perhaps the most physically taxing job in the federal government. His mind was as bright and energetic as it was at age thirty, with the added benefit of now being "a repository of experimental knowledge." The vice president could draw upon this fund of knowledge, and "his mind remained elastic and firm, his judgment sound and decisive; his perceptions acute, and his body strong and vigorous." If Clinton was too old to be president, why did the congressional caucus almost unanimously nominate him to be vice president? Supporters compared him with other venerable statesmen, such as George Washington, who was sixty-five years old when he left the presidency, and Benjamin Franklin, who made Clinton look like "a middle aged man."[222] Madison, derided as "this juvenile Franklin," was merely attempting unfairly "to sweep off from the political stage, a man of sterling worth, eminently qualified to serve his country, in the perilous times which threaten it"—a man to whom the illustrious Washington had turned for "aid and counsel . . . in the most perilous moments of distress, when our independence was most jeopardized."[223] Turning Clinton's age into an advantage, "Nestor" suggested that no one under sixty-five ought to be elected president until a constitutional amendment limiting the president's term was adopted. Far better that "three successive [old] Presidents should die in the chair, than that one young or middle aged man should get into it, who, with a common share of ambition, using the means within his reach, and aided by that sycophancy which will ever occupy the atmosphere of so much power, would be able to make himself a tenant for life, and thereby saddle the nation with a monarchy."[224] Using an old technique from Clinton's last gubernatorial campaign, Americans were asked whether Clinton should have a man "placed over his head, who was receiving correction from a school-master, while he was engaged in the strife of armies."[225]

Clintonians saw "a kind of fitness in the Vice-president's stepping to the Presidential chair." Such a regular succession "highly harmonizes with the feelings of the American mind." As important as this regular rotation of men was, it was even more important that there be a rotation in the states that provided the president.

Clintonians denounced the congressional caucus as an oracle from the capitol aimed at muting the voice of the American people and as a violation of the spirit and the letter of the Constitution, because members of Congress were expressly forbidden to be presidential electors. The caucus, by nominating candidates, was in effect electing the next president of the United States.[226]

As he had been since 1787, George Clinton was criticized because he had opposed the ratification of the Constitution. Madison, of course, was uniformly praised for his role in drafting and adopting the Constitution. But Clinton's New York supporters discovered a novel way to reverse these images. As part of the general campaign to discredit Madison, Clintonians charged that Madison had been an arch-Federalist in the Constitutional Convention of 1787, in the ratification debate, in the first federal Congress, and even as secretary of state he counseled the president to expand the powers of the central government.

The proceedings of the Constitutional Convention were still unknown to Americans. None of the delegates' notes had yet been published. Madison himself refused to publish his notes, by far the most substantial record of what took place at the Philadelphia meeting. Using Robert Yates's yet unpublished notes from the convention, "A Citizen of New-York" (Edmund Genêt) charged that Madison was the real danger to the Constitution. The Virginia Plan introduced into the convention in May 1787 provided for the creation of a government "on the principles of unity and consolidation, to the total exclusion of state governments." This was the proposal advocated by Madison. Rather than electing a man president who had wanted "to prostrate our state governments, which are the pillars of our federation," Americans should give their "votes to the one who hath never deviated and who is now what he always hath been, an energetic supporter of American federation, but an enemy to consolidation and monarchy."[227]

In the area of foreign policy Clintonians argued that Madison, despite his years as secretary of state, was just as inexperienced as Clinton. Madison was "the *mere organ or mouth piece* of Mr. Jefferson." The diplomatic papers signed by Madison were really the work of Jefferson—the experienced diplomat—"and *merely copied* by his *chief clerk* James Madison."[228] Madison, according to Clintonians, was "a man of good talents, probably a second or third rate." He was an honest man, but "*destitute of nerve*," and "*easily played upon*." He was no match for Bonaparte. An acknowledged Francophile, Madison would not have an independent American foreign policy. Clinton, on the other hand, was "the skillful pilot, the brave general, and the energetic statesman." He would "protect you from foreign and domestic foes, and consult your happiness, independence, and glory; place Clinton at your head and you are safe. . . . strengthen the arm of Government, and let Clinton guide the bark."[229] Napoleon would never deal seriously with a government led by "lenient philosophers," but with "old soldiers at our head, will treat us with more respect." George Clinton was the man for the job. His name was "the collective idea of military and civic virtue, of prudence and firmness. . . ."[230]

Clinton had experienced America's vulnerability directly. During the winter of 1806–1807, Clinton's youngest daughter, Maria, was dangerously ill. Beginning in January, Maria started to show signs of improvement, and her physicians felt that her life was no longer in danger. Clinton, however, saw "Symptoms still remaining that give me much Anxiety." The vice president watched over his twenty-one-year-old daughter as she slowly, "almost imperceptibly," regained her health. By the beginning of June 1807, Maria could sit up a half hour in a day.[231] By the end of June, Clinton decided that he and Maria should return home to New York via boat rather than overland. Travelling by revenue cutter, the vice president's ship was accosted by a British man-of-war. Newspapers reported the affront, which occurred only months after the *Leopard–Chespeake* affair in which a number of American seamen had been killed and wounded. At least one newspaper reported that the vice president's cutter had been fired upon thirty-five times.

President Jefferson congratulated Clinton on his "escape from British violence." Jefferson took this act of aggression very seriously and asked Clinton to write explaining the details of what had happened. He also requested that affidavits be obtained from the captain of the cutter and others that would be forwarded to our minister in London who would make a formal complaint to the British government. Clinton had the affidavits forwarded to Washington, but he realized that the administration's foreign and defense policies were inept.[232]

Madison's foreign policy was based on his "adoptive child, the embargo." This "unmanning policy" had stagnated the spirit and energy of the country and had brought America to the brink of war. Clinton had a bolder, more effective plan—a "dignified plan of neutrality." He would fortify our seaports and raise a well-disciplined army to protect both the south and the north. An effective naval force—not merely the administration's gunboats—would be stationed in each of the country's principal harbors. Ministers to courts that treated America with disrespect would be recalled. American merchants would be warned if the government could not protect them, and they would be allowed to arm their vessels. America's expansionist plans in Florida and in Canada would be delayed until new land was needed for settlement. Clinton would limit diplomatic negotiations—fewer "notes, memorials, and pamphlets on the imaginary law of nations" would be written. His tracts would be written "with swords, cannon and bayonets, on human skin." And finally, he would embargo nothing, because "the interference of government in mercantile transactions" always does more harm than good.[233]

The newspaper and pamphlet campaign won support for Clinton throughout the country. In Pennsylvania, many Republicans had long disliked Madison. He had been one of the driving forces in the drafting and adoption of the U.S. Constitution, thus alienating the state's numerous Antifederalists. Clinton's Antifederalism gained adherents. In the first Congress Madison supported programs that were anathema to many Pennsylvanians, including moving the nation's capital to the banks of the Potomac. Madison had been largely invisible in the "reign of terror" under the Adams administration, when Republican newspaper editors had been intimidated and prosecuted under the Sedition Act. When he emerged from his retirement from federal service and became secretary of state, he kept many Federalists in office, endorsed the compromise over the fradulent Yazoo land purchases in Georgia, and supported the embargo that financially debilitated the state. Pennsylvanians also had a stake in getting presidents elected from states other than Virginia.

In Philadelphia, the *Democratic Press* strongly opposed the congressional caucus even before it met. After Madison's nomination, the paper attacked the constitutionality of the caucus and printed essays supporting Clinton as president. Editor William Duane of the influential *Aurora* favored Clinton as his first choice and Monroe as his second, but conceded that the caucus nomination ought not to be renounced. "It is certainly not a period to bicker about men; and if we can only ensure the pursuit of the same system of policy that has been pursued under *Jefferson*, it is a very subordinate consideration at this moment which is the man." Pennsylvania Republicans would "not divide—they will support the choice made in the usual manner, since no other or better manner had been provided by the constitution."[234] Some believed that Duane took this lukewarm position merely to be contrary to his rival, the *Democratic Press*.

A number of Pennsylvania congressmen adamantly supported Clinton.

Samuel Maclay led a "flying squad" that worked tirelessly for Clinton's nomination and bitterly denounced the caucus system. When the "Democratic Conference" met at Lancaster on March 7 and 8, 1808, a compromise slate of presidential electors was chosen, consisting of supporters of Clinton and Madison. They were designated "the friends of Jefferson, and of democratic principles."[235] As the election approached, however, the state Republican committee sensed that Clinton could only be elected president if he received Federalist backing. Unwilling to elect a president so tainted, most Pennsylvania Republicans reluctantly abandoned their first choice and endorsed Madison, who received all of Pennsylvania's twenty electoral votes.[236]

In New York, the Livingstons, Lewisites, and Burrites all supported Madison. Chancellor Livingston encouraged Madison to save America from not only foreign aggression but also "from the disgrace of falling into the hands of ignorant dotage at home."[237] Although sympathetic to Clinton, Governor Tompkins was unwilling to support a losing cause and alienate the incoming Madison administration. As a face-saving gesture for both Clinton and the legislature, it was agreed to split the state's electoral vote. Madison received thirteen votes and Clinton six—the only electoral votes cast for Clinton as president.

By refusing to accept the decision of the caucus, some Republicans felt that Clinton had betrayed the party and therefore should not remain its vice presidential candidate. Virginia presidential electors John Preston and Philip Norborne Nicholas wrote to Senator Wilson Cary Nicholas, Madison's campaign manager, asking for advice. They felt committed only to Madison's presidential candidacy. Because Clinton had never accepted the caucus' vice presidential nomination, they felt "entirely at liberty to do as we may think best with respect to the Vice President."[238] Senator Nicholas, however, advised the electors to vote for Clinton.

> At the same time I can not conceal from you, its being the wish of a number of our friends that he should be set aside. This proceeds from dissatisfaction at Mr. Clinton's conduct. It is believed he should have acquiesced in the nomination of Mr. Madison, that he should have declared whether he would accept of the office of Vice President or not. It is suspected he is alienated from the republicans. This is believed from his own deportment, and from the conduct of his friends and the editors of papers that are supposed to be under the direction of D[eWitt] Clinton. Among the warm friends of Mr. Clinton are to be found the bitterest enemies of the administration and its measures. The reasons that induce me to think that he ought to be elected are, that he was nominated by the caucus at this place, and that nomination not having been revoked, if he is not elected there will not in future be any reliance upon such nominations, all confidence will be lost and there can not be the necessary concert.[239]

Nicholas also suggested that the only way in which Clinton would not be elected vice president would be for Virginia to withhold its support. Such an act would add to the jealousy that Republicans in other states felt toward Virginia. He thought that Virginia should defer to Pennsylvania's wishes on the vice presidency. Pennsylvanians had generally supported Clinton for president, but they had accepted the caucus' nomination. Virginia should do the same.

When the Virginia electors met, most of them were inclined to oppose Clinton. Nicholas' letter, which had been shown privately to a few of them, was then read to all of them. Enthusiastically, the electors voted unanimously for Madison for president; reluctantly they all voted for Clinton as vice president. Nationally, Madison and Clinton were easily elected. Madison defeated Pinckney 122 to 47. Clinton received 113 electoral votes for vice president to King's 47, while John Langdon, Madison, and Monroe each got three votes.

43. The Lamented Patriot

George Clinton did not attend the inaugural ceremonies for James Madison on March 4, 1809, and he was three days late in arriving for the congressional session that began on May 19. In fact, he had little desire to serve another term as vice president. Throughout the last three years of his life, he was troubled with various ailments that caused his periodical absence from the Senate. The death in 1810 of his daughter Cornelia, "who was very dear" to him, was a severe blow.[240]

Nevertheless, Clinton was one of the centers of opposition to President Madison. Years later, when Albert Gallatin was asked about the role of the vice presidency, he referred to Jefferson's conduct under President Adams and Clinton's under Madison. "I know that nothing can be more injurious to an Administration than to have in that office a man in hostility with that Administration, as he will always become the most formidable rallying point for the opposition."[241] A properly orchestrated coalition of anti-administration Republicans and Federalists in the Senate would have presented the president with many problems. But Clinton's age and health worked in Madison's favor, and the vice president did not serve effectively as an opposition leader.

Probably the most important act performed by Clinton as vice president occurred on February 20, 1811. By a one-vote margin (65 to 64), the House of Representatives had recently defeated a bill rechartering the Bank of the United States. Proponents of the measure, supported by President Madison and Secretary of the Treasury Gallatin, introduced a similar bill in the Senate, hoping that enough Republicans would join

Federalists to pass the measure, which would then be re-introduced in the House. Henry Clay led the Senate opposition. On the final vote, seven Federalists and ten Republicans favored recharter and seventeen Republicans opposed it. The decision was Clinton's. Voting as the old Republican he was, the vice president cast the deciding vote against rechartering the Bank of the United States.

Henry Clay drafted the vice president's speech accompanying his vote. Years later, Clay acknowledged his assistance, but refused to claim authorship: the speech represented the ideas and the philosophy of the vice president.[242] Clinton admitted that Congress had the constitutional authority to pass all laws necessary and proper for carrying into execution the powers specifically granted to the federal government. But the power to create a corporation was not expressly granted and should not be assumed by implication. He did not feel that his interpretation of the Constitution would "in any degree, defeat the purposes for which it was formed." On the contrary, to interpret the Constitution broadly would encourage "an inevitable tendency to consolidation, and affords just and serious cause of alarm." If it were found that the federal government needed this authority, "the Constitution happily furnishes the means for remedying the evil by amendment." The vice president ended by stating that, "In the course of a long life, I have found that Government is not to be strengthened by an assumption of doubtful powers, but by a wise and energetic execution of those which are incontestable; the former never fails to produce suspicion and distrust, while the latter inspires respect and confidence."[243] The principles that George Clinton espoused during the perilous days of the Revolution, during the Confederation years, and during the bitter dispute over the ratification of the Constitution were now invoked in the last important decision that he would make in public office.

* * *

As the nomination of presidential candidates for the election of 1812 approached, everyone realized that George Clinton would not be able to continue in office. As he lay on his deathbed, the president's wife lamented that "electioneering for his office goes on beyond description."[244] After an illness of about four weeks, George Clinton died of pneumonia at 9:00 A.M. on Monday, April 20, 1812. During his last weeks, he was attended by his daughter Maria, his nephew, Congressman George Clinton, Jr., and his son-in-law, Congressman Pierre Van Cortlandt, Jr., son of Clinton's longtime lieutenant governor.[245] He was seventy-three years old and had spent the last half century in the service of his country.

President *pro tempore* William H. Crawford announced the death to the Senate: "By this afflictive dispensation of Divine Providence the Senate is deprived of a President rendered dear to each of its members by the dignity and impartiality with which he has so long presided over their deliberations, and the nation bereaved of one of the brightest luminaries of its glorious revolution." Congress appointed a joint committee to report "measures proper to manifest the public respect for the memory of the deceased, and expressive of the deep regret of the Congress of the U.S. on the loss of a citizen so highly respected and revered."[246] On April 21, the House of Representatives and Senate met in a special morning session to settle the funeral arrangements. Both houses resolved that their presiding officers' chairs be shrouded with black for the remainder of the session and that their members wear black crepe on their left arm for thirty days. The entire Congress planned to attend the funeral later that day.

The arrangements committee, along with a detachment of District of Columbia cavalry met at O'Neal's boarding house, Clinton's last residence, at 2:00 P.M. A half hour later, the vice president's body was taken from his room to lie in state at the Capitol until 4:00. At that time the funeral procession began its half-hour march to the congressional cemetery near the navy yard. The procession started with cavalry and marines followed by the congressional chaplains and Clinton's physician. The hearse followed with eight Revolutionary War veterans as pall bearers. Members of the Clinton family followed the hearse, and in turn were followed by President Madison, the officers and members of the Senate and House of Representatives, the members of the cabinet and officers of the government, and "a concourse of people greater than ever has been gathered together" in Washington. Shops closed so that everyone could attend. "A general gloom pervaded all ranks of Society." The *National Intelligencer* ended its account of the funeral by stating that "When a CLINTON descends to the tomb of his ancestors, it is fit that the whole nation bewail the general loss, and history immortalizes his name. Hallowed be the ashes of the honored dead!"[247]

In New York City the common council set Tuesday, May 19, as a day of public tribute to the memory of the deceased vice president. A lengthy procession of public officials, militia, and private citizens marched from city hall to the Presbyterian church on Wall Street, arriving between noon and one o'clock. Prayers and music were followed by a eulogy delivered, surprisingly, by Gouverneur Morris. The bells of the city's churches tolled and minute guns fired at the battery and at Fort Columbus on Governor's Island. Shops closed and business was suspended as a bereaved city said farewell to "one of its brightest and worthiest pillars and ornaments."[248] A poem commemorated the occasion:[249]

Clinton is Dead! the good, the great!
    The patriot firm—the soldier brave
Whose arm upheld a drooping state,
    Sinks, full of honours, to the grave.

Through a long life, where glory's light
    Sublimely mark'd his fair career,
No stain occurs, his fame to blight;
    No spots upon our Sun appear.

Then, sacred be his cherished Name!
    With Washington's forever join'd,
Our deepest reverence, they shall claim,
    In holy union ever twin'd.

And, o'er his narrow house of Death,
    Shall hang, of greenest laurels wove,
A still renewing glory-wreath,
    The tribute of his country's love.

Three eulogies were delivered in New York City. No record remains of the one given at a meeting of Tammany by Jonal Mumford. The other two, by Gouverneur Morris and Elbert Herring, were published as pamphlets. Gouverneur Morris spoke at the Presbyterian church on May 19 at the request of the common council of the City of New York.[250] Morris and Clinton had read law with William Smith in the early 1760s. The two men respected each other greatly and were friends throughout the Revolution, but "a difference of political opinion, has since wrought a separation."[251] During the 1780s, Morris was a leading nationalist. In the Constitutional Convention he was among the most powerful advocates for a national government. In the 1790s he remained a staunch Federalist. The choice of Morris was peculiar, and Morris admitted that his oration was "coldly delivered and better received than such speaking deserved."[252] It is illuminating to compare these orations from political foe and friend. Morris began his oration with the bleak recognition that "Another soldier of the revolution is gone." Those who loved the vice president should feel not sorrow over his death, but relief. He was a great man who contributed much to the glory of America in his youth, but "bending beneath the weight of age, he was doomed to behold her in a wretched condition which he could not amend, which he could not but deplore." The bulk of the oration then outlined Clinton's life. Occasionally an anecdote or an amplification by Morris illustrated Clinton's perspective. Clinton, Morris said, was elected to the Second Continental Congress but attended little. "He had an aversion to councils, because (to use his own words) the duty of looking out for danger makes men cowards." During the Revolution, he suppressed the tories, gallantly defended the Highlands forts which had a profound impact on the unfolding drama at Saratoga, and raised supplies from an indigent and exhausted people for the starving Continental army.

In one area, Morris claimed that he and Clinton saw eye to eye. Clinton's gubernatorial career was "directed by a conviction that the foundations of society repose on the rights of property; a sacred regard to which can alone secure all others. . . . from the moment property becomes insecure, the incentives to industry are removed, and the principles of temperance and frugality destroyed." Not many of Clinton's opponents would have disagreed with this political philosophy; not many of them would have described Clinton in these terms.

Morris dealt bluntly with Clinton's vice presidency. Although he regularly presided over the senate, "to share in the measures of administration was not his part. To influence them was not in his power." His sense of duty and propriety, however, "induced him to be silent." As a soldier, he believed "the sword more powerful than the pen," consequently he opposed the theoretical foreign policy of embargoes. You cannot blame "an old man," Morris suggested, "for preferring measures, sanctioned by experience, to projects, however, wise, which have seldom been tried, and, when tried, have failed of their proposed object."

Elbert Herring's eulogy was delivered on May 20 at a meeting of the George Clinton Society. The society began meeting well before it formally adopted a constitution and rules on July 26, 1812, the seventy-third birthday of the late governor. It met regularly on the first Tuesday of each month and was dedicated to promoting the interest and disseminating the political principles of republicanism. Members also agreed "to support the constitution, laws and liberties of the United States of America, against all enemies foreign and domestic."[253] The preamble to its constitution reads like an oration honoring the memory of the deceased governor.

Herring's oration was far more complimentary than Morris'. All were saddened by Clinton's death, but his mourners could be heartened that his was an eminently useful life. Herring proposed to look at Clinton's life "and the virtues which stamped the hero and formed the patriot" to determine how this man became "a father of his Country." Herring described George Clinton as his friends saw him:

> Undissembling and unassuming, his manners were a transcript of his mind, denoting that genuine simplicity, peculiarly adapted to republican character. More intent on performance than on profession, his words left no impression of dubiousness, but seemed to partake of action as they flowed from his lips, and to give form and body to the subject of discourse. There was nothing evasive, ambiguous, or subtle, in his public or private deportment. His frankness resulted from a love of truth, which was conspicuous in all his actions. His modest deportment proceeded from natural feelings, and was cherished by just perceptions of its

suitableness. Conversant with affairs of state, and exalted in political station, he retained a courteous and unaffected freedom of demeanor, that made him accessible to all who sought his intercourse. . . . His habits were untainted by voluptuousness, unstained by luxury, and in conjunction with many original traits, caused him strongly to resemble the eminent men in the early period of Roman history.

Elected as the state's first governor during a time of peril and crisis, Clinton rose to the occasion with "more than an ordinary exercise of firmness, intelligence and valor." When duty called, Clinton "held danger in contempt." His maxim was "that his country not only had a claim on his services, but a right to life itself in her defence. . . . In the camp and in the cabinet, he equally evinced a composure and self possession, that bespoke a reliance on his own powers to meet occurring exigency. . . . His presence inspired confidence; his activity prompted dispatch, his ingenuity suggested expedients."

In peace Clinton "was the practical statesman, sound in judgment, prompt in execution, determined in purpose." He was not a philosopher, "but the morality of politics was familiar to him." In domestic relations, he knew that government must be limited by a constitution and laws; and in foreign relations, that his country's actions should be based on national power and a sense of right.

* * *

No matter when George Clinton lived, his greatness of character would have revealed itself. The perspicuity that taught him to seize the moment and choose the right means to an end, the wisdom to explore the entire range of possible actions and their consequences, the inventiveness that allowed him to develop solutions to seemingly impossible problems, the valor as a soldier and the courage that produced firmness as a politician, and the "unconquerable spirit of patriotism" that encouraged him to serve his country in times of danger would have set him apart from ordinary men. But to have these characteristics converge in a man during monumental events and epic crises adds luster to Clinton's glory.

George Clinton helped win America's independence. Subsequently he devoted his life to securing the triumph of republicanism, what we would today call democracy, uncontrolled by wealth or corruption. That America in 1812 was a democratic and diverse society and was on the verge of an enormous economic expansion was in no small degree due to Clinton's influence. His legacy was a vibrant nation of states and people, just beginning to develop its unlimited potential of political and economic freedom.

Notes

Introduction

1. Hamilton to James Madison, New York, May 19, 1788, Harold C. Syrett, ed., *The Papers of Alexander Hamilton* (27 vols., New York, 1961–1987), 4: 649.

2. Clermont, September 7, 1788, Livingston Papers, New-York Historical Society [NHi].

3. See John P. Kaminski, "The Governor and the Commander in Chief: A Study in Admiration and Friendship," Stephen L. Schechter and Richard B. Bernstein, eds., *New York and the Union: Contributions to the American Constitutional Experience* (Albany, 1990), 408–22.

4. Duane to Clinton, Princeton, August 12, 1783, Harold Hastings, ed., *Public Papers of George Clinton . . .* (10 vols., New York and Albany, 1899–1911), 8: 234.

5. Hamilton to Robert R. Livingston, German Town, Pa., August 7, 1777, Syrett, 1: 308.

6. Hamilton to Robert Morris, Albany, August 13, 1782, *ibid.*, 3: 137–38.

7. Hamilton to Clinton, Philadelphia, February 14, 1783, Syrett, 3: 255–56.

I — Preparing for Leadership

1. Charles Clinton's diary of the voyage is printed in *Olde Ulster* (10 vols., Kingston, N.Y., 1905–14), 4: 175–80.

2. Quoted in E. Wilder Spaulding, *His Excellency George Clinton, Critic of the Constitution* (New York, 1938), 6.

3. George Clinton to Charles Clinton, Camp near Fort Ontario, August 4, 1760, L. W. Smith Collection, Morristown National Historical Park.

4. William Smith, *Memoirs* (2 vols., New York, 1956), 2: 60n.

5. Gilbert D. B. Hasbrouck, "Governor George Clinton," New York State Historical Association *Quarterly*, I (1920), 145.

6. Spaulding, 30–33.

7. For McDougall and the legislature's actions, see Roger J. Champagne, *Alexander McDougall and the American Revolution in New York* (Schenectady, N.Y., 1975), 27–40.

8. Thomas Jones, *History of New York During the Revolutionary War*, ed. Edward Floyd De Lancey (2 vols., New York, 1879), 2: 326.

9. To Charles DeWitt, February 27, 1770, quoted in Spaulding, 30.

10. Jones, 2: 326.

11. *Ibid.*

12. *Ibid.*, 2: 326.

13. *Ibid.*, 2: 328; Hasbrouck, 147.

14. Edward Rutledge to John Jay, Philadelphia, June 29, 1776, Richard B. Morris, ed., *John Jay: The Making of a Revolutionary, Unpublished Papers 1745–1780*, 1 (New York, 1975), 280.

15. Jones, 2: 328.

16. *An Oration in Honor of the Memory of George Clinton* (New York, 1812), 10.

17. *Ibid.*, 2: 327–28.

18. November 1776, *Public Papers*, 1: 430.

19. To Colonel Charles DeWitt, New Windsor, January 9, 1776, *Public Papers*, 1: 217.

20. To Colonels Pawling and Snyder, Fort Montgomery, April 27, 1777, *Public Papers*, 1: 745.

21. To John McKesson, *Public Papers*, 1: 241.

22. March 3, 1777, *Public Papers*, 1: 643.

23. March 8, 1777, *Public Papers*, 1: 655.

24. May 22, 1777, *Public Papers*, 1: 836–37.

25. George Clinton to George Washington, Fort Montgomery, June 19, 1777, *Public Papers*, 2: 43.

26. George Clinton to Israel Putnam, Fort Montgomery, July 9, 1777, *Public Papers*, 2: 92–93.

27. Charles Z. Lincoln, ed., *Messages from the Governors* . . . (10 vols., Albany, 1909), 2: 8.

28. President Abraham Ten Broeck to President John Hancock, Kingston, March 18, 1777, Papers of the Continental Congress, Item 67, New York State Papers, 1775–88, National Archives. Clinton's commission is in the collection of the Museum of The City of New York.

29. George Clinton to George Washington, New Windsor, April 18, 1777, L. W. Smith Collection, Morristown National Historical Park.

II — THE WARTIME GOVERNOR

1. John Jay to Leonard Gansevoort, Kingston, June 5, 1777, Henry P. Johnston, ed., *The Correspondence and Public Papers of John Jay* (4 vols., New York, 1891), 1: 141.

2. Henry Beekman Livingston to Robert R. Livingston, June 30, 1777, Robert R. Livingston Papers, NHi.

3. Johnston, *Jay*, 1: 141.

4. Kingston, June 2, 1777, *Public Papers*, 1: 855–56.

5. John Jay to Philip Schuyler, Esopus, June 20, 1777, Johnston, *Jay*, 1: 142–43. Alfred F. Young, *The Democratic Republicans of New York: The Origins, 1763–1797* (Chapel Hill, N.C., 1967), 23.

6. Morris Graham to George Clinton, Little Nine Partners, June 16, 1777, *Public Papers*, 2: 36.

7. Johnston, *Jay*, 1: 142n–43n. William Smith stated that George Clinton even lost votes when people incorrectly voted for "General Clinton," because such a ballot was registered for James Clinton, George's older brother who had seniority as a general. *Memoirs*, 1: 172.

8. Young, 24.

9. Quoted in Staughton Lynd, *Class Conflict, Slavery, and the United States Constitution* (Indianapolis, Ind., 1967), 38–40.

10. Schuyler to Jay, Albany, June 30, 1777, Johnston, *Jay*, 1: 144.

11. To John Jay, Fort Edward, July 14, 1777, *ibid.*, 1: 146–47.

12. Quoted in Don R. Gerlach, *Proud Patriot: Philip Schuyler and the War of Independence, 1775–1783* (Syracuse, 1987), 233. Gerlach then states that throughout the remainder of the war, Schuyler and Clinton "enjoyed an easy friendship." I tend to think that they enjoyed an uneasy friendship, one in which Schuyler always resented the fact that Clinton was sitting "in the Chair of Government" that was rightfully his.

13. George Clinton to Philip Schuyler, New Windsor, August 7, 1777, Clinton Papers, Library of Congress.

14. *Public Papers*, 2: 88–89.

15. Fort Montgomery, July 11, 1777, *Public Papers*, 2: 105–6.

16. Syrett, 1: 297.

17. Fort Montgomery, July 26, 1777, *Public Papers*, 2: 140–41. Clinton was true to his word and returned in the fall to take command in the defense of Forts Clinton and Montgomery.

18. August 4, 1777, John C. Fitzpatrick, ed., *The Writings of George Washington from the Original Manuscript Sources, 1745–1799* (39 vols., Washington, D.C., 1931–1944), 9: 15.

19. White Plains, July 12, 1777, *Public Papers*, 2: 106–7.

20. August 2, 1777, *Public Papers*, 2: 161–62.

21. August 4, 1777, *Public Papers*, 2: 175–76.

22. August 1777, New York State Library.

23. *Messages from the Governors*, 2: 10–11. It was easy for Clinton to project this personal philosophy to a federal-state context, where the federal government would have only those powers delegated to it.

24. *Ibid.*, 12.

25. To Major General Israel Putnam, New York, November 9, 1777, Syrett, 1: 357.

26. Hoffman Nickerson, *The Turning Point of the Revolution Or Burgoyne in America* (Boston and New York, 1928), 343.

27. Troyer Anderson, *The Command of the Howe Brothers During the American Revolution* (New York, 1936), 261.

28. Philip Schuyler to George Washington, Saratoga, July 7, 1777, Washington Papers, Library of Congress.

29. Quoted in Bernhard Knollenberg, *Washington and the Revolution: A Reappraisal* (New York, 1940), 19.

30. Hamilton to Robert R. Livingston, German Town, August 7, 1777, Syrett, 1: 306–9.

31. *Ibid.*

32. Washington to Israel Putnam, August 11, 1777, Fitzpatrick, 9: 5, 56.

33. George Clinton to James Duane, August 27, 1777, Knollenberg, 20.

34. George Washington to President John Hancock, Camp 26 Miles from Philadelphia, October 10, 1777, Papers of the Continental Congress, Item 152, Letters from George Washington, National Archives.

35. George Washington to President John Hancock, Head Quarters, October 13, 1777, Papers of the Continental Congress, Item 152, Letters from George Washington, National Archives.

36. This account of the loss of the forts is taken from George Clinton's letters to the Council of Safety and to George Washington, October 7 and 9, 1777, *Public Papers*, 2: 380–95. See also George Clinton to Benjamin Lincoln, New Windsor, October 8, 1777, L. W. Smith Collection, Morristown National Historical Park.

37. Samuel Holden Parsons to Governor Jonathan Trumbull, Danbury, Conn., October 7, 1777, Charles S. Hall, *Life and Letters of Samuel Holden Parsons* (Binghampton, N.Y., 1905), 118.

38. Isaac Q. Leake, *Memoir of the Life and Times of General John Lamb* (rep. ed., New York, 1971), 174–77.

39. One of these spies was Daniel Taylor, who, unfortunately for him, stumbled upon some militiamen dressed in British uniforms. The Americans brought Taylor to Governor Clinton, where Taylor was seen to swallow something. A strong dose of tarter emetic was administered which produced a small silver ball. Again Taylor seemingly swallowed the missle. The governor threatened to hang Taylor immediately and cut him open on the spot. Taylor produced the silver bullet which was fastened together at the middle with a screw. Several days later, Taylor was tried, convicted, and hanged on an apple tree within sight of a smoldering Kingston.

40. See note 35.

41. Samuel Holden Parsons to Governor Jonathan Trumbull, Danbury, Conn., October 7, 1777, and Peekskill, October 9, 1777, Hall, *Life and Letters of Parsons*, 118, 119.

42. Leake, *Lamb*, 179.

43. Gouverneur Morris to Philip Schuyler, Kingston, October 8, 1777, Schuyler Papers, New York Public Library.

44. Gouverneur Morris to Robert R. Livingston, Kingston, October 8, 1777, Livingston Papers, NHi.

45. Samuel Holden Parsons to Governor Jonathan Trumbull, Danbury, Conn., October 7, 1777, and Peekskill, October 9, 1777, Hall, *Life and Letters of Parsons*, 118, 119.

46. George Dudley Seymour, *Captain Nathan Hale and Major John Palsgrave Wyllys* (New Haven, 1933), 189–90.

47. Philadelphia County, October 15, 1777, Fitzpatrick, 9: 372.

48. George Washington to General Israel Putnam, October 19, 1777, Fitzpatrick, 9: 401.

49. George Clinton to Benjamin Lincoln, Hurley, October 22, 1777, *Public Papers*, 2: 471–72.

50. Irving Brant, for instance, denigrated Clinton's military reputation that had been established by the surrender of two forts. "Election of 1808," in Arthur M. Schlesinger and Fred L. Israel, eds., *History of American Presidential Elections, 1789–1968* (4 vols., New York, 1971), 195.

51. *New York Journal*, April 18, 1792.

52. *An Oration in Honor of the Memory of George Clinton* (New York, 1812), 10–11.

53. George Clinton to President Henry Laurens, Poughkeepsie, September 9, 1778, Papers of the Continental Congress, Item 67, New York State Papers, 1775–88, National Archives. On March 26, 1778, General Jedidiah Huntington wrote Clinton telling him that the court over which he was to preside would sit the next day. Huntington sent the governor a list of the areas to be examined. Clinton Papers, State Historical Society of Wisconsin.

54. Spaulding, 85; Clinton to Henry Laurens, September 9, 1778, Papers of the Continental Congress, Item 67, II: 134, National Archives.

55. Leake, *Memoir of John Lamb*, 179.

56. Hamilton to Putnam, New Windsor, November 9, 1777; and Hamilton to Washington, New Windsor, November 10, 1777, Syrett, 1: 356–60. Unbeknownest to Hamilton or Putnam, on November 5 Congress had relieved Putnam of his command and reassigned him to the main army under Washington.

57. January 22, 1778, *Messages from the Governors*, 2: 19.

58. George Clinton to George Washington, Poughkeepsie, December 20, 1777, *Public Papers*, 2: 589–91. The chain was to be 500 yards long with "each Link about two feet long, to be made of the best sterling Iron, two Inches and one Quarter square." *Ibid.*, 708n–9n.

59. Fishkill, June 1, 1779, *Public Papers*, 5: 6.

60. Philadelphia, August 18, 1779, *Public Papers*, 5: 199.

61. George Clinton to the New York Delegates to Congress, Poughkeepsie, July 8 and September 7, 1778, James Duane Letterbook, Schenecdaty County Historical Society.

62. *Public Papers*, 3: 409 *passim*.

63. George Clinton to New York's delegates to Congress, Poughkeepsie, February 9, 1779, Papers of the Continental Congress, Item 67, New York State Papers, 1775–88, National Archives.

64. Governor Clinton, Speech to the legislature, September 7, 1780, *Messages from the Governors*, 2: 106.

65. *Ibid.*, 124.

66. October 25, 1777, Fitzpatrick, 9: 429.

67. Jay to George Clinton, Philadelphia, February 19, 1779, L. W. Smith Collection, Morristown National Historical Park.

68. Manour Livingston, September 22, 1778, *Public Papers*, 4: 67.

69. George Clinton to Abraham Ten Broeck, Poughkeepsie, June 11, 1778, *Public Papers*, 3: 447–48. Unadilla is about 100 miles southwest of Albany.

70. Account of a speech of the Oneida and Tuscorora Indians delivered to Robert Cochran at Fort Schuyler on September 28, 1778, *Public Papers*, 4: 131–32.

71. Clinton to Butler, Poughkeepsie, September 8, 1778, *Public Papers*, 4: 12–13.

72. To Colonel Goose Van Schaick, Saratoga, May 28, 1780, *Public Papers*, 5: 766–67.

73 George Clinton to James Clinton, Poughkeepsie, June 20, 1779, L. W. Smith Collection, Morristown National Historical Park.

74. *Public Papers*, 5: 769–70, 789–96, 816–19; 6: 351–55.

75. George Clinton to Robert R. Livingston, Poughkeepsie, July 7, 1780, Livingston Papers, NHi.

76. Clinton to General Heath, Poughkeepsie, September 9, 1781, *Public Papers*, 7: 315–16.

77. Philip Schuyler to Abraham Ten Broeck, Saratoga, November 3, 1780, *Public Papers*, 6: 377.

78. Philip Schuyler to George Clinton, Saratoga, May 21, 1781, *Public Papers*, 6: 898–99.

79. Poughkeepsie, April 13, 1783, Washington Papers, Library of Congress.

80. George Clinton to Udny Hay, June 29, 1779, *Public Papers*, 5: 103–4; George Clinton to the New York Delegates to Congress, New York, February 23, 1785, PCC, Item 67, II, 483–88, National Archives. Robert R. Livingston to George Clinton, Philadelphia, July 31, 1782, and George Clinton to Robert R. Livingston, Poughkeepsie, August 5, 1782, Livingston Papers, NHi.

81. George Washington to George Clinton, Valley Forge, February 16, 1778, Fitzpatrick, 10: 469.

82. Congressional Committee to George Clinton, Camp near Valley Forge, February 17, 1778, *Public Papers*, 2: 766–67.

83. To James Reed, to Congressional Committee, to George Washington, Poughkeepsie, February 24, 1778, n.d., March 5, 1788, *Public Papers*, 2: 799–800, 823–24, 866.

84. Middlebrook, May 3, 1779, *Public Papers*, 4: 796. In his funeral oration for Clinton, Gouverneur Morris referred to the governor's remarkable ability "to squeeze, supplies for that starving continental army, whose paper resources were but as chaff; matter for the sport of winds, not for the support of war." *An Oration, in Honor of the Memory of George Clinton*, 12–13.

85. Philip Schuyler to George Clinton, Morristown, N.J., May 26, 1780, *Public Papers*, 5: 760–61.

86. On May 13, 1778, Governor Clinton wrote Henry Laurens, President of Congress that "The favorite Plan of Henry Clinton, for subjugat'g America, is to possess Hudson's River & thereby destroy the communication between the Eastern & Southern States & I should not be surprised to hear that their whole force was collected & employed for that purpose." *Public Papers*, 3: 302.

87. George Washington to George Clinton, New Windsor, January 4, 1781; George Clinton to George Washington, January 5, 1781, *Public Papers*, 6: 547–51.

88. *Public Papers*, 6: 571–73.

89. January 16, 1781, Fitzpatrick, 21: 113–14.

90. George Washington to George Clinton, New Windsor, January 1781, *Public Papers*, 6: 592–93; to Robert Howe, West Point, January 22, 1781, Fitzpatrick, 21: 128–29.

91. George Clinton to George Washington, Poughkeepsie, January 26, 1781, *Public Papers*, 6: 597–98.

92. To George Washington, Albany, January 31, 1781, *Public Papers*, 6: 603.

93. Washington to Clinton, Dobbs's Ferry, August 10, 1781, Fitzpatrick, 22: 491–92.

94. Clinton to Schuyler, Poughkeepsie, August 14, 1781, *Public Papers*, 7: 193–95.

95. *Public Papers*, 2: 860–64.

96. *Ibid.*

97. Syrett, 1: 436.

98. Valley Forge, March 12, 1778, *ibid.*, 1: 439.

99. George Washington to George Clinton, Headquarters, Ramapaugh, June 27, 1780, *Revolutionary Relics, or Clinton Correspondence . . .* (New York, 1842), 7.

100. *Messages from the Governors*, 2: 107.

101. To Alexander Hamilton, September 16, 1780, Syrett, 2: 433.

102. Philadelphia, November 14, 1780, Paul H. Smith et al., eds., *Letters of Delegates to Congress, 1774–1789* (Washington, D.C., 1976–), 16:333.

103. PCC, Item 67, II: 344–59, National Archives.

104. *Ibid.*

105. *Messages from the Governors*, 2: 127.

106. Poughkeepsie, November 24, 1781, Papers of the Continental Congress, Item 67, New York State Papers, 1775–88, National Archives; and *Public Papers*, 7: 520–22.

107. Philadelphia, September 11, 1782, *Public Papers*, 8: 38.

108. Hamilton to Clinton, Philadelphia, [January 12], 1783, Syrett, 3: 240.

109. Poughkeepsie, October 14, 1783, Washington Papers, Library of Congress.

110. To Benjamin Walker, Schuykill, February 4, 1783, New York State Library.

111. Nicholas Fish to Henry Glen, Camp Ver Planks Point, September 11, 1782, Misc. Mss, Library of Congress.

112. To George Clinton, Philadelphia, March 18, 1783, *Public Papers*, 8: 89–90.

113. For the Newburgh conspiracy, see Richard H. Kohn, *The Eagle and Sword* (New York, 1975) and his "The Inside History of the Newburgh Conspiracy: America and the Coup D'Etat," *William and Mary Quarterly*, 3rd ser., 27 (1970), 187–220.

114. Mount Vernon, November 25, 1784, Fitzpatrick, 27: 501.

115. Mount Vernon, November 5, 1786, June 9, 1787, *ibid.*, 29: 53, 230. Clinton's copy of his account with Washington is in the L. W. Smith Collection, Morristown National Historical Park.

116. Mount Vernon, April 20, 1785, *ibid.*, 28: 134.

117. George Clinton to George Washington, Greenwich, December 17, 1795, Washington Papers, Library of Congress.

118. George Clinton to George Washington, Greenwich, March 7, 1796, Washington Papers, Library of Congress.

119. Poughkeepsie, April 17, 1783, *Public Papers*, 8: 144–47. The published letter is incorrectly dated April 7 and is very badly transcribed. The manuscript recipient's copy, dated April 17, is in the Washington Papers at the Library of Congress.

120. *Public Papers*, 8: 134–35.

121. Benson to Clinton, Poughkeepsie, April 17, 1783, *Public Papers*, 8: 140–44.

122. To George Washington, Poughkeepsie, October 14, 1783, Washington Papers, Library of Congress.

123. George Washington to George Clinton, Rocky Hill, October 23, November 2, 1783, Fitzpatrick, 27: 205, 228.

124. *New Hampshire Gazette*, December 27, 1783; printed from the original (with slight variations from the *New Hampshire Gazette* printing) in the *New York Journal*, November 26, 1787.

125. A broadside listed the order of the fireworks exhibition as well as the council's prohibition on lights. A copy of this broadside in the Henry Knox Papers, Massachusetts Historical Society, indicates that the celebration was delayed until December 2.

126. *Ibid.*, January 3, 1784.

127. *Ibid.*

128. New York *Independent Journal*, December 8, 1783.

129. Mount Vernon, December 28, 1783, Fitzpatrick, 27: 287–88. On January 20, 1784, Governor Clinton wrote a letter to the Marquis de Lafayette describing the entry into New York City and paraphrasing Washington's letter to him. (New York State Library)

III — SHAPING THE EMPIRE STATE

1. Robert R. Livingston to George Clinton, Philadelphia, June 29, 1780, and Stephen Lush to George Clinton, Albany, April 12, 1780, *Public Papers*, 5: 614–15, 896. Clinton to Robert R. Livingston, Poughkeepsie, July 7, 1780, Livingston Papers, NHi.

2. Clinton to Livingston, Poughkeepsie, November 29, 1782, Livingston Papers, NHi.

3. Thomas Tillotson to Robert R. Livingston, Clermont, December 15, 1782, April 27 and June 1, 1783, and Margaret Beekman Livingston to Robert R. Livingston, Clermont, April 30, 1783, Livingston Papers, NHi. The *New York Gazette*, June 9, 1783, reported that Clinton received 3,584 votes to Schuyler's 643 and Paine's 520. Ten precincts had turned in their ballots contrary to the law, and the inspectors rejected them. The *Gazette* stated, however, that the ten precincts had voted proportionately to the rest of the state.

4. Van Rensselaer to Clinton, June 7, 1783, quoted in Don R. Gerlach, *Proud Patriot: Philip Schuyler and the War of Independence, 1775–1783* (Syracuse, 1987), 499.

5. *Public Papers*, 8: 230–32. Tryon County was later renamed Montgomery.

6. Gerlach, *Proud Patriot*, 499–500.

7. *Assembly Journal*, March 13, 1781, pp. 63–67.

8. Philadelphia, March 11, 1781, James Duane Letterbook, Schenecdaty County Historical Society.

9. William Floyd to George Clinton, Philadelphia, February 18, 1783, and William Floyd and Alexander Hamilton to George Clinton, Philadelphia, March 5, 1783, *Public Papers*, 8: 75, 81–85.

10. James Clinton to George Washington, Little Britain, April 10, 1782, L. W. Smith Collection, Morristown National Historical Park.

11. Speech to the legislature, January 21, 1784, *Messages from the Governors*, 2: 196–98.

12. For a justification of the movement for Vermont independence based upon the social compact theory, see Ira Allen's address to the inhabitants of Vermont, Norwich, July 13, 1779, *Public Papers*, 5: 132–43. See also Chilton Williamson, *Vermont in Quandary, 1777–1791* (Montpelier, Vt., 1949); and Matt Bushnell Jones, *Vermont in the Making, 1750–1777* (Cambridge, Mass., 1939).

13. Egbert Benson to John Jay, Poughkeepsie, July 6, 1779, Johnston, *Jay*, 1: 211–12.

14. George Clinton to Congress, Albany, February 5, 1781, Papers of the Continental Congress, Item 67, II: 344, National Archives.

15. Clinton to Chittenden, n.p., n.d., *Public Papers*, 2: 633.

16. For representations from Vermonters wanting to remain under New York's jurisdiction, see *Public Papers*, 3: 16, 170–72; George Clinton to the New York Delegates to Congress, Poughkeepsie, June 6, 1778, James Duane Letterbook, Schenectady County Historical Society.

17. Clinton to Henry Laurens, Poughkeepsie, April 7, 1778, *Public Papers*, 3: 144–46.

18. Morris to Clinton, Philadelphia, June 6, 1779, *Public Papers*, 3: 419–20.

19. Clinton to Morris, Poughkeepsie, July 7, 1778, and Clinton to Henry Laurens, Poughkeepsie, July 8, 1778, *Public Papers*, 3: 530–32, 533–35; Clinton to the Delegates to Congress, Poughkeepsie, September 7, 1778, James Duane Letterbook, Schenecdaty County Historical Society.

20. *Public Papers*, 4: 173–74.

21. *Public Papers*, 4: 792–95.

22. *Public Papers*, 4: 800–802.

23. *Public Papers*, 4: 814–16.

24. Poughkeepsie, May 18, 1779, *Public Papers*, 4: 836.

25. Samuel Minott to George Clinton, Brattleborough, May 25, 1779, *Public Papers*, 4: 846–47.

26. May 29, 1779, *Public Papers*, 4: 858–59.

27. *Public Papers*, 5: 7–10. The committee consisted of Oliver Ellsworth and Jesse Root both of Connecticut, Timothy Edwards of Massachusetts, John Witherspoon of New Jersey, and Samuel J. Atlee of Pennsylvania.

28. Philadelphia, June 2, 1779, *Public Papers*, 5: 12.

29. Clinton to President John Jay, Camp Highlands, June 7, 1779, *Public Papers*, 5: 54–57.

30. June 7, 1779, *Public Papers*, 5: 59.

31. Samuel Minott to Clinton, Brattleborough, June 8, 1779; Micah Townsend to Clinton, Brattleborough, June 9, 1779, *Public Papers*, 5: 63–65, 67–70.

32. Philadelphia, June 14, 1779, *Public Papers*, 5: 84–85.

33. Poughkeepsie, June 23, 1779, *Public Papers*, 5: 93–95.

34. *Public Papers*, 5: 97–98.

35. Micah Townsend to Clinton, Brattleborough, July 5, 1779, *Public Papers*, 5: 108–12.

36. Samuel Minott to George Clinton, Brattleborough, July 28, 1779, *Public Papers*, 5: 156–58.

37. Egbert Benson to John Jay, July 6, 1779, *Public Papers*, 5: 114–15.

38. Jay to Clinton, Philadelphia, August 27, 1779, *Public Papers*, 5: 117.

39. Jay to Clinton, Philadelphia, September 2, 1779, Edmund C. Burnett, ed., *Letters of Members of the Continental Congress* (8 vols., Washington, D. C., 1921–1936), 4: 400.

40. Worthington C. Ford et al., eds., *Journals of the Continental Congress, 1774–1789* (34 vols., Washington, D. C., 1904–37), 15: 1097.

41. *Public Papers*, 5: 301–2.

42. *Public Papers*, 5: 325–26, 483–91.

43. Memorial of Charles Phelps, *Public Papers*, 7: 632.

44. Samuel Minott to George Clinton, Brattleborough, April 11, 1780, *Public Papers*, 5: 605–8.

45. Samuel Minott to George Clinton, Brattleborough, May 2, 1780, *Public Papers*, 5: 671–75.

46. Clinton to Delegates in Congress, Poughkeepsie, May 9, 1780, James Duane Letterbook, Schenecdaty County Historical Society.

47. Jenifer to Governor Thomas Sim Lee, Philadelphia, June 5, 1780, Emmet Collection, 9495, New York Public Library, quoted in Richard B. Bernstein, *Are We To Be A Nation? The Making of the Constitution* (Cambridge, Mass., 1987), 86.

48. Clinton to New York Delegates to Congress, Kingston, June 14, 1780, James Duane Letterbook, Schenecdaty Historical Society; Clinton to Samuel Minott, Kingston, June 16, 1780, *Public Papers*, 5: 834–35.

49. Scott to Clinton, Philadelphia, September 26, 1780, *Public Papers*, 6: 254–55.

50. Clinton to James Duane, Poughkeepsie, October 29, 1780, *Public Papers*, 6: 346–47.

51. James Duane to George Clinton, Philadelphia, November 14, 1780, James Duane Letterbook, Schenectady County Historical Society.

52. Poughkeepsie, October 31, 1780, *Public Papers*, 6: 356.

53. George Clinton to James Clinton, Poughkeepsie, August 7, 1781, *Public Papers*, 7: 173–74; and May 8, 1781, The Pierpont Morgan Library.

54. *Public Papers*, 6: 430–31.

55. Udny Hay to [Nathanael Greene], Poughkeepsie, November 19, 1781, H. P. McCullough Collection, University of Vermont Library; Philip Schuyler to Alexander Hamilton, Saratoga, November 12, 1780, L. W. Smith Collection, Morristown National Historical Park.

56. *Assembly Journal*, February 27, 1781. The state constitution gave the governor the power to prorogue the legislature "from time to time, provided such prorogations shall not exceed sixty days in the space of any one year."

57. Poughkeepsie, April 6, 1781, *Public Papers*, 6: 741–45.

58. Clinton to James Duane, Poughkeepsie, April 6, 1781, *Public Papers*, 6: 741–45.

59. Clinton to James Duane, Poughkeepsie, April 6, 1781, *Public Papers*, 6: 744–45. Egbert

Benson felt the same way. Congress should "*judicially* declare that from the *Evidence*" it appears that Vermont should be free. This "kind of *pious* Fraud" would allow New York a peaceable way out of this impossible situation. Egbert Benson to Robert R. Livingston, Poughkeepsie, February 1782, Livingston Papers, NHi.

60. *Public Papers*, 6: 613–19; Ezra L'Hommedieu to John Tayler, Philadelphia, August 11, 1781, H. P. McCullough Collection, University of Vermont Library; Philip Schuyler to Robert R. Livingston, Albany, February 1, 1782, Livingston Papers, NHi.

61. *Public Papers*, 7: 265–68, 402–4, 414–15, 554–59, 576, 611–13, 615–18, 623–24.

62. Syrett, 3: 204–5.

63. Floyd and Hamilton to Clinton, Philadelphia, December 9, 1782, *Public Papers*, 8: 56–57.

64. Clinton to Hamilton, Poughkeepsie, December 29, 1782, Syrett, 3: 229–31.

65. Hamilton to Clinton, Philadelphia, January 1, 12, 1783, Syrett, 3: 236, 241.

66. Clinton to William Floyd, Kingston, February 6, 1783, *Public Papers*, 8: 64–65.

67. Clinton to Alexander Hamilton, Kingston, February 24, 1783, Syrett, 3: 266–67.

68. Clinton to William Floyd, Kingston, February 23, 1783, *Public Papers*, 8: 79–81.

69. *Ibid.*

70. Clinton to Hamilton and Floyd, Kingston, February 25, 1783, Syrett, 3: 275–76.

71. Jonathan Blanchard to Josiah Bartlett, Annapolis, June 6, 1784; and Richard Dobbs Spaight to the Governor of North Carolina, Annapolis, July 23, 1784, LMCC, 7: 545, 573.

72. Williamson to Duane, Annapolis, June 8, 1784, LMCC, 7: 546–47.

73. Annapolis, April 9, 1784, LMCC, 7: 487.

74. Ephraim Paine to Robert R. Livingston, Annapolis, May 24, 1784, LMCC, 7: 535.

75. Quoted in DeAlva Stanwood Alexander, *A Political History of the State of New York* (New York, 1906), 1: 23.

76. *Public Papers*, 1: 783.

77. *Public Papers*, 1: 796.

78. *Public Papers*, 2: 854–59; 7: 275–76, 280–81.

79. Clinton to John Jay, March 1779, *Public Papers*, 4: 642.

80. For analyses of the confiscation program, see Alexander C. Flick, *Loyalism in New York* (New York, 1901); Staughton Lynd, *Class Conflict, Slavery, and the United States Constitution* (Indianapolis, Ind., 1967), ch. 2; Harry B. Yoshope, *The Disposition of Loyalist Estates in the Southern District of the State of New York* (New York, 1939); Catherine Snell Crary, "Forfeited Loyalist Lands in the Western District of New York-Albany and Tryon Counties," *New York History*, 25 (1954), 239–58; and E. Wilder Spaulding, *New York in the Critical Period, 1783–1789* (New York, 1932), ch. 6.

81. George Clinton to Robert R. Livingston, Poughkeepsie, January 7, 1780, Livingston Papers, NHi.

82. Jay to Clinton, Aranjues, 21 Miles from Madrid, May 6, 1780, Johnston, *Jay*, 1: 314–15.

83. Robert R. Livingston to John Jay, Clermont, August 30, 1784, *ibid.*, 3: 434–35.

84. Robert R. Livingston to John Jay, New York, January 25, 1784, Livingston Papers, NHi.

85. Floyd to Clinton, Philadelphia, March 17, 1783, *Public Papers*, 8: 86–89.

86. Papers of the Continental Congress, Item 67, II: 465–67, National Archives.

87. New York *Independent Gazette*, December 13, 1783, January 3, 1784.

88. *Ibid.*, October 28, 1784.

89. Jay to Clinton, October 25, 1779, Richard B. Morris, ed., *John Jay: The Making of a Revolutionary, Unpublished Papers 1745–1780*, 1: 659–60. Jay repeated his advice in a letter from Madrid on July 14, 1780, *ibid.*, 1: 791.

90. Jay to Clinton, October 1779, *Public Papers*, 5: 314.

91. Robert R. Livingston to Clinton, Philadelphia, November 30, 1779, *Public Papers*, 5: 383.

92. *Ibid.*

93. Clinton to Robert R. Livingston, Poughkeepsie, January 7, 1780, Livingston Papers, NHi and printed in *Public Papers*, 5: 445–46.

94. *Public Papers*, 5: 499–502, 6: 203–5.

95. Circular Letter to the States, Philadelphia, September 10, 1780, *Public Papers*, 6: 189–90.

96. New York Delegates to George Clinton, Philadelphia, March 11, 1781, James Duane Letterbook, Schenecdaty County Historical Society.

97. George Clinton to the New York Delegates, Albany, March 28, 1781, *ibid.*

98. Philadelphia, October 9, 1782, *Public Papers*, 8: 41–43.

99. Philadelphia, October 30, 1782, *Public Papers*, 8: 49.

100. James Duane and Ezra L'Hommedieu to George Clinton, Princeton, October 16, 1783, *Public Papers*, 8: 261–63.

101. New York Senate's response to Governor Clinton's speech, October 21, 1784, printed in the *New York Journal*, October 28, 1784.

102. *Public Papers*, 8: 108–9.

103. Hamilton and Floyd to Clinton, Philadelphia, April 9, 1783, Syrett, 3: 321.

104. Hamilton to Clinton, Philadelphia, June 1, 1783, *ibid.*, 3: 372.

105. Washington to Clinton, August 12 and 17, 1783, Fitzpatrick, 27: 97–98, 105.

106. Clinton to Washington, Poughkeepsie, August 13, 1783, Washington Papers, Library of Congress.

107. Washington to Clinton, Rocky Hill near Princeton, August 29, 1783, *ibid.*, 27: 120–21.

108. L'Hommedieu to Clinton, Princeton, September 3, 1783, *Public Papers*, 8: 248–50.

109. *Ibid.*

110. Hamilton to Clinton, Albany, October 3, 1783, Syrett, 3: 464–69.

111. LMCC, 7: 487–88.

112. Paine to Clinton, Annapolis, April 29, 1784, LMCC, 7: 504–5.

113. Clinton to Fish, New York, March 19, 1784, Nicholas Fish Misc. Mss, Library of Congress.

114. Andrew Cunningham McLaughlin, "The Western Posts and the British Debts," American Historical Association *Annual Report for 1894* (Washington, D. C., 1894), 415–28.

115. Paine to Robert R. Livingston, Annapolis, May 24, 1784, Livingston Papers, NHi and LMCC, 7: 534–35.

116. Hugh Williamson to James Duane, Annapolis, June 8, 1784, LMCC, 7: 546–47.

117. *Ibid.*, 487–88, 504–5, 545.

118. Hamilton to George Washington, Philadelphia, April 9, 1783, LMCC, 7: 129.

119. Hamilton to Clinton, Philadelphia, May 14, 1783, Syrett, 3: 354–55.

120. "A Rough Hewer," *New York Journal*, March 17, 1785.

121. Schuyler to Abraham Ten Broeck, Jacob Cuyler, Leonard Gansevoort et al., New York, February 19, 1786, New York State Library.

122. Schuyler to Abraham Ten Broeck, New York, March 19, 1786, New York State Library.

123. Gorham to James Warren, New York, March 6, 1786, "Warren–Adams Letters," Massachusetts Historical Society *Collections* (1925), 2: 270.

124. *Ibid.*

125. John Williams to his Friends in Washington County, January 29, 1788, John P. Kaminski and Gaspare J. Saladino, eds., *Commentaries on the Constitution* (Vol. 16 of *The Documentary History of the Ratification of the Constitution* [Madison, Wis., 1986]), 4: 200. An "Extract of a letter from a gentleman in New-York, to his friend in Connecticut," in the *Norwich Packet*, November 8, 1787, took the opposite position: "Tho' we are sensible, that the harbour of New-York is so commodiously situated for trade, that we might reap great profits from duties on

articles which are exported from hence into other states. But we may not think too much of our own particular interest to the injury of the whole.—At the same time I must confess myself at last convinced by these patriots in this state who maintain, that the port of New-York, having been saved by the united arms of all the states, ought to be free for all."

126. Melancton Smith's Defense of New York's Action on the Impost, n. d., Smith Papers, New York State Library.

127. Monroe to Clinton, New York, August 16, 1786, LMCC, 8: 430–31.

128. Clinton to the President of Congress, New York, August 26, 1786, Papers of the Continental Congress, No. 67, II: 545–47, National Archives.

129. Worthington C. Ford et al., eds., *Journals of the Continental Congress, 1774–1789* (34 vols., Washington, D.C., 1904–37), 31: 556n.

130. To Governor Richard Caswell, New York, August 24, 1786, LMCC, 8: 452.

131. King to Elbridge Gerry, New York, August 26, 1786, LMCC, 8: 454.

132. Mitchell to William Samuel Johnson, Wethersfield, August 9, 1786, LMCC, 8: 418.

133. In fact, Clinton in January 1786 had restated his 1777 pledge to adhere to a strict separation of powers under the state constitution. At the end of the April 1785 session, the senate voted to adjourn to meet in Kingston on a day to be assigned by the governor. The assembly disagreed and resolved to meet at a time and place to be determined by Clinton. The senate accepted the assembly's version of the adjournment. On November 16, 1785, Clinton called the legislature to meet in New York City on January 6, 1786. When a quorum assembled, Clinton told the legislators that they probably had violated the constitution by giving him the authority to call the legislature. The executive, he said, should only exercise that authority on "extraordinary occasions." (*Messages from the Governors*, 2: 251–52.) Clinton suggested the passage of an act setting a general date and meeting place for future legislatures. In March 1786, the legislature provided that future legislatures meet on the second Tuesday of every January unless called earlier by the governor. If no place could be agreed upon, the legislature should convene where it last sat.

134. Mitchell to Jeremiah Wadsworth, New York, January 24, 1787, LMCC, 8: 531. Clinton was confident that the legislature would support his refusal to call a special session. Shortly after the debate over censuring him, Clinton reported that the legislature had "finished all the little Ettequette such as Answers Addresses, etc. & go on as cordially as could be expected." That cordiality, however, was expected to end when Philip Schuyler arrived on January 25. The governor now supposed "the senate Room will ring with mealavent Rhapsody and feigned Patriotism, [where] hitherto it has been blessed with singular Harmony." George Clinton to Christopher Tappen, New York, January 26, 1787, L. W. Smith Collection, Morristown National Historical Park.

135. *Messages from the Governors*, 2: 264.

136. "Rough Carver," "Some Observations on the present Political situation of the United States," New York *Daily Advertiser*, September 3, 1787.

137. Madison to George Washington, New York, February 21, 1787, Robert A. Rutland et al., eds., *The Papers of James Madison* (Chicago and Charlottesville, Va., 1962-), 9: 285.

138. "Leo," New York *Daily Advertiser*, February 27, 1787.

139. Philip Schuyler to Henry Van Schaack, New York, March 13, 1787, in Henry Cruger Van Schaack, *Memoirs of the Life of Henry Van Schaack . . . during the American Revolution* (Chicago, 1892), 150.

140. *The Debates and Proceedings of the Convention of New-York . . .* (New York, 1788), 111.

141. "H.G." VII, New York *Daily Advertiser*, March 23, 1789, quoted in Syrett, 5: 277–78.

142. Blount to Governor Richard Caswell, New York, January 28, 1787, LMCC, 8: 533.

143. Hamilton to Robert Morris, Albany, August 13, 1782, Syrett, 3: 138.

144. Alexander Hamilton to Robert R. Livingston, April 25, 1785, Syrett, 3: 608–9.

145. Hamilton to Robert Morris, August 13, 1782, Syrett, 3: 137–38.

146. *New York Packet*, November 10, 1785.

147. New York *Daily Advertiser*, April 21, 1786.

148. John Jay to Thomas Jefferson, New York, August 13, 1785, Julian P. Boyd et al., eds., *The Papers of Thomas Jefferson* (Princeton, 1950–), 8: 52.

149. For complaints of the shortage of circulating money, see Peter Elting to Peter Van Gaasbeck, New York, February 24, 1786; Peter W. Yates to Peter Van Gaasbeck et al., Albany, May 22, 1786; John Dumont to Peter Van Gaasbeck, Peerpack, January 3, 1784, March 24, 1785, all in the Van Gaasbeck Papers, Senate House Museum, Kingston, N.Y.

150. *New York Packet*, February 13, 1786.

151. Petitions from the City and County of Albany, February 2, 1785, and from the Inhabitants of Hillsdale in Albany County, February 24, and March 2, all in the New York State Library.

152. Schuyler to John Tayler, March 24, 1784, Tayler Papers, NHi.

153. Robert R. Livingston, Opinion against issuing bills of credit, March 1786, Livingston Papers, NHi.

154. George Dangerfield, *Chancellor Robert R. Livingston of New York, 1746–1813* (New York, 1960), 214.

155. "Honestus," *New York Packet*, March 27, 1786.

156. New York *Daily Advertiser*, August 1, 1786.

157. William Barton, *The True Interest of the United States* (Philadelphia, 1786), 18.

158. *Ibid.*, 13.

159. Poughkeepsie *Country Journal*, February 2, 1786.

160. Abraham Yates Notes, New York Public Library.

161. "Honestus," *New York Packet*, March 27, 1786; "Mercator," New York *Daily Advertiser*, April 22, 1786.

162. *New York Packet*, March 6, 1786.

163. *Journal of the Assembly of the State of New York* (New York, 1784), 51, 26; *Journal of the Senate, of the State of New York* (New York, 1784), 95.

164. John Lansing, Jr., to Abraham Ten Broeck, New York, January 28, 1786, Ten Broeck Papers, Albany Institute of History and Art.

165. Clinton to Robert Boyd, New Windsor, February 25, 1777, *Public Papers*, 1: 630–31.

166. Address to the legislature, Poughkeepsie, October 13, 1778, *Public Papers*, 4: 157.

167. See Livingston's draft of Clinton's first address to the legislature delivered on September 10, 1777, in the Livingston Papers, NHi. George Clinton to Livingston, Poughkeepsie, January 7, 1780, *ibid.*

168. Morris to Clinton, Philadelphia, February 20, 1779, *Public Papers*, 4: 585.

169. George Clinton to James Duane, Poughkeepsie, May 15, 1779, L. W. Smith Collection, Morristown National Historical Park.

170. Robert A. Becker, *Revolution, Reform, and the Politics of American Taxation, 1763–1783* (Baton Rouge, La., 1980), 160–65, 226-27; Edward Countryman, "'Out of Bounds of the Law': Northern Land Rioters in the Eighteenth Century," ed. Alfred F. Young, *The American Revolution: Explorations in the History of American Radicalism* (De Kalb, Ill., 1976), 61.

171. Robert R. Livingston to George Clinton, May 21, 1780, February 20, 1787; and Clinton to Livingston, Poughkeepsie, July 7, 1780, Livingston Papers, NHi.

172. *Messages from the Governors*, 2: 199, 219.

173. Speech to the legislature, January 21, 1784, *ibid.*, 2: 198.

174. *Ibid.*, 2: 253, 255–56.

175. "Gustavus," *New York Packet*, April 13, 1786; Mat: Visscher to Abraham Yates, Jr., March 6, 1786, Abraham Yates Papers, New York Public Library.

176. Philip Schuyler to General Ten Broeck, New York, March 19, 1786, and Schuyler to Stephen Van Rensselaer, New York, March 22, 30, 1786, New York State Library; Schuyler to Leonard Gansevoort, New York, March 22, 1786, de Coppet Collection, Princeton University.

177. To Peter Van Gaasbeck, New York, April 21, 1786, Van Gaasbeck Papers, Senate House Museum, Kingston.

178. *New York Gazetteer*, May 26, 1786.

179. *New York Packet*, May 25, 1786.

180. William Van Ingen to Henry Glen, Albany, March 23, 1786, Henry Glen Papers, New York State Historical Association Library.

181. To William Petty, the Marquis of Lansdown, New York, April 16, 1786, John Jay Misc. Papers, Princeton University.

182. Hamilton to Robert Livingston, April 25, 1785, Syrett, 3: 609.

183. In October 1779, Jay recommended Hugh Hughes as sheriff of the City and County of New York, and appointive positions for John Lamb and William Malcolm. Jay to Clinton, *Public Papers*, 5: 315.

184. Johnston, *Jay*, 3: 151–52.

185. New York *Independent Journal*, April 2, 1785; *New York Journal*, April 7, 1785, February 9, July 26, 1786.

186. Johnston, *Jay*, 3: 154–56.

187. Schuyler to Stephen Van Rensselaer, New York, January 16, 1786, New York State Library.

188. Schuyler to Abraham Ten Broeck, Jacob Cuyler, and Leonard Gansevoort, New York, February 19, 1786, Schuyler Papers, New York State Library.

189. *New York Gazetteer*, July 28, 1786; *New Jersey Journal*, August 2, 1786.

190. *New York Journal*, August 24, 1786.

191. Hamilton Speech in Assembly, February 1787, Syrett, 4: 90; Nicholas Hoffman to John Williams, New York, November 2, 1787, John Williams Papers, New York State Library.

192. J. P. Brissot de Warville, *New Travels in the United States of America, 1788* (trans., Mara Soceanu Vamus and Durrand Echeverria, ed. Durrand Echeverria, Cambridge, 1964), 157. See also Melancton Smith, Speech in the New York Ratifying Convention, June 27, 1788, *Debates*, 94–96.

193. Merrill Jensen, *The New Nation: A History of the United States During the Confederation, 1781–1789* (New York, 1950), 215; *New York Packet*, November 18, 1788, March 10, 1789.

194. E. James Ferguson, "State Assumption of the Federal Debt During the Confederation," *The Mississippi Valley Historical Review*, 38 (1951), 418; New York *Daily Advertiser*, January 28, February 2, 1788.

195. *New York Morning Post*, January 21, 1788.

196. Providence *United States Chronicle*, March 15, 1787.

197. Clinton to the Senate, New York, February 19, 1787, *Messages from the Governors*, 2: 269.

198. *Journal of the Senate of the State of New-York* (New York, 1787), 35–36.

199. *New York Gazetteer*, February 26, March 19, 1787.

200. Benjamin Lincoln to George Clinton, Pittsfield, February 27, 1787, L. W. Smith Collection, Morristown National Historical Park.

201. *New York Gazetteer*, March 5, 1787; Rufus King and Nathan Dane to Governor James Bowdoin, New York, March 4, 1787; George Clinton to Benjamin Lincoln, Poughkeepsie, March 5, 1787, L. W. Smith Collection, Morristown National Historical Park.

202. New York *Independent Journal*, March 7, 1787.

203. Benjamin Lincoln to Governor James Bowdoin, Pittsfield, March 9, 1787, in the *New York Gazetteer*, March 22, 1787; General Orders in *New York Gazetteer*, March 12, 1787.

204. Lincoln to Bowdoin, Pittsfield, March 9, 1787, in the *New York Gazetteer*, March 22, 1787.

205. Van Schaack, *Memoirs*, 145.

206. Perhaps some of the misconception about Clinton's attitude toward the Shaysites stems from some false reports made for partisan political purposes during the gubernatorial

election of 1789. See the Exeter, N.H., *Freeman's Oracle*, March 31, 1789, in which an extract of a letter was printed saying that Clinton and Shays met in a tavern in mid-February 1789 and the governor "saluted him with all possible *politeness*. A circumstance," the letter writer said, "which was to the highest degree galling to every citizen."

207. Philip Schuyler to Henry Van Schaack, New York, March 13, 1787, Van Schaack, *Memoirs*, 150.

208 The following account of the doctors' riots is taken from the *New York Packet*, April 25, 1788; Victor DuPont to Pierre Samuel DuPont de Nemours, New York, April 18, 1788, Eleutherian Mills Historical Library; DeWitt Clinton to James Clinton, New York, April 25, 1788, New York State Library; William Heth Diary, April 14–15, 1788, Library of Congress; William Heth to Edmund Randolph, New York, April 16, 1788, Executive Papers, Virginia State Library; Noah Webster Diary, New York, April 13–15, 1788, New York Public Library; Paine Wingate to John Sullivan, New York, April 23, 1788, Peter Force Transcripts, Library of Congress; [John Vaughan] to [John Dickinson], n. d., Dickinson Papers, Library Company of Philadelphia; Levi Hollingsworth to Richard Dobbs Spaight, Philadelphia, April 22, 1788, Hollingsworth Letterbook, Historical Society of Pennsylvania. See also Paul A. Gilje, *The Road to Mobocracy: Popular Disorder in New York City, 1763–1834* (Chapel Hill, N.C., 1987).

IV — THE NEW CONSTITUTION

1. The bill was first printed in the *Providence Gazette*, January 6, 1787, and was reprinted in newspapers throughout the country.

2. *New York Journal*, October 19, 1786.

3. *New York Journal*, February 16, 1786.

4. "A Freeholder," *Hudson Weekly Gazette*, April 12, 1787.

5. For the postwar British trade policy, enunciated most strenuously by Lord Sheffield in his *Observations on the Commerce of the American States* (London, 1783), see Robert B. Bittner, The Definition of Economic Independence and the New Nation (unpub. Ph.D. dissertation, University of Wisconsin, 1970).

6. Merrill Jensen, John P. Kaminski, and Gaspare J. Saladino, eds., *Constitutional Documents and Records, 1776–1787* (vol. 1 of *The Documentary History of the Ratification of the Constitution*, Madison, Wis., 1976), 153–54.

7. *Ibid.*, 154–56.

8. *Journal of the Senate of the State of New-York* (New York, 1786), 49–50.

9. *Ibid.*, 103.

10. Robert C. Livingston's request for payment is dated September 21, 1786. On September 29, 1787, the state auditor and treasurer approved payment, and on October 9 Livingston acknowledged the receipt. Doc. #4045, New York State Library.

11. Livingston Papers, NHi.

12. Philip Schuyler to Henry Van Schaack, New York, March 13, 1787, in Van Schaack, *Memoirs*, 150.

13. *Ibid.*

14. Madison to Randolph and to Washington, New York, March 11 and 18, 1787, Rutland, *Madison*, 9: 307, 315.

15. Robert Yates to Abraham Yates, Jr., Philadelphia, June 1, 1787, Abraham Yates Papers, New York Public Library. Robert Yates ended his letter asking Abraham to communicate "my Respects to the Governor," an indication that it was Clinton alone to whom the confidential information was to be delivered.

16. Max Farrand, ed., *The Records of the Federal Convention of 1787* (3rd ed., 3 vols., New Haven, Conn., 1927), 1: 249–50, 257–57.

17. Farrand, 1: 282–83.

18. See John P. Kaminski, "New York: The Reluctant Pillar," in Stephen L. Schechter, ed., *The Reluctant Pillar: New York and the Adoption of the Federal Constitution* (Troy, N. Y., 1985), 63.

19. Luther Martin, "Genuine Information," Baltimore *Maryland Gazette*, January 4, 1788, Kaminski and Saladino, *Commentaries*, 3: 255.

20. Walter Rutherfurd believed that Clinton "had a hand" in convincing Yates and Lansing to write their letter. To John Rutherfurd, January 15, 1788, Rutherfurd Collection, NHi.

21. Yates and Lansing's letter to Governor Clinton, dated December 21, 1787, was printed in the New York *Daily Advertiser* and the *New York Journal* on January 14, 1788. The *Journal* reprinted it in the Thursday issue (January 17) which received wider distribution. By the end of January, six other New York newspapers had printed the letter, and by March 10 the letter had been printed in newspapers throughout the country. For Yates and Lansing's letter, see Kaminski and Saladino, *Commentaries*, 3: 366–70.

22. Carrington to James Madison, Manchester, Va., February 10, 1788, Rutland, *Madison*, 10: 493–95.

23. For an excellent account of the newspaper coverage of the Federal Convention, see John K. Alexander's *The Selling of the Constitutional Convention: A History of News Coverage* (Madison, Wis., 1990).

24. Robert Yates to Abraham Yates, Jr., June 1, 1787, Abraham Yates Papers, New York Public Library.

25. Hamilton's essay in the New York *Daily Advertiser*, July 21, 1787, is printed in Kaminski and Saladino, *Commentaries*, 1: 136–38. Within less than two months, at least eighteen newspapers reprinted it throughout the United States.

26. Kaminski and Saladino, *Commentaries*, 1: 138. Within a month, this paragraph was reprinted in at least fifteen newspapers throughout the country.

27. Humphreys to Hamilton, New Haven, September 1, 1787, Syrett, 4: 242.

28. "Impromptu," *Northern Centinel*, September 3, 1787.

29. "Rough Carver," New York *Daily Advertiser*, September 3–4, 1787.

30. "An Admirer of Anti-Federal Men," New York *Daily Advertiser*, July 26, 1787.

31. "A Republican," *New York Journal*, September 6, 1787, quoted in Kaminski and Saladino, *Commentaries*, 1: 139–40. The poem is quoted from Charles Churchill's *The Apology. Addressed to the Critical Reviewers* (London, 1761).

32. "An Old Soldier," Lansingburgh *Northern Centinel*, September 10, 1787.

33. "Rusticus," *New York Journal*, September 13, 1787.

34. *New York Journal*, September 20, 1787.

35. "Inspector," *New York Journal*, September 20, 1787.

36. Hamilton to Washington, [11–15 October 1787], Syrett, 4: 280–81.

37. Washington to Hamilton, Mount Vernon, October 18, 1787, *ibid.*, 4: 284.

38. "Inspector," *New York Journal*, September 20, 1787.

39. *Ibid.*, October 4, 1787.

40. *Ibid.*, October 18, 1787.

41. New York *Daily Advertiser*, September 15, 1787.

42. Quoted in Linda Grant De Pauw, *The Eleventh Pillar: New York State and the Federal Constitution* (Ithaca, N. Y., 1966), 74–75.

43. *Norwich Packet*, April 25, 1787.

44. Marinus Willett to John Tayler, New York, September 23, 1787, New York State Library.

45. Linda De Pauw disputes Clinton's authorship of the "Cato" series and suggests Abraham Yates, Jr., as a more likely author. (*Eleventh Pillar*, 283–92.) De Pauw's primary argument against Clinton is that he was not sufficiently well read to produce these essays; yet, Federalist essayist Dr. Charles McKnight argued a contrary position. "Examiner," as McKnight penned himself, "expected to have seen numberless quotations from the most sensible and approved political

writers in favor of what he ["Cato"] advanced, this being the method he promised to pursue; instead of which he has totally neglected Grotius, Puffendorf, Sydney, Locke, Hume, and others equally celebrated, confing himself to one or two thread-bare quotations from Baron Montesquieu which have appeared before in several recent publications." "Examiner" also discounted "Cato's" criticisms because "Cato" had "declared against the new constitution before he ever saw it"-a reference to Clinton's alleged statements against the Federal Convention in July 1787. (*New York Journal*, December 14, 1787.) "Curtius" II, New York *Daily Advertiser*, October 18, 1787, also criticized "Cato" because he had *pre-determined* that they [the delegates to the Federal Convention] should *do no good.* Other contemporary references to Clinton's authorship are given short shrift by De Pauw. One newspaper item ignored by De Pauw states that both "Cato" and "Rough Hewer" (Clinton and Abraham Yates) were in Poughkeepsie at the time of the legislative session, where they were both "using their utmost endeavours to create jealousy among the people." (Lansingburgh *Northern Centinel*, January 15, 1788, Kaminski and Saladino, *Commentaries*, 3: 569.)

46. "Cato" I, *New York Journal*, September 27, 1787, Kaminski and Saladino, *Commentaries*, 1: 255–57.

47. "Cæsar" I, New York *Daily Advertiser*, October 1, 1787, Kaminski and Saladino, *Commentaries*, 1: 287–88. Jacob E. Cooke unconvincingly argued against Hamilton's authorship of the "Cæsar" essays ("Alexander Hamilton's Authorship of the 'Caesar' Letters," *William and Mary Quarterly*, 3rd ser., XVII [1960], 78–85.

48. "Cato" II, *New York Journal*, October 11, 1787, Kaminski and Saladino, *Commentaries*, 1: 369–72.

49. "Cæsar," New York *Daily Advertiser*, October 17, 1787, Kaminski and Saladino, *Commentaries*, 1: 395–99.

50. "Curtius" II agreed with "Cæsar" that "Cato's" essay was "a declamatory attempt to excite the prejudices of the ignorant, and the distrust of the jealous." (New York *Daily Advertiser*, October 18, 1787.)

51. "Cato" III, *New York Journal*, October 25, 1787, Kaminski and Saladino, *Commentaries*, 1: 473–77.

52. "Cato" IV, *New York Journal*, November 8, 1787, Kaminski and Saladino, *Commentaries*, 2: 7–11.

53. "Cato" V, *New York Journal*, November 22, 1787, Kaminski and Saladino, *Commentaries*, 2: 182–85.

54. *Ibid.* and "Cato" VI, *New York Journal*, December 13, 1787, Kaminski and Saladino, *Commentaries*, 2: 428–32.

55. "Cato" VII, *New York Journal*, January 3, 1788, Kaminski and Saladino, *Commentaries*, 3: 240–43.

56. *Pennsylvania Herald*, September 25, 1787.

57. Elias Boudinot to William Bradford, Jr., Elizabethtown, New Jersey, September 28, 1787, Wallace Papers, Historical Society of Pennsylvania; printed in Merrill Jensen, John P. Kaminski and Gaspare J. Saladino, eds., *The Documentary History of the Ratification of the Constitution* (Madison, Wis., 1976–), 3: 134–35.

58. Edward Carrington to Thomas Jefferson, New York, October 23, 1787, Kaminski and Saladino, *Commentaries*, 1: 439.

59. Edward Carrington to William Short, New York, October 25, 1787, Kaminski and Saladino, *Commentaries*, 1: 469.

60. James Madison to Thomas Jefferson, New York, October 24, 1787, Kaminski and Saladino, *Commentaries*, 1: 451.

61. James Madison to William Short, New York, October 24, 1787, Kaminski and Saladino, *Commentaries*, 1: 454.

62. John Stevens, Jr., to John Stevens, Sr., New York, October 1, 1787, Stevens Family Papers, New Jersey Historical Society.

63. Arthur Lee to John Adams, New York, October 3, 1787, Adams Family Papers, Kaminski and Saladino, *Commentaries*, 1: 308.

64. Philadelphia *Independent Gazetteer*, November 24, 1787.

65. *Pennsylvania Journal*, December 19, 1787.

66. "A Freeholder," *Brunswick Gazette*, February 10, 1789, Den Boer, *Elections*, 3: 122.

67. Lewis Morris to Lewis Morris, Jr., Morrisania, March 31, 1788, New York State Library.

68. Henry Knox to George Washington, New York, May 25, 1788, Washington Papers, Library of Congress.

69. Nicholas Gilman to John Sullivan, New York, March 22, 1788, Kaminski and Saladino, *Commentaries*, 4: 462.

70. Samuel A. Otis to Caleb Davis, New York, May 27, 1788, Davis Papers, Massachusetts Historical Society.

71. "A Real Federalist," Providence *United States Chronicle*, March 27, 1788.

72. John Adams to George Clinton, London, March 26, 1788, Kaminski and Saladino, *Commentaries*, 4: 481. Adams was not yet fully aware of Clinton's stance on the Constitution nor did he fully commit his own opinion to Clinton. "It is expected in Europe," the diplomat wrote, "that the new Constitution for the United States will soon be adopted by all. It is a general opinion that the old one, stood in great need of a Reform, and that the projected Change, will be much for our Prosperity, a fœderal Republick of independent sovereign states was never known to exist, over a large Territory, innumerable Difficulties have been found in those which have been tried in Small Countries. The Question really Seems to be, whether the Union shall be broken; or whether all shall come under one sovereignty." Ever the diplomat, Adams told Clinton that "The Union is an object of such Magnitude: that every Thing but constitutional Liberty should be sacrificed to it."

73. Abigail Adams Smith to Abigail Adams, New York, June 15, 1788, [Caroline Amelia (Smith) DeWindt], ed., *Correspondence of Miss Adams, Daughter of John Adams . . .* (New York, 1842), 80–81.

74. *New York Journal*, January 3, 1788; James Madison to Edmund Randolph and to George Washington, New York, January 20, 1788, Rutland, *Madison*, 10: 398–99; Walter Rutherfurd to John Rutherfurd, January 8, 15, 1788, Rutherfurd Collection, NHi; Samuel A. Otis to Elbridge Gerry, January 2, 1788, Kaminski and Saladino, *Commentaries*, 3: 216; Richard Sill to Jeremiah Wadsworth, Albany, January 12, 1788, Wadsworth Correspondence, Connecticut Historical Society.

75. *New York Journal*, January 3, 1788, and December 5, 1787, respectively.

76. Clinton Speech, January 11, 1788, *Messages from the Governors*, 2: 282.

77. Philip Schuyler to Stephen Van Rensselaer, Poughkeepsie, January 27, 1788, New York State Library.

78. For the debates in the assembly and in the senate, see the New York *Daily Advertiser*, February 12 and 8, 1788, respectively. See also Kaminski, "The Reluctant Pillar," 73–77.

79. Abraham Bancker to Evert Bancker, Kingston, April 2, 1788, Bancker Family Correspondence, NHi.

80. Five years later, "A Citizen of Dutchess" asserted that Van Gaasbeck acquired his prominence by giving credit to other Ulster residents and never took "any coercive measures to force payments to him, but left every man to discharge his debts as he thought fit." *New York Journal*, April 7, 1792.

81. Peter Van Gaasbeck to Major Severyn Bruyn, Kingston, March 12, 1788, Van Gaasbeck Papers, Senate House Museum, Kingston. The Poughkeepsie slate included: Governor Clinton, his older brother James, Assemblyman Cornelius C. Schoonmaker, Dirck Wynkoop, Ebenezer Clark, and John Cantine.

82. *Ibid.*

83. *New York Journal*, February 29, 1788. After the meeting, about 100 revellers burned the new Constitution and an effigy of Alexander Hamilton.

84. Peter Van Gaasbeck to Major Severyn Bruyn, Kingston, March 12, 1788, Van Gaasbeck Papers, Senate House Museum, Kingston.

85. See a draft of a letter dated March 20, 1788, written by Van Gaasbeck under the pen name Jno. J. Ao. Modes to Cornelius C. Schoonmaker in the Van Gaasbeeck Papers, Senate House Museum. Outraged at the rumor, Addison traced its origin to a conversation between John C. Wynkoop and Peter Van Gaasbeck at the former's house in Kinderhook in early March. Wynkoop told Addison that he had described him as "an antifoederalist, but that I entertained so favorable an opinion of your Candor and Good sense, that if you should be chosen a delegate in Convention you would then be convinced of the Propriety of Adopting the Constitution, and give your vote in its favor. This [Wynkoop] remarked, was my opinion of all sensible, candid and Good Men when the wisdom, Importance, and Necessity of the plan should be Clearly explained." Wynkoop, however, assured Addison that he "never told Mr. Gaasbeck that you was a foederal man or that you had in Conversation with me in your house, or elsewhere, or ever expressed your self to that respect." Wynkoop to Addison, Kinderhook, April 7, 1788, Van Gaasbeck Papers, Senate House Museum. Van Gaasbeck, however, remembered the conversation differently. Wynkoop, according to Van Gaasbeck, asked "if the People of Kingston were unanimously opposed to the New system," to which Van Gaasbeck replied that they were. Wynkoop then asked "if it was as Represented that Mr. Addison was a very strong antifederal, to which [Van Gaasbeck] Reply'd that People thought so." Wynkoop expressed his surprise because several months before he had brought the first copy of the Constitution to Esopus, where he and Addison discussed it. At that time Addison appeared to be a Federalist. Peter Van Gaasbeck to John Wynkoop, April 17, 1788, Van Gaasbeck Papers, Senate House Museum.

86. Severyn T. Bruyn to Peter Van Gaasbeck, Bruynswyke, March 23, 1788, Van Gaasbeck Papers, Senate House Museum.

87. Cornelius C. Schoonmaker to Peter Van Gaasbeck, April 4, 1788, Van Gaasbeck Papers, Senate House Museum.

88. *Ibid.*

89. *Ibid.*

90. Peter Van Gaasbeck to Cornelius C. Schoonmaker, Kingston, March 31, 1788, Van Gaasbeck Papers, Senate House Museum.

91. Schoonmaker's letter to Van Gaasbeck on April 3 has not been found. He referred to that letter when he wrote Van Gaasbeck the next day. Schoonmaker to Peter Van Gaasbeck, April 4, 1788, Van Gaasbeck Papers, Senate House Museum.

92. Schoonmaker to Van Gaasbeck, April 4, 1788, Van Gaasbeck Papers, Senate House Museum.

93. *Ibid.*

94. Schoonmaker to Peter Van Gaasbeck, April 7, 1788, Franklin D. Roosevelt Collection, Franklin D. Roosevelt Library, Hyde Park.

95. Melancton Smith to Cornelius C. Schoonmaker, New York, April 6, 1788, John Lamb Papers, NHi.

96. Draft Circular in the Peter Van Gaasbeck Papers, Senate House Museum.

97. "A Dutchess County Anti-Federalist": To the Antifederalists of Ulster County, Poughkeepsie *Country Journal*, April 8, 1788.

98. *Ibid.*

99. *New York Journal*, June 12, 1788.

100. Peter Elting to Peter Van Gaasbeck, New York, April 14, 1788, Van Gaasbeck Papers, Senate House Museum.

101. Samuel B. Webb to Joseph Barrell, New York, April 27, 1788, Webb Family Collection, Yale University Library.

102. Samuel B. Webb to Catherine Hogeboom, New York, April 27, 1788, Webb Family Collection, Yale University Library.

103. "One of Yourselves," New York *Daily Advertiser*, May 1, 1788. Also published as a broadside dated "April 30, 1788."

104. "Extract of a Letter from a Gentleman at New-York, to his Friend in this Town, dated April 30, 1788," *Maryland Journal*, May 9, 1788.

105. Samuel B. Webb to Catherine Hogeboom, New York, May 4, 1788, Webb Family Papers, Yale University Library.

106. Morgan Lewis to Margaret Beekman Livingston, New York, May 4, 1788, Robert R. Livingston Papers, NHi.

107. *Ibid.*

108. Abraham Baldwin to Seaborn Jones, New York, June 5, 1788, Stokes Autograph Collection, Yale University Library.

109. "Extract of a letter from New York, July 20, 1788," *New Hampshire Spy*, July 29, 1788.

110. "Extract of a letter from a gentleman in New York, to his friend in this City, dated May 24," Charleston, S.C. *Columbian Herald*, June 19, 1788.

111. Robert R. Livingston to Marquis de Lafayette, Clermont, September 17–22, 1788, Livingston Papers, NHi.

112. Vaughan to Dickinson, n.d., Dickinson Papers, Free Library of Philadelphia.

113. Alexander Hamilton to James Madison, New York, May 19, 1788, Syrett, 4: 649.

114. Abraham Yates, Jr., to Abraham G. Lansing, New York, June 15, 1788, Yates Papers, New York Public Library.

115. Richard Platt to Winthrop Sargent, New York, June 14, 1788, Sargent Papers, Massachusetts Historical Society.

116. Alexander Hamilton to Gouverneur Morris, New York, May 19, 1788, Syrett, 4: 651.

117. Abraham Yates, Jr., to Abraham G. Lansing, New York, June 15, 1788, Yates Papers, New York Public Library.

118. The account of convention activities that follows is taken from Francis Childs's *Debates*.

119. John Lansing, Jr., to Abraham Yates, Jr., Poughkeepsie, June 19, 1788, Gansevoort–Lansing Papers, New York Public Library; David Gelston to John Smith, June 21, 1788, John Smith Misc. Mss, NHi.

120. Abraham G. Lansing to Abraham Yates, Jr., June 22, 1788, Yates Papers, New York Public Library.

121. Robert Yates to George Mason, Poughkeepsie, June 21, 1788, Emmet Collection, New York Public Library.

122. Alexander Hamilton to James Madison, June 19, 1788, Rutland, *Madison*, 11: 156.

123. William Duer to James Madison, New York, June 23, 1788, Madison Papers, Library of Congress.

124. George Clinton to Abraham Yates, Jr., Poughkeepsie, June 28, 1788, Yates Papers, New York Public Library.

125. DeWitt Clinton to Charles Tillinghast, Poughkeepsie, June 27, 1788, DeWitt Clinton Papers, Columbia University Libraries.

126. Samuel B. Webb to Joseph Barrell, New York, July 1, 1788, Webb Family Papers, Yale University Library.

127. Abraham G. Lansing to Abraham Yates, Jr., Poughkeepsie, June 29, 1788, Yates Papers, New York Public Library.

128. George Clinton Papers, Bancroft Transcripts, New York Public Library.

129. *Ibid.*

130. "Specious and plausible" might at first seem contradictory, but they are not. Clinton was in essence saying that Federalists were demagogues who used a seemingly "plausible" argument, but in reality their position was "specious."

131. *Ibid.*

132. *Debates*, 109–10.

133. *Debates*, 109–11.

134. For Hamilton's speech, see *Debates*, 112–19.

135. DeWitt Clinton to Charles Tillinghast, Poughkeepsie, July 2, 1788, DeWitt Clinton Papers, Columbia University Libraries.

136. Philip Schuyler to Stephen Van Rensselaer, Poughkeepsie, July 2, 1788, Henry Ford Museum Bicentennial Collection, Dearborn, Michigan.

137. John Jay to George Washington, Poughkeepsie, July 4–8, 1788, Washington Papers, Library of Congress.

138. Abraham Bancker to Evert Bancker, Poughkeepsie, July 12, 1788, Bancker Family Correspondence, NHi; DeWitt Clinton to Charles Tillinghast, Poughkeepsie, July 12, 1788, DeWitt Clinton Papers, Columbia University Libraries.

139. George Clinton Papers, Bancroft Transcripts, New York Public Library.

140. *Ibid.*

141. *Ibid.*

142. *Ibid.*

143. *Ibid.*

144. Abraham Yates, Jr., to Abraham G. Lansing, New York, June 29, 1788, and to George Clinton, New York, June 27, 1788, Yates Papers, New York Public Library.

145. Abraham G. Lansing to Abraham Yates, Jr., July 20, 1788, Yates Papers, New York Public Library.

146. *Ibid.*

147. "Copy of a Letter from Poughkeepsie, dated Friday, July 25, 1788," New York *Independent Journal*, July 28, 1788 (supplement).

148. Alexander Hamilton to James Madison, [July 2, 1788], Rutland, *Madison*, 11: 185.

149. Most historians give little credence to the secessionist movement threatened by New York's southern counties. Nevertheless, a substantial body of evidence exists that such a secession was contemplated and it affected Antifederalist behavior in the convention. See Morgan Lewis to Tench Coxe, New York, July 29, 1788, Coxe Papers, Historical Society of Pennsylvania; Evert Bancker to Abraham Bancker, New York, July 24, 1788, Bancker Family Correspondence, NHi; Oliver Wolcott, Sr., to Oliver Wolcott, Jr., Litchfield, July 23, 1788, and Jeremiah Wadsworth to [Oliver Wolcott, Sr.], New York, July 15, 1788, both in the Wolcott Papers, Connecticut Historical Society; William Ellery to Benjamin Huntington, Newport, July 28, 1788, Bright Papers, Jervis Public Library, Rome, N.Y. New Hampshire Congressman Nicholas Gilman wrote that the southern part of New York "are highly federal and are greatly incensed against the Governor and his party—they threaten a dereliction of the government and if they should be unable to bring over the Country party, I am inclined to think that a secession of this City and the Islands will absolutely take place" (Gilman to John Langdon, New York, July 15, 1788, John G. M. Stone Collection, Annapolis, Md.). If the convention failed to ratify the Constitution, Samuel B. Webb predicted "there will be a seperation of the State." A week later he wrote that "the Southern District are determined on a seperation to join the union" (Webb to Catherine Hogeboom, New York, July 6, 13, 1788, Samuel B. Webb Papers, Yale University Library). From Poughkeepsie, John Jay wrote to George Washington that "The Unanimity of the southern District, and their apparent Determination to continue under the Wings of the Union operates powerfully on the Minds of the opposite Party" (Jay to Washington, July 4, 1788, Washington Papers, Library of Congress).

150. Melancton Smith to Nathan Dane, Poughkeepsie, June 28, 1788, Dane Papers, Beverly Historical Society.

151. Nathan Dane to Melancton Smith, New York, July 3, 1788, John Wingate Thornton Collection, New England Historic Genealogical Society.

152. *Ibid.*

153. Samuel Osgood to Melancton Smith and Samuel Jones, New York, July 11, 1788, National Park Service, Collections of Federal Hall National Memorial, New York City.

154. Melancton Smith to Nathan Dane, Poughkeepsie, [c. July 15, 1788], John Wingate Thornton Collection, New England Historic Genealogical Society.

155. Zephaniah Platt to William Smith, Poughkeepsie, July 28, 1788, Museum, Manor of St. George, Mastic Beach, Long Island, N.Y.

156. Abraham Bancker to Evert Bancker, Poughkeepsie, June 28, 1788, Bancker Family Correspondence, NHi; Alexander Hamilton to James Madison, [Poughkeepsie, July 2, 1788], Rutland, *Madison*, 11: 185.

157. William Kent, ed., *Memoirs and Letters of James Kent . . .* (Boston, 1898), 304, 306.

158. "Copy of a Letter from Poughkeepsie, dated Friday, July 25, 1788," New York *Independent Journal*, July 28, 1788 (supplement).

159. Kent, *Memoirs*, 311–12.

160. Nicholas Gilman to John Langdon, New York, July 17, 1788, John G. M. Stone Collection, Annapolis, Md.

161. "H. G." XII (Alexander Hamilton), New York *Daily Advertiser*, April 7, 1789, Gordon Den Boer, ed., *The Documentary History of the First Federal Elections 1788–1790* (4 vols., Madison, Wis., 1976–1990), 3: 431–34.

162. Clinton's letter is in RG 11, National Archives. It was read in Congress on July 30.

163. The text of the circular letter is printed in DenBoer, *Elections*, 1: 44–45.

164. Richard Penn Hicks to John Dickinson, New York, July 15, 1788, Logan Papers, Historical Society of Pennsylvania.

165. Victor du Pont to Pierre Samuel du Pont de Nemours, New York, July 26, 1788, Victor du Pont Papers, Eleutherian Mills Historical Library.

166. St. Jean de Crevecoeur to William Short, New York, February 20, 1788, Short Papers, Library of Congress.

167. Samuel B. Webb to Catherine Hogeboom, New York, July 13, 1788, Webb Family Papers, Yale University Library.

168. James Johnston to Peter Van Gaasbeck, New York, August 4, 1788, Van Gaasbeck Papers, Senate House Museum, Kingston.

169. James Madison to George Washington, New York, August 11, 24, 1788, Den Boer, *Elections*, 1: 83, 100.

170. Edmund Randolph to James Madison, Richmond, August 13, 1788, *ibid.*, 1: 88.

171. James Madison to George Washington, New York, September 14, 1788, *ibid.*, 1: 139.

172. Henry Lee to George Washington, New York, September 13, 1788, Washington Papers, Library of Congress.

173. *Pennsylvania Gazette*, 6, 13 August 1788, *ibid.*, 1: 46.

174. For an elaboration on this thesis, see Kenneth R. Bowling, " 'A Tub to the Whale': The Founding Fathers and Adoption of the Federal Bill of Rights," *Journal of the Early Republic*, 8 (1988), 223–51.

175. Edward Carrington to James Madison, Richmond, November 9–10, 1788, Den Boer, *Elections*, 4: 88.

176. Alexander Hamilton to James Madison, New York, November 23, 1788, *ibid.*, 4: 94.

177. Manuscript circular, Lamb Papers, NHi.

178. Eight newspapers from Boston to Edenton, N.C., printed this item (Den Boer, *Elections*, 4: 112–13).

179. James Madison to Thomas Jefferson, Philadelphia, December 8, 1788, *ibid.*, 4: 109.

180. Edward Carrington to James Madison, Richmond, December 19, 1788, *ibid.*, 4: 115. See also Carrington to Henry Knox, Richmond, December 30, 1788, *ibid.*, 4: 119.

181. Edward Carrington to James Madison and to Henry Knox, Richmond, December 30,

1788, both in *ibid.*, 4: 120. Carrington was defeated by John Pride who voted for Washington and Clinton.

182. Carrington to Jeremiah Wadsworth, Richmond, January 16, 1789, *ibid.*, 4: 142.

183. St. Jean de Crevecoeur to Thomas Jefferson, New York City, January 5, 1789, *ibid.*, 4:129; Baltimore *Maryland Gazette*, February 14, 1789.

184. See especially the *Federal Gazette*, December 13, 1788.

185. Philadelphia *Federal Gazette*, December 26, 1788, January 3, 1789; *Pennsylvania Gazette*, December 31, 1788.

186. Baltimore *Maryland Gazette*, December 30, 1788.

187. *Ibid.*, January 2, 1789.

188. Litchfield *Weekly Monitor*, January 26, 1789. See also *Massachusetts Centinel*, February 18, 1789.

189. "A Real Federalist," Philadelphia *Independent Gazetteer*, January 6, 1789. A manuscript copy of this essay, in Charles Tillinghast's handwriting, is in the Lamb Papers, NHi.

190. "A Friend to Good Government," New York *Daily Advertiser*, January 26, 1788.

191. *Journal of the Senate of the State of New-York* (Albany, 1788), 4.

192. *Albany Gazette*, December 26, 1788.

193. *Journal of the Senate*, 14–17.

194. *Ibid.*, 18.

195. New York *Daily Advertiser*, April 7, 1789, printed in Syrett, 5: 295–97.

196. Hamilton to James Madison, [New York, November 23, 1788,] *ibid.*, 5: 235.

197. See Young, *Democratic Republicans*, 124–26; and Tadahisa Kuroda, "New York and the First Presidential Election: Politics and the Constitution," *New York History*, 69 (July 1988), 319–51.

198. St. Jean de Crevecoeur to Thomas Jefferson, New York, January 5, 1789, Den Boer, *Elections*, 3: 277.

199. Hamilton to Theodore Sedgwick, [New York, January 29, 1789,] Syrett, 5: 251.

200. Hamilton to James Wilson, New York, January 25, 1789, *ibid.*, 5: 248.

201. Joshua Atherton to John Lamb, Amherst, N.H., February 23, 1789, Den Boer, *Elections*, 4: 182.

202. David Ramsay to John Adams, March 1789, Adams Papers, Massachusetts Historical Society.

203. Samuel A. Otis to Nathan Dane, New York, March 28, 1789, Den Boer, *Elections*, 4: 209. Otis did not believe that the governor's enemies would succeed.

204. Comte de Moustier to Comte de Montmorin, New York, February 4, 1789, *ibid.*, 3: 403–4.

205. Abraham Yates, Jr., to Melancton Smith, Albany, March 18, 1789, *ibid.*, 3: 442–43.

206. Robert R. Livingston to St. Jean de Crevecoeur, Clermont, December 27, 1788, *ibid.*, 3: 252.

207. St. Jean de Crevecoeur to Thomas Jefferson, New York, January 5, 1789, *ibid.*, 3: 276–77.

208. Samuel A. Otis to Paine Wingate, New York, January 20, 1789, *ibid.*, 3: 252n.

209. John Randolph to St. George Tucker, New York, February 19, 1789, St. George Tucker Papers, Library of Congress.

210. Morris sensed the futility of his situation and announced his withdrawal from the race in the New York *Daily Advertiser* on February 28.

211. DeWitt Clinton to Charles Clinton, New York, November 25, 1788, and "Extract of a letter from New-York, January 12," *Pennsylvania Mercury*, January 17, 1789, Den Boer, *Elections*, 3: 212, 323.

212. New York *Daily Advertiser*, February 2, 1789. Van Cortlandt's announcement ran in the newspaper for more than a month.

213. The Albany Committee of Correspondence to John Jay and Richard Varick, January 31, 1789, Schuyler Papers, New York Public Library.

214. Crevecoeur to Thomas Jefferson, New York, January 5, 1789, Den Boer, *Elections*, 3: 276.

215. Alexander Hamilton to the Supervisors of the City of Albany, New York, February 18, 1789, Syrett, 5: 261.

216. *Albany Gazette*, April 24, 1789.

217. This committee was the only time that Hamilton and Burr collaborated during their political careers. James Kent described Burr as an Antifederalist—a man "who has always been regarded as unfriendly to the government [i.e., the Constitution] and its administration." James Kent to Theodorus Bailey, January 27, 1791, Kent, *Memoirs*, 40.

218. Alexander Hamilton to Pierre Van Cortlandt, New York, February 16, 1789, Syrett, 5: 254.

219. Hamilton to the Supervisors of the City of Albany, New York, February 18, 1789, *ibid.*, 5: 255–61.

220. For the charge that only six of the twenty-three men who voted to nominate Yates at a Newburgh meeting were qualified to vote for governor, see "A Citizen," *Albany Register*, April 6, 1789. For Henry K. Van Rensselaer's charge that a reported Antifederalist meeting at Newburgh was "an absolute falshood . . . undoubtedly designed to deceive the public," see the *Albany Gazette*, April 24, 1789.

221. *New York Journal*, March 26, 1789; and Peter Van Gaasbeck to Abraham B. Bancker, Kingston, February 26, 1789, Den Boer, *Elections*, 3: 499.

222. *Goshen Repository*, March 24, 1789.

223. New York *Weekly Museum*, March 21, 1789.

224. New York *Daily Advertiser*, February 18, 1789.

225. *Ibid.*, February 19, 1789.

226. Lansingburgh *Federal Herald*, March 2, 1789.

227. Even Jacob Cooke in his favorable biography of Hamilton seems baffled by this demagoguery. Jacob Ernest Cooke, *Alexander Hamilton* (New York, 1982), 68–69.

228. Henry Van Schaack to Theodore Sedgwick, Pittsfield, March 9, 1789, Den Boer, *Elections*, 3: 504.

229. "Philopas," Lansingburgh *Federal Herald*, April 20, 1789.

230. This lengthy essay in the form of a biography was reprinted in the *New Hampshire Spy*, April 10.

231. "H. G.," New York *Daily Advertiser*, March 11, 1789, Syrett, 5: 265–66.

232. "H. G.," New York *Daily Advertiser*, March 14, 17, 1789, Syrett, 5: 269–70, 271.

233. "H. G.," New York *Daily Advertiser*, March 18, 1789, Syrett, 5: 273.

234. "H. G.," New York *Daily Advertiser*, April 8, 1789, Syrett, 5: 299. Compare this statement with Hamilton's earlier charge that Clinton wanted "to establish *Clintonism* on the basis of *Antifederalism*." Hamilton to James Madison, [July 2, 1788], Rutland, *Madison*, 11: 185.

235. Three years later, Hamilton felt it his "religious duty to oppose" Aaron Burr's candidacy for the vice presidency. Hamilton to Rufus King, New York, September 23, 1792, Syrett, 12: 413–14.

236. "A Citizen," Lansingburgh *Federal Herald*, March 30, 1789.

237. *Albany Gazette*, March 13, 1789.

238. *New York Journal*, April 9, 1789; Syrett, 5: 324–25.

239. See Alexander Hamilton's address to the Electors of the State of New York, *New York Journal*, April 9, 1789, Syrett, 5: 326–27; "A Citizen," Lansingburgh *Federal Herald*, March 30, 1789; "An Independent Elector," *Goshen Repository*, March 31, 1789.

240. "A Citizen," Lansingburgh *Federal Herald*, March 30, 1789.

241. "Verus," New York *Daily Advertiser*, February 21, 1789 (reprinted from a non-extant issue of the *Albany Gazette*).

242. *Goshen Repository*, March 31, 1789. "No Party Man" asked Clinton's opponents if there ever had been a government ancient or modern in which "the chief magistrate or governor thereof, was not at the head of a party." *New York Journal*, March 12, 1789.

243. "A Citizen," Lansingburgh *Federal Herald*, March 30, 1789. James Kent described Yates "as a much more virtuous, more independent & more advisable Man" than Clinton. Kent to Simeon Baldwin, Poughkeepsie, March 26, 1789, Den Boer, *Elections*, 3: 496.

244. Alexander Hamilton to the Independent and Patriotic Electors of the State of New-York, April 7, 1789, printed in the *New York Journal*, April 9, 1789, and Syrett, 5: 317–29.

245. *New York Journal*, March 26, 1789.

246. "Cassius," Poughkeepsie *Country Journal*, March 3, 1789. These passages were reprinted as an "Extract of a letter from Albany dated February 9," Lansingburgh *Federal Herald*, March 30, 1789.

247. "Brutus," *New York Journal*, March 19, 1789.

248. "A Freeholder of the Southern District," *New York Journal*, March 19, 1789. According to a preface, this essay had been submitted to Francis Childs's *Daily Advertiser*, "but, the printer refused to admit the piece, unless he had permission to expunge some part of it." The author withdrew it from Childs and submitted it to Thomas Greenleaf's newspaper.

249. *Ibid*. On March 4, 1789, the *Daily Advertiser* printed a piece charging that Clinton had embezzled public funds. Antifederalists immediately denounced the slander. Federalists accused their opponents of planting the strawman, but this charge was refuted. "A Friend to Truth," *Daily Advertiser*, March 5, 1789; "A Mechanic": To the Mechanics of the City of New-York, April 28, 1789, (broadside) New York State Library.

250. *Ibid*.; "Truth" and "Junius," *New York Journal*, February 26, April 2, 1789.

251. "Brutus," *ibid*., March 19, 1789.

252. *Ibid*., March 19, 1789. A reference to Philip Schuyler and his son-in-law Alexander Hamilton. See also "A Yeoman," *ibid*., March 26, 1789.

253. *Pennsylvania Packet*, May 8, 1789.

254. "Extract of a letter from a gentleman in New-York, to his friend in this city, dated April 9," Fredericksburg *Virginia Herald*, April 23, 1789.

255. David Gelston to John Smith, April 27, May 7, 1789, John Smith Papers, NHi; Jeremiah Van Renssalaer, Chairman of the Albany Republican Committee to the Republican Committee of Kingston, April 23, 1789, New York State Library.

256. Quoted in Spaulding, 188.

257. Clermont, April 1789, Livingston Papers, NHi.

258. Monthly meteorological tables appear in the *New York Daily Gazette*. The April table was printed on May 6, 1789.

259. James Duane to William North, New York, May 2, 1789, Colburn Autograph Collection, Massachusetts Historical Society.

260. Schuyler to Hamilton, Albany, May 20, 1789, Syrett, 5: 339.

261. James Duane to Philip Schuyler and Volkert P. Douw, New York, June 5, 1789, Den Boer, *Elections*, 3: 514.

262. A tabulation of the vote by precinct for the counties is located in the Livingston Papers, NHi.

263. The report appeared in the *New York Daily Gazette*, May 30, 1789. In Westchester, New Rochelle lost 320 votes, York-Town 230, and Yonkers 280. Another 111 votes were lost in Warwick, Orange County. If the missing votes had been divided in the same proportional fashion between the two candidates as occurred throughout the other towns in those two counties, Westchester would have given Yates an additional 473 votes to Clinton's 357, while Orange would have given Yates an additional 12 votes and Clinton an additional 99. The net effect would have given Yates a majority of only 29 of the lost votes, narrowing Clinton's total majority to 400.

264. William Grayson to Patrick Henry, New York, June 12, 1789, William Wirt Henry, ed., *Patrick Henry: Life, Correspondence and Speeches* (3 vols., reprint edition, New York, 1969), 3: 393–94.

265. *Pennsylvania Packet*, June 10, 1789

V—A State Republican Leader

1. Alexander White to Horatio Gates, New York, July 23, 1789, Gates Papers, NHi.

2. To George Read, July 28, 1789, Den Boer, *Elections*, 3: 554.

3. Hamilton also backed King's candidacy as a U.S. senator and King became a staunch supporter of the secretary of the treasury.

4. Margaret Beekman Livingston to Robert R. Livingston, Clermont, April 1789, Den Boer, *Elections*, 3: 497.

5. Young, *Democratic Republicans*, 252–54.

6. James Kent to Theodorus Bailey, New York, January 16, 1791, Kent Papers, Library of Congress.

7. Troup to Hamilton, January 19, 1791, Syrett, 7: 445.

8. Clinton to Monroe, February 16, 1791, Monroe Papers, Library of Congress.

9. Morgan Lewis to Robert R. Livingston, Philadelphia, January 24, 1791, Livingston Papers, NHi.

10. Robert R. Livingston to Morgan Lewis, New York, January 27, 1791, Livingston Papers, NHi.

11. *Ibid.*

12. William Duer to Alexander Hamilton, January 19, 1791; James Tillary to Hamilton, [January 20], 1791, Syrett, 7: 614–16.

13. *Ibid.*; Troup to Hamilton, January 19, 1791, Syrett, 7: 442–45.

14. Philip Schuyler to John B. Schuyler, January 26, 1791, Schuyler Family Papers, New York Public Library.

15. *Laws of the State of New York*, 14 sess., chap. 42.

16. Hamilton to Unknown, September 21, 1792, and Hamilton to John Steele, Philadelphia, October 15, 1792, Syrett, 12: 408, 568.

17. New York *Columbian Gazetteer*, November 18, 1793.

18. George Clinton to John Smith, Albany, February 1, 1804, New York State Library.

19. George Clinton to James Monroe, New York, February 16, 1790, draft on third page of letter from Monroe to Clinton dated January 17, 1790, Clinton Papers, Box 39, New York State Library.

20. Robert R. Livingston to Janet Montgomery, January 15, 1790, Livingston Papers, NHi. Various members of the chancellor's family were among the largest speculators.

21. New York *Daily Advertiser*, March 10, 1790.

22. James Watson to James Wadsworth, January 16, 1791, Wadsworth Papers, Connecticut Historical Society.

23. James Kent to Theodorus Bailey, February 27, 1791, Kent, *Memoirs*, 41–42.

24. According to a newspaper report, Van Gaasbeck "bore a grudge in his heart against a certain family in Kingston, who are friends of the old Governor, because they hindered him to make himself a Congressman" in 1790 and because Van Gaasbeck's request for a land grant of 55,000 acres at one shilling per acre was rejected by the land office, in preference to another offer at three shillings per acre. Just before an Esopus meeting in late March, Van Gaasbeck allegedly swore "that, as he had now a chance, he was determined to leave no stone in the country unturned to get Clinton out of office, even if he should put one of his greatest enemies into it, such as Jay, with whom . . . he some time ago had a monstrous family dispute, and that it is even not yet settled." *New York Journal*, April 18, 21, 1792.

25. Moss Kent to James Kent, Springfield, County of Otsego, February 7, 1792, James Kent Papers, Library of Congress.

26. Isaac Ledyard to Alexander Hamilton, February 1, 1792, Syrett, 11: 2.

27. *Ibid.*

28. William Wilcocks, *New York Journal*, August 15, 1792.

29. Leonard Gansevoort to Peter Gansevoort, New York, February 11, 1792, L. W. Smith Collection, Morristown National Historical Park.

30. "Extract of a letter from New York, per stage," *Albany Gazette*, February 13, 1792; John Jay to John C. Dongan, New York, February 27, 1792, Johnston, *Jay*, 3: 413–14.

31. James Kent to Moss Kent, Poughkeepsie, March 1, 1792, James Kent Papers, Library of Congress.

32. Van Gaasbeck to Burr, March 28, 1792, Mary-Jo Kline, ed., *Political Correspondence and Public Papers of Aaron Burr* (2 vols., Princeton, N.J., 1983), 103–4.

33. Peter Van Schaack to John C. Wynkoop, Kinderhook, March 13, 1792, Van Schaack Papers, Library of Congress.

34. James Kent to Moss Kent, Poughkeepsie, March 1, 1792, James Kent Papers, Library of Congress.

35. *Ibid.*

36. Remsen to Jefferson, New York, April 23, 1792, Boyd, *Jefferson*, 23: 452. Remsen had just returned to New York City from Philadelphia after resigning as chief clerk in the Department of State.

37. From James Clinton, New York, March 15, 1792, L. W. Smith Collection, Morristown National Historical Park.

38. John C. Wynkoop to Peter Van Schaack, Kingston, February 23, 1792, Van Schaack Papers, Library of Congress.

39. John Livingston to Walter Livingston, Manor Livingston, November 13, 1791, Robert R. Livingston Papers, NHi.

40. John Livingston to Walter Livingston, Manor Livingston, February 16, March 1 and 7, 1792, Robert R. Livingston Papers, NHi; Peter R. Livingston to Peter Van Schaack, April 1, 1792, Van Schaack Papers, Library of Congress.

41. Manor Livingston, March 7, 1792, Robert R. Livingston Papers, NHi.

42. Peter Van Schaack to Peter Van Gaasbeck, April 12, 1792, Van Gaasbeck Papers, Senate House Museum.

43. *Ibid.*

44. John C. Wynkoop to Peter Van Schaack, Kingston, February 23, 1792, Van Schaack Papers, Library of Congress.

45. Joshua Mersereau to Alexander Hamilton, Elizabeth Town, N.J., April 29, 1792, Syrett, 11: 344. John Pintard had earlier referred to New York's Antifederalists as "Copperheads." Pintard to Elisha Boudinot, New York, June 10, 1788, Boudinot–Pintard Papers, NHi.

46. Dongan to Jay, February 27, 1792, Johnston, *Jay*, 3: 413n.

47. John Jay to John C. Dongan, *ibid.*, 3: 414.

48. *Ibid.*, 415.

49. Peter Van Schaack to John C. Wynkoop, Kinderhook, March 13, 1792, Van Schaack Papers, Library of Congress.

50. "Tammany," The Guardian, No. V, *New York Journal*, March 28, 1792.

51. *New York Journal*, April 21, 1792.

52. *Ibid.*

53. Peter Van Schaack to Messr. Dole and Tibbots, March 26, 1792, Van Schaack Papers, Library of Congress.

54. John C. Wynkoop to Peter Van Schaack, Kingston, April 17, 1792, Van Schaack Papers, Library of Congress. On March 30, 1785, the Council of Revision rejected a gradual-emancipation bill because (1) it deprived free blacks the right to vote and by implication the right to hold office; (2) "it holds up a doctrine which is repugnant to the principle on which the

United States justify their separation from Great Britain, and either enacts what is wrong, or supposes that those may rightfully be charged with the burdens of government, who have no representative share in imposing them"; (3) it would create a "class of disenfranchised and discontented citizens" who could become dangerous to the state and the constitution; (4) through inter-marriage thousands of people in the future might be deprived of their rights; and (5) it disenfranchised without cause free blacks that had "hitherto been entitled to vote . . . in direct violation of the established rules of justice, and against the letter and spirit of the constitution, and tends to support a doctrine which is inconsistent with the most obvious principles of government, that the Legislature may arbitrarily dispose of the dearest rights of their constituents." *Messages from the Governors*, 2: 237–39. Clinton, Chancellor Livingston, and Judge John Sloss Hobart signed this report.

55. "Tammany": The Guardian No. IV, *New York Journal*, March 21, 1792.

56. Peter Van Schaack to Messrs. Dole and Tibbots, March 26, 1792, Van Schaack Papers, Library of Congress.

57. "To the Independent Electors," *New York Journal*, March 24, 1792.

58. *New York Journal*, March 24, 1792.

59. Peter Van Schaack to John C. Wynkoop, Kinderhook, March 13, 1792, Van Schaack Papers, Library of Congress.

60. Peter Van Schaack to Messrs. Dole and Tibbots, March 26, 1792, Van Schaack Papers, Library of Congress.

61. *New York Journal*, September 1, 1792.

62. James Tillary to Alexander Hamilton, New York, March 6, 1792, Syrett, 11: 110.

63. "Cato," *New York Journal*, April 4, 1792.

64. In October 1792 New York City newspapers published a circular letter from former army officers asking Congress for their back pay. Governor Clinton was inadvertently listed as a member of the committee of officers that wrote the address. Subsequently the newspapers announced the error, saying that Clinton was not at the meeting and that he had already publicly renounced all claims on the United States for his military service. The governor, however, let it be known that he would "cooperate in any measures, consistent with his station, to procure justice to the officers and soldiers of an army with whom he so long and so honorably served." *New York Journal*, October 17, 20, 1792.

65. "An Independent Citizen," *New York Journal*, February 25, 1792.

66. *New York Journal*, March 7, 1792.

67. "Tammany": The Guardian No. IV, *New York Journal*, March 21, 1792.

68. Meeting in the town of Beekman on April 9, 1792, *New York Journal*, April 14, 1792.

69. *New York Journal*, March 7, 1792.

70. This anonymous circular letter to representatives of various counties was written by Chancellor Livingston. It was printed in the *New York Journal*, March 24, 1792. A draft is in the Livingston Papers, NHi.

71. Quoted in *New York Journal*, April 21, 1792.

72. From George Clinton, New York, March 4, 1792, L. W. Smith Collection, Morristown National Historical Park.

73. *New York Journal*, April 18, 1792.

74. Peter Van Schaack to Messr. Dole and Tibbots, March 26, 1792, Van Schaack Papers, Library of Congress.

75. *New York Journal*, April 21, 1792.

76. "Copy of a letter from a gentleman in Orange county, to his friend in this city [New York], dated April 1, 1792," *New York Journal*, April 18, 1792.

77. Robert Troup to John Jay, New York, May 6, 1792, Johnston, *Jay*, 3: 422–23.

78. Robert Troup to John Jay, New York, May 20, 1792, *ibid.*, 424.

79. Thomas Jefferson to James Madison, Philadelphia, June 10, 1792, Boyd, *Jefferson*, 24: 50.

80. James Kent to Moss Kent, Poughkeepsie, June 13, 1792, James Kent Papers, Library of Congress.

81. George Clinton to James Clinton, New York, May 2, 1792, Museum of The City of New York.

82. Robert Troup to John Jay, New York, May 20, 1792, Johnston, *Jay*, 3: 424.

83. *Ibid.*, 425–26.

84. Thomas Tillotson to Robert R. Livingston, New York, June 9, 1792, Livingston Papers, NHi.

85. Robert Troup to John Jay, New York, June 10, 1792, Johnston, *Jay*, 3: 428–29. James Kent also charged that Burr had "shamefully prostituted his talents to serve a desperate and abandoned party. To Moss Kent, Jr., June 15, 1792, Kent, *Memoirs*, 45.

86. Aaron Burr to Jacob Delamater, New York, June 15, 1792, Kline, *Burr*, 125–26.

87. Aaron Burr to James Monroe, Philadelphia, September 10, 1792, *ibid.*, 135–36.

88. Robert Troup to John Jay, New York, June 10, 1792, Johnston, *Jay*, 3: 429.

89. The majority report of the canvassers was signed by Melancton Smith, Daniel Graham, Jonathan N. Havens, David M'Carty, Thomas Tillotson, David Gelston, and Pierre Van Cortlandt, Jr., the son of the lieutenant governor. The minority report was signed by Samuel Jones, Isaac Roosevelt, and Leonard Gansevoort. The final canvasser, Joshua Sands, signed his own dissenting report a few days later. All of the reports appeared in the New York City newspapers during the third week in June.

90. Sarah Jay to John Jay, New York, June 10, 12, 1792, Johnston, *Jay*, 3: 431–33.

91. John Jay to Sarah Jay, East Hartford, June 18, 1792, *ibid.*, 3: 434–35.

92. James Kent to Moses Kent, March 22, 1793, Kent Papers, Library of Congress.

93. New York, June 13, 1792, Johnston, *Jay*, 3: 434.

94. Herman Hoffman, Jacob I. Hurmanance, and William Wheeler to Peter Van Schaack, Red Hook, June 16, 1792, Van Schaack Papers, Library of Congress.

95. *New York Journal*, July 4, 1792.

96. *New York Journal*, June 20, July 14, 1792.

97. Robert Troup to Peter Van Gaasbeek, New York, June 25, 1792, New York State Library.

98. *New York Journal*, July 14, 1792.

99. *New York Journal*, July 7, 1792.

100. *New York Journal*, July 14, 1792.

101. William Wilcocks to George Clinton, *New York Journal*, July 7, 1792.

102. Rufus King to Alexander Hamilton, New York, July 10, 1792, Syrett, 12: 21.

103. Chancellor Livingston agreed with this assessment: "it is easier to set a house on fire than to say where the flames shall stop." Robert R. Livingston to Edward Livingston, Clermont, July 20, 1792, Livingston Papers, NHi.

104. Alexander Hamilton to Rufus King, Philadelphia, June 28, July 25, 1792, Syrett, 11: 588–89; 12: 99–100.

105. Robert Troup to Alexander Hamilton, New York, August 24, 1792, *ibid.* 12: 272.

106. Robert R. Livingston to Edward Livingston, Clermont, June 19, 1792, Livingston Papers, NHi.

107. Robert R. Livingston to Edward Livingston, Clermont, October 1, 1792, Livingston Papers, NHi.

108. *New York Journal*, July 7, September 22, 1792.

109. *New York Daily Gazette*, June 12, 1792.

110. Robert Troup to Peter Van Gaasbeck, New York, June 25, 1792, New York State Library.

111. Ebenezer Foote to ?, June 27, 1792, Katherine Foote, *Ebenezer Foote, The Founder* (Delhi, N.Y., 1927), 44.

112. Rufus King to Alexander Hamilton, New York, July 10, 1792, Syrett, 12: 21.

113. Thomas Jefferson to James Madison, Philadelphia, June 21, 1792, Rutland, *Madison*, 14: 325.

114. James Madison to Thomas Jefferson, Orange, June 29, 1792, Rutland, *Madison*, 14: 332.

115. "The Respondent," No. V, *New York Journal*, September 5, 1792.

116. Morgan Lewis to Robert R. Livingston, Johnstown, July 4, 1792, Livingston Papers, NHi.

117. Edward Livingston to Robert R. Livingston, New York, July 14, 1792, Livingston Papers, NHi.

118. Benjamin Walker to Alexander Hamilton, New York, July 12, 1792, Syrett, 12: 30.

119. *Ibid*.

120. *New York Journal*, July 18, August 1, 1792.

121. New York *Daily Gazette*, June 19, 1792.

122. *New York Journal*, July 18, 1792.

123. *New York Journal*, July 14, 1792. For a compilation of town and county meetings with their resolutions, see "Commission book on election of 1792," New York State Library (#15117).

124. According to Edward Livingston, the addresses to Jay and his responses "have injured him with the moderate men of his own Party and I much question whether he Will not find that in Case of any violent measures he has calculated too much on the nerves of his New Patriots." (Edward Livingston to Robert R. Livingston, New York, July 14, 1792, Livingston Papers, NHi.) "P.Q." seconded Livingston. "The language of the nominal Governor secretly fed the violence of his party, by his cunning replies to the violent addresses of the north." *New York Journal*, July 21, 1792. See also "Aristides," the resolutions of an Ulster County meeting held on September 8, and "A Farmer," *New York Journal*, August 8, September 26, 1792, and January 16, 1793.

125. "Lucius" condemned Van Rensselaer for serving as an inspector of elections in Water Vliet, chiefly inhabited by his tenants. "In order to prevent them from voting against Mr. Jay and himself, and to mark out for vengeance those that had the audacity to oppose his inclination, he produced a peculiar kind of silk paper, with which the ballots were formed; by which means, and his official station as inspector (as one of the inspectors receives the ballots from the hands of the electors) he was able to tell immediately, whether his unfortunate tenants had voted their landlord for lieutenant governor." *New York Journal*, June 30, 1792. See also "Cato," *New York Journal*, July 25, 1792.

126. "The Republican" No. II stated that "The uniform, obstinate, and unrelenting opposition of Gen. Schuyler, and his adherents to Governor Clinton, ascertains beyond doubt the truth of the remark—This opposition is not the being of yesterday—it is coeval with the organization of our government, and may be traced from Mr. Schuyler's first unsuccessful competition for the magistracy, down to Mr. Jay's late defeat. In his third essay, "The Republican" said that "Every candid and impartial man, who has marked the commencement and progress of the opposition to the decision of the canvassers, must have considered General Schuyler as the spring that set the whole machinery in motion. He was in this city at the close of the canvass; and made every effort to stimulate his party to ribaldry and clamor." *New York Journal*, September 1, 8, 1792.

127. Silas Talbot to Enos Hitchcock, New York, December 15, 1792, New York State Library.

128. Loring Andrews to Peter Van Schaack, Stockbridge, October 9, 1792, Van Schaack Papers, Library of Congress.

129. Moss Kent to Peter Van Schaack, Springfield, October 12, 1792, Van Schaack Papers, Library of Congress.

130. William Cooper to Peter Van Schaack, October 1, 1792, Cooper Manuscripts, New York State Historical Association.

131. Thomas Tillotson to Robert R. Livingston, Albany, January 11, 1793, Livingston Papers, NHi.

VI—A National Republican

1. Alexander Hamilton to Rufus King, Philadelphia, July 25, 1792, Syrett, 12: 99.

2. Alexander Hamilton to John Adams, Philadelphia, June 25, 1792, *ibid.*, 11: 559.

3. John Beckley to James Madison, Philadelphia, August 1, 1792, Rutland, *Madison*, 14: 346.

4. *New York Journal*, September 1, 1792.

5. *New York Journal*, October 3, 1792.

6. Benjamin Rush to Aaron Burr, Philadelphia, September 24, 1792, Kline, *Burr*, 137.

7. Alexander Hamilton to George Washington, Philadelphia, September 23, 1792, Syrett, 12: 418.

8. Rufus King to Alexander Hamilton, New York, September 17, 1791, *ibid.*, 12: 387.

9. Melancton Smith and Marinus Willett to James Madison and James Monroe, New York, September 30, 1792, Rutland, *Madison*, 14: 379–81.

10. John Nicholson to James Madison, Philadelphia, October 3, 1792, *ibid.*, 14: 376–77.

11. John Beckley to James Madison, Philadelphia, September 2, 10, 1792, *ibid.*, 14: 356, 362.

12. James Monroe to James Madison, Fredericksburg, October 9, 1792, *ibid.*, 14: 377–79.

13. Draft letters, Philadelphia, September 21 and 26, 1792; Hamilton to Rufus King, September 23, 1792; Rufus King to Hamilton, New York, September 27, 1792; Hamilton to Charles Cotesworth Pinckney, Philadelphia, October 10; and Hamilton to John Steele, Philadelphia, October 15, Syrett, 12: 408, 413–14, 480, 493, 544, 567–68.

14. For the role of John Beckley in behind-the-scenes Republican politics, see Edmund Berkeley and Dorothy Smith Berkeley, *John Beckley: Zealous Partisan in a Nation Divided* (Philadelphia, 1973); Noble E. Cunningham, Jr., "John Beckley: An Early American Party Manager," *William and Mary Quarterly*, 3rd ser., 13 (1956), 40–52; and Philip Marsh, "John Beckley-Mystery Man of the Early Jeffersonians," *Pennsylvania Magazine of History and Biography*, 72 (1948), 54–69.

15. John Adams to Charles Francis Adams, Philadelphia, February 14, 1795, Kent, *Memoirs*, 67.

16. "Plain Sense" charged that Burr had given his opinion in favor of Clinton's 1792 reelection as a payoff for Burr's 1791 election to the U.S. Senate, and that Clinton now returned the favor by appointing Burr to the court. New York *Daily Advertiser*, October 29, November 14, 1792. Such sentiments were also expressed privately in a letter from James Kent to his brother Moss Kent on October 15 (Kent Papers, Library of Congress).

17. John Beckley to James Madison, Philadelphia, October 17, 1792, Rutland, *Madison*, 14: 383–85.

18. John Dawson to James Madison, Richmond, November 12, 1792, Rutland, *Madison*, 14: 405.

19. Robert R. Livingston to Edward Livingston, Clermont, October 4, 1792, Livingston Papers, NHi.

20. John Armstrong to Horatio Gates, January 12, 1792, Gates Papers, NHi.

21. John Dawson to James Madison, Richmond, November 12, 1792; William Overton Callis to James Madison, Richmond, November 19, 1792, Rutland, *Madison*, 14: 405, 409; and *North Carolina Journal*, December 19, 1792.

22. Reprinted in the *Fayetteville Gazette*, January 2, 1793.

23. *Virginia Gazette and General Advertiser*, November 28, 1792. See also an "Extract of a letter from Virginia," *North Carolina Journal*, October 24, 1792.

24. *North Carolina Journal*, November 14, 1792, reprinted in the Philadelphia *Independent Gazetteer*, November 24, 1792.

25. *North Carolina Journal*, October 24, 1792.

26. *Ibid.*

27. "Lucius," *New York Journal*, November 24, 1792; William Overton Callis to James Madison, Richmond, December 2, 1792, Rutland, *Madison*, 14: 420; and "A Republican Federalist," Philadelphia *Independent Gazetteer*, December 1, 1792.

28. *New York Journal*, December 12, 1792.

29. New York *Daily Advertiser*, December 8, 1792.

30. Fisher Ames to Timothy Dwight, Philadelphia, November 12, 1792, in W. B. Allen, ed., *Works of Fisher Ames* (2 vols., Indianapolis, 1983), 950–51. A week later, Ames described Clinton as a man "who would have trusted the issue [i.e., the ratification of the Constitution] to arms, and prevented New York from adopting it, who has kept an anti party alive there by his influence, and holds his governorship by a breach of the state constitution." Ames to George Richards Minot, Philadelphia, November 19, 1792, *ibid.*, 952.

31. John Beckley to James Madison, Philadelphia, September 2, 10, 1792, Rutland, *Madison*, 14: 356, 362.

32. George Clinton to Dr. Michael Leib, Greenwich, November 19, 1796, New York State Library.

33. Robert Gamble to Thomas Jefferson, Richmond, December 4, 1792, Boyd, *Jefferson*, 24: 698.

34. Archibald Stuart to Thomas Jefferson, Richmond, December 6, 1792, *ibid.*, 24: 705.

35. Alexander Hamilton to John Jay, Philadelphia, December 18, 1792, Syrett, 13: 338.

36. *New York Journal*, July 18, 1792.

37. Clinton also gravitated toward France because many of his political opponents supported Great Britain. Federalists realized that Great Britain was America's most important trading partner and that British capital supported American merchants and new manufactures. Federalists also knew that Hamilton's funding system depended on revenue derived from duties levied on British imports, and the Bank of the United States depended on the credibility of federally funded securities

38. *Messages from the Governors*, 2: 333.

39. *New York Journal*, May 11, 1793. On September 3, 1793, Collector of the Port of New York John Lamb reported to Clinton that two French privateers (*La Petite Democrat* and *Caramagnole*) had arrived. Lamb "thought it proper to communicate this information to your Excellency;-in order that you may take such steps respecting them, as you may deem proper." George Clinton Papers, State Historical Society of Wisconsin.

40. Cabinet Meeting of Washington, Jefferson, Knox, and Hamilton, Philadelphia, June 12, 1793, Syrett, 14: 534–36, 540; 15: 2–4.

41. *New York Journal*, August 10, 1793.

42. *Ibid.*, August 17, 1793.

43. George Washington to Alexander Hamilton, Philadelphia, August 10, 1793, Syrett, 15: 228–29; *New York Journal*, August 17, 1793.

44. New York *Columbian Gazetteer*, December 2, 1793.

45. Hugh Williamson to Alexander Hamilton, New York, October 24, 1793, Syrett, 15: 377.

46. *Ibid.*

47. *Messages from the Governors*, 2: 333–34.

48. *Ibid.*, 334.

49. *Ibid.*, 336–37, 339–40.

50. Robert R. Livingston to Edward Livingston, Albany, January 21, 1794, Livingston Papers, NHi.

51. New York *American Minerva*, March 11, 1794; *New York Journal*, August 17, 1793.

52. New York *Columbian Gazetteer*, March 31, 1794.

53. Letter from a committee appointed by a public meeting of citizens, addressed to John Watts, representative in Congress, March 3, 1794, New York *American Minerva*, March 5, 1794.

54. Alexander Hamilton to George Washington, Philadelphia, March 8, 1794, Syrett, 16: 134.

55. Letter from a committee appointed by a public meeting of citizens, addressed to John Watts, representative in Congress, March 3, 1794, New York *American Minerva*, March 5, 1794.

56. New York *American Minerva*, March 22, 1794; New York *Columbian Gazetteer*, March 24, 1794.

57. New York *Columbian Gazetteer*, March 27, 1794; New York *American Minerva*, March 27, 1794.

58. On one of the few days that George Clinton was able to attend the provincial convention that drafted New York's constitution in 1777, he voted with a minority of delegates against a resolution that would have allowed the governor alone to appoint the senators to the council.

59. See Howard Lee McBain, *DeWitt Clinton and the Origin of the Spoils System in New York* (New York, 1907). McBain characterized Clinton as "tactful, able, forceful."

60. Schuyler to John Jay, Albany, May 30, 1785, Jay Papers, Columbia University Libraries.

61. Edward Livingston to Robert R. Livingston, New York, September 29, 1793, Livingston Papers, NHi.

62. Thomas Tillotson to Robert R. Livingston, Albany, January 11, 1793, Livingston Papers, NHi; New York *Columbian Gazetteer*, January 16, 1794.

63. Thomas Tillotson to Robert R. Livingston, Albany, January 11, 1793, Livingston Papers, NHi.

64. John Addison to Peter Van Gaasbeck, February 15, 1794, and C. E. Elmendorph to Peter Van Gaasbeck, January 8, 1794, Van Gaasbeck Papers, Senate House Museum. See also McBain, *DeWitt Clinton and the Origin of the Spoils Systems in New York*.

65. New York *Herald*, October 13, 1794. Federalists reprinted Clinton's protest in the New York *Daily Advertiser* on April 7, 1801, when Governor Jay was advocating his sole power to nominate against a Republican-controlled council of appointment led by DeWitt Clinton.

66. *New York Herald*, October 13, 1794.

67. *Messages from the Governors*, 2: 360–61.

68. *Journal of the Assembly of the State of New-York* (Albany, 1794), 12–14; New York *Columbian Gazetteer*, January 27, 1794. Chancellor Livingston told his brother that "the legislature have hitherto amused themselves with triffles such as attacking titles etc." To Edward Livingston, Albany, January 21, 1794, Livingston Papers, NHi.

69. New York *Columbian Gazetteer*, March 20, 1794.

70. Robert R. Livingston to Edward Livingston, Albany, February 12, 1794, Livingston Papers, NHi; Philip Schuyler to Alexander Hamilton, New York, January 5, 1795, Syrett, 18: 18–20.

71. New York *Daily Advertiser*, January 26, 1795.

72. New York *Columbian Gazetteer*, June 9, 1794 (supplement).

73. New York *Daily Advertiser*, January 26, 1795.

74. See Beatrice G. Reubens, "State Financing of Private Enterprise in Early New York" (doctoral thesis, Columbia University, 1960).

75. George Clinton to DeWitt Clinton, December 13, 1803, DeWitt Clinton Papers, Columbia University Libraries.

76. George Clinton to Gilbert Livingston, Albany, March 26, 1804, Pierpont Morgan Library.

77. George Clinton to Mathias B. Tallmadge, Casper's Kill, October 22, 1804, Fraunces Tavern Museum.

78. George Clinton to Zephaniah Platt, Greenwich, February 7, 1800, Plattsburg Public

Library. Clinton also wrote very short, to-the-point, dunning letters: "Being under the necessity of raising a Considerable Sum of Money by the mid[d]le of december next, I will thank you if you will be pleased to discharge the Ballance due on your Bond before that Time." George Clinton to William Cross, Greenwich, October 27, 1799, L. W. Smith Collection, Morristown National Historical Park.

79. George Clinton to Zephaniah Platt, Greenwich, February 7, 1800, Plattsburg Public Library.

80. George Clinton to DeWitt Clinton, Greenwich, February 13, 1800, DeWitt Clinton Papers, Columbia University Libraries.

81. In 1801, Albert Gallatin explained that "the majority in the city of New York (on which, unfortunately, the majority in the State actually depends, that city making one-eighth of the whole)" was too tenuous for Republicans. To Thomas Jefferson, Washington, September 14, 1801, Henry Adams, ed., *The Writings of Albert Gallatin* (3 vols., Philadelphia, 1879), 1: 50–51.

82. Federalists found it difficult to nominate prominent New York City candidates to the legislature because the capital had just been moved permanently to Albany. Matthew Livingston Davis happily reported that the Federalist ticket included two grocers, a ship chandler, a baker, a potter, a bookseller, a mason, and a shoemaker. Kline, *Burr*, 423.

83. George Clinton to DeWitt Clinton, Albany, December 13, 1803, DeWitt Clinton Papers, Columbia University Libraries.

84. Matthew Livingston Davis' account, as quoted in Kline, *Burr*, 422.

85. Alexander Hamilton to John Jay, May 7, 1800, Syrett, 24: 465; Philip Schuyler to John Jay, New York, May 7, 1800, Johnston, *Jay*, 4: 270–72.

86. For the most thorough account of the nomination of a vice presidential candidate in 1800, see Kline, *Burr*, 430–34.

87. "Aristides" described Livingston's flawed reputation: "Whether *deafness* was among the influential objections to Chancellor Livingston's nomination, I do not know. But that there prevailed an uncommon want of confidence in his political stability, is certain. He was supposed, and justly, destitute of that solid and useful knowledge so essential to the character of a statesman. Instead of a man possessed of an energetic, vigorous mind, capable of steady application, and forcible inquiry, he was deemed a capricious, visionary theorist, eternally wandering in fancy's fairy fields. Heedless of important and laborious pursuits, at which his frivolous mind revolted, he was believed lamentably deficient in the practical knowledge of a politician. Although it was well known to his friends that these sentiments were generally entertained, so great was their solicitude upon the occasion, that with the consent of Mr. Burr, Mr. Livingston was first proposed to the meeting at Philadelphia, and rejected by a large majority." *An Examination of the Various Charges Exhibited Against Aaron Burr, Esq. Vice-President of the United States; and a Development of the Characters and Views of His Political Opponents* (Philadelphia, 1803), 25–26.

88. George Clinton to DeWitt Clinton, December 13, 1803, DeWitt Clinton Papers, Columbia University Libraries.

89. George Clinton to DeWitt Clinton, Albany, December 17, 1803, DeWitt Clinton Papers, Columbia University Libraries.

90. George Clinton to DeWitt Clinton, Albany, December 13, 1803, DeWitt Clinton Papers, Columbia University Libraries; and James Nicholson's Memorandum, December 26, 1803, *American Historical Review*, 8 (1903), 511–13. The manuscript of Nicholson's memoranda is in the DeWitt Clinton Papers, Columbia University Libraries.

91. Philip Schuyler to Alexander Hamilton, Albany, September 29, 1800, Syrett, 25: 123–24.

92. New York *Daily Advertiser*, February 28, 1801. Van Rensselaer, Philip Schuyler's brother-in-law, was the former co-chairman of the Albany County Republican Society during the debate over the ratification of the U.S. Constitution.

93. George Clinton to DeWitt Clinton, New York, January 13, 1801, DeWitt Clinton Papers, Columbia University Libraries.

94. George Clinton to DeWitt Clinton, Albany, November 16, 1803, DeWitt Clinton Papers, Columbia University Libraries.

95. William P.H. Beers to Ebenezer Foote, Albany, August 29, 1800, Foote Papers, Library of Congress.

96. New London, Conn., *Bee*, November 26, 1800.

97. C. E. Elmendorf to Ebenezer Foote, Kingston, January 27, 1801, Foote Papers, Library of Congress; and George Clinton to DeWitt Clinton, New York City, January 13, 1801, DeWitt Clinton Papers, Columbia University Libraries. Watson was formerly speaker of the assembly, a state senator, and a U.S. senator. Federalist Robert Troup told Rufus King that "I hardly know a man that has been so long in public life who is less esteemed." (October 2, 1798, King Papers, NHi.)

98. This Albany committee's address "To the Independent Electors of the State of New-York" was first printed in the *Albany Centinel*. "A Federalist" had it reprinted in the New York *Daily Advertiser* on March 4, 1801, so that he could respond to it in the same issue. In his response, he accused Chancellor Livingston, "the celebrated *Junius* (or *Julius*, if you please) of Columbia," of being the author. According to "A Federalist," Livingston, "tho' disclaiming 'a free Agency,' is zealously devoted to brighten the chains which has linked him to his present friends, and to atone for past errors by the boldness and avidity with which he promulgates his new creed."

99. New York *Daily Advertiser*, March 4, 1801.

100. *Ibid.*

101. "A Federalist," New York *Daily Advertiser*, March 4, 1801.

102. Albany Nominating Meeting, 3 March 1801, printed in the New York *Daily Advertiser*, March 13, 1801; and "A Federalist," New York *Daily Advertiser*, March 4, 1801.

103. "X," New York *Daily Advertiser*, April 20, 1801.

104. A meeting at Reuben Hatch's Inn in Rensselaerville, Albany County, on Tuesday, March 17, 1801, New York *Daily Advertiser*, April 11, 1801.

105. "Triangle" and "Brutus," New York *Daily Advertiser*, April 17, 27, 1801. The son of James Clinton, DeWitt Clinton was George Clinton's nephew. Ambrose Spencer was James Clinton's son-in-law. See also Hamilton's Address to the Electors of the State of New-York, [March 21, 1801], Syrett, 25: 370.

106. Van Rensselaer's supporters argued that his whole estate was in land, so that he would never agree to levy a land tax. New York *Daily Advertiser*, April 11, 1801. John Jay had called for a statewide tax on November 1, 1796 and August 9, 1798. On April 1, 1799, the legislature enacted a direct tax on real and personal property.

107. New York *Daily Advertiser*, May 13, 1801.

108. "A Federalist," and "An Honest Man," New York *Daily Advertiser*, March 4, 23, 1801.

109. "X," New York *Daily Advertiser*, April 20, 1801.

110. Broadside signed by Samuel Stringer, Chairman, Committee-room Albany, 20th April 1801.

111. Newark *Centinel of Freedom*, April 28, 1801.

112. Alexander Hamilton to James A. Bayard, Albany, February 22, 1801, Syrett, 25: 340–41.

113. Aaron Burr to Joseph Alston, New York, April 27, 1801, Kline, *Burr*, 572n. "An Elector" condemned Republicans for betting, suggesting that they were trying to give the impression that Clinton was unbeatable so that those voters who always want to be on the winning side would vote for him. New York *Daily Advertiser*, April 27, 1801.

114. Alexander Hamilton, Campaign Speech, New York, April 21, 1801, Syrett, 25: 382.

115. Barent Gardenier to Alexander Hamilton, Kingston, March 24, 1801, Syrett, 25: 373. Clinton carried Ulster by 400 votes.

116. Francis Crawford to Ebenezer Foote, New Windsor, March 7, 1801, Foote Papers, Library of Congress.

117. New York *Daily Advertiser*, June 8, 1801 (supplement); Aaron Burr to William Eustis, New York, April 29, 1801, and Burr to Samuel Smith, New York, May 2, 1801, Kline, *Burr*, 573, 575.

118. New York *Daily Advertiser*, June 8, 1801 (supplement).

119. Thomas Jefferson to George Clinton, Washington, May 17, 1801, Paul Leicester Ford, ed., *The Works of Thomas Jefferson* (New York and London, 1905), 9: 254–55.

120. George Clinton to Thomas Jefferson, Albany, January 20, 1804, Jefferson Papers, Library of Congress.

121. Albert Gallatin to Thomas Jefferson, September 14, 1801, Henry Adams, ed., *The Writings of Albert Gallatin* (3 vols., Philadelphia, 1879), 1: 49–52.

122. Aaron Burr to George Clinton, July 22, 1801, Kline, *Burr*, 611–13.

123. George Clinton to DeWitt Clinton, Albany, October 24, December 1, 1801, DeWitt Clinton Papers, Columbia University Libraries.

124. John Wood, *A Full Exposition of the Clintonian Faction* . . . (Newark, 1802), 7.

125. *Ibid.*, 9.

126. "Aristides," *An Examination*, 6, 8.

127. *Ibid.*, 22.

128. George Clinton to DeWitt Clinton, Albany, December 13, 1803, DeWitt Clinton Papers, Columbia University Libraries.

129. Stephen L. Mitchell to Mrs. Mitchell, Washington, December 21, 1803, in "Dr. Mitchell's Letters from Washington: 1803–1813," *Harper's New Monthly Magazine*, LVIII (1879), 740–55 (748). Mitchell thought it "Lamentable . . . that all the characters villified in it are *Republicans*. I think such tokens of schism and rupture must give great pleasure to the *Federalists*. And it is to be expected they will foment it by all the means in their power."

130. George Clinton to Thomas Jefferson, Albany, December 22, 1803, Jefferson Papers, Library of Congress.

131. Thomas Jefferson to George Clinton, Washington, December 31, 1803, H. A. Washington, ed., *The Writings of Thomas Jefferson* (8 vols., Washington, 1854), 4: 520–21.

132. George Clinton to Thomas Jefferson, January 20, 1804, Jefferson Papers, Library of Congress.

133. *Ibid.*

134. George Clinton to John Smith, Albany, February 1, 1804, New York State Library.

135. John Armstrong to DeWitt Clinton, Clermont, June 24, 1802, DeWitt Clinton Papers, Columbia University Libraries.

136. George Clinton to DeWitt Clinton, Albany, September 17, 1803, DeWitt Clinton Papers, Columbia University Libraries.

137. George Clinton to DeWitt Clinton, Albany, February 25, 1803, DeWitt Clinton Papers, Columbia University Libraries.

138. In a letter introducing his nephew to President Jefferson, Governor Clinton wrote that "It is reasonable to conclude that I feel a partiality for him as well from the consanguinity that exists between us as from his having at a very early period of Life been of my Family in the confidential Capacity of my private Secretary; But I can with great Truth assure you that these Considerations have no influence upon me in giving you his Character—His present Appointment [as senator] (which was by a very large majority) as well as the different elective Offices which he had previously filled afford good Evidence of his possessing the Confidence of his Fellow Citizens—His political Principles are pure and he has too much Integrity ever to deviate from them, nor will you find him destitute of Talents & Information." Albany, February 9, 1802, Jefferson Papers, Library of Congress.

139. George Clinton to DeWitt Clinton, Albany, February 16, 1803, DeWitt Clinton Papers, Columbia University Libraries.

140. George Clinton to DeWitt Clinton, Albany, September 3, 1803, DeWitt Clinton Papers, Columbia University Libbraries.

141. George Clinton to DeWitt Clinton, Albany, January 26, 1803, DeWitt Clinton Papers, Columbia University Libraries.

142. George Clinton to DeWitt Clinton, Albany, February 16, 1803, DeWitt Clinton Papers, Columbia University Libraries.

143. *Ibid.*

144. George Clinton to DeWitt Clinton, Albany, February 18, 1803, DeWitt Clinton Papers, Columbia University Libraries.

145. George Clinton to DeWitt Clinton, Albany, February 16, 1803, DeWitt Clinton Papers, Columbia University Libraries.

146. George Clinton to DeWitt Clinton, Albany, February 25, 1803, DeWitt Clinton Papers, Columbia University Libraries.

147. George Clinton to DeWitt Clinton, Albany, September 17, 1803, DeWitt Clinton Papers, Columbia University Libraries.

148. DeWitt Clinton to George Clinton, Washington, January 11, 1803, in the appendix to James Renwick, *Life of DeWitt Clinton* (New York, 1854), 309–11.

149. *Messages from the Governors*, 2: 522–23.

150. George Clinton to DeWitt Clinton, Albany, January 26, 1803, DeWitt Clinton Papers, Columbia University Libraries.

151. *Ibid.*

152. *Journal of the Senate of the State of New-York* (Albany, 1803), 8.

153. George Clinton to DeWitt Clinton, Albany, February 1, 1803, DeWitt Clinton Papers, Columbia University Libraries.

154. *Journal of the Assembly of the State of New-York* (Albany, 1803), 44.

155. George Clinton to DeWitt Clinton, Albany, February 3, 16, 1803, DeWitt Clinton Papers, Columbia University Libraries.

156. Speech to the Legislature, Albany, January 25, 1803, *Messages from the Governors*, 2: 523.

157. George Clinton to DeWitt Clinton, Albany, February 2, 1804, DeWitt Clinton Papers, Columbia University Libraries.

158. *Messages from the Governors*, 2: 541.

159. George Clinton to DeWitt Clinton, Albany, November 16, 1803, DeWitt Clinton Papers, Columbia University Libraries; and George Clinton to John Smith, Albany, December 25, 1803, New York State Library.

   Six months before he retired, Governor Clinton purchased an estate at the mouth of Jan Casper's Kill at Poughkeepsie. The Clintons had lived in Poughkeepsie from 1778 to 1783, and the governor looked forward to returning to live near old friends such as Gilbert Livingston and James Tallmadge, Jr. Because the old stone house on the estate was small, the governor eagerly planned to build a new retirement house—a fifty by forty-five-foot brick structure. For over two years, the governor searched for artisans and laborers who could build the house and also lay out the grounds and outlying buildings according to Clinton's design. As the structure took shape, Clinton made numerous alterations that contributed to the delay. So eager was he to inhabit his new home that the family moved in before the plastering had been finished. This would be George Clinton's last permanent residence.

160. George Clinton to John Smith, Albany, February 1, 1804, New York State Library.

161. DeWitt Clinton to Thomas Jefferson, New York, November 26, 1803, Jefferson Papers, Library of Congress.

162. Thomas Jefferson to DeWitt Clinton, Washington, December 23, 1803, DeWitt Clinton Papers, Columbia University Library.

163. George Clinton to Gilbert Livingston, Albany, March 17, 1804, L. W. Smith Collection, Morristown National Historical Park.

164. Hamilton tried to convince Rufus King that he was the only Federalist who might be

elected governor. King, however, refused to accept Hamilton's overtures partly because the governor's office had been sapped of energy. Alexander Hamilton to Rufus King, Albany, February 24, 1804, and King to Hamilton, New York, March 1, 1804, Syrett, XXVI, 195, 208.

165. Lansing continued his public denunciation of the Clintons in the 1807 election. Writing from Washington, Vice President Clinton sadly admitted that "Lansing has discovered a Depravity of heart & weakness of Mind beyond any Thing I coud have expected. His last publication is extreamly weak & wicked, tho I think it best to suspend making any remarks upon it till the heat of party Spirit subsides a little." Three weeks later, Clinton felt himself "degraded in having had an Agency" in Lansing's appointment as chancellor. George Clinton to DeWitt Clinton, Washington, May 12, June 2, 1807, DeWitt Clinton Papers, Columbia University Libraries.

166. George Clinton to DeWitt Clinton, Albany, February 25, 1803, DeWitt Clinton Papers, Columbia University Libraries.

167. Hamilton to Rufus King, Albany, February 24, 1804, Syrett, 26, 195.

168. George Clinton to Thomas Jefferson, Albany, January 20, 1804, Jefferson Papers, Library of Congress.

169. George Clinton to DeWitt Clinton, Albany, April 14, 1804, DeWitt Clinton Papers, Columbia University Library.

170. George Clinton to DeWitt Clinton, Albany, Thursday, 5 P.M., April 27, 1804, DeWitt Clinton Papers, Columbia University Library.

171. George Clinton to Thomas Jefferson, Albany, May 7, 1804, Jefferson Papers, Library of Congress.

172. Henry Rutgers to DeWitt Clinton, Albany, April 30, 1804, DeWitt Clinton Papers, Columbia University Libraries.

173. Everett Somerville Brown, ed., *William Plumer's Memorandum of Proceedings in the Senate, 1803–1807* (New York, 1923), 451, 452–53.

174. George Clinton to Thomas Jefferson, Albany, January 20, 1804, Jefferson Papers, Library of Congress.

175. The Twelfth Amendment was adopted on June 15, 1804.

176. George Clinton to Caesar A. Rodney, Albany, March 10, 1804, L. W. Smith Collection, Morristown National Historical Park. Congressman Rodney had informed Clinton of his nomination in a letter dated February 26, the day after the caucus.

177. Gideon Granger to DeWitt Clinton, March 27, 1804, DeWitt Clinton Papers, Columbia University Libraries.

178. Samuel Smith to Unknown, Washington, February 25, 1804, John G. M. Stone Collection, Annapolis, Md.

179. Clinton arrived in Washington on December 11, 1805. The next day he commented to New Hampshire Senator William Plumer "that he actually thought our habits, manners, customs, laws, & country were much preferable to the southern States." *Plumer's Memorandum*, 348–49. Near the end of his first term as vice president, he referred to Washington as "the Sink of Corruption." George Clinton to Edmund C. Genêt, Casper's Kill, August 21, 1808, New York State Library.

180. *Plumer's Memorandum*, 634–35. While Maria was dangerously ill, the vice president reported that "I fear a Melancholly Event which is likely to take Place in the Family where we lodge (I mean the death of Mr. Beckley who is very ill & I think cannot survive through the succeeding Night) may have a very unfavorable Effect upon her tho I rely greatly on her Fortitude & Patience." To DeWitt Clinton, Washington, April 8, 1807, DeWitt Clinton Papers, Columbia University Libraries.

181. *Ibid.*, 352–53.

182. Charles Francis Adams, ed., *Memoirs of John Quincy Adams* (12 vols., Philadelphia, 1874–77), 1: 385.

183. *Plumer's Memorandum*, 634–35.

184. *Ibid.*, 450. See p. 593 for another criticism of Clinton.

185. Theodorus Bailey to Unknown, New York, July 17, 1805, L. W. Smith Collection, Morristown National Historical Park.

186. Nathan Langford to DeWitt Clinton, New York, February 27, 1806, DeWitt Clinton Papers, Columbia University Libraries.

187. James Fairlie to DeWitt Clinton, New York, February 20, 1806, DeWitt Clinton Papers, Columbia University Libraries.

188. James Fairlie to DeWitt Clinton, New York, February 26, 1806, DeWitt Clinton Papers, Columbia University Libraries.

189. Goerge Clinton to DeWitt Clinton, Washington, n.d., DeWitt Clinton Papers, Columbia University Libraries.

190. *Ibid.*

191. George Clinton to DeWitt Clinton, Washington, December 24, 1806, DeWitt Clinton Papers, Columbia University Libraries.

192. George Clinton to DeWitt Clinton, Washington, December 27, 1806, DeWitt Clinton Papers, Columbia University Libraries.

193. George Clinton to DeWitt Clinton, Washington, December 28, 1806, DeWitt Clinton Papers, Columbia University Libraries.

194. George Clinton to DeWitt Clinton, Washington, January 17, 1807, DeWitt Clinton Papers, Columbia University Libraries.

195. Pierre C. Van Wyck to Anthony Lamb, New York, January 14, 1808, Lamb Papers, Library of Congress.

196. George Clinton to DeWitt Clinton, Washington, May 12, 1807, DeWitt Clinton Papers, Columbia University Libraries.

197. George Clinton to DeWitt Clinton, Washington, February 13, 1808, DeWitt Clinton Papers, Columbia University Libraries; "A Citizen of New-York" (Edmund Genêt), *Communications on the Next Election for President of the United States, and on the Late Measures of the Federal Administration* (New York, 1808), 12–13; *Albany Gazette*, October 27, 1808.

198. George Clinton to DeWitt Clinton, Washington, February 23 and 26, 1808, DeWitt Clinton Papers, Columbia University Libraries.

199. Spaulding, 288.

200. Adams, *Memoirs*, 1: 478.

201. *Ibid.*

202. "Nestor," *An Address to the People of the American States . . .* (Washington, 1808), 22–23.

203. George Clinton to DeWitt Clinton, Washington, March 5, 1808, DeWitt Clinton Papers, Columbia University Libraries. This letter was printed in several pamphlets and newspapers.

204. George Clinton to DeWitt Clinton, Washington, February 13, 1808, DeWitt Clinton Papers, Columbia University Libraries.

205. Samuel L. Mitchell to his wife, Washington, Jaunary 25, 1808, "Dr. Mitchell's Letters," 752.

206. Samuel L. Mitchell to his wife, Washington, November 23, 1807, "Dr. Mitchell's Letters," 752. Clinton felt that Mitchell was an unreliable supporter. On February 13, Clinton warned DeWitt that "Mitchell's Vanity and Love of popularity I fear often leads him to give too favourable Account of our Prospects & Measures tho actuated by no bad Motive." Two weeks later, the vice president felt that Mitchell had abandoned him "by advising his Friend to an acquiescence in the Bradlean Convention Nomination—It is like him. He is [—] & deceitful & never fails to do us more hurt than good from his inordinate Vanity which makes him the [—] & Dupe of the designing on all occasions." George Clinton to DeWitt Clinton, Washington, February 13 and 26, 1808, DeWitt Clinton Papers, Columbia University Libraries.

207. Copy, George Clinton to DeWitt Clinton, Washington, February 18, 1808, DeWitt Clinton Papers, Columbia University Libraries.

208. George Clinton to DeWitt Clinton, Washington, April 10, 1808, DeWitt Clinton Papers, Columbia University Libraries.

209. A report in the *Albany Gazette*, October 27, 1808, quoting from Madison's *Washington Monitor*, suggested that New York was about to destroy "the Clinton faction which like a worthless fungus disfigures her political character."

210. Josiah Masters to Edmund C. Genêt, Washington, March 1, 1808, New York State Library.

211. John Randolph to Joseph H. Nicholson, George Town, February 20, 1808, L. W. Smith Collection, Morristown National Historical Park.

212. *Ibid.*, March 24, 1808.

213. Stephen Mitchell to his wife, Washington, April 1, 1808, "Dr. Mitchell's Letters," 753.

214. George Clinton to Edmund C. Genêt, Casper's Kill, August 21, 1808, New York State Library.

215. John Thierry Danvers, *A Picture of a Republican Magistrate of the New School . . .* (New York, 1808), 82, 85.

216. *Ibid.*, 87, 88.

217. Samuel Eliot Morison, "First National Nominating Convention," *American Historical Review*, 17 (1911), 753–58.

218. Timothy Pickering to Killian K. Van Rensselaer, Wenham (near Salem), September 26, 1808, Pickering Papers, Massachusetts Historical Society.

219. "Thraso," *Aurora*, August 31, 1808.

220. "Nestor," *An Address to the People of the American States*, 5.

221. "A Citizen of New-York," *Communications*, 26–27.

222. *Ibid.*, 6–8, 19–20; Saunders Cragg, *George Clinton Next President, and our Republican Institutions Rescued from Destruction: Addressed to the Citizens of the United States: or James Madison Unmasked* (New York, 1808), 17, 19–20; "A Citizen of New-York," *Communications*, 6.

223. "Nestor," *An Address to the People of the American States*, 19–20.

224. *Ibid.*, 12–13, 31.

225. Cragg, *George Clinton Next President*, 32.

226. *Ibid.*, 14, 16, 43; Cragg, *George Clinton Next President*, 23; "A Citizen of New-York," *Communications*, 9, 33.

227. "A Citizen of New-York," *A Letter to the Electors of President and Vice-President of the United States* (New York, 1808), 4–6.

228. On the contrary, some diplomats and members of Congress believed that Madison had gained "a complete ascendancy" over Jefferson. Irving Brant, "Election of 1808," Arthur M. Schlesinger, Jr., and Fred L. Israel eds., *History of American Presidential Elections, 1789–1968* (4 vols., New York, 1971), 186.

229. Cragg, *George Clinton Next President*, 34, 37, 39–40.

230. "A Citizen of New-York," *Communications*, 31–32.

231. For Maria's illness, which Clinton described as a "Nervous Fever," see George Clinton to DeWitt Clinton, Washington, January 17, May 12, and June 2, 1807, DeWitt Clinton Papers, Columbia University Libraries.

232. Thomas Jefferson to George Clinton, Washington, July 6, 1807, and Clinton to Jefferson, New York, July 9, 1807, Jefferson Papers, Library of Congress.

233. "A Citizen of New-York," *Communications*, 25–26.

234. *Aurora*, January 28, March 28, 1808.

235. *Aurora*, March 10, 1808.

236. Sanford W. Higginbotham, *The Keystone in the Democratic Arch: Pennsylvania Politics,*

1800–1816 (Harrisburg, 1952), 155–63; Noble E. Cunningham, Jr., *The Jeffersonian Republicans In Power: Party Operations, 1801–1809* (Chapel Hill, 1963), 118–19.

237. Quoted in Brant, "Election of 1808," 193.

238. John Preston to Wilson C. Nicholas, November 15, 1808, Nicholas Papers, Library of Congress.

239. Wilson C. Nicholas to Philip N. Nicholas, Washington, December 3, 1808, Nicholas Papers, Library of Congress.

240. George Clinton to DeWitt Clinton, New York, March 8, 1811, DeWitt Clinton Papers, Columbia University Libraries.

241. Albert Gallatin to Walter Lowrie, Fayette County, Pa., October 2, 1824, Henry Adams, ed., *Writings of Gallatin* (3 vols., Philadelphia, 1879), 2: 296.

242. Robert V. Remini, *Henry Clay: Statesman for the Union* (New York, 1991), 71, and note 30.

243. *Abridgment of the Debates of Congress* . . . (New York, 1857), 4: 311.

244. Allen C. Clark, *Life and Letters of Dolly Madison* (Washington, D.C., 1914), 130.

245. For a transcript of Clinton's account with the U.S. treasury, in which Van Cortlandt was given power of attorney five days before the vice president died, see L. W. Smith Collection, Morristown National Historical Park.

246. Washington *National Intelligencer,* April 21, 1812.

247. *Ibid.,* April 21, 23, 1812. In 1908 Clinton's remains were exhumed and in a solemn ceremony reinterred in the cemetary of the Old Dutch Church in Kingston, New York.

248. *New-York Weekly Museum,* May 23, 1812.

249. Excerpts taken from "Clara," *New-York Weekly Museum,* May 23, 1812.

250. Gouverneur Morris, *An Oration, in Honor of the Memory of George Clinton* . . . (New York, 1812). Morris seems to have been the eulogist of choice in New York City at this time. In 1804 his eulogy of Alexander Hamilton also received a mixed reception.

251. The quotation is taken from a brief biography of Clinton that appeared in the *Washington Expositor.* The biography was reprinted in Saunders Cragg's *George Clinton Next President,* 24, and "Nestor's" *An Address to the People of the American States,* 2.

252. Anne Cary Morris, ed., *The Diary and Letters of Gouverneur Morris* (2 vols., New York, 1888), II, 541.

253. *Constitution and Rules of the George Clinton Society Established 26th July, 1812* (New York, 1913), 11.

Bibliography of Short Titles

Adams, *Memoirs*—Charles Francis Adams, ed., *Memoirs of John Quincy Adams* (12 vols., Philadelphia, 1874–77).

Boyd, *Jefferson*—Julian P. Boyd et al., eds., *The Papers of Thomas Jefferson* (Princeton, 1950–).

"A Citizen of New-York," *Communications*—"A Citizen of New-York" (Edmund Genêt), *Communications on the Next Election for President of the United States, and on the Late Measures of the Federal Administration* (New York, 1808).

Cragg, *George Clinton Next President*—Saunders Cragg, *George Clinton Next President, and our Republican Institutions Rescued from Destruction: Addressed to the Citizens of the United States: or James Madison Unmasked* (New York, 1808).

Debates—*The Debates and Proceedings of the Convention of New-York . . .* (New York, 1788).

Den Boer, *Elections*—Gordon Den Boer, ed., *The Documentary History of the First Federal Elections 1788–1790* (4 vols., Madison, Wis., 1976–1990). Volume 1 was edited by Merrill Jensen and Robert A. Becker.

De Pauw, *Eleventh Pillar*—Linda Grant De Pauw, *The Eleventh Pillar: New York State and the Federal Constitution* (Ithaca, N. Y., 1966).

"Dr. Mitchell's Letters"—"Dr. Mitchell's Letters from Washington: 1801–1813," *Harper's New Monthly Magazine*, LVIII (1878–1879), 740–55.

Farrand—Max Farrand, ed., *The Records of the Federal Convention of 1787* (3rd ed., 3 vols., New Haven, Conn., 1927).

Fitzpatrick—John C. Fitzpatrick, ed., *The Writings of George Washington from the Original Manuscript Sources, 1745–1799* (39 vols., Washington, D.C., 1931–1944).

Gerlach, *Proud Patriot*—Don R. Gerlach, *Proud Patriot: Philip Schuyler and the War of Independence, 1775–1783* (Syracuse, 1987).

Hall, *Life and Letters of Parsons*—Charles S. Hall, *Life and Times of Samuel Holden Parsons* (Binghampton, N.Y., 1905).

Johnston, *Jay*—Henry P. Johnston, ed., *The Correspondence and Public Papers of John Jay* (4 vols., New York, 1891).

Kaminski, "The Reluctant Pillar"—John P. Kaminski, "New York: The Reluctant Pillar," in Stephen L. Schechter, ed., *The Reluctant Pillar: New York and the Adoption of the Federal Constitution* (Troy, N. Y., 1985), 48–117.

Kaminski and Saladino, *Commentaries*—John P. Kaminski and Gaspare J. Saladino, eds, *Commentaries on the Constitution* (Vols. 13–17 of *The Documentary History of the Ratification of the Constitution*, Madison, Wis., 1976–).

Kent, *Memoirs*—William Kent, ed., *Memoirs and Letters of James Kent . . .* (Boston, 1898).

Kline, *Burr*—Mary-Jo Kline, ed., *Political Correspondence and Public Papers of Aaron Burr* (2 vols., Princeton, N.J., 1983).

Knollenberg—Bernhard Knollenberg, *Washington and the Revolution: A Reappraisal* (New York, 1940).

Leake, *Memoir of John Lamb*—Isaac Q. Leake, *Memoir of the Life and Times of General John Lamb* (rep. ed., New York, 1971).

LMCC—Edmund C. Burnett, ed., *Letters of Members of the Continental Congress* (8 vols., Washington, D. C., 1921–1936).

Messages from the Governors—Charles Z. Lincoln, ed., *Messages from the Governors . . .* (10 vols., Albany, 1909).

NHi—New-York Historical Society.

Plumer's Memorandum—Everett Somerville Brown, ed., *William Plumer's Memorandum of Proceedings in the Senate, 1803–1807* (New York, 1923).

Public Papers—Harold Hastings, ed., *Public Papers of George Clinton . . .* (10 vols., New York and Albany, 1899–1911).

Rutland, *Madison*—Robert A. Rutland et al., eds., *The Papers of James Madison* (Chicago and Charlottesville, Va., 1962-).

Smith, *Letters*—Paul H. Smith et al., eds., *Letters of Delegates to Congress, 1774–1789* (Washington, D.C., 1976–).

Spaulding—E. Wilder Spaulding, *His Excellency George Clinton, Critic of the Constitution* (New York, 1938).

Syrett—Harold C. Syrett, ed., *The Papers of Alexander Hamilton* (New York, 27 vols., 1961–1987).

Van Schaack, *Memoirs*—Henry Cruger Van Schaack, *Memoirs of the Life of Henry Van Schaack . . . during the American Revolution* (Chicago, 1892).

Young, *Democratic Republicans*—Alfred F. Young, *The Democratic Republicans of New York: The Origins, 1763–1797* (Chapel Hill, N.C., 1967).

Index